EX LIBRIS

Valerie Strauss

Knossos:
A Labyrinth of History

M. S. F. Hood

KNOSSOS

A Labyrinth of History

Papers presented in honour of Sinclair Hood

Edited by

DON EVELY
HELEN HUGHES-BROCK
NICOLETTA MOMIGLIANO

THE BRITISH SCHOOL AT ATHENS

1994

Published by
The Managing Committee of the British School at Athens

© The British School at Athens and the individual authors 1994

ISBN 0 904887 15 4

This book is available direct from
Oxbow Books, Park End Place, Oxford OX1 1HN
(Phone: 0–865–241249; Fax: 0–865–794449)

and

The David Brown Book Company
PO Box 5605, Bloomington, IN 47407, USA
(Phone: 812–331–0266; Fax: 812–331–0277)

Front Cover: Cnossos, silver tetradrachm (c.100 B.C.):
reverse — square labyrinth
Ashmolean Museum. Given by Sir A.J. Evans (17.10.1935)
***
Back Cover: Rachel and Sinclair Hood (Courtesy of Dictynna Hood)
***
Title page: Crocus pattern, LM IB hemispherical cup, Knossos

Typeset by Oxbow Books
Printed at Alden Press Limited,
Oxford and Northampton, Great Britain

Contents

Preface and Abbreviations		vii
List of Illustrations		ix
Foreword BY JOHN BOARDMAN		xv
Greetings from the British School at Athens BY RICHARD TOMLINSON		xvii
Bibliography of the Works of Sinclair Hood		xix

1. The Early Millennia: Continuity and Change in a Farming Settlement
   BY J.D. EVANS — 1

2. Knossos before the Palaces: An Overview of the Early Bronze Age (EM I–III)
   BY D. WILSON — 23

3. The Early History of the Palace at Knossos (MM I–II)
   BY J.A. MACGILLIVRAY — 45

4. An Old Palace Period Knossos State?
   BY G. CADOGAN — 57

5. Knossos in the New Palace Period (MM III–LM IB)
   BY W.-D. NIEMEIER — 71

6. Late Minoan II to the End of the Bronze Age
   BY M.R. POPHAM — 89

7. Urns with Lids: The Visible Face of the Knossian 'Dark Age'
   BY J.N. COLDSTREAM — 105

8. On Knossos and her Neighbours (7th Century to Mid-4th Century B.C.)
   BY G. HUXLEY — 123

9. Archaic, Classical and Hellenistic Knossos — A Historical Summary
   BY P.J. CALLAGHAN — 135

10. Roman Knossos and the Colonia Julia Nobilis Cnossus
    BY S. PATON — 141

11. The Inscribed Documents at Bronze Age Knossos
    BY J.-P. OLIVIER — 157

12. Sealings and Sealed Documents at Bronze Age Knossos
    BY J. WEINGARTEN   171

13. The Minoan Roads of Knossos
    BY P.M. WARREN   189

Poem 'Ariadne' BY R.F. WILLETTS   213

Preface and Note on Abbreviations

In 1991, when we started our labyrinthine plot to honour Sinclair Hood, we faced two alternatives. The first was to produce a volume (or volumes) of papers collected from a wide circle of pupils and colleagues, each writing on a subject of his or her choice reflecting the interests of the honorand. For Sinclair Hood this kind of tribute would have been beyond us to produce. So wide are his interests and learning, so numerous his friends, his admirers and those who are proud to think of themselves as his pupils that the resulting work would have been as hefty and as many-sided as *The Palace of Minos*! We had therefore to take the second course and produce a structured volume on a specific and relatively restricted theme. The obvious theme was Knossos.

A book of this kind would also, we felt, be in its way more useful, though we were aware, not a little sadly, that this scheme meant leaving out many who might have liked to offer Sinclair their tribute. Thus it was that we invited a number of colleagues to contribute a chapter each on some period or aspect of Knossos in antiquity. The first ten chapters progress from the Neolithic to the Roman period. The last three chapters return to the Bronze Age settlement and treat of important specific aspects of it. The aim of the volume as a whole is to present an outline of the present state of our knowledge with some mention of current and outstanding problems and with pointers to future lines of enquiry.

Unlike many Festschrifts, this volume is not intended to celebrate a particular anniversary or occasion. But it is fitting that the date of its publication should coincide with the centenary of Sir Arthur Evans' first visit to Knossos, for the lion's share of the study and exploration at Knossos since the Second World War is associated with the name of our honorand.

The reader may notice some lack of agreement in the absolute dates assigned by contributors to the various Bronze and Iron Age phases. For example, LM IB ends in 1520/10 in Niemeier's contribution, and in *c*.1450 in Popham's. Such variations simply reflect the state of scholarship, and we have preferred to leave them as they are. Dates, indeed, are not the only controversial matters about which the contributors — and the editors — have agreed to disagree.

Nor have we tried to achieve consistency in the rendering of Greek names. Sometimes we used the form familiar from the principal publication of a site, sometimes that preferred by an individual contributor, sometimes one which we prefer ourselves. Some readers may sometimes disapprove, but we trust that none will be seriously confused.

Many people have played a part in this enterprise. It would not have been possible at all without the very generous and personal support of Malcolm Wiener and the Institute for Aegean Prehistory in New York and without the substantial contributions kindly made by the Hellenic Foundation and the Leventis Foundation. Magdalen College, Oxford, gave some financial assistance towards the honouring of a distinguished son. The Marc Fitch Foundation provided a much appreciated loan. David Brown and Gabriela Canseco of Oxbow Books gave much valuable advice on various matters.

Dr. Roger Moorey (Ashmolean Museum), Prof. Barry Cunliffe, Dr. J.J. Coulton, Dr. Gary Lock and Jennifer Lowe (Institute of Archaeology, Oxford) provided access to computing facilities and help with photographic services. Permission to use the coin illustrated on the front cover was kindly given by the Visitors of the Ashmolean Museum. The etchings and the illustration at p. xvi are the work of Jeff Clarke, a tribute which reflects three decades of association with the Hoods and Knossos. Illustrative material of a more personal nature was supplied in conspiratorial secrecy by Rachel, Dictynna and Mary Hood. Professor J.A. MacGillivray suggested the title of the volume. 'Ariadne' and the Labyrinth are reproduced here as an affectionate offering from the artist, Jane Willetts, and the poet, Professor Emeritus R.F. Willetts (and with kind permission from the Birmingham and Midland Institute, which first published them in 1991 in *Ironies and Hymns* by R.F. Willetts). Some of the typing was done by Lynda Smithson (Institute of Archaeology, Oxford), by Jan Scriven (Wolfson College, Oxford) and by Dr. Susan Sherratt. Our thanks are also due to the librarians at the Ashmolean and Bodleian Libraries, and to John Cordy for copy-editing the typescript. We should like to express our deep gratitude to all of them for their help, advice and patience.

Finally we should also like to thank Sinclair himself, for unwittingly providing his own Bibliography. He little knew, or so we trust, how often as he sat working in the Ashmolean Library parts of this volume were being stitched together by his side or behind his back! We sincerely hope that he enjoys the result.

Don Evely   Helen Hughes-Brock   Nicoletta Momigliano

Abbreviations

Most of the abbreviations used are the same as, or close to, those listed in *Amer.Journ.Arch.* 95 (1991), pp. 4–16, the notable exception being our *Kr.Chron.* for *Kretika Khronika*.

Cretological stands for Πεπραγμένα τοῦ ... Διεθνοῦς Κρητολογικοῦ Συνεδρίου [Proceedings of the ... International Cretological Congress]. The first of these is published in 3 volumes in *Kr.Chron.* 15–16 (1961–2).

PM stands for *The Palace of Minos at Knossos* by Sir Arthur Evans (4 vols.; London, 1921–36).

List of Illustrations

FIGURES

Frontispiece	M.S.F. Hood (courtesy of Dictynna Hood)
Title page	Crocus pattern, LM IB hemispherical cup Knossos (courtesy of M.R. Popham)
Chronological Chart	(based on S. Hood, *The Arts in Prehistoric Greece* (Harmondsworth, 1978), 15; and P. Warren and V. Hankey, *Aegean Bronze Age Chronology* (Bristol, 1989), 169)
Crete and Knossos	(General plan after S. Hood and D. Smyth, *Archaeological Survey of the Knossos Area* (2nd edn.; London, 1981), fig. 1; Palace plan after K.P. Foster, 'Reconstructing Minoan palatial faience workshops', in R. Hägg and N. Marinatos (eds.), *The Function of the Minoan Palaces* (Stockholm, 1987), fig. 1)

Boardman   illustration at end (courtesy of J. Clarke)

Clarke Plate I   Taverna Yard, Knossos (etching)

Evans
FIG. 1   Plan of the Palace, showing position of soundings
FIG. 2   N–S section of the site
FIG. 3   Contours of the natural hill before occupation; and the expansion of the settlement to the end of EN II
FIG. 4   Section of south side of area AC
FIG. 5   EN IIC building
FIG. 6   EN IIA building
FIG. 7   MN (solid) and LN buildings in the Central Court

Clarke Plate II   Taverna Yard, Knossos — with chair, amphora and lemon tree (etching and aquatint)

Wilson
FIG. 1   Findspots of principal EM IA–B deposits at Knossos
FIG. 2   Findspots of principal EM IIA–B deposits at Knossos
FIG. 3   Findspots of principal EM III deposits at Knossos

MacGillivray
FIG. 1   Schematic Plan of the Old Palace at Knossos (after *PM I*, fig. 152)
FIG. 2   Schematic Plan of the Old Palace at Knossos (drawn by L. Bernini)

Cadogan
FIG. 1   Sites in the Knossos region, with 800 m contour

1	Tylissos	7	Gournes
2	Kavrochori	8	Mt. Iuktas
3	Gazi	9	Archanes-Phourni
4	Giophyrakia	10	Archanes village
5	Poros	11	Vathypetro
6	Prasa	12	Kastelli
		13	Vorou

(drawn by D. Smyth and J. Clarke)

Clarke Plate III   Villa Ariadne, Knossos — Evans' Palm Trees (etching)

Niemeier
FIG. 1   Plan of the New Palace at Knossos (after A. Brown, *Arthur Evans and the Palace of Minos* (Bath, 1983), 9; after G. Cadogan)
FIG. 2   The Town and its Environs at Knossos (based on Hood and Smyth, *Survey of Knossos*, fig. 2)

C	Caravanserai	RV	Royal Villa
H CS	House of the Chancel Screen	SE H	South–East House
H HP	House of the High Priest	SH	South House
LP	Little Palace	SM X	Stratigraphical Museum Excavations
NW H	North–West House	TT	Temple Tomb
RR	Royal Road	UM	Unexplored Mansion

Popham
FIG. 1   Location of sites mentioned in the text
FIG. 2   The Town and its Environs at Knossos (as Niemeier FIG. 2)
FIG. 3   Pictorial sherds from LM Knossos. Scale 1:3

Clarke Plate IV   The Way to Silamos — Fig Tree (etching)

Coldstream
FIG. 1   Knossos: settlement pattern in the Early Iron Age (based on J.N. Coldstream, 'Knossos: an urban nucleus in the Dark Age?', in D. Musti *et al.* (eds.), *La Transizione dal Miceneo all'Alto Arcaismo; dal Palazzo alla Città* (Rome, 1991), fig. 1)
FIGS. 2, 3   PG necked pithoi. Scale 1:4
FIG. 4   PGB pithos 283.11. Scale 1:4
FIG. 5   PGB pithos 292.144, with lid 61. Scale 1:4
FIGS. 6, 7   Conical lids. Scale 1:3
FIGS. 8–14   Domed lids. Scale 1:3

Huxley
FIG. 1 Simplified plan of locations at Knossos (based on Hood and Smyth, *Survey of Knossos,* fig. 5)
FIG. 2 Locations in the neighbourhood of the Knossos valley, mentioned in the text

Callaghan
FIG. 1 Location of sites in Crete mentioned in the text (based on R.F. Willetts, *Everyday Life in Ancient Crete* (London, 1969), fig. 1)

Paton
FIG. 1 Plan of locations at Roman Knossos
FIG. 2 Roman Corinthian building from the North Cemetery, reconstruction, from front
FIG. 3 Roman Corinthian building from the North Cemetery, reconstruction, from side

Clarke Plate V Makryteichos, Knossos — Communications (etching)

Olivier
FIG. 1 Hieroglyphic and Linear A scripts. Hieroglyphic: seal (steatite: AM 1938.929/*CHIC* 203; from A.J. Evans, *SM* I, 158.P.49); 'medallion label' (clay: *CHIC* 39; from *SM* I, fig. 95). Linear A: tablet (clay: KN 1 a and b; from L. Godart, *GORILA* I, 256); ring (gold: KN Zf 13; after I. Athanassiadou, *GORILA* IV, 153). Scale 1:1, except ring at 4:1; seal at 2.5:1
FIG. 2 Linear B script. Tablets (clay):
a KN 114 verso - Room of the Chariot Tablets
b V 503 - West Magazine VIII, Scribe 115 (from L. Godart, *CoMIK* I, 55 and 183) Scale 1:1

Weingarten
FIG. 1 Minoan Neopalatial Sealing shapes (not to scale)
    A characteristic aspect   C additional characteristics
    B view of impression from   p profile
      a above   r reverse
      b below   * shape known in Protopalatial deposits also
      s side
    1 most common nodulus shape   2 *OJA* 7 (1988) = Class VI/B
FIG. 2 Seal impressions on EM III jar stopper (after S. Hood and V. Kenna, 'An Early Minoan III sealing from Knossos', *Cronache di Archeologia* 12 (1973), 104, fig. 2)
FIG. 3 a Medallion from Hieroglyphic Deposit (after *SM* I, 167.P.85)
b Roundel from Temple Repositories (after E. Hallager, 'The Knossos roundels', *BSA* 82 (1987), fig. 1). Scales about 1:1 and 1:2 respectively

Warren
FIG. 1 The Minoan roads of Knossos
FIG. 2 Royal Road West, joining the Royal Road under later staircase
FIG. 3 Stratigraphical Museum site, with east–west and north–south roads
FIG. 4 Minoan roads under central car park, west of Palace (1937 excavation). A, B see FIG. 5
FIG. 5 Plan of central preserved sections of Minoan roads under car park. A, B in FIG. 4

Clarke Plate VI Knossos — The Way Back (etching and aquatint)

Labyrinth illustration by Jane Willetts.

PLATES

Evans

PLATE 1
- a Mudbrick walls in Aceramic stratum, area ZE
- b Mudbrick building, Stratum IX, area AC
- c *Pisé* building, Stratum VII, area AC
- d MN building, area K/N

PLATE 2
- a EN I potsherd with *pointillé* decoration
- b EN II incised bowl
- c Ripple-burnished carinated bowl, MN
- d Two-handled jar, MN
- e Storage vessel, LN
- f Incrusted bowl from Sounding FF

PLATE 3
- a Clay figurine from Aceramic deposit, Stratum X
- b Clay figurines, later N
- c Stone male figurine, Stratum VIII pit
- d Clay seated male figurine, LN

PLATE 4
- a Bracelets and pendants
- b Disc beads and ?pendants
- c Stone mace-heads
- d Obsidian and chert, all levels
- e Obsidian blades from Sounding FF

PLATE 5
- a Clay spinning and weaving equipment
- b Stone axes
- c Bone spatulae
- d Bone double points, from ribs
- e Bone points, on ulnas
- f Bone 'chisels'

Popham

PLATE 6 Militarism at Knossos in LM II to early LM IIIA
- a Palace Style jar from Katsamba depicting helmets (Herakleion Museum)
- b bronze helmet (Herakleion Museum)
- c–f weapons and details of their decoration (M.S.F. Hood and P. de Jong, 'Late Minoan warrior-graves …', *BSA* 47 (1952), fig. 12.II.4; *PM IV.ii*, figs. 848–50)
- g fragment of a vase depicting swords or daggers (Ashmolean Museum)   Various scales

PLATE 7 Mycenaean features at Knossos in LM II to early LM IIIA
- a chamber tomb with long keyhole-shaped dromos (M.S.F. Hood and J.N. Coldstream, 'A Late Minoan tomb …', *BSA* 63 (1968), fig. 1)
- b squat alabastron (Hood and de Jong, *BSA* 47 (1952), fig. 10.I.9)
- c Linear B tablet listing a cuirass, chariot and horse (*CoMIK* I, 100.230)
- d Tomb of the Tripod Hearth (A.J. Evans, 'The prehistoric tombs of Knossos', *Archaeologia* 59 (1906), pl. 89)   Various scales

PLATE 8 Knossian vases of LM II to early LM IIIA
- a-b LM II 'Ephyraean'-type goblets
- c-d cups depicting floral sprays in LM II/III A1 and LM IIIA2
- e-f cups decorated with a frieze of flowers in LM II and early LM IIIA   Scale 1:3

PLATE 9		Knossian vases of LM II and early LM IIIA
	a–c	Palace Style jars
	d–e	LM II cups
	f	early LM IIIA cup a–c) no scale; rest 1:3
PLATE 10		Vases decorated with birds in LM II and early LM IIIA
	a	LM II jug from Katsamba
	b	LM IIIA alabastron from Phaistos
	c	LM II pyxis from the Unexplored Mansion
	d	LM IIIA1 cup fragments from the Palace
	e	LM IIIA pyxis from Mycenae b–e) scale 1:3
PLATE 11		Early LM IIIA vases
		a, b and d from Knossos
	c	from Prosymna in the Argolid
	e–f	from East Crete Scale 1:3
PLATE 12		LM IIIB (a–e) and LM IIIC (f–g) vases
	a	cup from the Little Palace
	b	mug from the Palace
	c	bowl from Phoenikia
	d	kylix from Milatos
	e	stirrup jar from the Palace
	f	restored drawing of the bowl from the Kephala tholos
	g	stirrup jar from Mouliana Scale 1:3

Coldstream

PLATE 13	a	EPG coarse pithos 285.58
	b	EPG kalathos J 37
	c, d	PGB pithos 283.11, with lid 283.31
PLATE 14	a	EG pithos G 6, with lid G7
	b	EG lid 107.138
	c	LM II oval-mouthed jar G 37
	d	MG pithos and lid Eph. 58
PLATE 15	a	LG pithos and lid Fortetsa 824
	b, c	PGB coarse lid with stamped decoration
PLATE 16	a	EG domed lid 293.123
	b	LG domed lid 163.2
	c	MG set of miniature domed lids from Tomb 134

Paton

PLATE 17		Villa Dionysos, mosaic panels (photos Michael Gough)
	a	Pan with pipes
	b	Maenad with flute
PLATE 18		Statue of Hadrian found in the Villa Dionysos in 1935, showing *bucrania* on the greaves and other joining fragments recently identified by D.E.H. Wardle (photo Graham Norrie)

Weingarten

PLATE 19	a	Seal impression on MM IB nodulus
	b	Hieroglyphic seal impression on Class VI, from South-East Pillar Room (*CHIC* 03–08)

PLATE 20	Seal impressions on two-sided oval nodulus, from South-East Pillar Room
	a double-axe (= *CHIC* 03?)
	b 'barley-corn' (= *CHIC* 08?)

PLATE 20   Seal impressions on two-sided oval nodulus, from South-East Pillar Room
         a   double-axe (= *CHIC* 03?)
         b   'barley-corn' (= *CHIC* 08?)

PLATE 21   Hieroglyphic deposit - crescents (after *SM* I, pl. iv)
         a P64   c P69   e P68
         b P65   d P60   f P63

PLATE 22   Look-alike seal impressions on noduli, from Temple Repositories: a and b

PLATE 23   Look-alike seal impressions on noduli, from Temple Repositories: a and b

PLATE 24   a   Class XII sealing
         b   Ring impressions:
             top – Knossos sealing (*PM IV.ii*, figs. 331 and 591)
             middle – Knossos matrix – photographically reversed (*PM II.ii*, fig. 498)
             bottom – Zakro sealing (*PM II.ii*, fig. 499)

Warren

PLATE 25   Knossos central area (photo Whittlesey Foundation, May/June 1976)
         1 Royal Road; 2 Royal Road West; 3, 4 West extensions of Royal Road; 5 Little Palace Road; 6 Car park roads; 7 Stepped Portico; 8 Viaduct

PLATE 26   Royal Road from west (23/7/73)

PLATE 27   Royal Road and Theatral Area, with branch road southeast to Palace (right). From west (21/8/73)

PLATE 28   Above. Royal Road West, with cobbled area and flanking walls: A Royal Road, B Staircase over Royal Road West. From south
         Below. Royal Road West, after restoration (test area below cobbles on right). From north

PLATE 29   Left. Royal Road West: road, cobbled drain and east flanking wall. From south
         Right. Staircase from Royal Road (foreground), over Royal Road West (top right). From north

PLATE 30   Early Minoan III cobbling or road (scale 0.5 m) below Royal Road West (left), with flanking wall of Royal Road West on top of cobbling. From west

PLATE 31   Stratigraphical Museum site, East–West Road, with drain. Above. Trench L (scale 1.0 m). Below. Trench M (scale 2.0 m). From east

PLATE 32   Left. Stratigraphical Museum site, North–South Road, with drain on left (scale 1.0 m). From north
         Right. Royal Road. Stone column base which had been built into later wall beside Minoan Staircase (pl. 29 right) (scale 0.5 m)

PLATE 33   West Court, East–West Road (causeway). From west (25/5/93)

PLATE 34   Above. Stepped Portico (scale by foundation column -A- 2.0 m). From northeast (27/5/93)
         Below. Stepped Portico (A) and area of side roads (B). From southeast (27/5/93)

PLATE 35   Above. Viaduct. From northeast (30/7/78)
         Below. Viaduct. From northwest (6/75: photo V. Hankey)

Chronological Chart (p. xxvi), Crete and Knossos plans (p. xxvii), Figs. 1 and 2 (Niemeier, Popham and Huxley), Fig. 1 (Callaghan) prepared by D. Evely.

Foreword

British archaeologists have enjoyed a distinguished record of excavation in Greek lands, and especially at the two most important Bronze Age sites — prominent at Mycenae, dominant at Knossos. The Knossian heritage began with Sir Arthur Evans a hundred years ago, but the succession is no less decisively associated with the name of Sinclair Hood. It was fitting, therefore, that the editors of this volume in his honour should mark his distinguished and continuing work at Knossos by inviting contributors to offer an account of the site and its development over the full range of its archaeological history, in terms both of discovery and of more specialised topics.

Sinclair Hood's work in Greece has by no means been confined to Knossos. When he came to the British School at Athens as a student in 1947 the British were excavating only at Bayrakli (Izmir) and he worked there for two seasons, and later, as School Director (1954–62), his work in Crete was punctuated by the excavations he conducted at Emporio in Chios, a project which has defined for the first time the archaeology of the island in some detail over three millennia of its history.

He is a prime example of a teacher who has never taught, at least in the narrower academic sense of the word. His instruction is tacit, by example; or explicit, and then informal, in the trench or museum, or over the dinner table. He has founded no 'Knossian School' of interpretation, and although he has been sharp to criticise and generous to applaud, it is by the balanced and basic archaeological skills that he has employed that he has influenced all thinking on that great site. If he has ever taken sides, it has been to support sober discussion and honest argument derived from the evidence rather than from preconceptions. Knossos, of all sites, calls for a breadth of approach which his wider studies, from Europe to Egypt, have put within his grasp. But there is beside this balance and breadth an infectious enthusiasm which makes working with him almost a family affair — no little due to the support and sympathetic presence of Rachel Hood. It does not often emerge in his writing, but it is well known to those who have enjoyed his company at work, and felt fired by it. Stamina also enters into the equation, and lesser mortals can sometimes find the pace too challenging.

Much current archaeological thinking tends to discount the value of excavation, while remaining totally dependent on it; but it is not merely the digging, but the manner of digging and publication that determines value. In these respects our honorand set standards which have directly or indirectly been followed in most subsequent work by British archaeologists in Greece, and have not been without their influence on the work of other Institutes and Greek colleagues. Hood came to Greece with excavation training in the most rigorous of schools, pioneered by Mortimer Wheeler and Kathleen Kenyon, with experience in both Britain and (also with Leonard Woolley) the Near East. Excavation methods in Greece had left, and in places still leave, something to be desired. Hood introduced a new regime, new methods and a heightened degree of attention to the record of the past that was being destroyed as it was uncovered: a sharp discipline of observation and recording in the course of excavation, of intensive study of finds — even the apparently most unrewarding assemblages of plain handmade pottery can yield to the treatment — and a meticulous control of publication that could gather the evidence of all sources without abandoning decisions largely to teams of 'experts'. His personal involvement in all aspects of excavation, recording and study are exemplary. These are qualities still rare in the conduct of excavation in Greece, and where they flourish still in British work, it is due wholly to his example.

Hood's own work at Knossos has served both to bring together the experience of the last hundred years, in the *Knossos Survey* and *Palace Plan* (both 1981), and to elucidate periods and problems by excavation in the Palace area and cemeteries, as well as by observation and analysis of, for example, the masons' marks in the Palace, with which he is still engaged. And he has added to this fieldwork a distillation of his understanding of the Greek Bronze Age in his volumes *The Home of the Heroes* (1967), *The Minoans* (1971) and *The Arts in Prehistoric Greece* (1978). It is a notable and growing academic record to which he has added innumerable more personal services through his patience with the over-eager, and his invariable good humour. This volume carries with it the admiration and good wishes not only of its contributors but of many scholars of many countries who have had good reason to be grateful to Sinclair Hood for his help, example and scholarly integrity.

J. Boardman

Greetings from the British School at Athens

I am delighted that the editors of this volume gave me, a dedicated non-Knossian, the opportunity to send the warmest of greetings to Sinclair and Rachel on behalf of the whole British School at Athens. Sinclair was Director of the School when I first became a full student, my subject, the architecture of the Macedonian vaulted tombs, very far removed from Crete. Yet I remember not only the support he gave me, but the percipient questions about the tombs, particularly whether they were royal. I could not say, and it had to wait over twenty years before Manolis Andronikos provided the answer for at least the examples under the great tumulus at Vergina. Later in that same first year I enjoyed another non-Knossian experience with Sinclair at Emporio, and so have happiest memories of a School excavation which, from the Director downward, seemed to involve the whole of the School. It is worth remembering how many of the small band of students under Sinclair's Directorship — and encouragement — have continued to dedicate themselves to the work of the School. Knossians and non-Knossians alike hold Sinclair and Rachel high in their affection and regard.

Richard Tomlinson
(Chairman of the Managing Committee of the British School at Athens)

Bibliography of the Works of Sinclair Hood

MARTIN SINCLAIR FRANKLAND HOOD MA, FBA, FSA

Born 31 January 1917
Education:
    Harrow School and Magdalen College, Oxford
    Degree in Modern History, 1938
    Diploma in Prehistoric European Archaeology, London 1947, after study under Dame Kathleen Kenyon and Professor V. Gordon Childe
    Student of the British School at Athens, 1947–8, 1951-3
    Student of the British Institute of Archaeology at Ankara, 1948–9

Assistant Director of the British School at Athens, 1949–51
Director of the British School at Athens, 1954–62
Geddes-Harrower Visiting Professor of Greek Art and Archaeology at the University of Aberdeen, 1969
Norton Lecturer for the American Institute of Archaeology, 1973
Visiting Fellow of the British School at Athens, 1981
Guest Scholar at the J. Paul Getty Museum (Malibu), Winter 1981-2
Elected Fellow of the Society of Antiquaries of London, 1953
Elected Fellow of the British Academy, 1983

Participated in excavations at:
    Dorchester (near Oxford): Roman settlement, 1937
    Southwark (London): Roman and Medieval, 1946
    *Compton (Berkshire): Roman burial ground and cremating place, 1946–7
    Dorchester (near Oxford): Neolithic and Bronze Age cemetery, 1947
    Tell esh Sheikh, 1948
    Old Smyrna, 1948–9
    Atchana, 1948–9
    *Tabara el Akrad, 1948–9
    Sakçe-Gözü, 1950
    Mycenae, 1950–2
    Jericho, 1952
    *Knossos, 1950–1, 1953–5, 1957–61, 1973, 1987
    *Chios: Kofina Ridge, 1952
    *Chios: Emporio, 1952–5
    Phylakopi (Melos), 1974–6
    Palaikastro (Crete), 1986

* As Director or Co-Director of the excavations

Bibliography

GENERAL WORKS

Chapter 7, 'The Home of the Heroes: The Aegean before the Greeks,' in S. Piggott (ed.), *The Dawn of Civilization* (London, 1961), 195–228.

The Home of the Heroes: The Aegean before the Greeks (London, 1967).

The Minoans: Crete in the Bronze Age (London, 1971).

The Arts in Prehistoric Greece (The Pelican History of Art; Harmondsworth, 1978).

EXCAVATION REPORTS AND NOTICES

(with Hilary Walton) 'A Romano-British cremating place and burial ground on Roden Down, Compton, Berkshire', *Transactions of the Newbury District Field Club* 9.i (1948), 10–62.

'Excavations at Tabara el Akrad, 1948–49', *Anat. Stud.* 1 (1951), 113–47.

FA 5 (1950), 143, no. 1633, Knossos excavations.

FA 6 (1951), 147, no. 1824, Knossos excavations.

FA 7 (1952), 112, no. 1448, Chios: Kofina Ridge and Emporio excavations.

(with P. de Jong) 'Light on the last and militarist phase of Minoan Crete', *Illustrated London News*, 12 January 1952, 58–60.

(with P. de Jong) 'Late Minoan warrior-graves from Ayios Ioannis and the New Hospital site at Knossos', *BSA* 47 (1952), 243–77.

FA 8 (1953), 115–16, no. 1617, (with J. Boardman) Chios: Emporio excavations; no. 1623, Knossos excavations.

(With M. Holland, A.G. Woodhead and A.J.B. Wace) 'Mycenae, 1939–1952, Part 2. The Perseia Fountain House', *BSA* 48 (1953), 19–29.

(with A.J.B. Wace and J.M. Cook) 'Mycenae, 1939–1952, Part 4. The Epano Phournos tholos tomb', *BSA* 48 (1953), 69–83.

FA 9 (1954), 140–1, no. 2022, Chios: Emporio excavations.

Foreword to J.K. Anderson, 'Excavation on the Kofina Ridge, Chios', *BSA* 49 (1954), 123.

'Excavating a traditional "birthplace" of Homer: discoveries covering four thousand years at Emporio, in the island of Chios', *Illustrated London News*, 30 January 1954, 159–61.

(with J. Boardman) 'Chios excavations, 1954', *Antiquity* 29 (1954), 21–3.

FA 10 (1955), 142–3, no. 1837, (with J. Boardman) Chios: Emporio excavations; no. 1838, Knossos excavations.

'Another warrior-grave at Ayios Ioannis near Knossos', *BSA* 51 (1956), 81–99.

FA 11 (1956), 120, no. 1954, Knossos excavations.

FA 12 (1957), 124–5, no. 2019, Knossos excavations.

(with J. Boardman) 'A Hellenic fortification tower on the Kefala ridge at Knossos', *BSA* 52 (1957), 224–30.

'The largest ivory statuettes to be found in Greece; and an early *tholos* tomb: discoveries during the latest Knossos excavations,' *Illustrated London News*, 22 February 1958, 299–301.

FA 13 (1958), 108–9, no. 1702, Knossos excavations.

(with P. de Jong) 'A Late Minoan III "kitchen" at Makritikhos (Knossos)', *BSA* 53–54 (1958-9), 182–93.

(with G. Huxley and N. Sandars) 'A Minoan cemetery on Upper Gypsades', *BSA* 53–54 (1958-9), 194–262.

(with J. Leatham) 'Sub-marine exploration in Crete, 1955', *BSA* 53–54 (1958–9), 263–80.

'A Minoan shaft-grave on the slopes opposite the Temple Tomb', *BSA* 53–54 (1958–9), 281–2.

'A Minoan shaft-grave in the bank with Hogarth's Tombs', *BSA* 53–54 (1958–9), 283–4.

FA 14 (1959), 114, no. 1802, Knossos excavations.

FA 15 (1960), 111–12, no. 1726, Knossos excavations.

(with J. Boardman) 'Early Iron Age tombs at Knossos (Knossos Survey **25**)', *BSA* 56 (1961), 68–80.

FA 16 (1961), 134–5, no. 1937, Knossos excavations.

'Knossos', *A.Delt.* 17.2 (1961–2), 294–6.

'Stratigraphic excavations at Knossos, 1957–61', *Cretological I, A'* 92–8.

'Sir Arthur Evans vindicated: a remarkable discovery of Late Minoan IB vases from beside the Royal Road at Knossos', *Illustrated London News*, 17 February 1962, 259–61.

'Excavations at Emporio, Chios, 1952–55', in *Atti del VI Congresso Internazionale delle Scienze Preistoriche e Protostoriche, Roma ... 1962*, ii (Firenze, 1965), 224–8.

(with J.N. Coldstream) 'A Late Minoan tomb at Ayios Ioannis near Knossos', *BSA* 63 (1968), 205–18.

'Excavations in Chios 1938–1955. Prehistoric Emporio and Ayio Gala' (2 vols.) (*BSA* Suppl. 15 and 16; London, 1981, 1982).

MISCELLANEOUS

'Mycenae, 1939–1952, Part 5. A Mycenaean Cavalryman', *BSA* 48 (1953), 84–94.

'Archaeology in Greece, 1954', *AR* 1 (1954), 3–19.

(with J. Boardman) 'British Excavations — Chios, 1954', *AR* 1 (1954), 20–3.

(with J. Boardman) 'Archaeology in Greece, 1955', *AR* 2 (1955), 3–38.

'Archaeology in Greece, 1956', *AR* 3 (1956), 3–23.

'Archaeology in Greece, 1957', *AR* 4 (1957), 3–25.

'Archaeology in Greece, 1958', *AR* 5 (1958), 3–22.

'The Minoan/Mycenaean question: some archaeological considerations', *London University Minoan Linear B Seminar*, Minutes of Meeting of 19 February 1958, 135–7.

'Alan John Bayard Wace' (obituary), *Gnomon* 30 (1958), 158–9.

Archaeological Survey of the Knossos Area (London, 1958).

'Archaeology in Greece, 1959', *AR* 6 (1959–60), 3–26.

'Schliemann's Mycenae albums', *Archaeology* 13.1 (1960), 61–5.

'*Tholos* tombs of the Aegean', *Antiquity* 34 (1960), 166–76.

'Archaeology in Greece, 1960–61', *AR* 7 (1960–61), 3–35.

'The Early Bronze Age chronology of the Aegean area with special reference to Troy,' in *Bericht über den V. Internationalen Kongress für Vor- und Frühgeschichte, Hamburg ... 1958* (Berlin, 1961), 398–403.

'The date of the Linear B tablets from Knossos', *Antiquity* 35 (1961), 4–7.

'Archaeology in Greece, 1961–62', *AR* 9 (1961–62), 3–31.

'The Knossos tablets: a complete view', *Antiquity* 36 (1962), 38–40.

'Stratigraphy of the Linear B tablets found at Knossos', *London University Mycenaean Seminar*, Meeting of 30 September 1964, 299–305.

'The find-place of the lid of Khyan at Knossos', *Nestor* 2, 80 (August 1964), 342–3.

'Inscribed cup from a Late Minoan IB deposit at Knossos', *Kadmos* 3 (1964), 111–13.

(with P. Warren and G. Cadogan) 'Travels in Crete, 1962', *BSA* 59 (1964), 50–99.

'A Late Bronze Age built tomb below the main road from Herakleion to Rethimno', *Kr.Chron.* 19 (1965), 105–10.

'Minoan sites in the far west of Crete', *BSA* 60 (1965), 99–113.

'"Last palace" and "reoccupation" at Knossos', *Kadmos* 4 (1965), 16–44.

(with P. Warren) 'Ancient sites in the province of Ayios Vasilios, Crete', *BSA* 61 (1966), 163–91.

'Date of the "reoccupation" pottery from the Palace of Minos at Knossos', *Kadmos* 5 (1966), 121–41.

'An aspect of the Slav invasions of Greece in the Early Byzantine period', *Sborník Národního Muzea v Praze* 20 (1966), 165–71.

'The last palace at Knossos and the date of its destruction', *SMEA* 2 (1967), 63–70.

(with M. Cameron) *Catalogue of Plates in Sir Arthur Evans' Knossos Fresco Atlas* (Farnborough, 1967).

'The Tartaria tablets', *Antiquity* 41 (1967), 99–113.

'Buckelkeramik at Mycenae?', in W.C. Brice (ed.), *Europa: Studien zur Geschichte und Epigraphik der Frühen Aegaeis. Festschrift für Ernst Grumach* (Berlin, 1967), 120–31.

'Some ancient sites in south-west Crete', *BSA* 62 (1967), 47–56.

'"Last palace" and "reoccupation" at Knossos,' in *Cretological II, A'* (Athens, 1968) 173–9.

'The Tartaria tablets', *Scientific American* 218.5 (May 1968), 30–7.

'The eruption of Santorin', in S.G.F. Brandon (ed.), *Milestones of History* in Ancient Empires (London, 1970), 33–9.

'The international scientific congress on the volcano of Thera, 15 — 23 September 1969', *Kadmos* 9 (1970), 98–106.

'Minoan civilization', in N.G.L. Hammond and H.H. Scullard (eds.), *The Oxford Classical Dictionary* (2nd edn.; Oxford, 1970), 692–3.

'The relative chronology of the Aegean in the Early and Middle Bronze Ages,' in *Actes du VII Congrès International des Sciences Préhistoriques et Protohistoriques, Prague ... 1966*, i (Prague, 1970), 605–8.

'Lerna and Bubanj', *Zbornik Narodnog Muzeja u Beogradu* 6 (1970), 83–90.

'An Early Helladic III import at Knossos and Anatolian connections,' in *Mélanges de préhistoire, d'archéocivilisation et d'ethnologie offerts à André Varagnac* (Paris, 1971), 427–36.

'Late Bronze Age destructions at Knossos,' in A. Kaloyeropoulou (ed.), *Acta of the 1st International Scientific Congress on the Volcano of Thera held in Greece ... 1969* (Athens, 1971), 377–83.

'The date of the final destruction of the Palace at Knossos', Columbia University Seminar on the Archaeology of the Eastern Mediterranean, Eastern Europe and the Near East, 11 March 1971 (privately circulated).

'The Tartaria tablets: reply to Mr David Whipp', *Antiquity* 47 (1973), 148–9.

'Mycenaean settlement in Cyprus and the coming of the Greeks,' in V. Karageorghis (ed.), *Acts of the International Archaeological Symposium 'The Mycenaeans in the Eastern Mediterranean', Nicosia ... 1972* (Nicosia, 1973), 40–50.

'An early oriental cylinder seal impression from Romania?', *World Archaeology* 5 (1973), 187–97.

'The Baden Culture in relation to the Aegean,' in B. Chropovský (ed.), *Symposium über die Entstehung und Chronologie der Badener Kultur* (Bratislava, 1973), 111–30.

'The eruption of Thera and its effects in Crete in Late Minoan I,' in *Cretological III, A'* (Athens, 1973) 111–18.

'Troy II and the Balkans', in *Actes du VIII Congrès International des Sciences Préhistoriques et Protohistoriques, Beograd ... 1971*, ii (Belgrade, 1973), 294–9.

'Cnosso', in *Enciclopedia dell'Arte Antica: Classica ed Orientale, Supplemento 1970* (Rome, 1973), 238–41.

(with V.E.G. Kenna) 'An Early Minoan III sealing from Knossos,' in *Antichità Cretesi: studi in onore di*

Doro Levi 1, *Cronache di Archeologia* 12 (1973), 103–6.

'Aegean Civilizations,' in *Encyclopaedia Britannica* (15th edn.) (1974), 111–23.

'Northern penetration of Greece at the end of the Early Helladic period and contemporary Balkan chronology,' in R.A. Crossland and A. Birchall (eds.), *Bronze Age Migrations in the Aegean* (London, 1974), 59–71.

'Primitive rock engravings from Crete', *The J. Paul Getty Museum Journal* 1 (1974), 101–11.

'The Mallia gold pendant: wasps or bees?', in F. Emmison and R. Stephens (eds.), *Tribute to an Antiquary: Essays Presented to Marc Fitch by Some of his Friends* (London, 1976), 59–72.

'Carbon 14 dates for the Aegean Bronze Age,' in *Programme et Résumés des Communications* for *IX Congrès International des Sciences Préhistoriques et Protohistoriques, Nice ... 1976* (Nice, 1976), 443.

'Minoan town-shrines?' in K.H. Kinzl (ed.), *Greece and the Eastern Mediterranean in Ancient History and Prehistory. Studies presented to Fritz Schachermeyr on the Occasion of his Eightieth Birthday* (Berlin and New York, 1977), 158–72, 285–8.

'Traces of the eruption outside Thera,' in C. Doumas and W.W. Phelps (eds.), *Thera and the Aegean World* I. *Papers presented at the Second International Scientific Congress, Santorini, Greece, August 1978* (London, 1978), 681–90. Summary as delivered in: II. *Papers and Proceedings* (London, 1980), 372–3.

'Discrepancies in ^{14}C dating as illustrated from the Egyptian New and Middle Kingdoms and from the Aegean Bronze Age and Neolithic', *Archaeometry* 20.2 (1978), 197–9.

'The early Mediterranean world c. 3000 to 1200 BC,' in G. Barraclough (ed.), *The Times Atlas of World History* (London, 1978), 66–7.

(with Rachel Maxwell-Hyslop) 'Dating Troy II' (London University Mycenaean Seminar, January 1979), *BICS* 26 (1979), 125–7.

'Shaft grave swords: Mycenaean or Minoan?' in *Cretological IV, A'1* (Athens, 1980) 233–42.

'The end of Minoan Crete,' letter to *The Times*, Friday 12 December 1980.

(with W. Taylor) *The Bronze Age Palace at Knossos: Plan and Sections* (*BSA* Suppl. 13; London, 1981).

(with D. Smyth) *Archaeological Survey of the Knossos Area* (2nd edn., revised and expanded; *BSA* Suppl. 14; London, 1981).

'Northern "barbaric" elements in early Greek civilization c 1200 – 500 B.C.', in P. Oliva and A. Frolíková (eds.), *Concilium Eirene XVI: Proceedings of the 16th International Eirene Conference, Prague ... 1982*, iii (Prague, 1983), 98–103.

'The Swedish Institute Symposium on Minoan Thalassocracy', *Kadmos* 22 (1983), 165–6.

'A Minoan Empire in the Aegean in the 16th and 15th centuries BC?', in R. Hägg and Nanno Marinatos (eds.), *The Minoan Thalassocracy: Myth and Reality. Proceedings of the Third International Symposium at the Swedish Institute in Athens ... 1982* (*Skrifter ... Svenska Inst. i Athen*, 4°, 32; Stockholm, 1984), 33–7.

'Games at Knossos?', in *Aux origines de l'Hellénisme. La Crète et la Grèce : Hommage à Henri van Effenterre* (Publ. de la Sorbonne, histoire anc. et méd. 15; Paris, 1984), 39–42.

'The "Country House" and Minoan Society', in O. Krzyszkowska and L. Nixon (eds.), *Minoan Society: Proceedings of the Cambridge Colloquium 1981* (Bristol, 1984), 129–35.

'The relative chronology of the Neolithic and the beginning of the Early Bronze Age in the Cyclades', in J.A. MacGillivray and R.L.N. Barber (eds.), *The Prehistoric Cyclades: Contributions to a Workshop on Cycladic Chronology* (Edinburgh, 1984), 26–30.

'Mycenaean vases in the J. Paul Getty Museum,' in *Occasional Papers on Antiquities 3. Greek Vases in* the *J. Paul Getty Museum* (*J. Paul Getty Museum* 2; Malibu, 1985), 1–16.

'Pigs or pulse? The pens at Knossos', *AJA* 89 (1985), 308–13.

'The primitive aspects of Minoan artistic convention,' in P. Darcque and J-C. Poursat (eds.), *L'iconographie minoenne. Actes de la Table Ronde d'Athènes ... 1983* (*BCH* Suppl. 11; Paris, 1985), 21–7.

'Cyprus and the Early Bronze Age circular tombs of Crete', in Πρακτικά τοῦ Β′ Διεθνοῦς Κυπριολογικοῦ Συνεδρίου Α´ (Lefkosia, 1985), 43–9.

'Warlike destruction in Crete c. 1450 BC,' in *Cretological V, A'* (Herakleion, 1985), 170–8.

'A Mycenaean Horns of Consecration,' in *Φίλια Ἔπη εἰς Γεώργιον Ε. Μυλωνᾶν* (Athens, 1986), 148–51.

'Mycenaeans in Chios,' in J. Boardman and C.E. Vaphopoulou-Richardson (eds.), *Chios: a Conference at the Homereion in Chios 1984* (Oxford, 1986), 169–80.

'Evidence for invasions in the Aegean Area at the end of the Early Bronze Age,' in G. Cadogan (ed.), *The End of the Early Bronze Age in the Aegean* (Cincinnati Classical Studies N.S. 6; Leiden, 1986), 31–68.

'Mason's marks in the palaces', in R. Hägg and Nanno Marinatos (eds.), *The Function of the Minoan Palaces. Proceedings of the Fourth International Symposium at the Swedish Institute in Athens ... 1984* (Skrifter ... Svenska Inst. i Athen, 4°, 35; Stockholm, 1987), 205–12.

'A horned altar at Knossos?', in *ΕΙΛΑΠΙΝΗ, Τόμος Τιμητικὸς γιὰ τὸν Καθηγητὴ Νικόλαο Πλάτωνα* (Herakleion, 1987), 355–8.

'An early British interest in Knossos', *BSA* 82 (1987), 85–94.

(with Judith Shackleton and J. Musgrave) 'The Ashmolean shell plaque (AM 1938.537)', *BSA* 82 (1987), 283–95.

'Some exotic pottery from prehistoric Greece', *Slovenská Archeológia* 36:1 (1988), 93–7.

'A baetyl at Gournia?', in *ΑΡΙΑΔΝΗ* 5: *Αφιέρωμα στον Στυλιανό Αλεξίου* (1989), 17–21.

'The Third International Congress on Santorini (Thera)', *Kadmos* 29 (1990), 84–6.

'Autochthons or settlers? Evidence for immigration at the beginning of the Early Bronze Age in Crete', in *Cretological VI, A'1* (Chania, 1990), 367–75.

'The Cretan element on Thera in Late Minoan Ia', in D.A. Hardy *et al.* (eds.), *Thera and the Aegean World III. Proceedings of the Third International Congress, Santorini, Greece ... 1989*, i *Archaeology* (London, 1990), 118–23.

'Settlers in Crete c. 3000 B.C.', *Cretan Studies* 2 (1990), 151–8.

'Schliemann's Mycenae album', in K. Demakopoulou (ed.), *Troy, Mycenae, Tiryns and Orchomenos. Heinrich Schliemann: The 100th Anniversary of his Death* (Athens, 1990), 113–21.

'Schliemann and Crete', in J. Hermann (ed.), *Heinrich Schliemann. Grundlagen und Ergebnisse moderner Archäologie 100 Jahre nach Schliemanns Tod* (Berlin, 1992), 223–9.

'Cretans in Laconia?', in J.M. Sanders (ed.), *ΦΙΛΟΛΑΚΩΝ. Lakonian Studies in honour of Hector Catling* (London, 1992), 135–9.

'Amber in Egypt', in C. Beck and J. Bouzek (eds.), *Amber in Archaeology: Proceedings of the Conference on Amber held at Liblice in October, 1990* (Czech Acad. of Scis.; Prague, 1994).

'Cnosso', in *Enciclopedia dell'Arte Antica: Classica ed Orientale* second Supplemento (Rome, date unknown).

28 short articles written for Aretê Encyclopedia of Archaeology, (Princeton: Aretê Publishing Co. Inc., date unknown).

FORTHCOMING (in hands of publishers or editors)

'Knossos' and 'Emborio' in Macmillan's *The Dictionary of Art*.

'The magico-religious background of the Minoan villa', in R. Hägg (ed.), *The Function of the 'Minoan Villa'. Proceedings of the Eighth International Symposium at the Swedish Institute at Athens ... 1992* (*Skrifter ... Svenska Inst. i Athen*, 4°; Stockholm, ?1994).

'Soundings in the Palace Area, 1973–1987', *BSA* 89 (1994).

(with Nicoletta Momigliano) 'Excavations of 1987 on the South Front of the Palace at Knossos', *BSA* 89 (1994).

'Schliemann's Mycenae albums', in G. Korres (ed.), *Archaeology and Heinrich Schliemann — A Century after his Death*.

'The Bronze Age context of Homer', in J. Carter and S. Morris (eds.), *The Ages of Homer*.

'The Minoan palace as residence of gods and men', in *Cretological VII*.

REVIEWS

74 published in various journals including:
American Journal of Archaeology
The Antiquaries Journal
Antiquity
The Classical Outlook
The Classical Review
Gnomon
Journal of Hellenic Studies

Chronological Chart

TIME	CRETE		KNOSSOS
500	EARLY BYZANTINE		5 — GRADUAL ABANDONMENT
	in the		
	ROMAN EMPIRE		
AD 0 BC			late 20's - COLONIA 0
			67 - CONQUEST BY METELLUS
	HELLENISTIC		183 - EUMENES II. TREATY
	CLASSICAL		
500	ARCHAIC		5
	LG; O	E	
	PG B; E/MG	I	DORIAN
	PG	A	
1000	Sub-M		TRANSITION 1
	IIIc		Post-
	IIIb LM	M	1200 - ?FALL Palatial
	IIIa²	I	1360 - FALL Mycenaeans
	II - IIIa¹ b	N	1425 - CONQUEST
1500	a	O	1500 - THERA Second
	III b	A	Palace
	a	N	
	II		First
	b MM		Palace
	I a		
2000			2
	III		
		M	
2500	II EM	I	Pre-
		N	Palatial
		O	
		A	
		N	
3000	I		3
	FN	N	
	LN	E	
4	MN	O	
		L	
	EN II	I	
5		T	
	EN I	H	
		I	
6	Aceramic	C	FIRST OCCUPATION
7000			7

Crete and Knossos

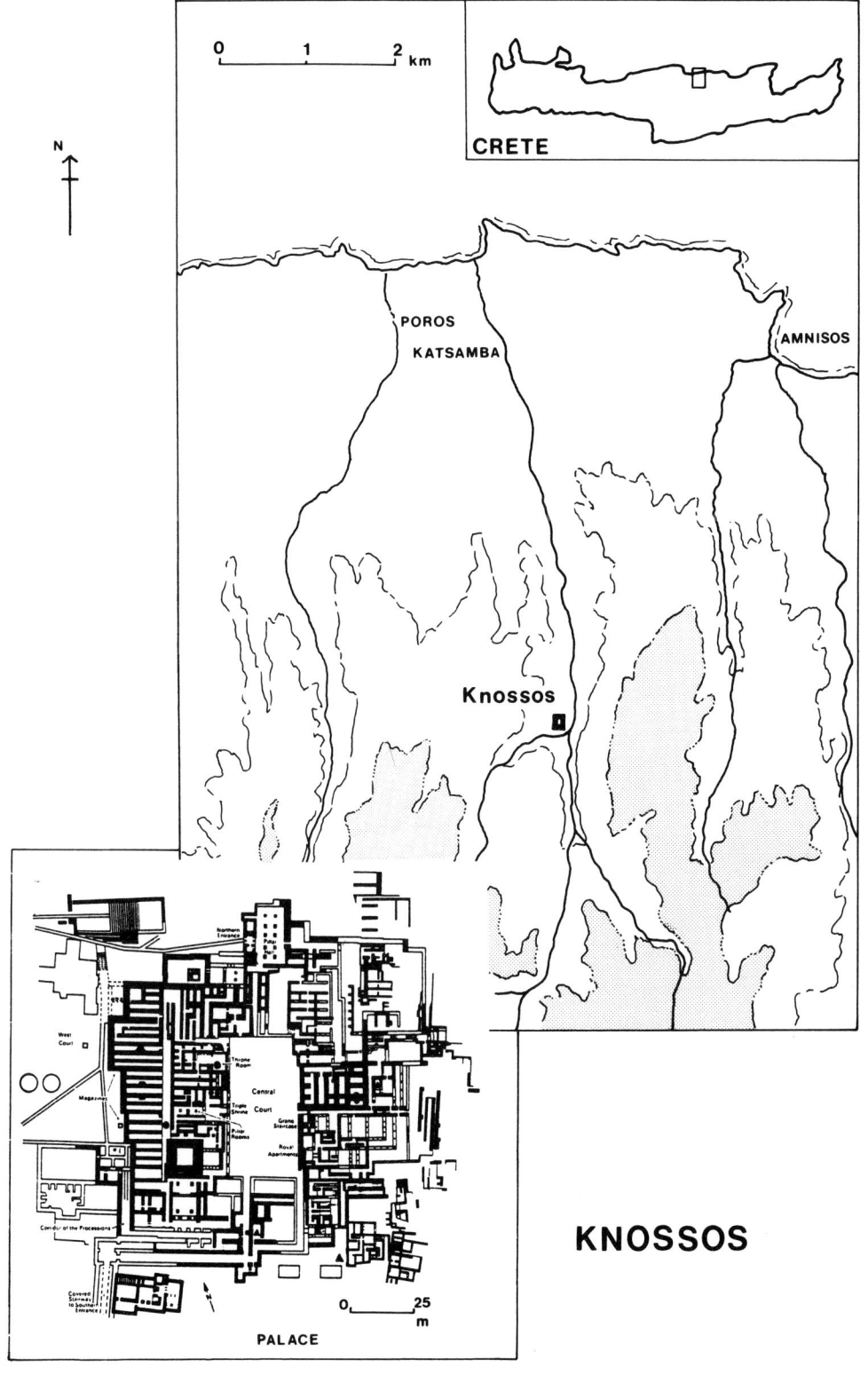

We all have our friends and acquaintances, but it happens that some meetings will fundamentally affect the very direction and quality of our lives. I first visited Crete to draw for Sinclair Hood at Knossos in October 1964, staying through till May 1965.

The brilliance of light and power of the landscape cast a long spell over my thoughts and responses, perhaps not to be broken, even in the face of the agitated mixture of increasing prosperity, progress, noise and despoliation that sharply increasing tourism and technology have brought to the island.

Several regular seasons in the early eighties working with Sinclair in recording the deteriorating masons' marks in the Palace of Knossos and its environs provided times in which ideas and images could take root, to be drawn on the spot during subsequent visits.

This group of etchings shown is most thankfully dedicated to Sinclair and Rachel Hood, without whose continuing support, encouragement and friendship these and many other ideas would never have reached fruition.

Jeff Clarke

PLATE I   Taverna Yard, Knossos (etching)

Chapter 1

The Early Millennia:
Continuity and Change in a Farming Settlement

J. D. EVANS

At some time near the end of the 8th, or in the earlier part of the 7th millennium B.C., a small group of people came to the low promontory formed by the junction of the valleys of the Vlykhia and the Kairatos streams which was much later to become the location of the Minoan Palace of Knossos. They built a small hamlet of mud-brick houses on the southern portion of it and began to farm the surrounding land, using the seed-corn and domestic animals that they had brought with them. Such were the unspectacular beginnings of human occupation on a site which was eventually to play a key role in the history of Crete and the Mediterranean world and inspire legends which continue to exercise their fascination today alongside the equally fascinating story recovered in this century by excavation.[1]

In most respects this little community and its way of life resemble those of other contemporary sites known to us in the Aegean area and beyond. That their stock of domesticated animals included, in addition to sheep, goats, pigs and dogs, small cattle which seem already considerably changed from the presumed wild ancestor, the *aurochs*, is not especially surprising, because similar cattle are present in a few more or less contemporary sites in northern Greece as well as at Çatal Hüyük in southern-central Anatolia. Considerably more so, however, is their possession, in addition to legumes and cereals like barley, both naked and hulled, and emmer and one-corn wheat, of fully developed breadwheat (*Triticum aestivum*), of which they apparently grew relatively pure crops. This is really unexpected, since the only other appearance of breadwheat in a roughly contemporary context is again at Çatal Hüyük.[2]

Where did these people come from? None of the various claims for pre-Neolithic occupation in Crete have so far proved to be reliable,[3] and the first settlement at Knossos is certainly earlier than any other Neolithic site yet identified on the island. For the present therefore we have to assume that

---

[1] The excavations on which this account is based were carried out in six seasons, the first four between 1957 and 1960 and the last two in 1969 and 1970. They were initiated by Sinclair Hood as part of his programme of stratigraphic excavations at Knossos, and he invited me to take over the direction after the first season. It is pleasant to be able to record here my gratitude to him for this, and also to all those who participated in the work itself.

[2] J. Mellaart, *The Neolithic of the Near East* (London, 1975), 98.

[3] For a recent summary and critique of these, see J.F. Cherry, 'The first colonization of the Mediterranean islands: a review of recent research', *JMA* 3.2 (1990), 158-9.

they were newcomers to Crete itself, as well as to Knossos. The low hill with its adjacent streams, and surrounded by a more than adequate area of good arable land,[4] would no doubt have seemed an ideal spot for a settlement to such a group exploring up the Kairatos valley from the coast five kms. to the north.

The part of the site on which the settlers chose to build their houses appears to have been a small kidney-shaped knoll at the southern end of the Kephala promontory, below which the land fell sharply to the stream beds on the south and west, also sloping away, but much more gently, towards the northwest and west (FIG. 3). The appearance of the hill has been considerably altered since then by the accumulation of occupation debris and periodic levelling (most drastically for the building of the Minoan Palaces), and finally by the dumping of earth from the archaeological excavations. Nevertheless, it has been possible to reconstruct the original form with some confidence by using measurements of the depth at which bedrock was encountered in numerous soundings which have been made since excavations began on the site (FIG. 2).[5]

The material remains found in the deposits overlying those of the initial settlement point to the continuous occupation of the site by the descendants of the first inhabitants over a period which we now know covers some three and a half millennia. This immensely long period is called Neolithic because of the absence of metal objects (at any rate until nearly the end of it), but four main subdivisions, Early Neolithic I, Early Neolithic II, Middle Neolithic and Late Neolithic have been recognised on the basis of changes in the form and decoration of the pottery at various times.[6]

ACERAMIC

The evidence for this earliest settlement at Knossos comes from three soundings (FIG. 1). Two of these were small ones: X, at the southernmost point of the Central Court of the Minoan Palace, and ZE, a little further to the south, just west of the ramp which leads into the court. The third was Area AC, lying just in the northern half of the court. The first two both lay over the knoll and revealed remains of walls made of unbaked mud-bricks. In X the deposit was truncated above the second course of bricks by Minoan levels, but in ZE it was some two metres thick and contained traces of four different building levels (PLATE 1.a).[7] Area AC was more extensive, 11 m. by 5 m.; here no building remains were found, but there was plentiful evidence of other activities, including threshing, corn grinding, digging pits and interring the bodies of a number of children of various ages.

All this suggests that the buildings were probably confined to the knoll, with the activities of the villagers spilling over on to the northern, and possibly the western slope (though not reaching the area covered by the West Court sounding AA/BB). The two southern soundings were too small to give any idea of the nature of the buildings or their density, though it seems probable that they may have had oblong rooms like the later ones at Knossos. It seems unlikely that these covered an area of more

---

[4] N. Roberts, 'The location and environment of Knossos', *BSA* 74 (1979), 240; M.R. Jarman, G.N. Bailey and H.N. Jarman (eds.), *Early European Agriculture: Its Foundations and Development* (Cambridge, 1982), 147, fig. 53.

[5] J.D. Evans, 'Neolithic Knossos: the growth of a settlement', *PPS* 37.2 (1971), 99.

[6] The tripartite division was originally made by Duncan Mackenzie in his paper 'The pottery of Knossos', *JHS* 23 (1903), 158-64. This was modified and refined by A. Furness in her article 'The neolithic pottery of Knossos', *BSA* 48 (1953), 94-134, who distinguished two separate Early Neolithic phases. Subsequent excavation has confirmed her findings.

[7] Evans (n. 5 above), 101–2.

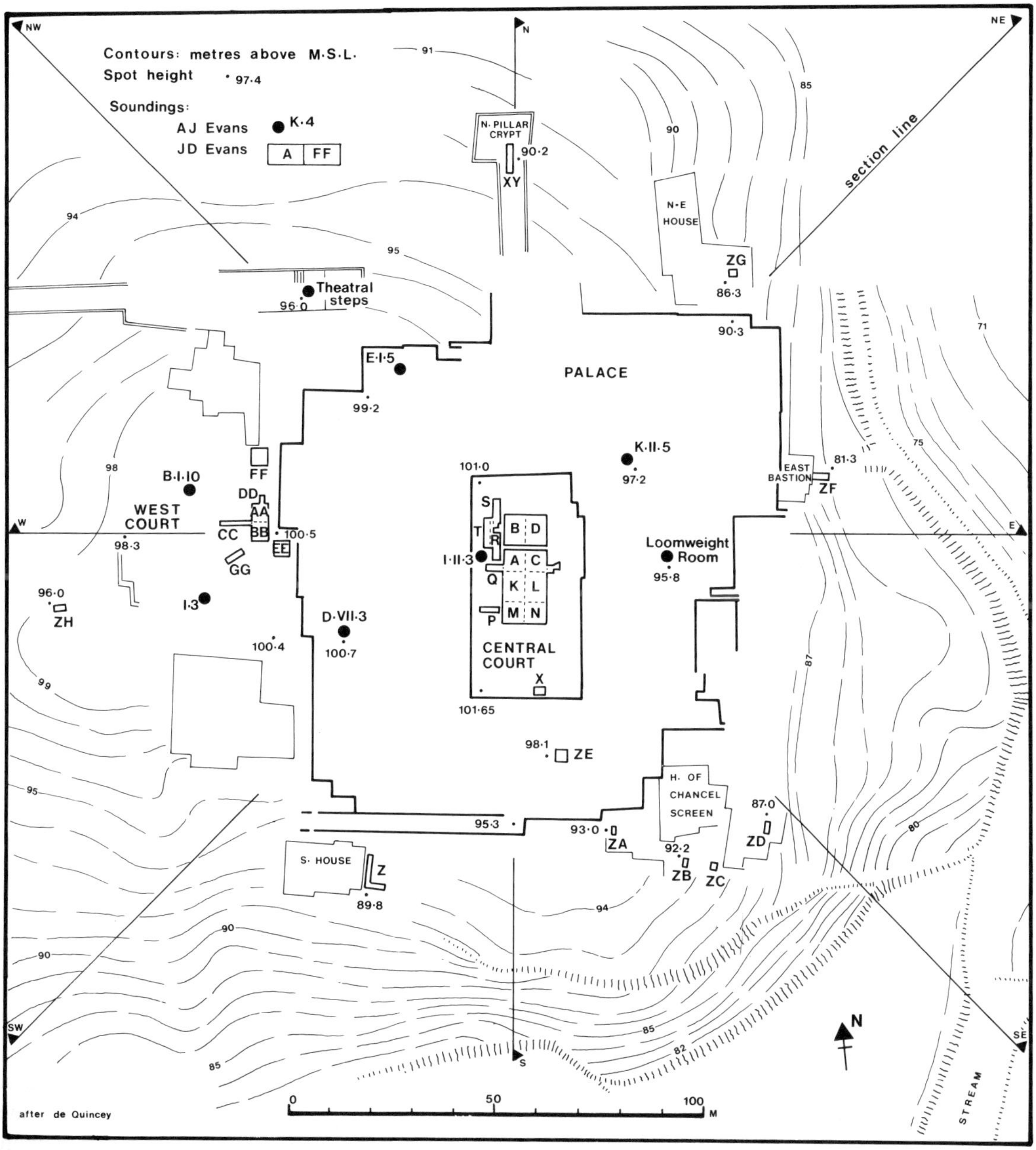

FIG. 1   Plan of the Palace, showing position of soundings

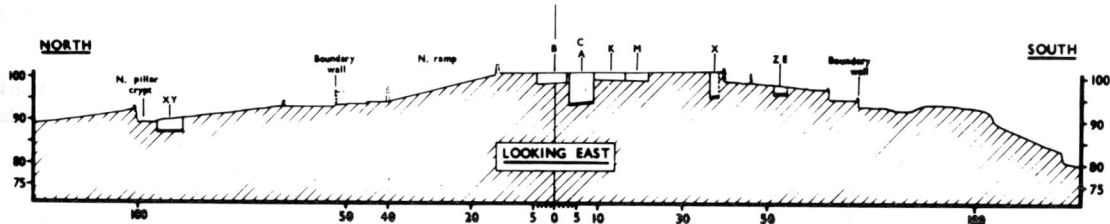

FIG. 2   N–S section of the site

than about 0.25 ha., so the population can hardly have numbered more than 100 and possibly was only in the range of 25 to 50 individuals (FIG. 3).[8]

TABLE I

Relation of strata to ceramic periods in Areas AC (see FIG. 4) and AA/BB

PERIOD	CENTRAL COURT Area AC	WEST COURT Area AA/BB	
Early Minoan		A	
Late Neolithic	I, II	B	
		C	(LN/MN)
Middle Neolithic	III A, B	D, E	
		F	(MN/EN II)
Early Neolithic II	IV	G	(EN IIA)
		H	(EN IIA/B)
		J	(EN IIB)
		K	(EN IIC)
Early Neolithic I	V–VII	L	(EN IA)
		M	(EN IB)
		N	(EN IC)
			(EN ID)
		P	(EN IE)
			(EN IF)
	VIII/IX		
Aceramic	X		

Note: Strata N and P in Area AA/BB each contain two separate stratigraphic units, which were notionally combined for convenience of pottery analysis.

As mentioned above, the area to the north of the knoll was shown by the excavations below the northern part of the Central Court not to have been built on in this first phase, but to have been used by the inhabitants for various activities.[9] A number of pits and smaller hollows had been dug into the bedrock, one at least of which seemed to have had a stone lining. Some of them yielded pieces of charcoal, carbonised grain and animal bones, others were filled with earth of a variety of colours. Over these and the rest of the natural surface was a thin layer of mainly blackish earth, varying in thickness from less than 20 cms. to about 40 cms. At several points thin layers of ash possibly represented the remains of fires raked out of some of the hollows (the use of small fire-pits was characteristic of later levels). In one area grain from a field of breadwheat had apparently been

---

[8] Given the very small percentage of the settlement area examined for each phase and the many unknowns, all estimates of population size are little more than guesses.

[9] J.D. Evans, 'Excavations in the Neolithic settlement of Knossos, 1957-60. Part I', *BSA* 59 (1964), 140, 142.

threshed. One side of this area was marked by a row of stake-holes, and the carbonised remains of some of the actual stakes were found to be still in the holes in which they had been set.

The bodies of several small children were also found in this area. They had been laid in a flexed position in the deposit. Apart from one foetus, their ages ranged from new-born to six or seven years old. Only one body, that of a child of four or five, had a more elaborate burial, being laid on its back in a flexed position in a small pit cut into the bedrock and covered with an oval slab of stone. This burial lay at some distance from the rest, but like them was devoid of any grave-goods.

In contrast to the advanced nature of their farming stock, the material equipment of this little community, or at least such of it as survives, was very simple. Obsidian, local chert and very occasionally rock crystal were utilised, mainly in the form of unretouched flakes, though there were occasional retouched or shaped pieces. Animal bones were made into points, spatulae (perhaps intended for scraping flour from querns; PLATE 5.c) and 'chisels' (possibly for removing meat from bones; PLATE 5.f); and pebbles from the river bed into small axes (PLATE 5.b). Figurines are represented (PLATE 3.a). For adornment they had beads and pendants of shell, baked clay and stone, and rarely stone bracelets (PLATE 4.a). The only material used which was not of local occurrence was obsidian, obtained from Melos.[10]

The dating suggested above for the first arrival of these settlers at Knossos depends on three radiocarbon dates, all from the Area AC (TABLE II: BM-124, BM-278 and BM-436). Two of them are from the tip of the same oak stake, which formed one of the row along one side of the threshing floor described above. The third was from a sample of the wheat itself. They are close enough to be adopted with some confidence.[11]

As already noted, the cultivation of breadwheat at this early date seems to indicate a link with Asia Minor, since breadwheat was also being cultivated at Çatal Hüyük. Asia Minor also has early examples of domesticated cattle, though it is not unique in this. The other domesticated plants and animals are not so helpful, being attested at more or less contemporary sites in Greece as well as in western Asia, often in widely scattered areas. The use of mud-brick for building could again point to Asia Minor, where it occurs earlier at Aceramic Hacilar and Aşikli Hüyük.[12]

Though admittedly none of this is very specific, taken as a whole it gives some support to the idea of southwestern Asia Minor as the most likely area for the settlers at Knossos to have originated from, though even if this is correct they might not have come directly from there to Crete, but possibly from one of the intervening islands, such as Karpathos. As yet, however, there are no finds from either the coastal areas of Turkey or the intervening islands which could help either to confirm or to rule out this hypothesis.

---

[10] C. Renfrew, J.R. Cann and J.E. Dixon, 'Obsidian in the Aegean', *BSA* 60 (1965), 237-8. The main source of supply of this material throughout the Neolithic period, as later, continued to be Melos. But three pieces from a group later analysed at Bradford University were found to correspond closely to pieces from the source in Giali (Dr. A. Aspinall, personal communication). Two of them are from EN I levels, the third is from the EN II period.

[11] The slightly lower date given by the grain sample is surprising, in view of the close association with the stake delimiting the threshing floor from which the other two were taken. It can only be partially explained by the greater age of the wood, since the oak stake was probably only 15-20 cms. in diameter. However, it is on the right side of the date for Stratum IX.

[12] J. Mellaart, *Excavations at Hacilar I*, (Edinburgh, 1970), 3-4; I.A. Todd, 'Aşikli Hüyük: a protoneolithic site in central Anatolia', *Anat. Stud.* 16 (1966), 139-63.

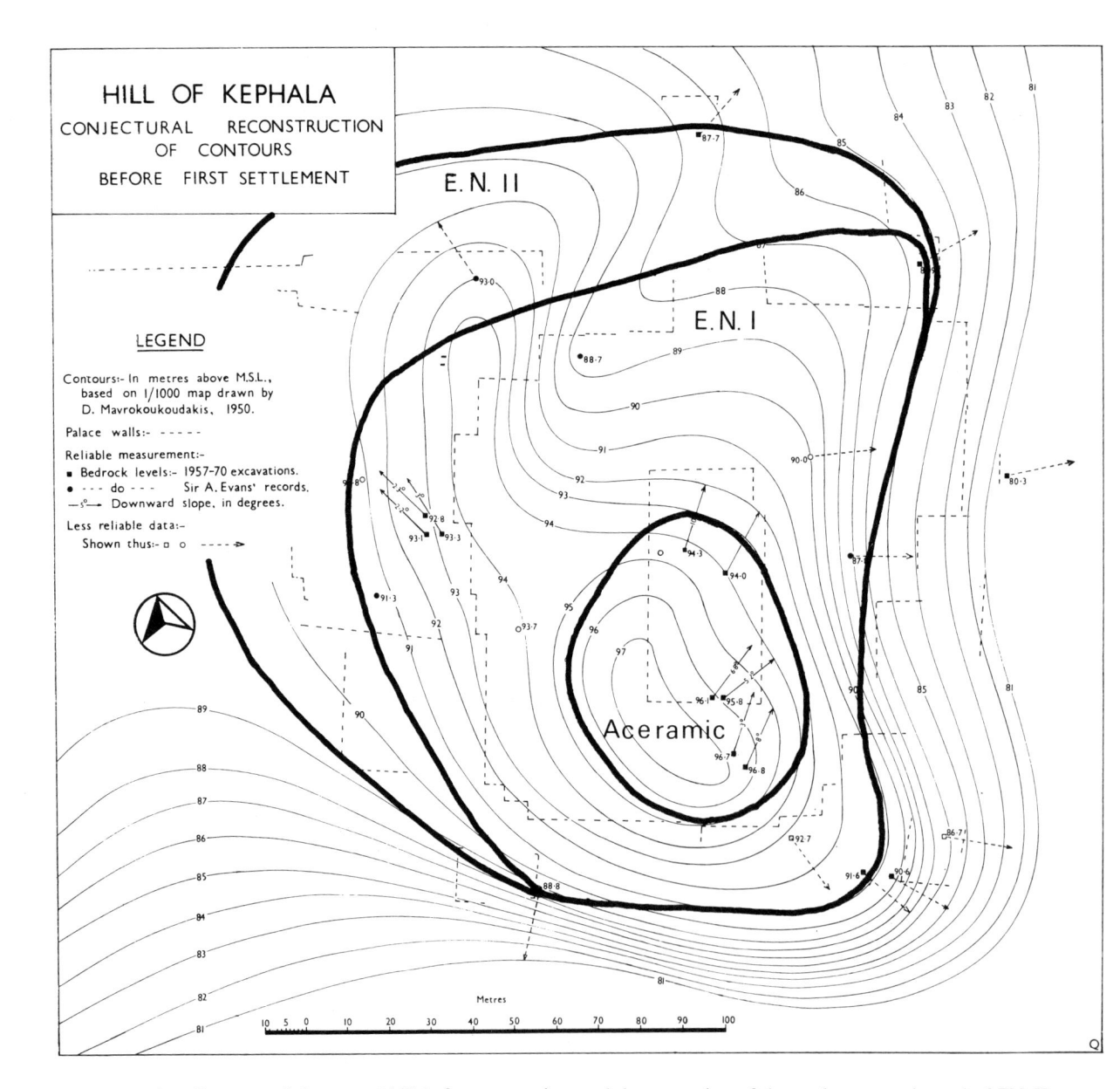

FIG. 3 Contours of the natural hill before occupation; and the expansion of the settlement to the end of EN II

EARLY NEOLITHIC I

In Area AC Stratum X, which contains the remains of the earliest settlement, lies below a later deposit, Stratum IX, which was up to a metre thick in parts, though considerably less in others, and which provides evidence of the expansion of the village and the beginning of pottery manufacture.[13] Part of a trapezoidal room which lay within the excavated area had mud-brick walls, like the earlier structures to the south, but now the bricks were fired (though perhaps only accidentally in the destruction of the building), and a good deal of stone, including old quernstones, was incorporated (PLATE 1.b). The eastern and western walls had separate inner and outer faces with a filling of broken bricks and stones between. There was evidence that the outer face of the east wall had originally been free-standing and was only later incorporated into the room. In the west wall an oval mortar seemed to have been used to pave a gap, perhaps originally a narrow doorway, but later filled up with stones. There were traces of several floors at different levels within this room. Some fragments of daub with impressions of wattles probably represent remains of a light roof.

In the deposit which surrounded these remains, and which consisted mainly of the multicoloured debris from tumbled mud-bricks walls, were found the first sherds of pottery and a number of small finds, mostly similar to those from the aceramic levels, except that bone spatulae are no longer represented, but the obsidian pieces this time include a lunate and a thumbnail scraper in addition to the unretouched flakes. There was also part of a clay female figurine and, more surprisingly, two small lumps of azurite and one of malachite. Virtually all of this material came to light outside the area enclosed by the building; its floors were clean, and this was found to be the norm in later buildings also.

Stratum VIII was only about 30 cms. thick over most of the area uncovered.[14] It again consisted chiefly of multicoloured mud-brick debris, which in the western part covered the slight remains of part of a room delimited on the east and west by traces of the bases of flimsy walls. On the northern half of the beaten earth floor were remains of what had probably been two domed ovens, one rectangular in plan, the other more oval. A little to the east was a circular pit, one metre in diameter, full of ash.

More pottery was found in this stratum than in the previous one, the total weight being about 50 kg. as against 15 kg. in Stratum IX; but this is still very little compared to the quantities in the later strata.[15] However, it was possible to reconstruct several complete vessels, whose variety of shape and details reinforce the impression made by the sherds from this and the preceding stratum that they are not the initial experiments of beginners, but belong to an already well established tradition of potting. Both fine and coarse wares are burnished, and sometimes have beaded rims and flap or wishbone handles or trumpet lugs. Fine ware pots may be decorated with incised patterns, generally enhanced by dots (*pointillé*) and filled with a white paste to make them stand out. Plastic decoration consisting of strips or knobs of clay occurs on fine or coarse wares.

Other finds again included bone points and 'chisels', while a trapeze (PLATE 4.d.1) and a thumbnail scraper figured among the obsidian pieces, all the rest being the usual unretouched flakes. The most striking finds from this stratum, however, were three marble figurines. One came from the deposit itself, the other two from one of two large pits which had been dug from the top of the deposit representing the destruction of the Stratum VIII building; the other pit yielded a complete pot. The larger of the two represents a standing figure, apparently male and possibly wearing a penis sheath, with the forearms raised over the chest (PLATE 3.c). No attempt has been made to represent the hands.

---

[13] Evans (n. 9 above), 144, 146.
[14] Ibid. 146, 148-50.
[15] Ibid., fig. 44.

The head and left leg are unfortunately missing. The other, much smaller, figure is again apparently male and represented in a sitting position. Remains of a V-shaped perforation in the middle of the back suggest that it may have been worn suspended from a cord.[16] It lacks the head, left leg and both arms. The skill displayed, particularly in the fashioning of the standing male figure, is unexpected, and is not matched by anything else from the later levels of Neolithic Knossos.

The next stratum, VII, documents a change in building techniques to what was to become the norm in the Knossos settlement until the end of the Neolithic. The building uncovered in excavating this stratum was apparently more complex in plan than those in the earlier ones, consisting of at least two rooms with possibly an open court and further rooms beyond the excavated area (PLATE 1.c). Instead of mud-brick, its walls consisted of *pisé*, partially reinforced at the base with stones. The floors were of beaten earth as before, and as bare of finds, but featuring a number of small circular hollows, some of which showed clear traces of the action of fire both inside and immediately around them. Not all were in use at the same time, since a number had been deliberately covered with fresh earth during the life of the building, and at least one overlapped an earlier one which had subsequently been filled in. In one of the two rooms uncovered a small area adjacent to one of the walls was outlined with stones. It had a burnt clay floor on which were found several fragments of a large pot. Between the rooms on the north was a cobbled area which surrounded a small circular depression. This may have been open to the sky and served for cooking, but the rooms were apparently roofed with branches covered with daub, like earlier structures.

Almost three times as much pottery was collected in this stratum as in the previous one. Though it was a deeper deposit (varying from about 40 cms. to a metre thick), much of it consisted of the yellowish clay from the *pisé* walls, which of course were barren of finds, so this increase in the quantity of sherds must be taken to indicate greatly increased production and use of clay vessels. In technique and style they were much the same as before, however, and the other finds, though not very numerous, also differed little from those of earlier levels. The most unusual was the head of a clay figurine, something of a rarity.

In Area AC, Strata VI and V provide evidence of the continuation of the life of the Knossos community with little apparent change in house-building techniques or artifacts.[17] No houses were actually built in the area excavated during this time, but quantities of stones and yellow clay were found, evidently derived from the dismantling of nearby buildings. Patches of pebble paving, fire-reddened circular hollows (some with a secondary smaller hollow in the centre),[18] and clay floors divided into compartments by kerbs or flimsy walls indicated much activity in what was evidently essentially an open space during this period. The deposit itself consisted largely of refuse dumped from the nearby buildings. Strata IX to V are said to represent the EN I period in the conventional sequence because no overall change in pottery style is apparent throughout, from its first appearance in Stratum IX to the top of Stratum V. During the later part of this time houses continued to be built by the methods introduced in Stratum VII, though no very substantial buildings were uncovered in Area AC during the two succeeding strata. Stone mace-heads (PLATE 4.c), the only significant addition to the material equipment attested during this time, first appear in Stratum VI.

---

[16] Ibid., pl. 66.4.
[17] Ibid. 155-61.
[18] Ibid., pl. 35.2 and 3.

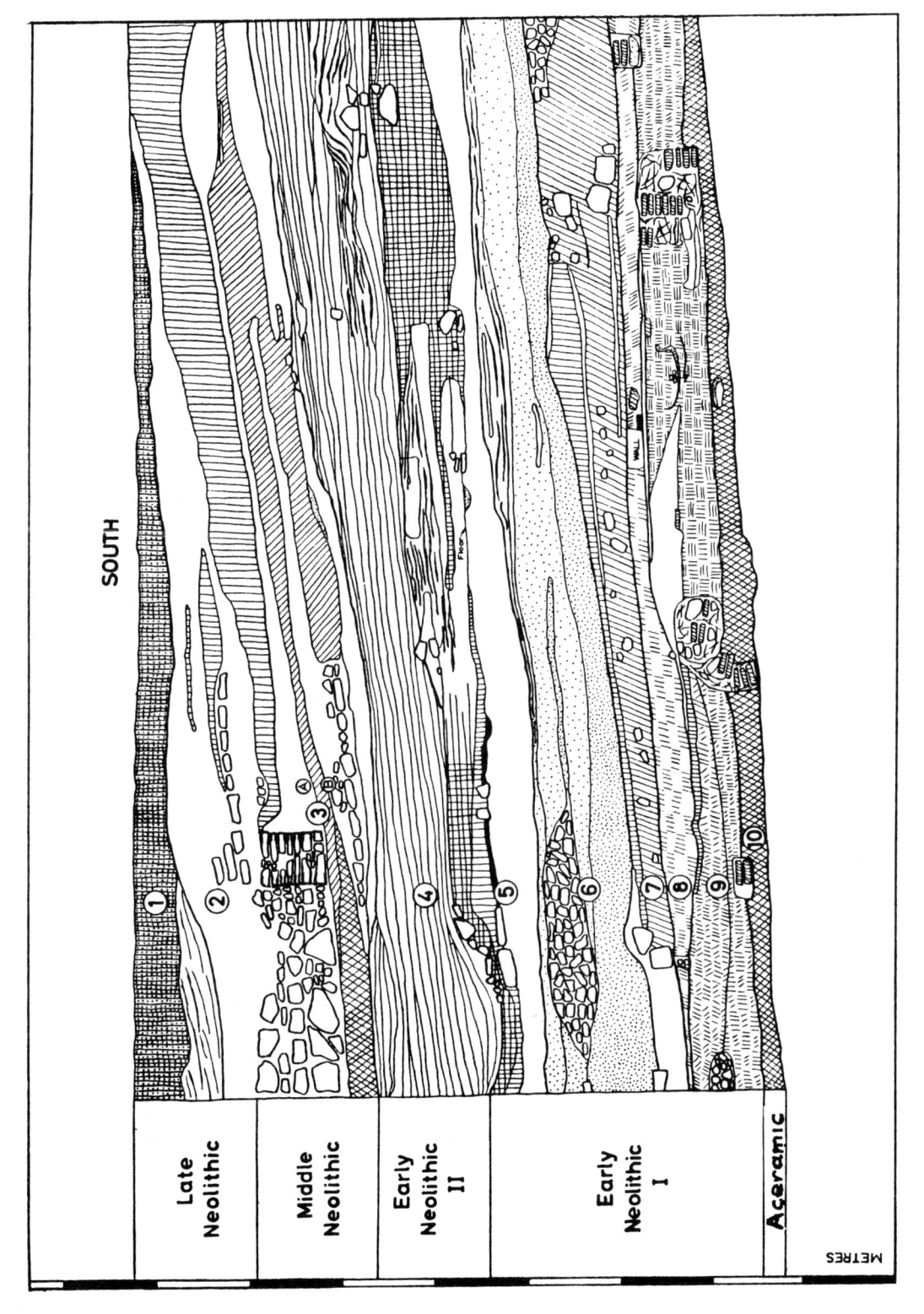

FIG. 4 Section of south side of area AC

The animal bones from the same strata, however, reveal that major changes took place in the proportion of domestic animals kept from the earliest settlement to the end of Stratum V, which must indicate changes in diet and no doubt also reflect the effect which the human and animal community was having on the local environment.[19] Most striking is the increase in the proportion of cattle to other animals, which was double the original ratio (6.5%) by Stratum VIII and which almost doubled again (to 22.7%) by Stratum V. Caprines increase steadily in numbers throughout, and still represent over 60% of the total animal bone in the later part of this period, though their relative value as a food source has declined over the same time from nearly 50% to a little under 25%. Pigs declined both in numbers and importance for food over the same period. The increase in numbers of cattle and decrease in pigs may reflect the progressive destruction of woodlands around the site and the corresponding spread of areas suitable for grazing animals. There is throughout no evidence to indicate any reliance on game.

Evidence for the expansion of the settlement during the EN I period is provided by the small soundings Z and ZG and Area AA/BB in the West Court, though unfortunately the remains found in them do not add much to our knowledge in other ways. The two first were both small. Z, near the Minoan South House, and ZG, near the North-East House, are both at points where the hill began to fall away steeply to the stream beds below, and both produced deposits of EN I pottery. These may represent simply middens at the edge of the settlement, but this at least implies that the outermost buildings are unlikely to have been far away. AA/BB, though considerably larger, also seems to lie at or near the western margin of the EN I settlement.[20] Here the two metres of deposit with EN I pottery which were found again seemed to consist mainly of refuse, though some rather nondescript remains of small structures were found about half way up. These however had *pisé* walls on stone foundations, which seems to imply that they cannot be earlier than Stratum VII in the Central Court sequence. Also the quantities of sherds from the lowest levels of the deposit in AA/BB (EN IF) are much greater than those found in Strata IX and VIII of Area AC. They are in fact very similar to those found in Stratum VII, though rather surprisingly the later levels do not match the further spectacular increases found in Strata VI and V in Area AC. It evidently took some time for the settlement to spread into the West Court area and substantial buildings did not appear in the excavated area until the beginning of EN II.

Taken as a whole, the evidence we have shows that before the end of EN I the Knossos settlement must have covered an area of 2 ha. What this means in terms of increase in the population is less easy to determine. Obviously there was some, but it is clear from the excavations that the buildings were never tightly packed together, as on many Near Eastern sites. Quite large areas were left open, or only occupied by flimsy auxiliary buildings, and this makes it difficult to make a very confident estimate of population size during any particular phase. However, it seems reasonable to assume that by the later part of the period the number of inhabitants was probably in the order of a few hundred.

The depth of the EN I deposit in the Central Court area, about three metres, indicates that the EN I period probably covered a considerable length of time, and this is confirmed by the radiocarbon dates (TABLE II). In radiocarbon years, they span a millennium and a half. The single determination for

---

[19] M.R. and H.N. Jarman, 'The fauna and economy of Early Neolithic Knossos', in P. Warren, M.R. and H.N. Jarman, N.J. Shackleton, and J.D. Evans, 'Knossos Neolithic, Part II', *BSA* 63 (1968), 241–64.
[20] Evans (n. 5 above), 107-9, figs. 4 and 6.

Stratum IX, when calibrated, indicates a probable date in the later 7th millennium B.C., which fits well with those for Stratum X. No date is available for Stratum VIII, but one for the lowest stratum (EN IF) of Area AA/BB in the West Court (BM–1371) points to a date in the middle or later 6th millennium for this phase, which, as suggested above, may be contemporary with Stratum VII in Area AC. A slightly later date, but still probably in the 6th millennium B.C., comes from a sample from Stratum VI (BM–273), and one from EN IE in the West Court (BM–1371) does not contradict this, though unfortunately the standard error is very large. One of the two dates for Stratum V (BM–274) is only slightly later (late 6th/early 5th millennium when calibrated), but the other (BM–126) is quite out of line with all the others and seems far too early. Discounting this, the other dates all suggest a duration between one and a half and two millennia for the EN I period.

EARLY NEOLITHIC II

Above the remains of the EN I period is a further four metres of deposit representing the accumulations of the Early Neolithic II, Middle Neolithic and Late Neolithic periods. Building remains found in the later strata are more substantial than in the earlier ones, which could mean a more rapid rate of accumulation. This is confirmed by the ten radiocarbon dates, which, when calibrated, span no more than about a millennium and a quarter at most. During this time, however, change becomes more noticeable than throughout the long EN I period, though there is still nothing which would indicate any disruption of the peaceful development of the Knossos community. The three periods into which it is conventionally divided are based on changes in pottery style and technology which, though part of a continuous process, allow us to distinguish the three well-marked phases we call EN II, MN and LN.

The EN II period evidently saw a further expansion of the settlement which seems to have been quite rapid. Traces of three superimposed buildings of this period, the lowest resting immediately on bedrock, were found in a small sounding, XY, well to the north of the Central Court of the later Palace.[21] So this area would seem to have been incorporated directly into the settlement at this time with no intermediate episode of rubbish tipping. Another small sounding, ZH, to the west of the limits of the West Court, also produced EN II pottery, but no remains of buildings.

In Area AC the period was represented by Stratum IV, a deposit from 1 to 1.5 m. thick consisting mainly of habitation refuse from structures which lay beyond the excavated area.[22] Below the West Court, however, in Area AA/BB parts of three successive buildings were uncovered (FIGS. 5 and 6), matching the three from XY, and together occupying a vertical depth of about 2.5 to 3 m. of deposit.[23] Each building appeared to consist of a number of small rectangular rooms, and all extended beyond the area of the excavations. They were of the by now normal construction of *pisé* walls on a stone foundation, which by this time has become quite substantial and about a metre high. Nevertheless, it seemed that they had sometimes to be strengthened using new material. The clay floors, in some cases renewed one or more times, occasionally contained small fire-reddened hollows, like those in the Stratum VII building. A number of doorways were observed, some of which had

---

[21] Evans (n. 9 above), 166, 168, fig. 15.
[22] Ibid. 164, 166.
[23] Ibid. 107-9, figs. 4 and 6.

FIG. 5   EN IIC building

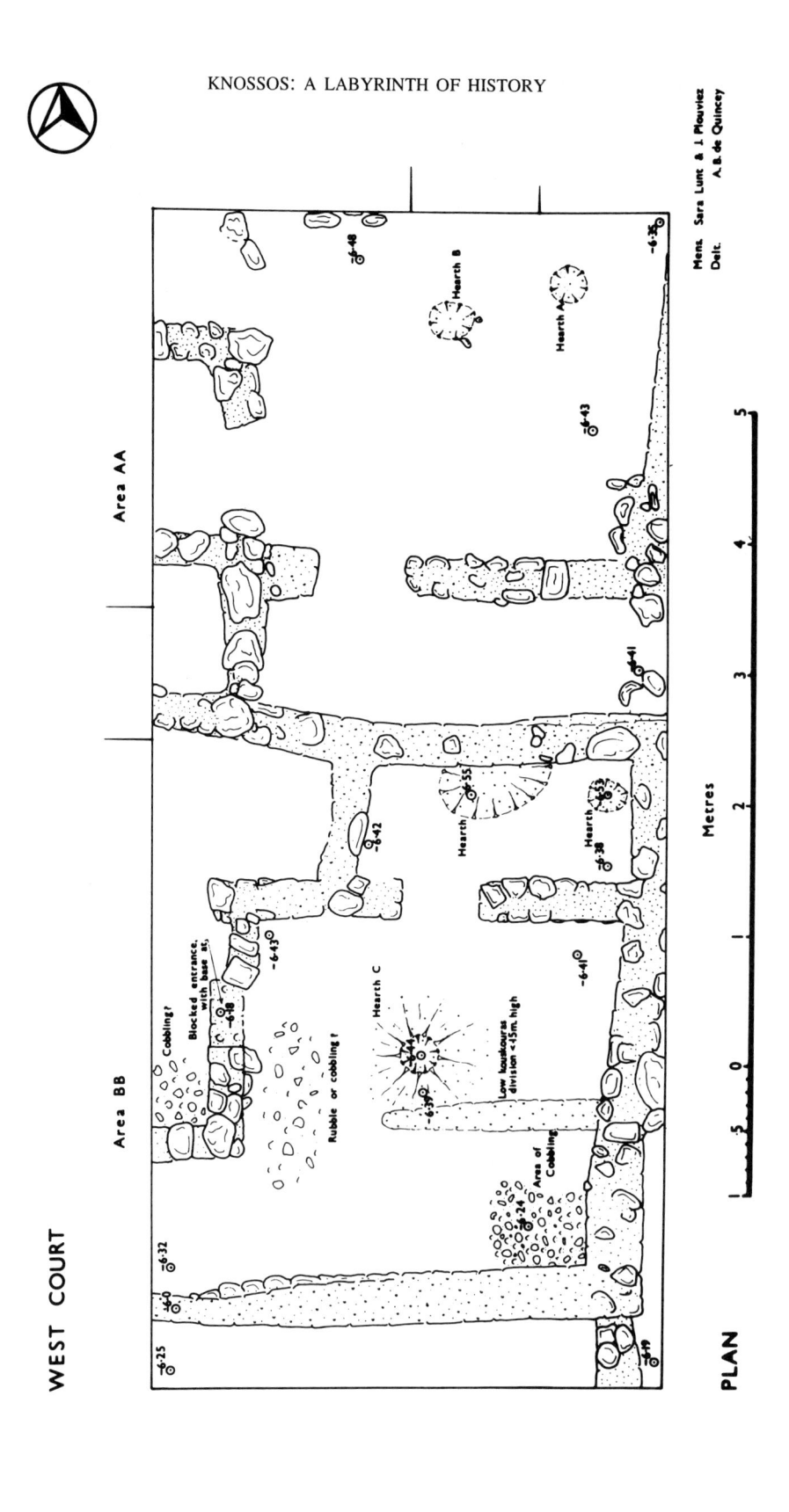

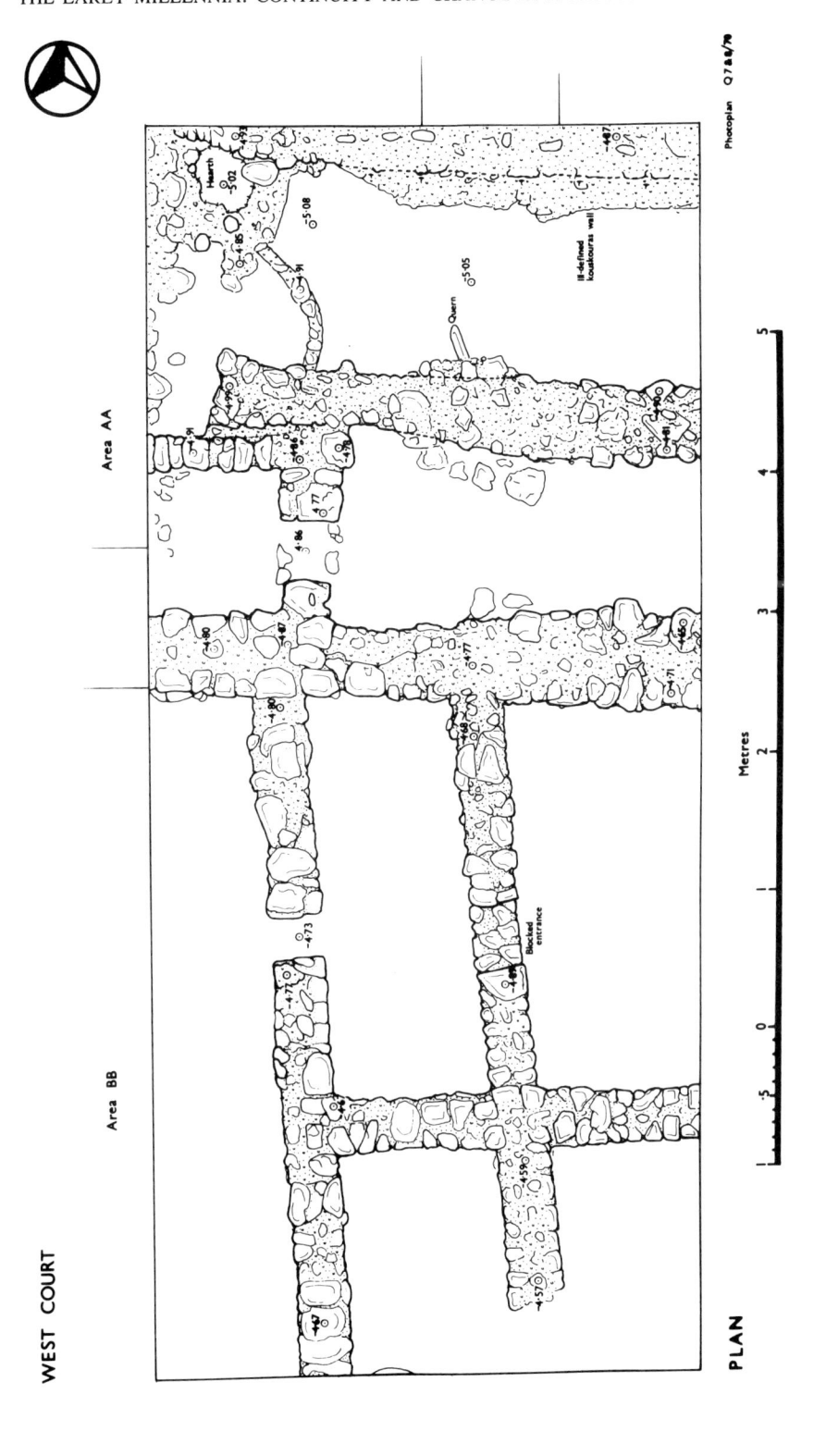

FIG. 6 EN IIA building

been blocked at some time during the occupation. Remains found in AC suggested that some structures might have had small enclosed yards attached.

The evidence from all outlying soundings indicated that during the EN II period the settlement occupied an area of at least 3 ha. (FIG. 3), covering the whole of the area occupied by the Minoan Palace and extending somewhat beyond this to the north and west. Expansion naturally had to be in these directions since the habitable area was bounded by the steep slopes to the south and east. As before, sizable parts of this area seem to have been open spaces, which were used for such activities as food preparation and cooking, as was attested by patches of pebble paving with animal bones on them and hollows with traces of fire and a rather greasy appearance. Rubbish from the houses was tipped in these areas, constantly raising the level, while the clay floors of the houses were kept clean.

The pottery which defines the limits of this period is most easily recognisable from the decoration of the fine wares. A number of new, but generally clumsily executed, incised patterns (PLATE 2.b) dominate in place of the more varied, often *pointillé*-filled ones of EN I (PLATE 2.a), and they occur much more frequently than the latter ever did on the fine wares.[24] A new technique of decorative ripple burnish was introduced during the course of the period. The coarse wares are now often unburnished or given only a perfunctory 'scribble burnish', perhaps as a decorative effect. Only rarely do they exhibit plastic decoration, which was much more common during EN I. The rest of the equipment shows little change apart from the first appearance of a type of flattened bar of terracotta with notched ends (PLATE 5.a, middle), of which two examples were found. These were probably used as shuttles in weaving, as Sir Arthur Evans realised long ago, and as such they represent the first surviving testimony to textile manufacture at Knossos, though this does not mean that it was not carried on earlier with equipment made entirely of perishable or unrecognisable materials. The first spindle-whorls (PLATE 5.a, top) made their appearance in levels transitional between EN II and MN. No less than twenty-two broken terracotta figurines, many certainly or probably female, one certainly male, and several fragments of animals, probably cattle, were found in the western half of Area AC in the EN II levels. Though such figurines are relatively common in the later strata, this is by far the greatest concentration found anywhere. It seems likely that they all come from the same building, which may have lain immediately to the north.

The EN II period probably mainly fell within the earlier part of the 5th millennium B.C., according to the three radiocarbon dates available (TABLE II, BM–719, BM–577 and BM–279). Its actual duration is difficult to determine, but it probably lasted several hundred years.

MIDDLE NEOLITHIC

The succeeding Middle Neolithic period has been explored over a considerably larger area than any of the earlier ones, especially below the Central Court, where substantial architectural remains have been found (FIG. 7; PLATE 1.d). Here portions of two multi-roomed buildings and a large, roughly square room, which may possibly be a more or less complete building, have been uncovered.[25] The

---

[24] D.K. Washburn, in her paper 'Symmetry analysis of ceramic design: two tests of the method on Neolithic material from Greece and the Aegean', in D.K. Washburn (ed.), *Structure and Cognition in Art* (Cambridge, 1984), 143, has convincingly demonstrated the sweeping nature of the change in pottery decoration from EN I to EN II. It is interesting to note that this coincided with what appears to have been a rapid expansion of the settlement, as noted above.
[25] Evans (n. 9 above), 172, 174, 176-8; (n. 5 above), 111, fig. 7, pl. viii.

more substantial of the multi-roomed buildings lay below the middle of the Central Court, to the south of the other two. It seemed to represent a more substantial version of the EN II buildings found in the West Court, and the aggregation of small rooms is evidently very similar in principle to that of the LN houses excavated by Sir Arthur Evans just below the surface of the Central Court. The massive stone foundations of the outer walls met at right angles and the whole building may have been rectangular, though unfortunately the eastern wall was not located. Inside, the space was divided into a number of small rooms, and there may also have been at least one unroofed area. In the debris which filled a narrow room in the northwestern corner of this building were found a number of clay loomweights (PLATE 5.a, bottom). It seems likely that they were stored, if not used, in this room, and their presence seems to establish the domestic character of the whole building.

The foundations of the part of the other multi-roomed house to the northwest of the one just described were a good deal flimsier and the rooms less regular. The skeletons of two children were found buried under the floors. Remains of portions of similar buildings were found in the MN levels below the West Court. The large square room, A, to the west of this house and north of the large rectangular house was evidently built before the other two, and may also represent something different. The internal measurements are about 4.5 × 4.5 m., the wall foundations are fairly thick, and it appears to be more or less detached. In the centre of the floor was a fire-reddened hollow; a square platform raised some 20 cms. above the level of the rest of the floor occupied one corner; and there were two small 'cupboards' containing the remains of pots. All these features are normal in houses, and none points to any special use; but into the top of the mound of yellow clay formed over the ruins by the collapsed *pisé* walls were sunk two pits which had been filled with pots, including a ladle, bowls, two hole-mouthed pots, one with a spout, and jars;[26] a deliberate burial of what looks like two sets of special equipment in the ruins of the room. As usual the floor was bare, but a couple of fragmentary human and one animal figurine found among the surrounding refuse remind one of the numerous figurines found in the preceding stratum, perhaps discarded from the predecessor of this building. Could this have been a shrine?

The pottery style of the MN period is characterised by the enormous popularity of ripple burnish on the fine wares (PLATE 2.c). Incised decoration is almost as popular as in EN II, but the hatched triangles, chevrons, zigzags and rectangles are as now precisely drawn as the EN II patterns were carelessly. Carinated bowls with a concave upper wall and ripple decoration dominate. The pots were superbly finished, but there is a certain monotony in both shapes and decoration (PLATE 2.d), though at least one new shape, the hole-mouthed pot, was introduced. Most coarse wares are not burnished, but have a smooth surface which may bear some decorative scribble burnish. Apart from the spindle-whorls and loomweights there are no novelties in the equipment, though clay disks cut from potsherds, possibly used as tallies or gaming pieces, which first appeared in Stratum VII, become very common, but rarer again afterwards.[27] Unworked fragments of rock crystal were also relatively common, after first appearing in the previous stratum. By this time the proportion of cattle seems to have risen to a peak, accounting for about 50% of the domesticated animals, but declining again rapidly in later strata.[28]

The MN appears to be represented everywhere by a single building level, though it is clear that,

---

[26] Evans (n. 9 above), fig. 20 and pls. 39.2 and 3; 42.5 and 6; 44.1, 2 and 5.
[27] Ibid. 235, pl. 58.1 and 2.
[28] Jarman, Bailey and Jarman (n. 4 above), 148.

as one might expect, not all the buildings were erected at exactly the same time. It is therefore likely to have been relatively short. Two of the three radiocarbon dates relating to the later part of it (BM–575 and BM–580) are only about a hundred years apart and when calibrated should fall somewhere in the later part of the 5th millennium B.C.; the third, however, BM–718, overlaps with dates for the EN II period.

LATE NEOLITHIC

The LN period is represented in the Central Court sequence by at least three building levels, if we include the houses excavated by Sir Arthur Evans, which are still the major architectural remains that can be attributed to it. Even so we cannot be sure that we have all of it because of terracing and levelling operations which clearly took place in Early Minoan times as well as for the erection of the later Palace. The surviving deposit varied in depth from around one to two metres, the deeper parts being in the eastern portion of the excavated areas. While most of it, even those parts which may have been put in as fill for levelling purposes, did not produce any post-Neolithic finds, there were signs of later disturbance in the top few centimetres. Two separate strata (II and I) were distinguishable within this accumulation.[29] In Area AA/BB in the West Court only about 0.75 m. of LN deposit was found below the Early Minoan building.[30] A bit further south, in Sounding EE, where LN levels were found immediately below the paving of the Court, the depth of the deposit belonging to this period was about 1.5 m. The later MN house in the middle of the Central Court was still in use at the beginning of the period, but not for long, since the corner of a similar multi-roomed house lying to the south and belonging to Stratum II was built over it. Otherwise the only building remains found in my excavations were those of short stretches of slight walls which can only be those of yards or working areas. The occurrence of pits and patches of pebble paving and the lack of other regular floors point in the same direction. The houses excavated by Sir Arthur Evans in 1923-4[31] are therefore the latest surviving Neolithic structures at Knossos. It has been shown that a deposit of yellow clay derived from old *pisé* walling which overlies the Stratum II deposits over much of the central and northern half of the Central Court passes beneath them, and they therefore belong to Stratum I. The main structure revealed is a complex of small rooms and perhaps open areas paved with pebbles. Evans distinguished two separate houses on the basis of two 'fixed hearths', or small raised platforms, which he found in separate rooms. If these were hearths, they represent an innovation. There was indeed a low platform in one corner of the single-roomed square building in Stratum III, but it was not a hearth. A fragment of a still later building was found overlying the eastern part of Evans' House A, where the ground sloped away, but only parts of two rooms survived.

Pottery style is again what defines the LN period. As usual, there is no sharp break with the previous style. The pottery of Stratum II has in some respects a transitional character, though the popularity of ripple burnish already shows a great decline. Firing techniques were clearly improving and new wares were developed, together with a greater variety of shapes and decoration. Improved firing eventually led to the complete abandonment of burnishing on coarse wares (PLATE 2.e), and the

---

[29] Evans (n. 9 above), 182, 184, 188.
[30] Evans (n. 5 above), 110-14, pl. viii.
[31] *PM II.i*, 1–21, fig. 8A.

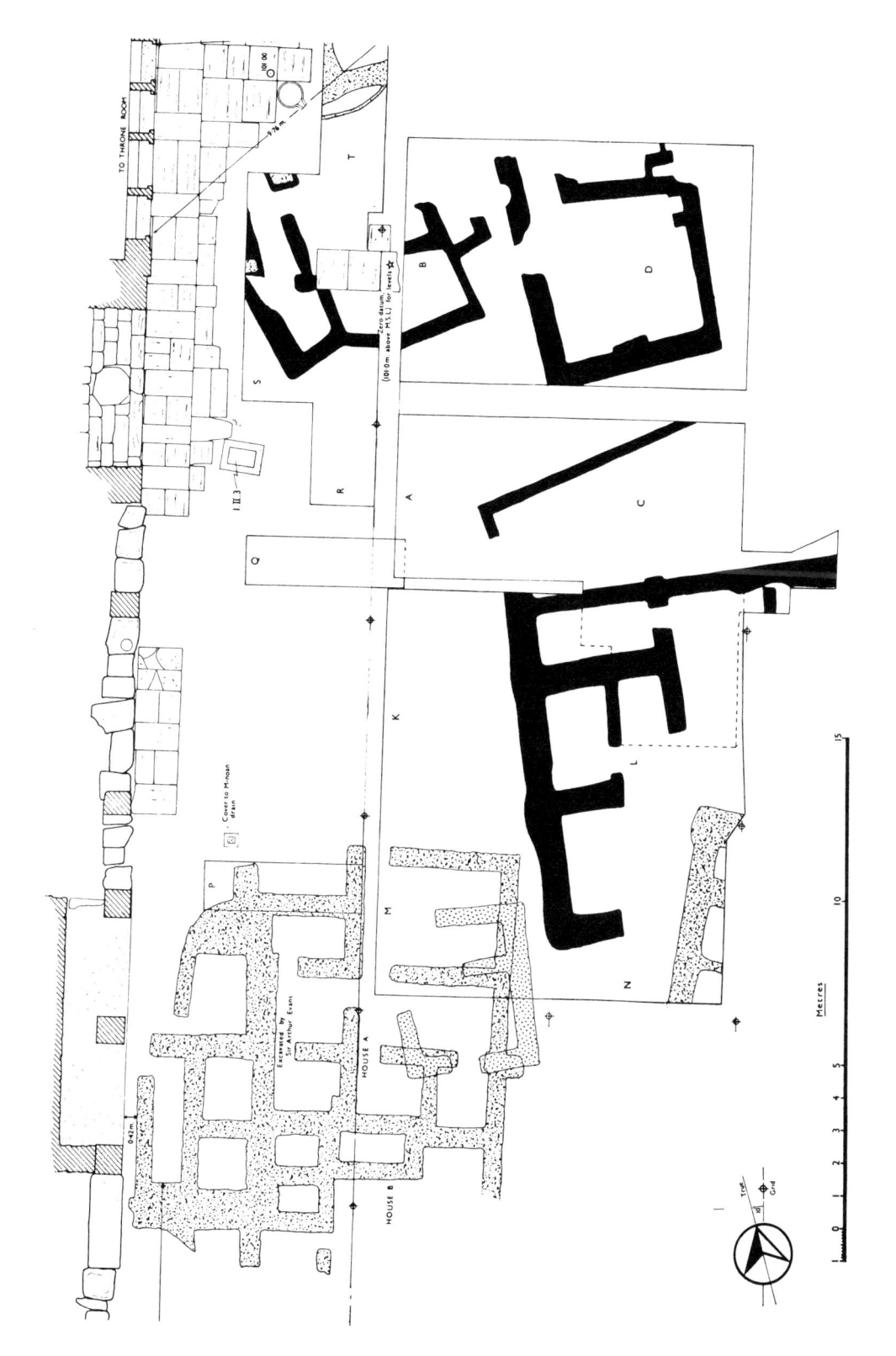

FIG. 7 MN (solid) and LN buildings in the Central Court

smoothed finish gradually gave way to one simply wiped over with a bunch of grass or coarse cloth. Fine wares were still generally finished by burnishing, but even some of these, particularly a fine grey ware, were left unburnished. New decorative techniques, such as pattern-burnish and channelling, were introduced, and old ones, like *pointillé* and applied decoration, were reintroduced in a somewhat different form.

Apart from pottery there is little change in the material equipment. Miniature vases, however, seem to be more common than before. Figurines (PLATE 3.b) representing humans and animals include a remarkable seated male figure in terracotta (PLATE 3.d), and a possible snake's head of the same material.[32] The beads and pendants of stone, shell, bone and terracotta found are of much the same types as in previous periods (see PLATE 4.b). Spindle whorls, sometimes decorated, of clay and occasionally of stone, are very common, and there are also clay spindle-whorls and loomweights. Small stone axes and adzes are still in use; a flat copper axe was found in Sir Arthur Evans' houses,[33] but unfortunately this cannot be regarded as a secure context and there are no supporting finds from the later excavations. Bone points are very numerous (see PLATE 5.d and e), and bone 'chisels' are still found. Small flakes of chert, obsidian and rock crystal continue to occur regularly, but there are, as in previous periods, very few tools: only very rarely small scrapers, lunates or blades. There are also querns and mortars, as always. Apart from the small quantity of obsidian all the materials used continue to be of local occurrence.

As has been already mentioned, much of the LN deposit under the central part of the Central Court had the characteristics of a fill or tip, and would probably have been needed to level the very uneven surface resulting from the destruction of MN and LN buildings there. The pottery was all of LN character, but includes pieces with decoration which is strikingly similar to that of some of the Phaistos Neolithic pottery, though no encrusted pieces are known here.[34] In the West Court, however, Sounding FF yielded a deposit of similar character which, in addition to pieces of similar type, also produced examples of other Phaistian decorative techniques, including this time a number of red encrusted pieces, trough spouts, and two examples of a Phaistian carinated bowl with very typical incised and red encrusted decoration (PLATE 2.f). A number of short obsidian blades also came from this deposit (PLATE 4.e).

The radiocarbon dates for the LN period are puzzling (TABLE II, BM–717, BM–581 and BM–579). One (BM–717) falls within the period covered by the EN II dates, the other two within that of the MN dates, calibrating to the second half of the 5th millennium B.C. or at the latest the very beginning of the 4th. Another date (BM–716), from FF, is substantially later, but unfortunately has a big standard error. When calibrated it suggests that this deposit probably belongs to the first half of the 4th millennium B.C. or the very end of the 5th.

There is unfortunately little evidence to show how far, and at what rate, the expansion of the settlement continued after the end of the EN II period. Late Neolithic sherds found in excavations along the Royal Road,[35] though not associated with building remains, imply occupation not far

---

[32] Evans (n. 9 above), fig. 60.16.
[33] Evans (n. 31 above), 14, fig. 3f.
[34] P.M. Fraser, 'Archaeology in Greece, 1969-70', *AR* 16 (1969-70), 28.
[35] M.S.F. Hood, 'Archaeology in Greece, 1961–62', *AR* 8 (1961–62), 27; H.W. Catling, 'Archaeology in Greece, 1971–72', *AR* 18 (1971–72), 21.

away, and if this inference is correct the LN settlement could have covered some 5 ha. There is as yet no evidence for the MN limits, but the settlement of this period certainly covered at least as much ground as was occupied during EN II. All that can be said about the size of the community during these periods is that it was probably never less than at the end of EN II, and could have been larger, reaching a maximum of perhaps a thousand or more by the LN.

There are differing views about the way in which the Knossian community developed from EN II onwards. My suggestion of continuous steady growth with gradually accelerating change and widening contacts[36] has recently been strongly challenged by Broodbank, who, acting on previous hints by Whitelaw and Bintliff,[37] has developed detailed arguments to demonstrate that a period of rapid growth and sudden cultural change, representing a radical transformation of the social structure, occurred during the EN II and MN periods.[38] This would correspond to the time when the settlement was expanding fastest, and may have slackened, along with its physical growth, in the LN. Change of this kind, Broodbank argues, matches observations of what tends to happen in farming communities of more than a few hundred people.[39] The case is cogently made out on the basis of the existing evidence, and would be well worth further testing.

The relationship of the Neolithic settlement to the succeeding Early Minoan one is another problem which is currently far from settled. The proliferation of settlements throughout Crete which took place during the Late Neolithic could imply some hiving off of population from Knossos, but there is no doubt that it still remained an exceptionally large one during that period. But what of FN Knossos, which is attested only by the deposit in Square FF? This may turn out to be mainly a question of terminology. Many traits characteristic of the FN pottery of Phaistos are already present in the later LN levels in both the Central Court and the West Court excavated in 1969 and 1970,[40] and I now believe it may have been misleading to isolate some of the material from FF as representing a separate phase because of a few special features which have not yet been found elsewhere. Thus a contraction of the settlement in the last Neolithic phase, as envisaged by Broodbank on the basis of the absence of these from the Royal Road soundings,[41] need not be inferred. Later levelling seems indeed to have destroyed any stratigraphical link with the EM settlement, but there are hints of continuity in the material from either side of the divide.[42] Neolithic Knossos is important in its own right as a Neolithic 'super-site', unique in Crete, but it is surely not coincidence that Knossos also became the most important Minoan centre. No doubt many other factors played a part in bringing this about, but it is at least possible that building on an unusually large and firmly established Late Neolithic community, with perhaps surviving traditions of its great antiquity and special position in the island's history, gave Knossos an initial advantage which contributed in some measure to its success in Minoan times.

---

[36] Evans (n. 5 above), 3.
[37] T.M. Whitelaw, 'The settlement of Fournou Korifi, Myrtos and aspects of Early Minoan social organisation' in O. Krzyszkowska and L. Nixon (eds.), *Minoan Society: Proceedings of the Cambridge Colloquium 1981* (Bristol, 1983), 340; J.L. Bintliff, 'Structuralism and the Minoan myth', *Antiquity* 58 (1984), 37.
[38] C. Broodbank, 'The Neolithic Labyrinth: social change at Knossos before the Bronze Age', *JMA* 5.1 (1992), 39–75.
[39] Ibid. 42.
[40] See n. 30 above. A detailed study of the Late Neolithic pottery of Knossos and its relation to the Phaistos Neolithic pottery and to Early Minoan pottery has been made by K. Manteli for her Ph.D thesis (University College, London, 1993).
[41] Broodbank (n. 38 above), 42.
[42] e.g. the continued popularity of 'wiped' coarse wares in the early part of EM.

TABLE II

C-14 dates for Neolithic Knossos

Lab. No.	Date BP	Context; Date	Material
BM–124	8050 ± 180	Area AC, St. X	Charcoal from oak stake
BM–278	7910 ± 140	Area AC, St. X	Charcoal from oak stake
BM–436	7740 ± 130	Area AC, St. IX	Carbonised grain
BM–272	7570 ± 150	Area AC, St. IX	Charcoal
BM–1372	6482 ± 161	Area AA/BB, EN IF	Charcoal (combined samples)
BM–273	6210 ± 150	Area AC, St. VI	Charcoal
BM–1371	6201 ± 252	Area AA/BB, EN IE	Charcoal (combined samples)
BM–126	7000 ± 180	Area AC, St. V	Charcoal
BM–274	6140 ± 150	Area AC, St. V	Charcoal
BM–719	5967 ± 41	Area AA/BB, EN IIA	Charcoal (combined samples)
BM–577	5884 ± 188	Area M, late EN II	Charcoal (combined samples)
BM–279	5680 ± 150	Area AC, St. IV	Charcoal (combined samples)
BM–718	5892 ± 91	Square EE, MN	Charcoal (combined samples)
BM–580	5522 ± 88	Squares AA, CC, late MN	Charcoal (combined samples)
BM–575	5636 ± 94	Area AA/BB MN/LN transition	Charcoal (combined samples)
BM–717	5806 ± 124	Square EE, LN	Charcoal
BM–581	5588 ± 145	Area K/N, LN	Charcoal (combined samples)
BM–579	5534 ± 76	Area SS/BB, LN	Charcoal (combined samples)
BM–716	5003 ± 213	Square FF, LN/FN	Charcoal

PLATE II Taverna Yard, Knossos — with chair, amphora and lemon tree (etching and aquatint)

Chapter 2

Knossos Before the Palaces:
An Overview of the Early Bronze Age (EM I–EM III)[1]

D. WILSON

INTRODUCTION

This paper is meant primarily to serve as a general cultural overview of Early Minoan Knossos. No other period of the Minoan settlement is so poorly preserved, owing largely to the very extensive intrusions made during the course of later building activity. For this reason, the summary I present here must be based largely on the ceramic evidence. This should not, however, be viewed as a drawback for any cultural reconstruction of the period, since detailed stylistic and petrographic ceramic analyses can provide a wealth of information not otherwise available from the archaeological record.[2] This survey will focus on the use of pottery to provide a framework for the cultural sequence of Knossos in Early Minoan and for the relative dating of specific events within the development of the Prepalatial settlement. I begin by outlining Arthur Evans' original definitions for the phasing of Early Minoan Knossos and review the later work led by Sinclair Hood which has made possible important revisions of the ceramic sequence. There follows a stylistic summary of the Early Minoan pottery phases at Knossos based on the principal defining deposits for each period. This forms a chronological framework for piecing together the extent of the Early Minoan settlement from scattered fill deposits and fragmentary architectural remains. Knossos is then placed within the perspective of its larger Cretan and Aegean context, as I review the evidence for inter-regional exchange and signs

---

Special Abbreviation:
SMK = J.D.S. and H.W. Pendlebury, E. Eccles and M. Money-Coutts, *A Guide to the Stratigraphical Museum in the Palace at Knossos. Parts I–III* (London, 1933–5).

[1] This paper has benefited greatly from the comments and criticisms of Gerald Cadogan, Peter Day, Nicoletta Momigliano, and Todd Whitelaw. I would also like to thank Sinclair Hood, Gerald Cadogan, and Peter Warren for allowing me to study their EM material on numerous occasions and sharing with me so much of what they know about this period. Barbara Bilyea patiently prepared the figure drawings for me, for which I am grateful. With my contribution to this volume, I would like to acknowledge my indebtedness to Sinclair Hood, who first introduced me to Early Minoan Knossos in 1978 and who has since been always generous both to me and to many others of his time and knowledge of Minoan Knossos.

[2] D.E. Wilson and P.M. Day, 'Ceramic regionalism in Prepalatial central Crete: the Mesara imports at EM I–EM IIA Knossos', in press; P.M. Day and D.E. Wilson, 'The ceramic sequence of Prepalatial Knossos: innovation and development in a regional potting centre', forthcoming.

of foreign contact. In the concluding section I make some observations on the possible bearing that points brought up in this paper may have for our understanding of the origins of palatial society at Knossos.

EVANS' CERAMIC PHASING OF EARLY MINOAN

In 1904 Duncan Mackenzie made a series of tests beneath the West Court of the Palace at Knossos from which he drew up a north–south section of his findings.[3] The 1904 West Court soundings and section provided for Evans what appeared to be an almost uninterrupted sequence of habitation levels for the Neolithic through Middle Minoan phases at Knossos.[4] Evans presented the evidence from the 1904 tests in that year reproducing Mackenzie's north–south section largely unchanged and showing three successive Early Minoan floor levels; it was upon this section that Evans based his tripartite division of Early Minoan.[5] Mackenzie, however, clearly noted that there was insufficient evidence in the form of floor deposits from his 1904 West Court tests to support a complete sequence for Early Minoan as published by Evans.[6] With the exception of the Early Houses excavated in 1908, relatively little Early Minoan was found after Mackenzie's Palace tests in 1904. Therefore, the West Court tests remained in 1921 the best, although incomplete, record for the Early Minoan settlement at Knossos. This is probably why Evans reprinted the West Court Section in his *Palace of Minos*, although he must have been aware of its limitations.[7] Evans had to resort largely to sites and deposits outside Knossos to define the EM I–III pottery sequence.[8] Nowhere beneath the West Court has there yet been found a continuous sequence for all phases of Early and Middle Minoan. A careful study of the pottery preserved from the 1904 West Court tests following roughly the north–south line of Mackenzie's original section records the following sequence for Early Minoan:[9] (1) a mixed fill of latest Neolithic and EM IIA above undisturbed Neolithic deposits at 2.80 m. (= Evans' 'EM I floor' or 'Sub-Neolithic'); (2) a pure fill deposit of EM IIA at about the 2.50 m. level (= Evans' 'EM II Stratum'); and (3) above the EM IIA fill there is not a consistent sequence from one test to the next, but at about the 1.50 m. level at least some of the material from tests 4, 9, 14, and 15 can now be assigned to EM III,[10] although Evans had earlier placed this deposit in his MM IA.[11]

---

[3] For the approximate location of the 1904 West Court tests, see D.E. Wilson, 'The pottery and architecture of the Early Minoan IIA West Court house at Knossos', *BSA* 80 (1985), fig. 1. For a list of the tests made in that year, see *SMK*, plan 4.B. Mackenzie's sketch of the N–S section appears opposite p. 44 of his daybook for 1904, the original copy of which is now in the Ashmolean Library, Oxford.

[4] A.J. Evans, 'The Palace of Knossos: Knossos excavations 1904', *BSA* 10 (1903–4), 1–62.

[5] Ibid., fig. 7; id., *Essai de classification des époques de la civilisation minoenne* (London, 1906).

[6] Mackenzie, Daybook 1904, 44; and letter to Evans of September, 1905, reproduced in L.R. Palmer, *The Penultimate Palace of Knossos* (Incunabula Graeca 33; Rome, 1969), 149–51.

[7] *PM I*, fig. 4.

[8] Ibid., 56–126.

[9] Unless otherwise noted, the terms EM I–III and MM IA are used in this paper as defined in G. Cadogan, P. Day, C. Macdonald, J.A. MacGillivray, N. Momigliano, T. Whitelaw and D. Wilson, 'Early Minoan and Middle Minoan pottery groups at Knossos', *BSA* 88 (1993), 21–8.

[10] N. Momigliano, 'MM IA pottery from Evans' excavations at Knossos: a reassessment', *BSA* 86 (1991), 185–91.

[11] *PM I*, 172. Compare this interpretation of the sequence with P. Warren and V. Hankey, *Aegean Bronze Age Chronology* (Bristol, 1989), 109 n. 5.

Evans was not able to refer directly to any stratified deposits to characterise EM I at Knossos, and defined the period largely on the basis of pottery groups from other sites.[12] He divided EM II into an early and a late phase: the former he defined at Knossos as the lower floor deposit beneath the South Front Early Houses, the latter as the final period (III) of the EM II settlement at Vasilike characterised by the predominance of Vasilike Ware.[13] He did not, however, cite any deposits at Knossos which might correspond to this final phase of EM II at Vasilike. Evans defined the EM III ceramic period at Knossos on the basis of the upper floor deposit from the South Front Early Houses.[14] He chose, however, to place later in MM IA other deposits which have since been shown to be contemporary with the upper floor of the Early Houses.[15]

PREPALATIAL KNOSSOS SINCE EVANS

After the series of Palace tests made at Knossos between 1904 and 1908, with a final presentation of the evidence by Evans in 1921, no further explorations to clarify the Early Minoan sequence were made for fifty years.[16] In 1957 Sinclair Hood began a programme of stratigraphic excavations along the Royal Road and found the most complete sequence of Early Minoan levels yet known for the Prepalatial settlement.[17] It is the strata from tests on the northern side of the Royal Road which for the first time provided evidence for the EM II–EM III ceramic sequence at Knossos. This sequence was independently confirmed by tests made outside the South Front of the Palace in 1960 in the area of the Early Houses. Here floor deposits which now best define the EM IIB ceramic phase at Knossos were found partly stratified beneath floor and fill deposits of EM III.[18] Elsewhere, in the North-East Quarter of the Palace, a chance discovery in 1958 of a deep well deposit produced the earliest Minoan pottery yet known from Knossos. Hood assigned the Palace Well deposit to an early phase of EM I, i.e. EM IA, but noted that no deposits had been found at Knossos which could be placed later in EM I, i.e. EM IB.[19]

These stratigraphic tests by Hood from 1957 to 1961 clarified and supplemented the Early Minoan sequence of pottery as initially presented by Evans. The Palace Well deposits provided the first ceramic evidence for an EM I phase at Knossos. The Royal Road North and the South Front Early Houses established the stylistic and stratigraphic distinctions between an EM II and an EM III phase. There still remained, however, a ceramic gap between the EM I Palace Well and EM II, and no clear definition of ceramic phases within EM II. Further tests in 1969 and 1972 provided evidence to address both these problems.

---

[12] *PM I*, 56–64.
[13] Ibid. 71–5.
[14] Ibid. 108. Evans never illustrated any of the material from this upper deposit.
[15] S. Andreou, 'Pottery Groups of the Old Palace Period in Crete' (Ph.D. dissertation, University of Cincinnati, 1978); Momigliano (n. 10 above), 268.
[16] The only exception is the 1930 excavation of Houses A and B beneath the kouloures in the West Court. For detailed bibliography, see Momigliano (n. 10 above), 206.
[17] S. Hood, 'Stratigraphic excavations at Knossos, 1957–61', *Cretological I, A'I* 92–8; and 'The Early Minoan periods at Knossos', *BICS* 13 (1966), 110–11.
[18] N. Momigliano (n. 10 above), 198–201, 268, for discussion of EM III.
[19] Hood (n. 17 above), 110; id., *The Minoans: Crete in the Bronze Age* (London, 1971), 37.

In 1969 John Evans made a number of tests beneath the West Court of the Palace at Knossos in the hope of finding deposits that might show the ceramic development from the latest Neolithic to Early Minoan. Although such a sequence was not found, he did uncover portions of a building, the West Court House, and associated deposits which have since been shown to mark the beginning of EM IIA at Knossos.[20] Further tests at the southern side of the Royal Road in 1972 by Warren uncovered parts of a substantial building with two successive floor deposits, both of which were assigned to EM IIA.[21] Hence what had up to 1969 been an ill-defined phase within EM II was now richly represented by the remains of two houses and their associated deposits. These two pottery groups made it possible to argue on stylistic grounds that the lower deposit beneath the South Front Early Houses does not belong in the earlier phase of EM II, as was originally thought by Sir Arthur Evans, but is later and represents EM IIB at Knossos.[22]

A test made north of the West Court House by John Evans in 1969, Trench FF, contained a small burnt fill deposit of EM I. The Trench FF group appears stylistically to fall between the EM IA Palace Well and the EM IIA West Court House deposits, hence providing the first possible ceramic evidence at Knossos for an EM IB phase.[23] Recent tests by Hood in 1987 behind the Throne Room (Room 46) and in the North-West Quarter (*SMK*, D.I.2, 6) of the Palace have uncovered further deposits of EM IB.[24]

To sum up, although Sir Arthur Evans argued for a tripartite division for Early Minoan, the limited evidence then known had made it impossible for him to describe fully the ceramic character of his successive phases. Hood was able, however, by 1961 to present the ceramic sequence for the Prepalatial settlement from EM I through MM IA. Further work since 1961 has focused on phasing and refining the ceramic development within EM I–MM IA. Both Hood[25] and Cadogan[26] suggested that there was a later phase of EM I at Knossos which post-dated the Palace Well group and might be contemporary with the Pyrgos Cave deposits. The existence of an EM IB phase at Knossos has now been confirmed by the Trench FF deposit, by the 1987 tests of Hood, and by recent study of material from various Palace tests made by Evans between 1903 and 1905.[27] Evans had been unable to phase the EM II deposits at Knossos, but later discoveries made it possible for Hood[28] and Warren[29] to argue for a ceramic development within EM II. Two phases of EM II, A and B, can

---

[20] J.D. Evans, 'The Early Minoan II occupation of Knossos: a note on some new evidence', *Anat. Stud.* 22 (1972), 115–28; Wilson (n. 3 above), 281–364.

[21] P. Warren, 'Knossos and the Greek mainland in the third millennium B.C.', *AAA* 5 (1972), 392–8.

[22] Cadogan *et al.* (n. 9 above); cf. Warren and Hankey (n. 11 above), 17.

[23] Wilson (n. 3 above), 359–64; cf. S. Hood, 'Autochthons or settlers? Evidence for immigration at the beginning of the Early Bronze Age in Crete', in *Cretological VI, A'1* (Chania, 1990), 368.

[24] H.W. Catling, 'Archaeology in Greece, 1987–88', *AR* 34 (1987–88), 69. My thanks to Sinclair Hood for permission to study the 1987 test material and make mention of it here. The 1987 tests in the North–West Quarter of the Palace are now being studied by Alan Peatfield for final publication.

[25] Hood (n. 17 above), 110; and (n. 19 above), 36–7.

[26] G. Cadogan, 'Early Minoan and Middle Minoan chronology', *AJA* 87 (1983), 508.

[27] A ware characterisation study of EM IB is now underway by the author and P.M. Day: 'A ceramic characterization of EMIB at Knossos', forthcoming.

[28] Hood (n. 19 above), 37–8.

[29] P. Warren, 'The first Minoan stone vases and Early Minoan chronology', *Kr.Chron.* 19 (1965), 7–43; id., (n. 21 above), 395–6; Warren and Hankey (n. 11 above), 15–17.

now be clearly distinguished at Knossos, and future study may help to characterise possible ceramic development within EM IIA. Finally, analyses by Andreou and Momigliano have provided a detailed ceramic picture of EM III at Knossos and have helped to clarify the succeeding MM IA phase.[30]

THE EARLY MINOAN POTTERY SEQUENCE AT KNOSSOS: MAIN DEPOSITS AND STYLISTIC SUMMARY[31]

1. Early Minoan IA (FIG. 1)

> Palace Well — North-East Palace Quarter — pure burnt fill deposit.
> Related deposits: material from mixed(?) fill deposits in 1987 test west of North Lustral Basin (*SMK*, D.I.2).[32]

The present sequence at Knossos indicates a marked stylistic break between the latest Neolithic and the earliest Early Minoan, represented by the EM IA Palace Well.[33] It is still not clear how much continuity, if any, there may be in fabric, shape or surface treatment from the latest Neolithic to EM IA.[34] Nor is it yet certain whether the latest Neolithic deposits preserved at Knossos represent the final ceramic phase here before the Palace Well group.[35] The upper levels of the deep soundings in the West Court (Trenches EE and FF) made by John Evans in 1969 and 1970 appear to represent the latest Neolithic at Knossos.[36] Because of a small group of sherds from Trench FF which are very similar in style to the FN of Phaistos, John Evans had initially suggested a ceramic phase at Knossos which post-dated the latest Neolithic beneath the Central Court (Stratum I).[37] He now believes, however, that the presence or absence of rare Phaistian FN features is not by itself a justifiable basis for the definition of a separate FN phase at Knossos.[38]

For the moment all that can be said with certainty is that the latest Neolithic of Knossos is at least in part contemporary with the FN of Phaistos.

---

[30] Andreou (n. 15 above); Momigliano (n. 10 above).

[31] The deposits by period cited here are a slight expansion on the list published in Cadogan *et al.* (n. 9 above) — to which the reader should refer for references. The ceramic summary presented here is based on these defining deposits. Detailed discussion of EM IIA and EM III pottery styles has already appeared elsewhere: Wilson (n. 3 above); Andreou (n. 15 above); Momigliano (n. 10 above). See also forthcoming studies by Hood and Cadogan for the entire EM sequence at Knossos and Wilson for EM IIB ware groups ('Ware groups of the EMIIB deposit from the South Front Early Houses at Knossos'). For the results of the 1993 tests in the area of the 'Early Houses', see N. Momigliano and D.E. Wilson, 'Knossos 1993: excavations outside the South Front of the palace', forthcoming. The most detailed survey to date of the EM ceramic sequence at Knossos is in Hood (n. 19 above), 36–9 and for Crete as a whole in P.P. Betancourt, *The History of Minoan Pottery* (Princeton, 1985), 23–63. A detailed study by ware and fabric group of the Prepalatial ceramic sequence at Knossos is now underway by Peter Day and the author (n. 2 above).

[32] See Catling (n. 24 above), 69, fig. 1.

[33] Hood (n. 23 above), 369.

[34] For results of current research in this area, see Day and Wilson (n. 2 above).

[35] For a review of the evidence at Knossos with further references, see D.E. Wilson, 'The Early Minoan IIA West Court House at Knossos' (Ph.D. dissertation, University of Cincinnati, 1984), 131–40. For the final Neolithic in Crete, see L. Vagnetti and P. Belli, 'Characters and problems of the final Neolithic in Crete', *SMEA* 19 (1978), 125–63; also Warren and Hankey (n. 11 above), 12–14.

[36] J.D. Evans, 'Neolithic Knossos: the growth of a settlement', *PPS* 37.2 (1971), 113–14; K. Manteli, 'The Transition from the Neolithic to Early Bronze Age in Crete' (Ph.D. dissertation, University of London, 1993).

[37] Evans, ibid. 114.

[38] See Evans in this volume — p. 19.

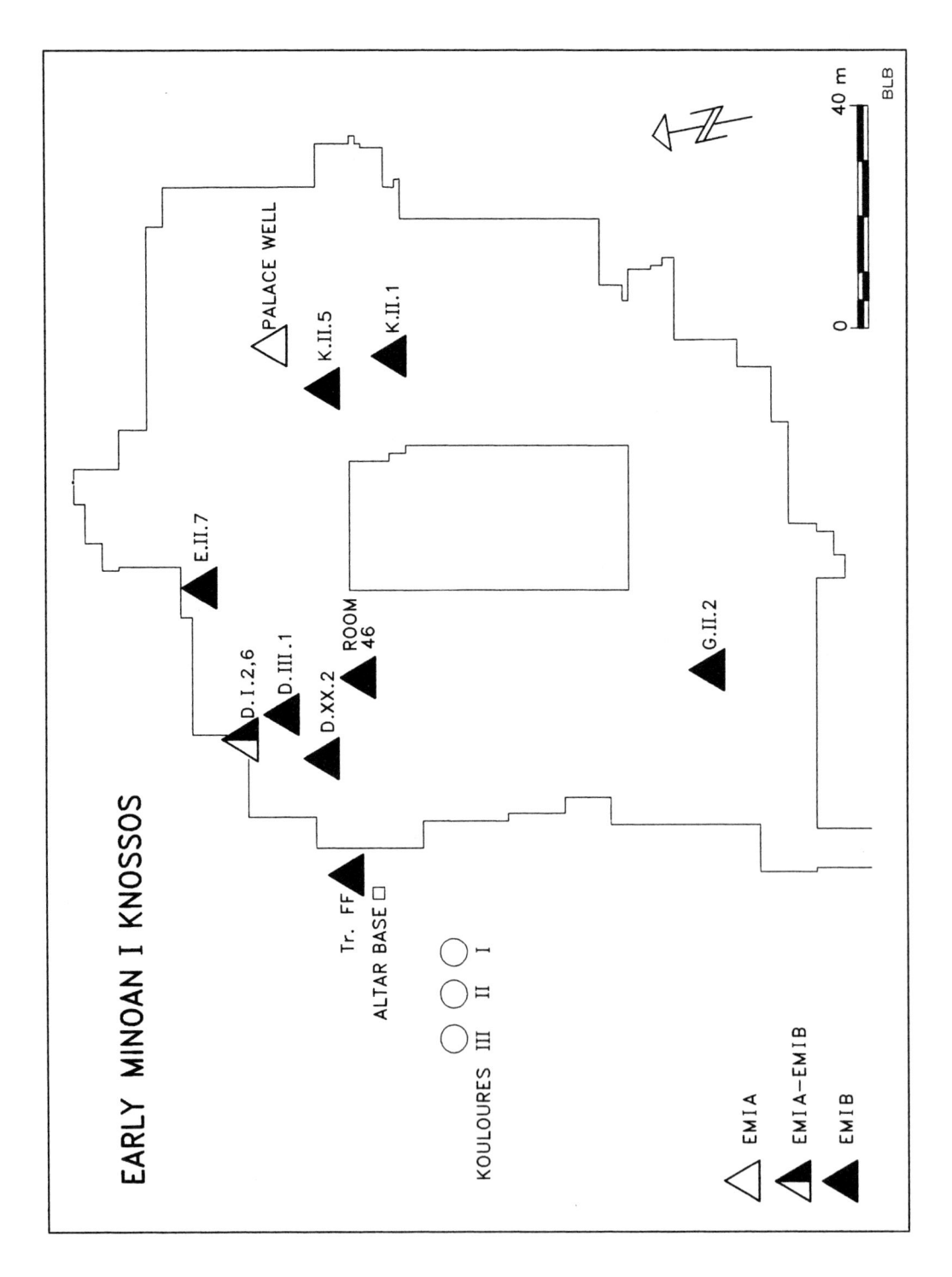

FIG. 1 Findspots of principal EM IA–B deposits at Knossos

The EM IA ceramic phase at Knossos, based on Hood's preliminary description of the Palace Well Group, is characterised by the following principal shapes and decoration:[39] (1) pattern-burnished pedestalled bowls[40] and chalices;[41] (2) burnished lids with cylindrical handles;[42] (3) large globular jugs with pinched-in spouts;[43] (4) deep bowls with carinated rounded bottoms;[44] (5) dark-on-light painted round-bottomed jugs with cutaway spouts;[45] (6) baking plates;[46] (7) deep bowls/open jars;[47] (8) pithoi with trickle-painted decoration.[48]

2. Early Minoan IB (FIG. 1)[49]

West Court-Trench FF (Level 4) — burnt fill deposit above latest Neolithic and below a mixed EM IIA-MM fill.
Related deposits: Magazine 16 (*SMK*, D.XX.2); Area of Pictographic Tablets (*SMK*, D.III.1); North-West Portico (*SMK*, E.II.7); deposits from tests made in 1987 west of North Lustral Basin (*SMK*, D.I.2, 6) and west of Throne Room (Room 46);[50] North-East Hall (*SMK*, K.II.5); Corridor of the Draught Board (*SMK*, K.II.1); the South Propylaeum (*SMK*, G.II.2).

The deposits which are used here to define an EM IB phase at Knossos represent fills, either pure or mixed with Neolithic and/or EM IIA (and in some cases later material). A convincing case on stylistic grounds, however, can be made for a distinct EM IB phase which falls between the EM IA Palace Well and the EM IIA West Court House deposits. Future study of the 1987 test material may provide the stratigraphic evidence for the phasing of EM I. The stylistic summary which follows is based on the assumed pure or largely homogeneous fill deposits from the Palace tests listed above. The occurrence in these deposits of new shapes, decorative techniques and fabrics not seen in the Palace Well presents a strong argument for this separate phase in EM I. The argument is furthered by certain stylistic affinities with the quite separate pottery of EM IIA.

The EM IB ceramic phase at Knossos is characterised in part by the following stylistic features:[51] (1) dark grey burnished ware chalices, usually with pattern-burnished decoration and a narrow waist with parallel grooving;[52] (2) dark-on-light painted ware jugs with cutaway or pinched-in spouts;[53]

---

[39] For full publication of the Palace Well pottery, see M.S.F. Hood and G. Cadogan, *Early Minoan Excavations at Knossos*, forthcoming.
[40] Hood (n. 23 above), fig. 1.2; id., 'Settlers in Crete c.3000 B.C.', *Cretan Studies* 2 (1990), fig. 1.
[41] Hood (n. 23 above), fig. 1.1.
[42] Ibid., fig. 2.17–18.
[43] Ibid., fig. 1.12; id., (n. 40 above), fig. 2.
[44] Hood (n. 23 above), fig. 1.8–9.
[45] Ibid., fig. 1.11; id., (n. 40 above), fig. 3.
[46] Hood (n. 23 above), fig. 1.10.
[47] Ibid., fig. 1.6–7.
[48] Ibid. 370.
[49] See Hood and Cadogan (n. 39 above); Wilson and Day (n. 2 above).
[50] Catling (n. 24 above), 68–9; S. Hood and W. Taylor, *The Bronze Age Palace at Knossos. Plans and Sections* (*BSA* Suppl. 15; London, 1981), no. 160 and Room 46.
[51] See Wilson (n. 3 above), 359–63, for initial publication of the Trench FF group, which this description follows. Also Wilson and Day (n. 2 above).
[52] Wilson (n. 3 above), FF1–4.
[53] Ibid., FF8, FF11, pl. 56 right.

(3) deep bowls/open jars[54] and jugs[55] with a heavily wiped or scored exterior surface; (4) baking plates in a cooking-pot ware;[56] and (5) pithoi.

The deep carinated bowl and large globular jug with pinched-in spout which are common in the EM IA Palace Well are rare by EM IB. New ware groups in EM IB include dark grey burnished ware with a reddish fabric and scored ware. There is a strong continuity in ware groups from EM IB to EM IIA. As for shapes, the pedestalled bowl, chalice, and jug with cutaway or pinched-in spout occur in both phases of EM I, although there are developments in form, as in the case of the chalice. In general, there does appear to be a greater discontinuity in ceramic traditions from EM IA to EM IB than from EM IB to EM IIA.[57]

3. *EM IIA* (FIG. 2)

West Court House — floor and associated fill deposits.
Related deposits: 1904–5 West Court Tests (*SMK*, B.I.4–6, 9, 15–17); Trench GG — 1969 test east of kouloura I;[58] Area of Pictographic Tablets (*SMK*, D.III.1); west of North Lustral Basin (*SMK*, E.I.7, 9); North-West Portico (*SMK*, E.II.7); North-East Magazines (*SMK*, K.I.4, 6–8); North-East Hall (*SMK*, K.II.5); Area of the Olive Press (*SMK*, M.III.1).

The earliest known ceramic phase of EM II Knossos is defined by the West Court House deposits, which have been described in detail elsewhere.[59] I summarise here those wares and shapes which continue from EM IB into EM IIA at Knossos and those which appear to be absent by the time of the West Court House. Most of the ware groups which occur in EM IIA have their origins in EM IB. These include dark grey burnished, dark-on-light, cooking pot and pithos wares.[60] Notably absent by EM IIA are vessels with a heavily wiped or scored exterior surface. A new introduction in EM IIA is red or black slipped ware, the first appearance of a surface treatment which would become standard by EM III.

The strong continuity in ware groups from EM IB is partly reflected in the range of shapes which continue into EM IIA: jugs with cutaway spout, baking plates, deep bowls/open jars, and pithoi. There are developments within this group, however, as for example with the jug which in EM IIA has a high beaked spout, three pellet feet, and often applied pellet 'eyes' on the spout neck. There are rare examples of the EM I type of pedestalled bowl and chalice in the West Court House deposits, but neither shape outlives this early phase of EM IIA. The West Court House deposits introduce a range of new shapes: the stemmed or low-pedestalled goblet, small rounded bowls, bowls with internally thickened rims, side-spouted deep bowls, basins/lekanai, large baking plates with burnished interior, and horned stands. There are not only more shapes in EM IIA, but also more techniques of surface treatment. Notable are vessels with a red or black slipped surface, the first use of white-on-dark painted decoration, and fine incised decoration. Overall or pattern-burnished surfaces continue

---

[54] Ibid., pl. 57 top photo: bottom row right.
[55] Ibid., FF13–14; pl. 57 top photo: top row right and bottom row middle.
[56] Ibid., FF16–18.
[57] Day and Wilson (n. 2 above).
[58] Wilson (n. 3 above), 291–2.
[59] Ibid.
[60] Day and Wilson (n. 2 above).

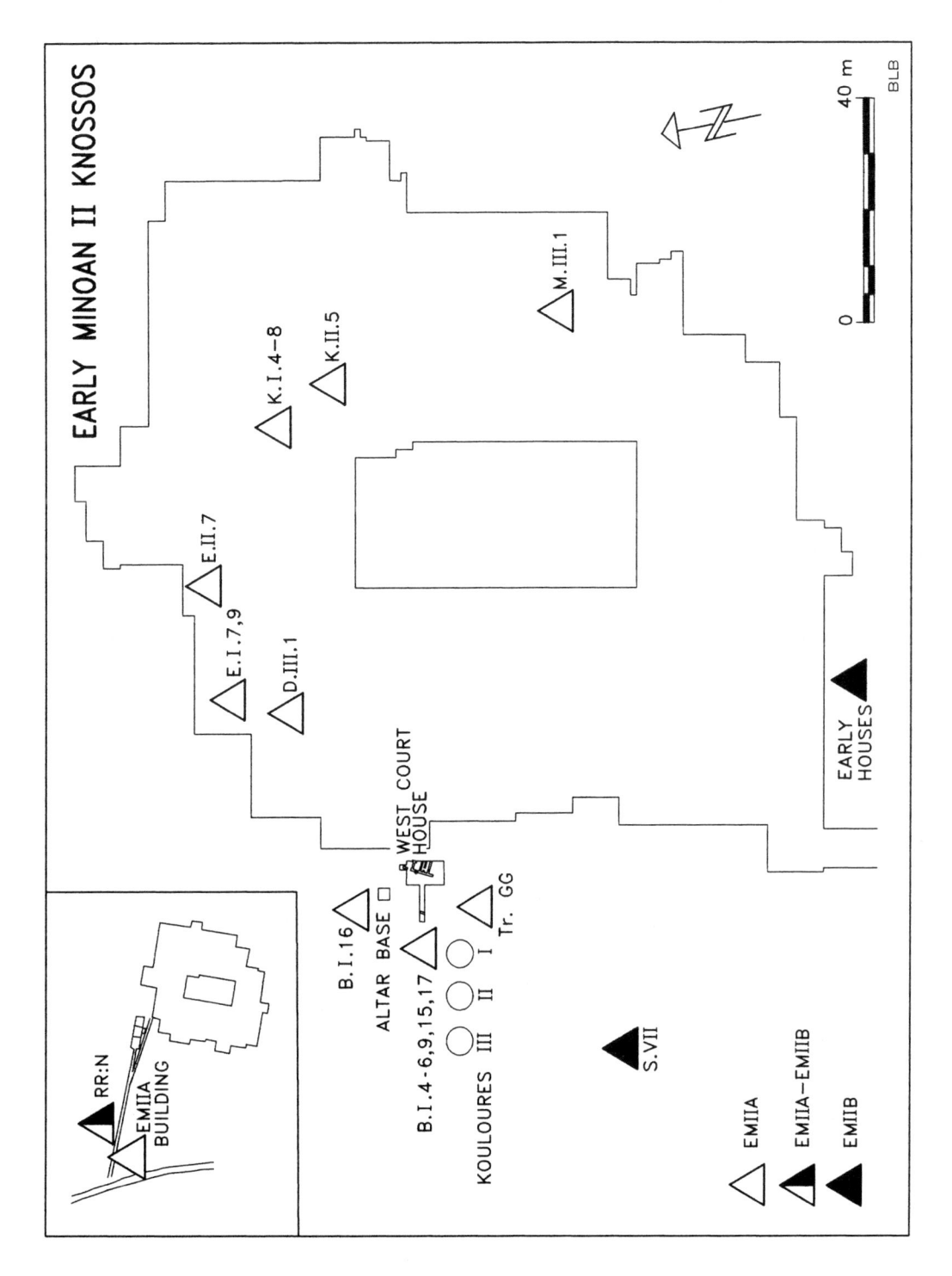

FIG. 2   Findspots of principal EM IIA–B deposits at Knossos

from EM I, but pattern-burnishing dies out before the end of EM IIA. Dark-on-light painted decoration is more common than in EM I and uses a greater range of decorative schemes and motifs.

There is a small group of EM IIA fill deposits at Knossos which appear to be stylistically homogeneous and are characterised by a sufficient number of features to suggest a post-West Court House phase for EM IIA.[61] The quantity of dark grey burnished ware falls off, while buff or red/black slipped wares correspondingly increase. Dark-on-light painted decoration continues, but the range of decorative schemes and motifs is not as rich as the West Court House repertoire. New bowl types appear which become common in EM IIB, namely the shallow bowl with rounded thickened rim or everted rim.[62] Although it might be argued that these EM IIA deposits are simply mixed fills of EM IIA and EM IIB, it is significant that not a single example of the ubiquitous EM IIB footed goblet has been found in any of them.[63]

4. EM IIB (FIG. 2)

South Front Early Houses – lower floor deposit found partly beneath an EM III floor.[64]
Related Deposits: Royal Road North, floor V;[65] building south of the West Court (area *SMK*, S.VII).[66]

In contrast to the strong ceramic continuity from EM IB to EM IIA at Knossos, the lower floor deposits from the Early Houses show a sharp break in style from EM IIA. The fabric in EM IIB becomes markedly standardised with most of the pottery assemblage represented by only two wares: dark-on-light painted and red or black slipped wares. Dark-on-light painted ware has a plain buff or burnished surface with a restricted range of decorative motifs: simple bands on bowls; cross-hatched triangles on the shoulder and triple chevrons on the necks of jugs. This simplified decorative scheme on jugs replaces the large cross-hatched 'butterfly' motifs and neck banding of EM IIA examples.[67] Gone is the lively and imaginative decorative style of EM IIA. There is also a relatively limited range of shapes: the most common is the footed goblet,[68] followed by the shallow bowl with rounded thickened rim,[69] two-handled bowl with a painted cross on base interior and/or exterior, the deep bowl with everted rim,[70] and jug.[71] There are roughly equal amounts of red or black slipped ware,

---

[61] North–West Portico (Test 2: *SMK*, E.II.7); North–East Magazines (*SMK*, K.I.5). The deposits from the Royal Road: South EM IIA building may belong with this group, although their relationship to the West Court House pottery is not yet clear from the preliminary publications (Warren n. 21 above). final publication of the Royal Road: North floor VI deposits (Hood and Cadogan n. 39 above) will also resolve their relative position within EM IIA (Wilson n. 35 above, 168–73).

[62] See Wilson (n. 3 above), P247 fig. 27, for example of shallow bowl from mixed deposit above the West Court House.

[63] e.g. *PM I*, fig. 40: second row from top.

[64] See n. 31 above. The EM III South Front House is labelled as 'Early Houses' in Hood and Taylor (n. 50 above), 13, no. 2. For a new plan and discussion of this building, see Momigliano and Wilson (n. 31 above).

[65] Hood and Cadogan (n. 39 above); Wilson (n. 35 above), 205–6.

[66] Found in the 1993 excavations in the area to the southwest of the Palace, just south of the West Court and west of the South-West House. I am grateful to Dr. Colin Macdonald for permission to make mention of this find here.

[67] e.g. Wilson (n. 3 above), P218 and P221.

[68] *PM I*, fig. 40: top, second, and bottom rows.

[69] Ibid., fig. 40: top and bottom rows.

[70] Ibid., fig. 40: third row.

[71] Ibid., fig. 40: top row.

with or without white painted decoration, whose shape repertoire includes the footed goblet, two-handled bowl with incurving or everted rim, and jug.[72] A shape which might be specific to this ware is the side-spouted jar with pouring handle ('teapot'). These two wares make up well over half the total number of vessels in EM IIB. Vasilike ware, which has traditionally been viewed as a type-fossil of EM IIB Crete, is rare at Knossos and probably all of it is imported.[73]

To sum up, a comparison between EM IIA and EM IIB shows clear differences. The stemmed or low-pedestalled goblets and small rounded bowls of EM IIA are gone, while the large globular EM IIA jug on three pellet feet has been replaced by a smaller more ovoid-shaped flat-bottomed jug. Among the new shapes in EM IIB are the footed goblet, shallow bowl, two-handled bowl with everted rim, and the side-spouted jar ('teapot'). The most significant change in the assemblage of wares from EM IIA is the disappearance of dark grey burnished ware, which had already begun to die out before the end of EM IIA. This brings an end to a very long-lived tradition of dark burnished pottery going back to the beginning of the Neolithic at Knossos. Lastly, as regards decoration, the dark-on-light decorative technique which predominated in EM IIA now occurs in equal quantities with the white-on-dark one. Neither pattern-burnishing nor incised decoration continues into EM IIB.

5. *EM III* (FIG. 3)

> South Front Early Houses — floor and fill deposits associated with the South Front House.[74]
> Related pottery groups:[75] Houses A, B, and C and well to north of House A, all beneath the West Court; the Upper East Well deposit; deposit from North Quarter of City; Royal Road North deposits.

The EM III ceramic phase has been discussed in detail elsewhere. Here I make only general comments regarding developments from EM IIB to EM III.[76] There is a greater break in ceramic traditions between EM IIA and EM IIB than between EM IIB and EM III in shapes, fabrics and surface decoration. Indeed, EM IIB may be viewed as the beginning of the ceramic developments which would go on to form the Old Palace period pottery style. Within this context EM III is simply a continuation of the new developments noted in EM IIB. This is most clearly shown in the increased standardisation of fabrics and ware groups. Red or black slipped ware, which became common in EM IIB, now predominates, while the dark-on-light painted ware loses ground. White painted decoration on a black or red slipped ground, which had become common in EM IIB, is now the norm, with curvilinear motifs replacing the geometric rectilinear decoration of EM II. The greatest continuity of shape is seen in the goblet series, although footed goblets now have straight sides rather than the rounded profile of EM IIB.[77] New cup shapes are the flat-bottomed goblet/tumbler and the one-

---

[72] Ibid., fig. 40: top and third rows.
[73] Wilson and Day (n. 2 above).
[74] Hood and Cadogan (n. 39 above); Momigliano (n. 10 above), 198–204, 268, for analysis of material excavated in 1908. For the most recent finds in this area, see Momigliano and Wilson (n. 31 above).
[75] See Momigliano (n. 10 above), for detailed discussion of these groups and their attribution to EM III/MM IA (i.e. EM III).
[76] Andreou (n. 15 above); Momigliano (n. 10 above).
[77] Compare *PM I*, fig. 40: 2nd row, with Momigliano (n. 10 above), fig. 30 types 1–4.

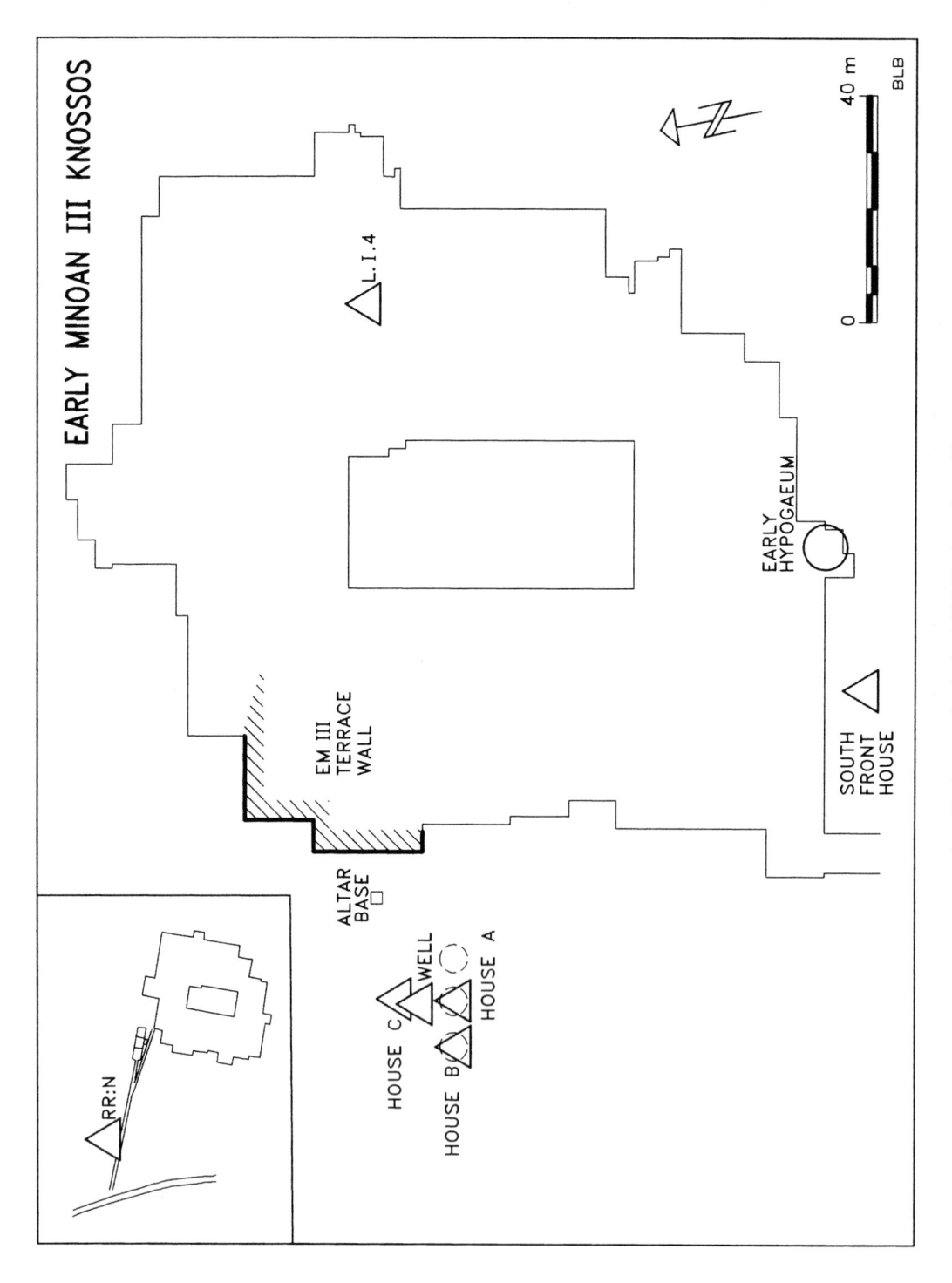

FIG. 3   Findspots of principal EM III deposits at Knossos

handled rounded cup.[78] Two other important new shapes are the two-handled side-spouted jar and the bridge-spouted jar.[79] Among those shapes which continue from EM IIB into EM III are the beaked jug, now often with a rope band at the neck base, and the shallow bowl with everted rim, which replaces the bowl with thickened rounded rim of EM IIB.[80] Last but not least, there is evidence for the early use of the potter's wheel in EM III, although it is restricted to certain shape types within the goblet series.[81]

THE EXTENT OF THE PREPALATIAL SETTLEMENT

The Palace Well provides the only substantial deposit of EM IA at Knossos. It appears that virtually the entire settlement of this period was cleared away during later building. This certainly happened in the area beneath the West Court where, except for the small deposit in Trench FF, the EM I occupation levels are not preserved, but rather there is EM IIA stratified directly above the latest Neolithic.[82] The recent Palace tests in 1987 west of the North Lustral Basin (*SMK*, D.I.2) provide the only significant body of EM IA material outside the Palace Well (FIG. 1).[83] The hopes of finding any architecture or floor deposits associated with the beginning of Minoan Knossos are slim. If the settlement was concentrated on the top of the hill and immediately adjacent slopes, later expansion in Early Minoan and building in the Palatial periods will have destroyed all of it. As long as this critical gap in the archaeological record remains, it will be virtually impossible to resolve the question of what (or who) caused the marked cultural change at Knossos from the latest Neolithic to Early Minoan I.[84]

Our knowledge of EM IB at Knossos is slightly better, based as it is on the distribution of known deposits beneath the Palace. With the possible exception of the 1987 tests west of the North Lustral Basin (*SMK*, D.I.2), nowhere are any of the EM IB deposits stratified above EM IA. There are no floor deposits or any associated architecture for this period. It is thus impossible to discuss building or settlement plan or the extent and nature of occupation at Knossos in EM IB. All that can be said for the present is that the EM IB material is largely preserved under the northern half of the Palace (FIG. 1). As with the EM IA settlement, virtually all traces of occupation in this period appear to have been removed in later building. Indeed much of this levelling and clearance on the site may have occurred at the beginning of EM IIA, when there is evidence for large-scale levelling and cutting down into Late Neolithic levels.

Should the paucity of evidence for EM I at Knossos be interpreted as a decline in the size of the settlement after the latest Neolithic and before renewed growth in EM IIA? Or is it equally fair to

---

[78] Momigliano (n. 10 above), fig. 30 types 1–2 and fig. 31 types 1–4.
[79] Ibid., figs. 35–6.
[80] Ibid., figs. 32–3.
[81] This hinted at in Momigliano (n. 10 above), 247–9, 264–5, but discussed in detail by P.M. Day, 'Revolutions in ceramic technology: the introduction of the potter's wheel in Crete', forthcoming.
[82] Wilson (n. 3 above), 281–7, 359–60.
[83] See n. 24 above. I have noted only a handful of single stray sherds of EM IA from scattered mixed deposits beneath the Palace.
[84] For a recent discussion of this problem see Hood (n. 23 above).

argue that the settlement size and population remained steady from the Neolithic to Early Minoan?[85] To assume from the scarcity of evidence for EM I that it was a period when the settlement shrank and cultural development suffered a setback might be unjustified, for the ceramic technology develops with significant innovations during the course of it.[86]

It is difficult to assess how significant the changes were which occurred in EM IIA at Knossos against our comparatively obscure picture of EM I. In any case, our evidence for the EM IIA settlement at Knossos is much richer.[87] The 1969 tests beneath the West Court show at least two building phases within EM IIA. The earlier is represented by the remains of the West Court House — a substantial building whose first floor rooms would have stood roughly at the level of the later Palace in the area of the West Magazines.[88] This suggests that much of the area of the later Palace at the level of the Central Court would have formed the core of the Prepalatial settlement, and there is evidence for terracing of buildings both in the area of the West Court and outside the South Façade. At a point still early in EM IIA the upper floor rooms of the West Court House were levelled, perhaps to make clear an open public area bordered by a terrace wall to the west also built at this time.[89]

A series of tests made beneath the West Court in 1904–5 show that the EM IIA town continued to the west of the West Court House.[90] A consistent sequence is found in all five tests: (1) a hard grey stratum at 3 m. below the West Court which marks the upper limit of the undisturbed Neolithic deposits and probably represents part of the same cutting which was made down to the Neolithic strata at the beginning of EM IIA for new building in this area, which included the West Court House; (2) a possible floor/yard level at 2.5 m. below the West Court, which corresponds to the yard level adjacent to the basement rooms of the West Court House; (3) above this yard level about a meter of EM IIA fill which may be part of a large-scale terracing operation that included the levelling of the West Court House and construction of the terrace wall to the east. While the area over the fill in the West Court House basements appears to have remained open from this time onward, to the west of the EM IIA terrace wall building continued at a lower level from EM III to the end of the Old Palace period. In addition to this evidence from beneath the West Court, tests in the northern half of the Palace point to the same large-scale reorganisation of the settlement in EM IIA. Deep pure EM IIA fills stratified directly above hard-packed Neolithic occupation levels were found in a series of tests widely spaced beneath the northern half of the Palace: Area of the Pictographic Tablets (*SMK*, D.III.1), North Lustral Basin (*SMK*, E.I.7, 9), North-West Portico (*SMK*, E.II.7), North-East Magazines (*SMK*, K.I.4–8), North-East Hall (*SMK*, K.II.5), and Area of the Olive Press (*SMK*,

---

[85] See C. Broodbank, 'The Neolithic labyrinth: social change at Knossos before the Bronze Age', *JMA* 5.1 (1992), 68–9 for brief discussion of the merits of these two views, and T.M. Whitelaw, 'Lost in the labyrinth? Comments on Broodbank's "social change at Knossos before the Bronze Age" ', *JMA* 5.2 (1992), 229–43.

[86] Day and Wilson (n. 2 above).

[87] For earlier discussion of the extent of the EM II settlement at Knossos, see P. Warren, 'Knossos and its foreign relations in the Early Bronze Age', in *Cretological IV, A'2* (Athens, 1981), 628–37.; T.M. Whitelaw, 'The settlement at Fournou Korifi, Myrtos and aspects of Early Minoan social organization', in O. Krzyszkowska and L. Nixon (eds.), *Minoan Society: Proceedings of the Cambridge Colloquium 1981* (Bristol, 1983), 339–40; Wilson (n. 35 above), 36–45.

[88] Wilson (n. 3 above), 282–93.

[89] Ibid. 290–1, fig. 1.

[90] Tests 1, 2, 6, 12, 14 (*SMK*, B.I.4–6, 9, 15–17, and plan 4.B); Wilson (n. 35 above), 175–80. Pendlebury *et al.* (n. 3 above), plan 4.B.

M.III.1) (FIG. 2).⁹¹ These fills would have served to level up the steep slopes of the Prepalatial hill and extend the area for building on the hilltop to the north and northeast.

The southernmost extent of the EM IIA settlement may be traced to the area immediately outside the South Façade of the Palace. From the EM IIB floors of the Early Houses (stratified directly above Neolithic) were found rare sherds of EM IIA. These might simply be part of a fill brought in from elsewhere on the site to terrace the area for building in EM IIB or they may represent EM IIA occupation strata which were levelled out for the initial construction of the Early Houses. Virtually all of the pre-Palace settlement on the south and southeast slopes of the hill was removed in later deep cutting and construction in the palatial periods.⁹² The furthest known extent of the EM IIA settlement to the northwest is marked by the Royal Road South and North deposits.⁹³ Portions of a large EM IIA house stood south of the later Royal Road;⁹⁴ the earliest floor level (floor VI) found in tests on the northern side of the road is probably contemporary.⁹⁵

The sequence of pure EM IIA fills stratified above Late Neolithic, found in numerous widespread tests cited above, may argue for two separate phases of large-scale terracing and building in EM IIA. The West Court House was terraced directly into the LN levels, with all traces of the intervening EM I settlement cleared away. This pattern of rebuilding at the very beginning of EM IIA may have been repeated across the site. Shortly after its construction the West Court House was itself levelled as a part of a major reorganisation of the settlement plan to extend the area for building on top of the hill with an open court area on the west and further building on the slopes below. The clearing of the hilltop in EM IIA would establish the basic ground level upon which the later EM IIB–MM settlements and Palace were built. For this reason EM IIA is well represented and preserved at Knossos in the form of deep terrace fills.

In relative terms we know as little about the EM IIB settlement as we do about that of EM I. Although small quantities of EM IIB pottery are found in mixed deposits from various tests beneath the Palace, the only stratified floor deposits come from the southern and northern edges of the known Prepalatial settlement. The southernmost extent of the settlement is marked by the remains of two buildings. One lies beneath the EM III South Front House, a second further west just to the south of the West Court.⁹⁶ In tests made in 1987 to explore the northeast limits of an EM III terrace wall, a stone-paved ramp was found to the southwest of the North Lustral Basin; it lay above an EM IIA deposit and partly beneath the EM III terrace wall fill.⁹⁷ This may be a ramp or roadway leading up to the top of the hill from the north; it may have been built as early as the rebuilding programme in EM IIA or it may

---

[91] *SMK*, plans D, E, K, M; Wilson (n. 35 above), 181–99.

[92] Evans (quoting Mackenzie) made mention of Early Minoan being found in a test by the first pillar of the Stepped Corridor with a sequence of Neolithic, 'strata representing the three Early Minoan periods', and MM IA (*PM II.i*, 146 n. 3). These observations cannot now be verified from the kept sherds in the Stratigraphical Museum at Knossos.

[93] Finds of EM II material from the Stratigraphical Museum excavations (S. Hood and D. Smyth, *Archaeological Survey of the Knossos Area* (2nd. edn.; *BSA* Suppl. 14; London, 1981), no. 188) may, however, extend the western limits of the known settlement at this time (information kindly supplied by Professor Peter Warren). See also Warren, this volume p. 205.

[94] Warren (n. 21 above); Hood and Smyth, ibid., no. 216.

[95] Hood (n. 17 above), 93; Hood and Smyth, ibid., no. 215.

[96] Hood and Cadogan (n. 39 above); Momigliano and Wilson (n. 31 above). Reference to EM sherds, including Vasilike ware, from the area of the House of the High Priest (M.S.F. Hood, 'Archaeology in Greece, 1957', *AR* 4 (1957), 21) was later corrected to a context north of the South House (Hood and Smyth, n. 93 above, 56, no. 296).

[97] FIG. 3: at northeast end of EM III terrace wall fill; Catling (n. 24 above), 69, fig. 94.

belong in EM IIB. On the north side of the Royal Road, the floor (floor V) above the EM IIA level and below the EM III deposits also belongs in this period. Later building on the top of the hill and surrounding slopes has destroyed all earlier traces of the EM IIB settlement beneath the Palace.

Architectural remains of the EM III settlement (FIG. 3) are preserved only in those areas which escaped disturbance when the first Palace was built in MM IB. Beginning at the southern edge of the settlement are the fill and floor deposits associated with the substantial South Front House. More problematic is the date of the Early Hypogaeum found beneath the South Porch of the Palace: it may be as early as EM III and hence contemporary with the South Front House or it may belong later in MM IA, but still pre-date the First Palace.[98]

Portions of three EM III houses (A, B and C) and a well were found beneath and to the north of the West Court kouloures.[99] Remains of what appears to be an extensive EM III terrace wall with an associated stone fill behind it have now been traced beneath the West Façade of the Palace from a point just south of Magazine XI, whence it runs north to the northwest angle of the Palace and then east to a point just southwest of the North Lustral Basin (FIG. 3).[100] This terrace wall may have formed the foundations for a building or buildings which stood on the top of the hill in EM III above the level of the Houses A, B and C to the southwest on a lower terrace.[101] The most substantial deposit of EM III found elsewhere beneath the Palace is from the Upper East Well in the North-East Quarter just west of the Court of the Stone Spout.[102] Outside the Palace to the northwest at the southern side of the Royal Road and at right angles to it Warren found a north–south section of paved road with a flanking wall which can be placed in EM III.[103] This road appears to mark the first construction in this area. Further afield are the finds of EM III by Warren in the Stratigraphical Museum excavations west of the Palace[104] and an EM III deposit found in the North Quarter of the city about half a km. north of the Palace.[105]

---

[98] Momigliano (n. 10 above), 195–8, and MacGillivray in this volume. The 'Early Paving' between the South Front House and the Early Hypogaeum can now be dated to an early phase of the Old Palace period: see Momigliano and Wilson (n. 31 above).

[99] Momigliano (n. 10 above), 185–94, 206–39.

[100] The northeast limits of the wall could not be traced into the 'Initiatory Area', but the associated fill was found (Sinclair Hood, pers. comm.). A.J. Evans, 'The Palace of Knossos', *BSA* 7 (1900–1), 48–9, 56–7 and pl. 2, for north face of wall; *PM I*, fig. 109, for northwest corner of wall; Hood and Taylor (n. 50 above), no. 122; Catling (n. 24 above), 69, fig. 96; N. Momigliano, 'The "Protopalatial Façade" at Knossos', *BSA* 87 (1992), 167, 171, pl. 8a.

[101] Hood and Smyth (n. 93 above), 6–8; this wall was later reused as the foundations for the First Palace façade (Catling, n. 24 above, 69). MacGillivray (this volume) suggests that the Northwest Platform may be later and be associated with the construction of the First Palace at Knossos, perhaps late in MM IA.

[102] *SMK*, L.I.4; see EM III pottery summary above for references. For a related deposit from the 'Room of the Jars' in the Royal Pottery Stores, and north of the 'Magazines of Giant Pithoi' (*SMK*, L.III.8), see N. Momigliano, 'Knossos 1902, 1905: Early and Middle Minoan deposits from the Room of the Jars', forthcoming.

[103] Hood and Smyth (n. 93 above), no. 216; P. Warren, 'Knossos', *A.Delt.* 27.B'2 (1972), 627–9.

[104] Hood and Smyth (n. 93 above), no. 188; P. Warren, 'The genesis of the Minoan Palace' in R. Hägg and N. Marinatos (eds.), *The Function of the Minoan Palaces: Proceedings of the Fourth International Symposium at the Swedish Institute in Athens ... 1984* (*Skrifter ... Svenska Inst. i Athen*, 4°, 35; Stockholm, 1987), 53 n. 41; N. Momigliano, 'MMIA Pottery from Evans' Excavations at Knossos' (Ph.D. dissertation, University of London, 1989), 154 and Appendix 1, no. 29, where Momigliano dates some of Warren's 'MM IA' to EM III.

[105] Hood and Smyth (n. 93 above), no. 232; Momigliano (n. 10 above), 176–84. A few sherds of EM come from a box of Neo-LM material whose context is labelled as a test made in 1908 about three-quarters of a km. northwest of the Palace to the east of the Roman amphitheatre (*SMK*, V.1908/3); however, the provenance of this box of sherds may be in doubt (Hood and Smyth, n. 93 above, 6, no. 110). The uncertain context and the paucity of material does not make a very strong case for EM occupation in this area.

PREPALATIAL KNOSSOS: INTER-REGIONAL EXCHANGE AND FOREIGN CONTACTS

Before the Early Bronze Age began, Knossos was largely isolated from the rest of the Aegean. Melian obsidian is found from the earliest aceramic levels onward through the Neolithic, but this need not indicate more than the most sporadic contacts with Melos made at a time when that island itself was not inhabited.[106] Apart from obsidian, there is no certain evidence of foreign imports at Knossos before EM IIA. Three stone vases from the LN houses beneath the Central Court may be of Egyptian origin, but this is not certain.[107]

There is no evidence of any foreign contact in EM IA, although the scarcity of material for this period at Knossos leaves the question open. For contact with the rest of Crete there is only a single piece of evidence — a fine grey ware vessel from the Mesara found in the Palace Well.[108] There is considerably more evidence for contacts with the Mesara in EM IB, represented by nearly a dozen imports which compare closely with EM I examples from Phaistos.[109] Elsewhere in central and eastern Crete at this time there are striking signs of contact with the EB I Cyclades. There does not, however, appear to be a single example at Knossos of any of the vases of Cycladic type that are found in contemporary deposits at the Pyrgos and Kyparissi burial caves[110] and in the large cist grave cemetery at Aghia Photia in east Crete.[111] This is in marked contrast to the Cycladic imports found at later EM IIA Knossos. One possible explanation is that the fashion for Cycladic or Cycladic-type vessels was restricted to burial use, or it may simply be that the EM IB sample at Knossos is too small to say anything definite one way or the other.

The greatest percentage of ceramic imports at Prepalatial Knossos occurs in EM IIA with a marked increase in pottery from the Mesara and the first certain foreign imports in the form of Cycladic pottery. Although imports of pottery from the Mesara can now be traced back to EM I at Knossos, the only sizeable body of it before the Old Palace period occurs in EM IIA. These Mesara imports to Knossos are represented largely by a group of fine painted ware side-spouted bowls[112] and fine grey ware stemmed goblets and pyxides.[113] All were probably luxury wares and their limited range of shapes suggests that they were introduced for some specialised domestic function.

Virtually all the imports of pottery from the Cyclades before Middle Minoan at Knossos occur in EM IIA contexts. No fewer than thirty EC II vessels have now been identified, over half being jars

---

[106] R. Torrence, 'The obsidian quarries and their use', in C. Renfrew and M. Wagstaff (eds.), *An Island Polity: the Archaeology of Exploitation in Melos* (Cambridge, 1982), 220–1; ead., *Production and Exchange of Stone Tools: Prehistoric Obsidian in the Aegean* (Cambridge, 1986), 214–16; Broodbank (n. 85 above), 48.

[107] Warren, *Minoan Stone Vases* (Cambridge, 1969), 106; 109, A.5,10; 112, G.6. The suggestion that a copper axe from the same houses is an import (Vagnetti and Belli, n. 35 above, 155) would have to be confirmed by analysis of the metal; the context of the axe is, in any case, not secure (see Evans, this volume, p. 18). A 'slip of ivory' from a LN context at Knossos (J.D. Evans, 'Excavations in the Neolithic settlement of Knossos, 1957–60. Part I', *BSA* 59 (1964), 188, pl. 62.1, no. 13) has been re-identified as shell (O. Krzyszkowska, 'Ivory in the Aegean Bronze Age: elephant tusk or hippopotamus ivory?', *BSA* 83 (1988), 228 n. 60).

[108] Hood and Cadogan (n. 39 above); Wilson and Day (n. 2 above).

[109] Wilson and Day (n. 2 above).

[110] S. Xanthoudides, 'Μέγας πρωτομινωϊκὸς τάφος Πύργου', *A.Delt.* 4 (1918), figs. 7.33, 35; 8.49–50; 9.67–69, 73; S. Alexiou, 'Πρωτομινωϊκαὶ ταφαὶ παρὰ τὸ Κανλὶ Καστέλλι Ἡρακλείου', *Kr.Chron.* 5 (1951), fig. 1 no. 9, pl. 14.

[111] K. Davaras, *Hagios Nikolaos Museum* (Athens, n.d. [1982?]), figs. 3, 4, 6, 9.

[112] e.g. Wilson (n. 3 above), fig. 15: P98–103. See Wilson and Day (n. 2 above) for detailed publication and discussion.

[113] e.g. Wilson (n. 3 above), fig. 13: P81–84 and pl. 32 top left; Wilson and Day (n. 2 above).

and as many as another third sauceboats.[114] Shape, decoration and fabric may argue for a western Cycladic origin for as many as half — certainly for five broad-streak painted ware jars from Melos.[115] At least some of the imported island material, however, is central Cycladic, including decorated sauceboats which compare closely with examples from Keros.[116] Non-ceramic Cycladic imports include rare examples of marble bowls, at least one of which comes from an EM IIA context.[117]

There may have been no direct contact between Knossos and the Greek Mainland before the end of the Early Bronze Age.[118] The Urfirnis sauceboat has traditionally been considered an exclusively Mainland Helladic pottery type, but recent work in the Cyclades suggests an island source of manufacture for some of these vessels.[119] Of the dozen or so Urfirnis sauceboats now known from Knossos, at least half appear from their fabric and surface treatment to be from the same potting centre or region. This group is similar in fabric to sauceboats from both Ayia Irini on Kea and Phylakopi on Melos.[120] There may be a western Cycladic potting centre responsible for at least some of the Knossian, Melian and Keian sauceboats.[121] Even if the Urfirnis sauceboats from Knossos should prove to be of Mainland origin, they probably reached Crete via the western Cyclades.[122]

---

[114] A study of the Cycladic imports at Knossos from the Prepalatial and Old Palace periods is now underway by J.A. MacGillivray and the author. For earlier discussion of Minoan–Cycladic contacts in the Early Bronze Age, see P. Warren, 'Early Minoan–Early Cycladic chronological correlations', in J.A. MacGillivray and R.L.N. Barber (eds.), *The Prehistoric Cyclades: Contributions to a Workshop on Cycladic Chronology* (Edinburgh, 1984), 55–62. In spite of the possible stylistic links, the vases which Warren argues are exports to the islands from Crete may not be Minoan (Wilson and Day n. 2 above).

[115] Examples of these Melian jars have also been identified by the author from Period II contexts at Ayia Irini on Kea. See D.E. Wilson and M. Eliot, *Keos IX. Ayia Irini: Periods I–III* (Mainz, forthcoming).

[116] Wilson (n. 3 above), 358–9; for Keros, see F. Zaphiropoulou, ''Οστρακα ἐκ Κέρου', *AAA* 7 (1975), 79–84.

[117] *SMK*, E.I.7, (box no. 620); P. Warren, 'Knossos and its foreign relations in the Early Bronze Age', in *Cretological IV, A'2* (Athens, 1981), 628–37.

[118] For an earlier survey of possible Minoan and Mainland contacts in the Early Bronze Age, see J.B. Rutter and C.W. Zerner, 'Early Hellado-Minoan contacts', in R. Hägg and N. Marinatos (eds.), *The Minoan Thalassocracy: Myth and Reality, Proceedings of the Third International Symposium at the Swedish Institute in Athens ... 1982* (Skrifter ... Svenska Inst. i Athen, 4°, 32; Stockholm, 1984), 75–7. Aside from the Urfirnis sauceboat which is discussed above, only a few seals and amulets can suggest even the most sporadic and indirect contacts between Crete and the Mainland before the Middle Bronze Age: see ibid. 75, Appendix IA(4), IB(1)–(2). The earliest certain Mainland import at Knossos may be the MH I Grey Minyan ware bowl from an early MM IA fill below the lower MM IA floor of the Royal Road South basements: see Cadogan *et al.* (n. 9 above), for date of fill; and Rutter and Zerner, op. cit. 77 and Appendix IIA(1) with full references. For Minoans at Kastri, see J.N. Coldstream and G.L. Huxley, *Kythera. Excavations and Studies conducted by the University of Pennsylvania Museum and the British School at Athens* (London, 1972), 275–6. The origin of the settlers who founded Kastri on Kythera in EM IIB is not known, although the excavators argue for a west Cretan initiative (ibid. 309). It has been suggested that Kythera before the Middle Bronze Age may have been only a seasonal camp used by west Cretan Fishermen (Rutter and Zerner, op. cit. 76). If this was so, then Kastri was not initially established as a stepping-off point for trade with the Mainland.

[119] D.E. Wilson, 'Kea and East Attike in Early Bronze II: beyond pottery typology', in J.M. Fossey (ed.), *ΣΥΝΕΙΣΦΟΡΑ McGILL. Papers in Greek Archaeology and History in Memory of Colin D. Gordon* (Amsterdam, 1987), 39; Wilson and Eliot (n. 115 above).

[120] This was indicated by the author's macroscopic study of Keian and Melian examples.

[121] Warren (n. 21 above), 397, and (n. 117 above), 631, who argues for a Mainland Argive origin. I have not studied the Urfirnis sauceboats from the Lera and Platyvola Caves of west Crete (see Rutter and Zerner, n. 118 above, Appendix IA(2)–(3) for full references) and therefore have no view on their possible origin, although I do believe that they are also non-Minoan.

[122] See below p. 42–3.

Of unknown origin but of considerable significance are the fragments of two clay objects with seal impressions from EM IIA fill levels below the West Court.[123] The fabric of both sealings (if that is what they are) does not appear to be local and may even be of non-Cretan origin; the seal designs bear a general resemblance to EB II Cycladic seal impressions with concentric circle or spiraliform motifs. Likewise unique, and somewhat more exotic, is the fragment of a hippopotamus tusk of Egyptian origin found in the EM IIA fill above the West Court House.[124] An obsidian bowl from EM IIA levels at the southern side of the Royal Road may come from Egypt,[125] and will if so be the earliest Egyptian stone vase found at Knossos in a Minoan context.[126]

Compared to the rich assemblage of imports found at EM IIA Knossos, EM IIB presents a somewhat stark picture. Beginning within the island, imports from the Mesara have virtually disappeared and east Crete may be at least one of the sources for wares of non-local fabric at Knossos. Possible east Cretan imports include Vasilike ware goblets, bowls and jars.[127] Again in sharp contrast to EM IIA, there may not be a single import from the Cyclades in either EM IIB or EM III. The only possible signs of foreign contact in EM IIB come in the form of two Egyptian stone vases from the South Front Early Houses. The first is an Early Dynastic import found in the EM IIB Room 1 floor deposit,[128] the second a VIth Dynasty jar from a mixed EM IIB–EM III fill.[129] Since stone vases normally have a long lifespan as heirlooms, both vessels may have arrived at Knossos before EM IIB. If most, or all, of the rare Near Eastern and Egyptian imports were coming to Crete via the Cyclades in the Early Bronze Age, then these two stone vases may have been imported to Knossos in EM IIA, the only period of certain foreign contacts before the beginning of the Middle Minoan period at Knossos.

In EM III east Crete continues to be at least one source of imported wares at Knossos, which include vessels with a distinctive reddish fabric apparently belonging to a 'Lasithi group'.[130] There are only rare imports from the Mesara in this period. As was noted above, there are no apparent imports from the Mainland and only a single example from the Cyclades.[131] Across the island as a whole no Near Eastern imports have been found in firmly dated EM III contexts.[132] Just at that time when settlements, both in the islands and on the Mainland, began to pick up at the beginning

---

[123] Wilson (n. 35 above), 210–11, SMV.865–866. See Weingarten in this volume, p. 174

[124] O. Krzyszkowska, 'Ivory from hippopotamus tusk in the Aegean Bronze Age', *Antiquity* 48 (1984), 123–5.

[125] Warren (n. 117 above), 633–5; Warren and Hankey (n. 11 above), 125, fig. 1.

[126] Warren (n. 117 above), 632–3, believes that Egyptian stone vases of Early Bronze Age type, but found in later post-EM or unstratified contexts, may originally have reached Knossos not long after their time of manufacture. However, there do not appear to be any cogent reasons for this view, as L. Pomerance has convincingly argued ('The possible role of tomb robbers and viziers of the 18th dynasty in confusing Minoan chronology', in *Cretological IV, A'2* (Athens, 1981), 447–53).

[127] Day and Wilson (n. 2 above).

[128] Warren (n. 107 above), 110, C.1; id., (n. 117 above), 633; Warren and Hankey (n. 11 above), 125, fig. 2.

[129] Warren (n. 117 above), 633.

[130] Momigliano (n. 10 above), 261–4, Fabric III. See Day and Wilson (n. 2 above) for analyses and further discussion of this ware and other possible imports.

[131] A crescent-shaped jar handle of a type common in the Middle Bronze Age Cyclades and occurring as early as Phylakopi I.ii–iii context in the islands, was found in a foundation fill asociated with the EM III South Front House (Momigliano and Wilson n. 31 above). Two vases from the 'lower' floor of House B suggest Cycladic affinities in style, but neither appears to be an import (Momigliano, n. 10 above, 227–8, nos. 60–61, pl. 50).

[132] Cadogan (n. 26 above), 513. The imported bridge-spouted jar from a tomb at Lapithos in Cyprus can belong in Knossian terms to either EM III or MM IA (ibid. 513; Momigliano, n. 10 above, 228 with further references).

of the Middle Bronze Age, we see contacts resumed between Crete and the rest of the Aegean with central Cretan MM IA exports to Phylakopi and Lerna Va.[133]

CONCLUSIONS

Knossos from its inception at the beginning of the Neolithic was to hold a pre-eminent position as the largest settlement in Crete until nearly the end of the Bronze Age and it certainly did so in Early Minoan.[134] But was it only physical size which distinguished Knossos from other settlements in the Prepalatial period, or was the site also unique in the level of its social organisation? Whitelaw has suggested that later Palatial settlements such as Knossos had already crossed some major organisational thresholds by the opening of Early Minoan.[135] Is there any substantive evidence for the nature and level of social organisation of Knossos then and any possible signs of any marked social change within the Early Bronze Age?

It may never be possible to address these questions for EM I, although the quality of the Palace Well pottery shows anything but a cultural regression at this time. There is, however, a sufficient body of evidence in EM IIA to suggest a large-scale reorganisation of the settlement which may reflect some significant social change. Fragmentary and scattered as the evidence for EM IIA is, it does strongly suggest a major replanning of the settlement which included new construction at its centre. The principal aim appears to have been to increase the area for building on the levelled hilltop with houses of the surrounding settlement terraced into the slopes below. This ambitious building programme clearly argues for a central authority at Knossos with sufficient means to initiate such a scheme and organise the considerable manpower necessary to carry it out. Might this programme have included a large central structure or structures on the hilltop, marking some change in the social organisation of the settlement? The nature and relative degree of this change in EM IIA are difficult to assess owing to the paucity of evidence for EM I and EM IIB, but there are other clear signs of something unusual happening at this time.

There is a dramatic increase in the quantity of ceramic imports in EM IIA at Knossos from elsewhere in Crete, most of the pottery coming from the Mesara.[136] This argues for not only a specialisation in pottery production for central Crete, but a new trade in luxury wares from the Mesara to Knossos. The first ceramic imports at Knossos from outside the island also occur in EM IIA, with a small but significant body of material from the Cyclades.[137] These Cycladic imports may be anomalous at EM Knossos, with only one certain example appearing before the Old Palace period in an EM III context. At least half these imported vessels may be western Cycladic in origin, with

---

[133] For the Cyclades, see Cadogan (n. 26 above), 509, and J.B. Rutter, 'Some observations on the Cyclades in the later third and early second millennia', *AJA* 87 (1983), 72–3. For Hellado-Minoan contacts in MH I/MM IA, see Rutter and Zerner (n. 118 above), 77–80 and Appendix II.

[134] See Broodbank (n. 85 above), for summary of Neolithic evidence; and Whitelaw (n. 87 above), 337–40, for size comparison with other EM settlements.

[135] Whitelaw (n. 87 above), 340. For the Neolithic origins of social complexity at Knossos, see Broodbank (n. 85 above), but see also Whitelaw (n. 85 above).

[136] Wilson and Day (n. 2 above).

[137] Other sites in north-central and east Crete do show signs of Cycladic contact earlier in EM IB, and future excavations may prove the same at Knossos.

Melos as one certain source. Although these imports at Knossos are rare in themselves, they may reflect a more substantial trade in other commodities, especially metals.[138] Looking further afield, it has already been suggested above that the Near Eastern and Egyptian imports to Knossos before MM may all have arrived in EM IIA. These Near Eastern imports are so rare that for the moment they are better viewed as exotic oddities rather than as evidence for even the most sporadic eastern contacts. It cannot be mere coincidence that they reached Knossos in that period of Early Minoan when the only certain foreign contacts with the Aegean occur.

By EM IIB Knossos had established contacts further afield within Crete, evidenced for example by the imports of Vasilike ware from east Crete. This does not, however, necessarily imply a growth in inter-regional contacts for Knossos in EM IIB, since at this time imports from the Mesara seem to have virtually disappeared. Indeed, imported pottery from the Mesara at Knossos was to remain a rarity until after the beginning of the Old Palace period. Further study may suggest reasons for this apparent shift in exchange patterns between Knossos and the rest of Crete. For the moment what is clear is that there are no apparent foreign imports at Knossos in EM IIB and only one certain example in EM III.

Knossos appears, then, to have been largely isolated from the rest of the Aegean during the Prepalatial period, except for a relatively short span of time in EM IIA.[139] But could this apparent absence of Aegean imports from EM IIB through possibly to as late as MM IA be due simply to the accidents of preservation? The relative chronology of Knossos and the West Aegean in EB II suggests at least one possible scenario for a cessation of contacts between Knossos and the rest of the Aegean until the beginning of the Middle Bronze Age. From EM IIA contexts at Knossos there occur island imports which belong to a developed phase of EC II, including Urfirnis and decorated sauceboats and Melian broad-streak painted ware jars.[140] This would suggest that at least part of EM IIB at Knossos was contemporary with the final phase of EB II in the west Aegean, i.e. the period of the Kastri-Lefkandi I-Ayia Irini III groups and possibly Lerna IIId (House of Tiles phase) in the Argolid.[141] This was a period of at least some disruptions in exchange and trade within the Cyclades and was to end with the destruction and/or abandonment of many settlements. There followed in EB III a period of at least reduced settlement in the Cyclades, if not an actual break in occupation.[142] This period of isolation for Knossos and Crete as a whole from the rest of the Aegean from later EB II until after the beginning of the Middle Bronze Age probably reflects the cultural setback in the

---

[138] Gale has shown the western Cycladic island of Kythnos to be a major source of copper for EM Crete (N.H. Gale, 'The provenance of metals for EBA Crete — local or Cycladic?', in *Cretological VI, A'1* (Chania, 1990), 299–316). For a discussion of the metals trade between the Cyclades and Attica in EB II, see Wilson (n. 119 above), 44–6. See too J.L. Davis, 'Review of Aegean prehistory I: the islands of the Aegean', *AJA* 96 (1992), 704, for summary and further references.

[139] This break in contacts between Knossos and the rest of the Aegean from late EB II until the beginning of the Middle Bronze Age may have occurred over the whole of Crete. See Rutter and Zerner (n. 118 above), 76–7.

[140] All these ceramic types are found in well-stratified Period II contexts at Ayia Irini on Kea which itself was resettled after the beginning of EBII in the Cyclades: see Wilson and Eliot (n. 115 above).

[141] Ibid.

[142] For a summary of the evidence and further references, see Davis (n. 138 above), 754 n. 264.

western Aegean at this same time.[143] In contrast, there are no signs at Knossos of any destructions or disruptions in the cultural sequence after EM IA. Such apparent stability in the local community throughout most of EM must have been one of the contributing factors in the early emergence of palatial society at Knossos.

For the moment it must remain an open question whether the picture presented here of some major social change in EM IIA is real or is biased by our lack of evidence for EM I and EM IIB. We face a similar problem when trying to assess the evidence for EM III against the very meagre background of EM IIB. In spite of this, EM III may be viewed as another point of accelerated growth within the Prepalatial sequence.[144] Construction of the extensive EM III northwest terrace wall may represent part of a large-scale rebuilding programme comparable to that argued for EM IIA. This terrace wall may have formed the limits of a large foundation platform for a central building or buildings on the hilltop. This large-scale building programme was part of a new expansion of the settlement in EM III in areas both to the west and to the north of the later Palace.

While I agree with Cherry that the origins of Palatial society on Crete should not be viewed simply as a gradual incremental process over time, we have not necessarily to imagine a relatively sudden revolution in organisational change in MM I.[145] The evidence reviewed above would suggest an alternative model: a process of growth and social change always cumulative but moving at an uneven pace — slower, it would appear, in EM IIB, accelerated in the more innovative and outward-looking EM IIA and again in EM III. It is significant that analyses of the mortuary data from the cemeteries of Mallia, Gournia, and Mochlos show clear evidence of social ranking also beginning in EM IIA.[146] This provides independent evidence complementing that from Knossos for the rise of complex social organisation in EM IIA Crete. For the present our knowledge is simply too sparse to attempt a comparative assessment of the level of organisation or the rate of social change between EM settlements. Such an assessment, if and when it does become possible, might help to explain why in MM IB palatial society emerged at only a few exceptional sites on Crete. One question to focus on in future study of both Neolithic and Early Minoan Knossos is this: what accounts for the special, if not unique status, which was held on Crete from its earliest beginnings by this settlement?

---

[143] The Spedhos-type figurines from Archanes in EM III contexts in the Phourni tholos tomb C do not necessarily prove contacts with the Cyclades at this time (I.A. Sakellarakis, 'The Cyclades and Crete', in P. Getz-Preziosi (ed.), *Art and Culture of the Cyclades* (Chicago, 1977), 145–53; J.A. Sakellarakis and E. Sapouna-Sakellaraki, *Archanes* (Athens, 1991), 116–18). There is no independent evidence from the Cyclades to put this figurine type after EB II; all the imported Cycladic figurines in Crete could have reached the island before the end of EM II, if not before the end of EM IIA, and these would have survived as heirlooms in later contexts.

[144] K. Branigan, 'Some observations on state formation in Crete', in E.B. French and K.A. Wardle (eds.), *Problems in Greek Prehistory: Papers Presented at the Centenary Conference of the British School of Archaeology at Athens, Manchester, April 1986* (Bristol, 1988), 66–8.

[145] J. Cherry, 'Evolution, revolution and the origins of complex society in Minoan Crete', in Krzyszkowska and Nixon (n. 87 above), 33 ff.

[146] Whitelaw (n. 87 above), 337–40; J.S. Soles, 'Social ranking in prepalatial cemeteries', in French and Wardle (n. 144 above), 49–61; J.S. Soles, *The Prepalatial Cemeteries at Mochlos and Gournia and the House Tombs of Bronze Age Crete* (*Hesperia* Suppl. 24; Princeton, 1992), 255–8.

Chapter 3

The Early History of the Palace at Knossos (MM I–II)

J.A. MacGillivray

INTRODUCTION[1]

A landmark in the prehistory of early Aegean society was the appearance for the first time in Crete of the large, planned architectural complexes with internal courtyards, large-scale storage facilities and written archives labelled by their modern excavators as 'palaces'. The importance of the structures lies not only in their innovations, mechanical and architectural, but in the numerous and apparently abrupt changes in Cretan society signalled by their appearance.

The fact that major palaces were built at Knossos, Phaistos and Mallia in the Cretan Middle Bronze Age is undeniable. What remains to be sorted out, even after nearly a century of excavation in Crete, however, is exactly when, in what form, and most important of all, why and by whom?

This paper concentrates on the issues of 'when and in what form' using the example of Knossos. What follows is a historical outline; detailed discussion of pottery chronology and foreign relations are presented elsewhere.[2]

Before we begin, however, it is necessary to address two possible misunderstandings. The current terms 'Old' and 'New Palace' imply that there were two separate structures, one superimposed over the other. This was not the case. The Palace at Knossos was one building with a very long history and therefore numerous occasions when repair and renovation programmes were effected as a necessary response to natural stress and violent human intervention. A major event in the building's history seems to have been a seismic shock around 1780 B.C. which forced the authorities to undertake large-scale rebuilding over a century after the designer's original concept, and thus most

---

[1] It is with great pleasure and deep gratitude that I dedicate this very personal overview of the Knossos Old Palace to Sinclair Hood, who more than any other is responsible for the passion I share for Knossos and Minoan Crete. This paper is part guide to existing opinion and part new ideas of my own that are bound to be controversial and, one hopes, provide the sort of spark necessary to continue the debate on this wonderful building first introduced to me by Sinclair. Many and long discussions with a number of colleagues, especially Stella Chryssoulaki, Judith Weingarten and Malcolm Wiener, have helped to organise the thoughts presented here. An earlier version was read to the New York Aegean Bronze Age Colloquium on May 1st, 1992, and comments received then are gratefully acknowledged. The plan in FIG. 2 is the result of discussions with Stella Chryssoulaki and Lara Bernini, who also inked the drawing, in the spring of 1991 and should be taken as very much preliminary and provocative until a new programme of trials within the Palace at Knossos might be undertaken.

[2] J.A. MacGillivray, *Knossos: Pottery Groups of the Old Palace*, forthcoming.

probably to incorporate architectural innovations that may not have been in the original plan. Archaeologists use this event as a benchmark in Aegean prehistory, if only because it seems so obvious a horizon at Knossos, but then look for accompanying social or political change from one major architectural period to another. In fact, the event, which has not been proven to have affected the whole of the island, should be used only to support relative chronological dating and not be treated as the 'interregnum' it has become.

The second commonly held but questionable notion is that the Palace was first built as 'insulae', or separate blocks, and all at one time.[3] But we should remain alert to the fact that there are likely to have been stages of construction reflecting the relative urgencies and resources of the first proprietors and that completion may have taken as long as a generation. As we look back from the present, early history appears condensed and we tend to lose sight of real time. It seems fairly certain, as is discussed below, that an overall plan or concept existed and that the building was regarded as a single structure from the outset, even if not all parts were present from the very beginning.

CHRONOLOGICAL FRAMEWORK

Sir Arthur Evans devised a relative chronological framework modelled on the historical counterpart of Pharaonic Egypt and called it 'Minoan' after the most famous monarch Greek history preserved from Bronze Age Crete.[4] Like the Egyptian Kingdoms, the Minoan period was separated into early, middle and late stages. Unfortunately, there are no king lists from Crete and so the Minoan periods are purely artificial and have no relation to political events. When first conceived they were seen as formative, mature and decadent stages of a civilisation and thus were quite subjective. While no longer used to judge a period's 'worth', Evans' chronological scheme, in the absence of an acceptable radiocarbon-based absolute chronology, remains the only useful reference grid for Cretan prehistory. Absolute dates are forthcoming from comparison with Egypt, and it is those calendar years that are used here.[5]

Four events during the building's early history seem to have left their mark on the Palace site and allow us to speak of three intervening periods of time. The *first* event was probably the levelling of the tell which had accumulated during the four thousand and more years of occupation in the Neolithic and Early Bronze Ages. The latest ceramics found on floors that would seem immediately to pre-date this operation include the polychrome style of the late MM IA period.[6] The earliest pottery group within the Palace walls is the Vat Room Deposit, which does not give the impression

---

[3] *PM I*, 203.

[4] First presented in A.J. Evans, *Essai de classification des époques de la civilisation minoenne* (London, 1906), and elaborated on in *PM*. This system remains the most commonly used framework for the Cretan Bronze Age.

[5] The chronology used here is essentially that argued for in P. Warren and V. Hankey, *Aegean Bronze Age Chronology* (Bristol, 1989). The absolute dates are derived from the Egyptian chronology outlined by F. Arnold in his privately circulated, 'Tentative diagram of interconnections' (Metropolitan Museum of Art; New York, 1992). A more detailed explanation of the absolute dates for MM Crete is given by MacGillivray (n. 2 above).

[6] G. Cadogan, P. Day, C. Macdonald, J.A. MacGillivray, N. Momigliano, T. Whitelaw and D. Wilson, 'Early Minoan and Middle Minoan pottery groups at Knossos', *BSA* 88 (1993), 25–6, concerning Royal Road South, Basements, Lower Floor.

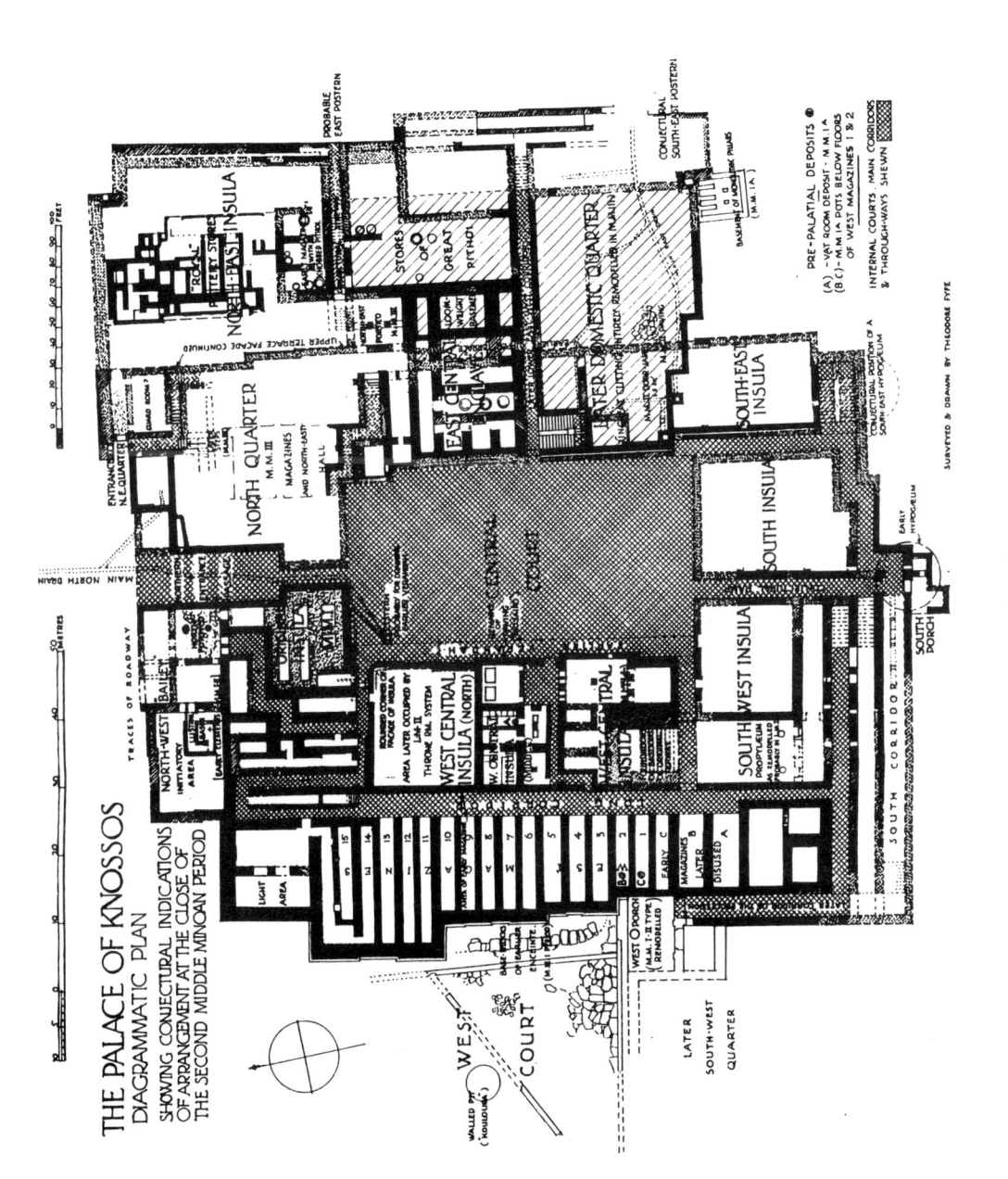

FIG. 1   Schematic Plan of the Old Palace at Knossos

of being very far removed in time from the ceramics of late MM IA[7] but contains certain elements that look forward to the end of the first period in the history of the Palace marked by the *second* event: burnt floor deposits in the Early West Magazines. The whole of the first period, which for convenience continues to be called MM IB, lasted about 40 years from 1910 to 1870 B.C.

The most useful groups we are able to refer to the event marking the end of the MM IB period are, as stated above, the burnt deposits in Early West Magazines A and 2, which contain pottery in very similar styles and fabrics to a large group of material from the middle floor of the Royal Road South Basements.[8] Taken as a whole they provide a comprehensive cross-section of the pottery in use during the first stage of occupation in the Palace. This allows us to identify MM IB ceramics which are now mixed with later groups from the East Wing of the Palace but which may have come from early floors in that wing. Their presence suggests that by the end of the MM IB period most, if not all, of the architectural elements that made up the East and West Wings of the Palace had been completed and were in use.

A *third* significant event in the history of the building is indicated by burnt deposits in the Royal Pottery Stores, the Early Olive Press floor and the early floor beneath the Room of the Stone Pier, all in the East Wing. A group with very similar pottery was found deposited on the upper floor of the Royal Road South Basements.[9] The ceramics from these deposits show a great deal of innovative advance on the previous period, including the frequent use of the potter's wheel to mass-produce forms 'thrown off the hump' and the very finest ceramics on earth at this time, called Egg-Shell Ware — almost certainly the clay imitations of silver vases used as exports.[10] The period between the second and third events is called MM IIA and lasts roughly the fifty years from 1870 to 1820 B.C.

The *fourth* event that interests us here may be the least well defined, perhaps because it is two events separated by a very short time span. I refer to what Evans interpreted as the seismic destruction of the Palace around 1780 B.C. The evidence is quite convincing: huge blocks from the southeast Palace angle thrown into the House of the Fallen Blocks and a similar stretch of gypsum wall along the Southern Enceinte found collapsed in the same direction.[11] The most dramatic evidence, however, to support the earthquake theory comes from Anemospilia near Archanes, roughly 10 kilometres south of Knossos, where a MM building collapsed during a religious ceremony.[12]

At Knossos, the programme of cleaning up and reconstruction following the earthquake was so thorough that no pure deposits have survived in the Palace. Instead, we find material that was probably in use during the final stage of the Old Palace period redeposited in great filling operations in the West Court 'kouloures', the Loomweight Basement and the houses at the southeast angle of the Palace.[13] As they were part of the rebuilding operations, it seems likely that they contain

---

[7] N. Momigliano, 'MM IA pottery from Evans' excavations at Knossos: a reassessment', *BSA* 86 (1991), 167–75.
[8] Cadogan *et al.* (n. 6 above), 26.
[9] Ibid. 26; MacGillivray (n. 2 above), Groups F and L.
[10] *PM I*, 241–2; J.A. MacGillivray, 'Pottery workshops and the Old Palaces in Crete', in R. Hägg and N. Marinatos (eds.), *The Function of the Minoan Palaces, Proceedings of the Fourth International Symposium at the Swedish Institute in Athens ... 1984* (*Skrifter ... Svenska Inst. i Athen*, 4°, 35; Stockholm, 1987), 277–8.
[11] *PM II.i*, 43, 348; *III*, 12, 14.
[12] I. Sakellarakis and E. Sapouna-Sakellaraki, 'Ἀνασκαφὴ Ἀρχανῶν', *PAE* 1979, 347–92; 'Drama of death in a Minoan temple', *National Geographic* 159 (1981), 205–22; eid., *Archanes* (Athens, 1991), 337–56.
[13] Cadogan *et al.* (n. 6 above), 26; MacGillivray (n. 2 above), Groups E, K and N.

elements of the subsequent Neopalatial period. This becomes clear when we compare a group from a destruction level in the town of Knossos, Trial KV,[14] with the earliest deposit in the Neopalatial houses on the Knossos Acropolis.[15] The former we use to define the end of the MM IIB period, the latter represents MM IIIA.[16] There are elements such as White-spotted Ware and Ridged cups in Group A on the Acropolis which are not found in the Trial KV material but occur in the filling deposits following the earthquake in the Palace. Evans used similar pottery to illustrate what he meant by MM IIIA ceramics.[17] This would place the post-seismic work programme in the MM IIIA period.[18]

In summary, the first main period of the Palace's history, known as the Old Palace Period, comprised three main ceramic phases, MM IB, MM IIA and MM IIB, and covered the period from c.1910 to 1780 B.C. after which major renovations were required following a strong earthquake.

NATURE OF THE EARLY PALACE

The earliest architecture in the Palace is the Northwest Platform overlooking the Northwest Treasury and Royal Road. Hood's excavations into the fill of the Northwest Platform in 1973 and 1987 produced pottery of the EM III or MM IA periods.[19] The construction of the wall contrasts sharply with the rest of the Palace façade. It is made up of small limestone blocks of uniform size laid out in regular courses looking like bricks with a mortar of pebbles and clay.[20] The technique is not found elsewhere at Knossos, not even in the contemporary Houses A and B below the West Court kouloures. It is so distinctive that one suspects it might represent an early attempt by a builder accustomed to working in regular or standardised bricks to execute a wall in stone. The wall may have been intended as a support for a mud-brick or rammed earth superstructure which together with the stone support would have been plastered over.

The Northwest Platform, on present ceramic evidence, was the first part of the Palace to be built. Hood cites an early construction date for the Platform in EM III as evidence that the earliest Palatial architecture at Knossos, which he suggests included the Early Keep, Protopalatial Façade and Early Hypogaeum, should be placed in the EM III period and not in MM IA as stated by Evans.[21] However, Branigan's re-evaluation of the date of the Early Keep presents convincing evidence that it was built when MM IB ceramics were in use,[22] and Momigliano has abolished the Protopalatial

---

[14] M.R. Popham, 'Trial KV (1969), a Middle Minoan building at Knossos', *BSA* 69 (1974), 181–94. The most comprehensive groups of ceramics to define the MM IIB period are those found in the destruction deposits of E. Fiandra's 'Period 3' at Phaistos, see Warren and Hankey (n. 5 above), 51–4.

[15] E.A. and H.W. Catling, and D. Smyth, 'Knossos 1975: Middle Minoan III and Late Minoan I houses by the acropolis', *BSA* 74 (1979), 21–7.

[16] Cadogan *et al.* (n. 6 above), 26–7.

[17] *PM I*, 413–14.

[18] There remain problems with the date of the earthquake at Knossos and the origins of the 'Ridged Cup', see Warren and Hankey (n. 5 above), 57.

[19] H.W. Catling, 'Archaeology in Greece, 1973–74', *AR* 20 (1973–74), 34; id., 'Archaeology in Greece, 1987–88', *AR* 34 (1987–88), 69.

[20] J. Raison, *Le Palais du second millénaire à Knossos I* (*Études Crétoises* 28; Paris, 1988), pl. 118a, b on the right.

[21] 'Palatial Crete', a paper read to the Centenary Conference of the British School at Athens in 1986.

[22] K. Branigan, 'The early keep, Knossos: a reappraisal', *BSA* 87 (1992), 153–63.

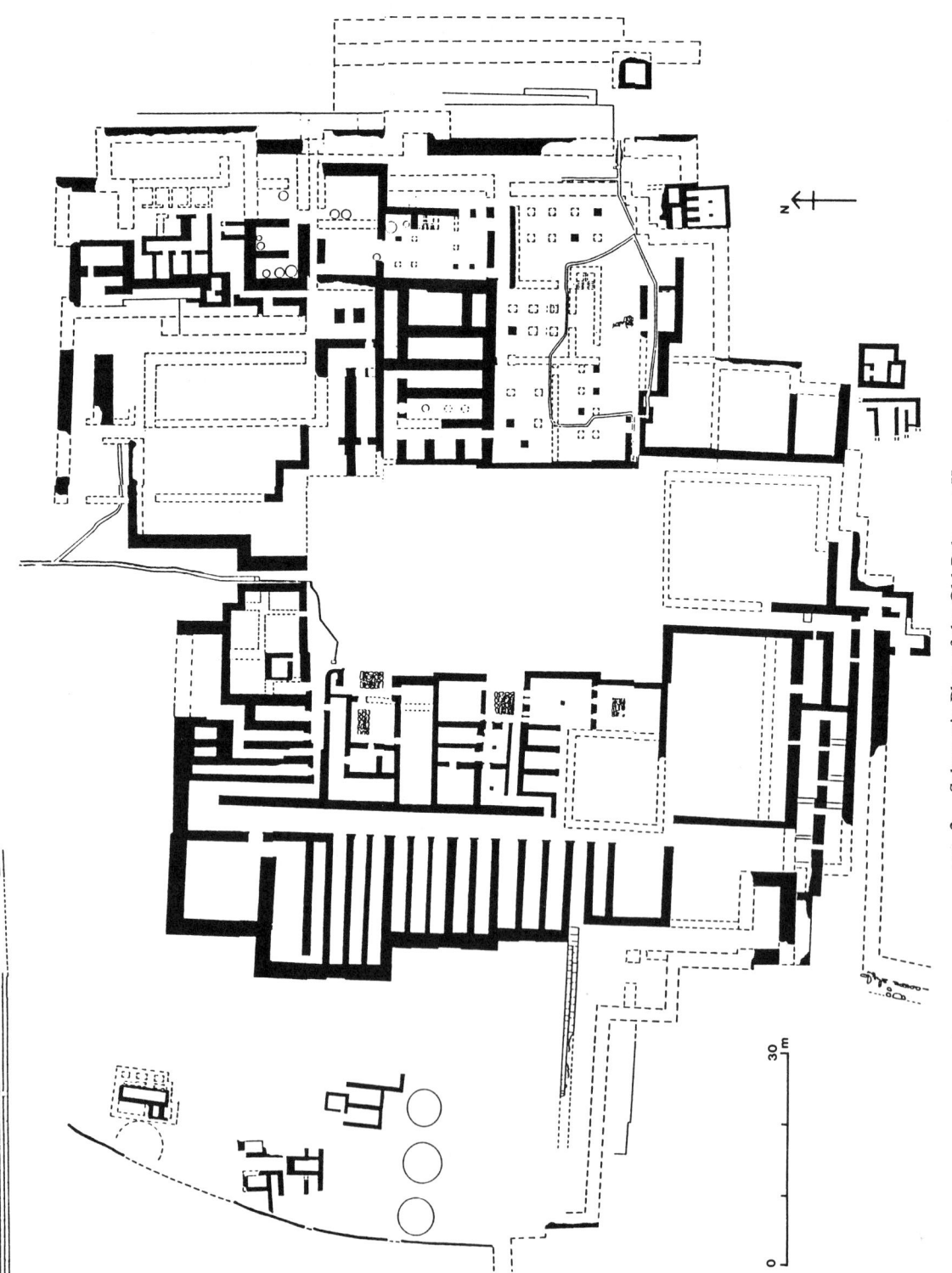

FIG. 2   Schematic Plan of the Old Palace at Knossos

Façade.[23] This leaves only the Early Hypogaeum,[24] which cannot be assigned a conclusive date but may have played a role in the life of the early Palace, as we shall see below. Until the finds from Hood's trials are fully published we cannot say exactly when the Northwest Platform was built, although the temptation is to place it in MM IA.[25]

It is interesting to note that the Monolithic Pillar Basement, in use at least as early as the MM IA period, was neither incorporated into the Palace design, since it had been set out on a different alignment, nor razed like the houses below the West Court at the time the Palace was built.[26] It remained in use well into the Neopalatial period, apparently just outside the Palace wall. Its survival may indicate the continuity of its cult function from MM IA into the Palace period.

Whatever else stood on the Kephala hill between the end of the EM IIB period and the end of MM IA, apart from the Northwest Platform and the Monolithic Pillar Basement, was cut away to make room for the Palace, an action that would have required either a very great deal of common good will on the part of those forced to relocate or a leader with an extraordinary amount of power. It is assumed here that the entire Kephala had not been given over to religious architecture removed when the Palace was built. This is suggested by the intentional preservation of the Monolithic Pillar Basement alone.

If, as Hood suggests, the Northwest Platform was in place first, might we assume that the construction of the Palace began at the northwest corner? Fyfe was quite confident that the Platform held a light area with double door leading into an enclosed space, as shown in FIG.1, perhaps a forerunner of the Minoan Hall. When the nearby North Keep was completed its cells may have served as granaries.[27] These two facilities, then, may have provided storage and ceremonial areas, perhaps reflecting the most important needs to be satisfied, if only temporarily, by the first proprietors while the rest of the Palace was under construction.

The foundation walls of both areas were most probably designed to support mud-brick walls. The foundations for the façades of the remainder of the Palace were built to support courses of gypsum blocks. Evans assumed that the gypsum blocks were put in place at an early stage of the building's history and many survived in position, at least as lower courses, into the Late Bronze Age.[28] The use of a building material that was specifically sought out for qualities other than pure support strength, cut into transportable blocks and trimmed into uniform dimensions to become luxurious, level courses in external walls was an important innovation in Crete at this time. It implies not only the existence of newly acquired skills in quarrying and engineering, but also a new desire for ostentatious and permanent architecture.

Gypsum was used to line entrances, like the South Corridor, and to create dramatic effect in stepped courses along the East Façade, where it would have been visible to traffic coming up the river from Poros, on the South Front, where travellers from inland would have first caught sight of the Palace, and in the West Façade above the town of Knossos. The material itself may have been

---

[23] N. Momigliano, 'The "Proto-palatial Façade" at Knossos', *BSA* 87 (1992), 65–75.

[24] *PM I*, 104–8; Momigliano (n. 7 above), 195–8.

[25] D. Wilson, in this volume, favours a construction date in EM III, which could mean that the Platform was not built as part of the Palace, but merely incorporated into the later design.

[26] *PM I*, 146, fig. 106; Momigliano (n. 7 above), 163–7; MacGillivray (n. 2 above), Group M.

[27] Branigan (n. 22 above), 163.

[28] *PM I*, 128, 209.

thought to hold supernatural qualities, as the mason's marks may indicate,[29] and in this respect could have been important for defining the sacred limits of the Palace. Gypsum seems to have been a feature primarily of the early building; replacement blocks following the earthquake of 1780 B.C. were generally cut from the nearby limestone quarries on Ailias.

As impressive as the new building itself were the access routes leading up to it. From the south, traffic would have crossed the Viaduct and Stepped Portico, both expensive constructions which could both facilitate and control access from the countryside.[30] From the west, traffic, possibly even wheeled, gained access through the town of Knossos along the direct and well paved, perhaps even formal or ceremonial, Royal Road.[31] The furthest extent of the Royal Road from the Palace was found in the Stratigraphical Museum excavations and shows that the line continues beyond even that point.[32] It is important to remember that the construction of the Royal Road must have forced the evacuation of very many households as it was engineered and cut along a line five metres wide and almost one kilometre long through the MM IA town. Like the Palace itself, such a project could only have been carried out with universal consent or by extreme force.

Adjacent to the Palace outside the West Façade was an apparent agglomeration of structures without clear definition.[33] New features erected in this area during the MM IB period were the three kouloures.[34] These large, circular, stone-lined storage pits were cut deep into the levels of the tell. Their interpretation as granaries has led to much speculation about social storage outside the walls of the Palace proper.[35] Built during the same ceramic period as the kouloures were the West and, most probably, Southern Enceinte walls defining the limits of the later West Court.[36] Not very impressive at the time of their discovery, they may have been strong limiting factors to access in the early Palace period, if the southern wall is anything to judge by. There, Evans found collapsed rows of large cut gypsum blocks, like those that were used in the façades of the Palace, but lying as they had fallen after the earthquake of 1780 B.C.[37] The Western Enceinte was found as a very unstable retaining wall without any external face. What is preserved, however, almost certainly represents only the backing of what would have been a gypsum wall over two metres high. The gypsum blocks might have been removed later or could have disintegrated as the crystalline stone does when exposed to moisture for many years. The kouloures, then, may not have been readily accessible to members of the public, but could have been for the temporary holding of materials, such as grain or cereals, not yet processed for long-term storage within the Palace. Their final use was as repositories for building debris and rubbish from the cleaning-up operations following the 1780 B.C. earthquake.[38]

---

[29] S. Hood, 'Mason's marks in the palaces', in Hägg and Marinatos (n. 10 above), 205–12.
[30] *PM II.i*, 140, fig. 71.
[31] *PM II.ii*, 572.
[32] P.M. Warren, 'Knossos: Stratigraphical Museum Excavations, 1978–1980. Part 1', *AR* 27 (1980–81), 73. It is my feeling that the paved way led to a gate at the town limits, at least in the early years of the Palace.
[33] *PM I*, 207; *II.ii*, 609. The overall understanding of Old Palace Period structures beneath the later West Court remains problematic, since Pendlebury's excavation notebooks have not been found and there remain unexcavated areas.
[34] *PM IV.i*, 61–6.
[35] K. Branigan, 'Social security and the state in Middle Bronze Age Crete', *Aegaeum* 2 (1988), 11–16.
[36] *PM IV.i*, 49–59, figs. 30, 34–5.
[37] Ibid. 58, fig. 35.
[38] H.W. and J.D.S. Pendlebury, 'Two Protopalatial houses at Knossos', *BSA* 30 (1928–30), 55 n. 1.

Within the Palace walls, we are hard put to it to conclude which features existed when and to speculate how rooms or wings might have been used, because of the later modifications in the structure. Evans' and Fyfe's observations on the dates of wall foundations allow us to accept their inference that the West Magazines and much of the West Wing were already in existence early in the history of the building — not however as insulae, as indicated on their plan (reproduced here in FIG. 1), but rather as one coherent unit with a long internal north-south corridor, as shown in a proposed schematic plan (FIG. 2).

The West Wing included the deep storage pits, perhaps for dry goods, in the Early Keep, the West Magazines, where large ceramic jars could have been used to store liquids such as oil or wine, an early version of the Throne Room System,[39] the Pillar Crypt and other ceremonial spaces associated with the Room of the Column Bases.[40] The whole of the ground floor seems to have been dedicated to ceremony and storage, very much as one might expect in a temple. It is not certain that the West Wing had an upper floor during this early period. There seem not to have been predecessors for the North-West Entrance System[41] or for the Stepped Porch[42] and no other indication of a stairway, although this need not preclude access to a second storey.

The East Wing preserves much less of its original character than the West, but surviving evidence suggests that it contained very little in the way of surplus agricultural storage facilities; only the Magazines of the Giant Pithoi[43] may represent such storage, although on a much smaller scale. The existing evidence for storage points to manufactured goods, for example high-quality ceramics in the Royal Pottery Stores and the sets of cups and jars from the deposit below the Room of the Olive Press.[44] Both groups contain products which we know were valued as export items throughout the Aegean and Near East.[45] There is no evidence that the pottery was manufactured in the Palace. Instead, it seems likely to have come from the Archanes region.

There are strong indications for weaving on the upper floors of the East Wing in the form of over 400 loomweights in the Loomweight Basement.[46] Textiles seem to have been an important part of life, if we accept that the origins for many design motifs and patterns preserved on pottery and probably imitated in wall painting came from the loom.[47]

The renovations in the East Wing in MM III were quite comprehensive, no doubt owing to the effects of the earthquake of 1780 B.C. Nonetheless, it is possible to identify square gypsum pillars

---

[39] As argued in S. Mirié, *Das Thronraumareal des Palastes von Knossos: Versuch einer Neuinterpretation seiner Entstehung und seiner Funktion* (Saarbrücker Beiträge zur Altertumskunde, 26; Bonn, 1979), but trials by S. Hood in 1987 may alter the plan and chronology somewhat: see Catling (n. 19 above — 1988), 69.

[40] J. Driessen, *An Early Destruction in the Palace at Knossos: a New Interpretation of the Excavation Field-Notes of the South-West Area of the West Wing* (Acta Archaeologica Lovaniensia, Monographiae 2; Leuven, 1990), 103–5, fig. 9.

[41] S. Hood and W. Taylor, *The Bronze Age Palace at Knossos. Plans and Sections* (BSA Suppl. 13; London, 1981), 19, nos. 148–9.

[42] Ibid. 17, no. 100.

[43] Ibid. 21, nos. 187–8.

[44] MacGillivray (n. 10 above), 273–8.

[45] For recent bibliography and discussion, see M.H. Wiener, 'The nature and control of Minoan foreign trade', in N.H. Gale (ed.), *Bronze Age Trade in the Mediterranean: Papers presented at the Conference held at Rewley House, Oxford ... 1989* (SIMA 90; Jonsered, 1991), 332.

[46] *PM I*, 248–51.

[47] *PM II.i*, 114, 195–208, fig. 117a; *IV.i*, 100, fig. 66. [Editors' note: see too E.J.W. Barber, *Prehistoric Textiles: the Development of Cloth in the Neolithic and Bronze Ages with Special Reference to the Aegean* (Princeton, 1991), 311–57.]

within the later walls in the Domestic Quarter.⁴⁸ The plan in FIG. 2 shows these in black and gives the hypothetical locations of other gypsum supports in a proposed reconstruction of the first plan of the area. There may have been four pillared halls in the areas to become the Grand Staircase, Hall of the Colonnades, Hall of the Double Axes and Court of the Distaffs. The Area of the Queen's Megaron seems to have been paved and may have served as an interior courtyard.⁴⁹ The evidence for what might have taken place in these halls when first built has long since been removed, but a clue may come from the so-called Drainage System.⁵⁰

Generally regarded as essential for the evacuation of rainwater from the Central Court, the waterway beneath the later Domestic Quarter does not make sense as a simple drain. Had it been built uniquely as a drain for the Court, one straight line from the area of the shafts to the East Exit would have served the purpose. In any case, the drain in the North Entrance Passage should have sufficed for evacuating the Central Court.⁵¹ The indirect route may have connected small, internal courts, as it does after MM III, but there is no evidence that these existed in the first plan. An alternative suggestion is that the underground system was a passage constantly filled with running water that could be drawn off at various points in the basement rooms it served. The implication is that fresh water in great quantities was required as part of the original plan for this part of the Palace.

It is certain that one of the sources that supplied the Palace with fresh water was the spring at Mavrokolyvo, roughly 500 metres to the southwest of the Palace in the Vlykhia gully.⁵² Near the source, Evans found a length of covered aqueduct of similar construction and dimensions to the Palace drainage system. Given the contours of the gully, it seems most likely that the water course arrived at the Palace near the Stepped Portico and South Corridor. The exposed section of aqueduct is roughly 100 metres above sea-level, the floor in the South Corridor roughly 97. Given the distance from the source and the drop in level, the water could have arrived at the Palace with some force.⁵³ It may not be fortuitous that the Early Hypogaeum was located in this area. A deep, circular vault cut out of the soft bedrock, the Early Hypogaeum was roughly 8.5 metres wide and 15 metres high.⁵⁴ It was designed to be entered and access to the very bottom was provided by steps cut into the rock. Unfortunately, for safety reasons, only a small part of the structure was explored and so many questions remain. However, it seems possible that the man-made cavern could have functioned as both a reservoir, ensuring a protected reserve, and a settling tank for water arriving at the Palace along the Mavrokolyvo aqueduct.

I suspect that the water did not stop at the South Porch, but was further directed into the Palace, perhaps with the system of terracotta pipes designed to increase the water pressure and force the water to run uphill, examples of which were found nearby.⁵⁵ Evans carried out very little investigation into

---

⁴⁸ *PM III*, 374–7, fig. 249, Plan E.

⁴⁹ *PM III*, 356–9, figs. 235–6.

⁵⁰ For recent re-investigation and full bibliography, see C. Macdonald and J. Driessen, 'The drainage system of the Domestic Quarter in the Palace at Knossos', *BSA* 83 (1988), 235–58.

⁵¹ *PM I*, 397, fig. 286.

⁵² *PM II.ii*, 462–3, fig. 273, map opp. 547; *III*, 252.

⁵³ An indication of such water pressure is provided by the painted image of a fountain from the House of the Frescoes, *PM III*, 253–4, pl. XXII. The painting may record something that existed within the Palace walls and not the fancy of the painter.

⁵⁴ *PM I*, 104–6, fig. 74.

⁵⁵ *PM I*, 141–3, fig. 104A.

the early levels of the South and South-East Insulae, where a water way would have been built to connect the South Porch with the Domestic Quarter.

It is possible that the East Wing was provided with a constant source of fresh running water. One reason for so much water could have been commercial, for example the washing, boiling and dyeing of the fabrics woven on the first floor looms. The large, well-aired halls could have been hung with drying wool. Such a proposal, however, would be in direct conflict with the evidence for how this area seems to have functioned after the renovations of MM III. The pier-and-door partitions and multiple 'polythyra' would seem better suited to ritual than to commercial behaviour, or for what Evans implied with his name for this suite — the 'Domestic Quarter'.[56] Without relying too much on Evans' image of Victorian palace life, it is quite possible to imagine the basement rooms as the private quarters of a palace in a society in which cleansing in running water was crucial for both ritual and hygienic reasons.

CONCLUSION

The Palace at Knossos may have been conceived both as place of worship and as storehouse for wealth — rather like an early temple, but also as the dwelling for the ruling family — like the contemporary palaces in the Near East. There is no precedent in the Aegean for such a building or the organisation required to construct and maintain it.

The range of possible functions we can assign to the early building with certainty is severely limited by lack of evidence, especially textual. However, one of its main roles would have been to impress outside viewers with the gypsum façades that glistened in the sunlight but at the same time controlled access to the interior through narrow passages. The limited access to the building may reflect the concerns of the first generations of rulers with maintaining their authority, both in the immediate region and beyond.[57]

The earthquake of c.1780 B.C. did not bring about the destruction of the building, but rather provided the opportunity for a new generation of Cretan architects to invent ways to deal with problems posed by the Cretan environment and to remedy some of the failings of the earlier structure. This new obsession with architectural innovation may account for the great increase in the number of house models and representations of buildings in the early stages of the Neopalatial period from MM IIIA onwards.[58] For example, gypsum may have been observed not to weather well and so was replaced by limestone. More wood and plastered mud-brick might have been introduced into the structure and used as a framework for lightweight building material because of the failure in seismic stress of the largely stone walls of the previous period. The discovery of the wooden frame may have led to the proliferation of the elaborate and highly original pier-and-door partition. But no matter how clever the new architects may have felt, they can have been in no doubt upon whose shoulders they stood in the Labyrinth of Daedalus at Knossos.

---

[56] N. Marinatos and R. Hägg, 'On the ceremonial function of the Minoan polythyron', *Op. Ath.* 16 (1986), 57–73.
[57] Discussed in J.A. MacGillivray, 'The Cretan countryside in the Old Palace period', in R. Hägg (ed.), *The Function of the 'Minoan Villa': Proceedings of the Eighth International Symposium at the Swedish Institute in Athens ... 1992* (Skrifter ... Svenska Inst. i Athen, 4°; Stockholm, in press).
[58] A. Lembesi, ''Ο οἰκίσκος τῶν 'Αρχανῶν', *Arch.Eph.* 1976, 12–43.

Chapter 4

An Old Palace Period Knossos State?

G. CADOGAN

Was there a distinctive Knossian cultural region in the Old Palace period that could have formed a Knossos state separate from the rest of Crete?

On the south side of the Royal Road[1] Sinclair Hood's excavations have revealed the most intelligible ceramic sequence for understanding the Old Palace period of Knossos, as a seminar held at Knossos in 1992 affirmed.[2] If Sinclair's translations of this sequence of deposits into Evans' Minoan terminology have moved up and down,[3] that reflects two things: the slippery nature of the problem (making a stout argument against dogmatic certitude in Minoan studies); and Sinclair's fearlessness about changing his mind in his several attempts to land this difficult catch.

Our knowledge of the hinterland of Knossos in the Old Palace period is less secure. It is possible to identify a Lasithi cultural region which probably indicates a Lasithi state centred on Mallia; and we may be able to identify other such regions or states, in the far east (Zakro cum Palaikastro) and

---

[1] S. Hood and D. Smyth, *Archaeological Survey of the Knossos Area* (2nd edn.; *BSA* Suppl. 14; London, 1981), 51, no. 216.
I have been fortunate to have worked with Sinclair Hood for more than thirty years. I have always found myself learning from him — about the archaeology of the Minoans or virtually any group in the world, and about history, politics (ancient or modern, local or global), civilisation, humane values and, not least, religion. It is rare that someone remains so young as Sinclair, so intense in his devotion to archaeology and everything else he values, and so willing to perceive a better explanation, or better policy, and to change his mind. His modesty combined with his pertinacious zeal for the truth (or the elimination of falsehood, which is often as far as we can go in archaeology) teaches us all. My life changed in the summer of 1960 when Sinclair made me Hugh Sackett's trench assistant in the excavations on the north side of the Royal Road. There I learnt what is now known as the British School at Athens method of digging, which was really Sinclair's system. (He would say that he was following Woolley's methods at Alalakh and, I expect, Kenyon's at Jericho.) It has revolutionised the quality of British excavation in Greece and the accuracy of reporting archaeological contexts and horizons (to use a favourite term of Sinclair's). There have been adaptations and refinements but from the Ionian Islands to Cyprus the system endures. How many fieldworkers are still putting their level numbers in triangles as they check their running sections, the record of what they did, against their final sections — the record of what they should have done!
I should like to thank Jeff Clarke for drawing the map (FIG. 1), and David Smyth for collecting the information for it. Numbers in bold in the text refer to sites shown on FIG. 1.
[2] G. Cadogan, P.E. Day, C. Macdonald, J.A. MacGillivray, N. Momigliano, T.M. Whitelaw and D.E. Wilson, 'Early Minoan and Middle Minoan pottery groups at Knossos', *BSA* 88 (1993), 21–8.
[3] See citations, ibid., under the heading 'Previous attributions'.

in the west (either Rethymno cum Chania or two separate units).[4] But what about Knossos? And if there was a Knossian cultural region or state, what was its relation to Phaistos and its surroundings of the Mesara plain, the Asterousia mountains and, as the new excavations at Monastiraki suggest, the southern part of the Amari valley to the west of Psiloriti?[5] Was there one large central Cretan cultural region, or were there two regions, Knossos and Phaistos?

The evidence is less than one would wish, making it difficult to construct a picture of the Middle Minoan hinterland of Knossos. Apart from those around Knossos and Archanes, far fewer research excavations have been undertaken in north-central Crete than in Lasithi and around the Bay of Mirabello, where their evidence is essential for assembling the probable Mallia-Lasithi cultural region. Collating the Archaeological Service's many rescue excavations, some of which have become research excavations (such as the recent work at Kastelli[6]), would release much new information and show, probably, that the Pediada and Malevisi districts — the continental part of Crete — were more densely settled and more prosperous in Minoan times than we now imagine. More surveys, to add to those of Knossos and Archanes, are needed.

Another constraint is our lack of knowledge of the Old Palace itself of Knossos, although new studies are improving matters.[7] The lack makes it particularly difficult to compare Knossos with Phaistos, where much more of the Old Palace is preserved with a complicated stratigraphical sequence, and large deposits of pottery and administrative documents (the *cretule*) have been published.

With these caveats I shall attempt to review the evidence for a distinct cultural region around Knossos in the Old Palace period, which may indicate a Knossos state.

THE EVIDENCE

Situation

Knossos, (FIG. 1), lies in low rolling country in central Crete near the north coast. The natural western limit to an extended Knossian territory (meaning one that stretched beyond the immediate surroundings of the Minoan town) is the Psiloriti massif and its outlying ranges, which run down to the north coast and were breached only by the opening of the new National Road to Rethymno and Chania. To the east the Lasithi massif dominates the horizon but is less of a barrier than Psiloriti. It is easy from Knossos to reach the flat country around Mallia at the northern foot of the Lasithi mountains, or to traverse their west and south sides. But the Lasithi peaks and the upland plain could well have been alien territory for

---

[4] G. Cadogan, 'Mallia and Lasithi: a palace-state', *Cretological VII* (forthcoming); id., 'Lasithi in the Old Palace period', *BICS* 37 (1990), 172–4.

[5] A. Kanta, 'Monastiraki', in J.W. Myers, E.E. Myers and G. Cadogan (eds.), *The Aerial Atlas of Ancient Crete* (Berkeley and London, 1992), 194–7.

[6] N. Demopoulou, ''Αρχαιολογικές ειδήσεις από την Πεδιάδα', *Lyktos* 2 (1986–7), 30–41.

[7] See J.A. MacGillivray's and P.M. Warren's papers in this volume. Among other recent contributions are K. Branigan, 'The early keep, Knossos: a reappraisal', *BSA* 87 (1992), 153–63, and N. Momigliano, 'MM IA pottery from Evans' excavations at Knossos: a reassessment', *BSA* 86 (1991), 149–271, and 'The "Proto-palatial façade" at Knossos', *BSA* 87 (1992), 165–75. Publications we await include J.A. MacGillivray's *Knossos: Pottery Groups of the Old Palace* (a preliminary account is 'Pottery workshops and the old palaces in Crete', in R. Hägg and N. Marinatos (eds.), *The Function of the Minoan Palaces. Proceedings of the Fourth International Symposium at the Swedish Institute in Athens ... 1984* (Skrifter ... Svenska Inst. i Athen 4°, 35; Stockholm, 1987), 273–9); and M. Panagiotaki's study of the rooms around the Temple Repositories.

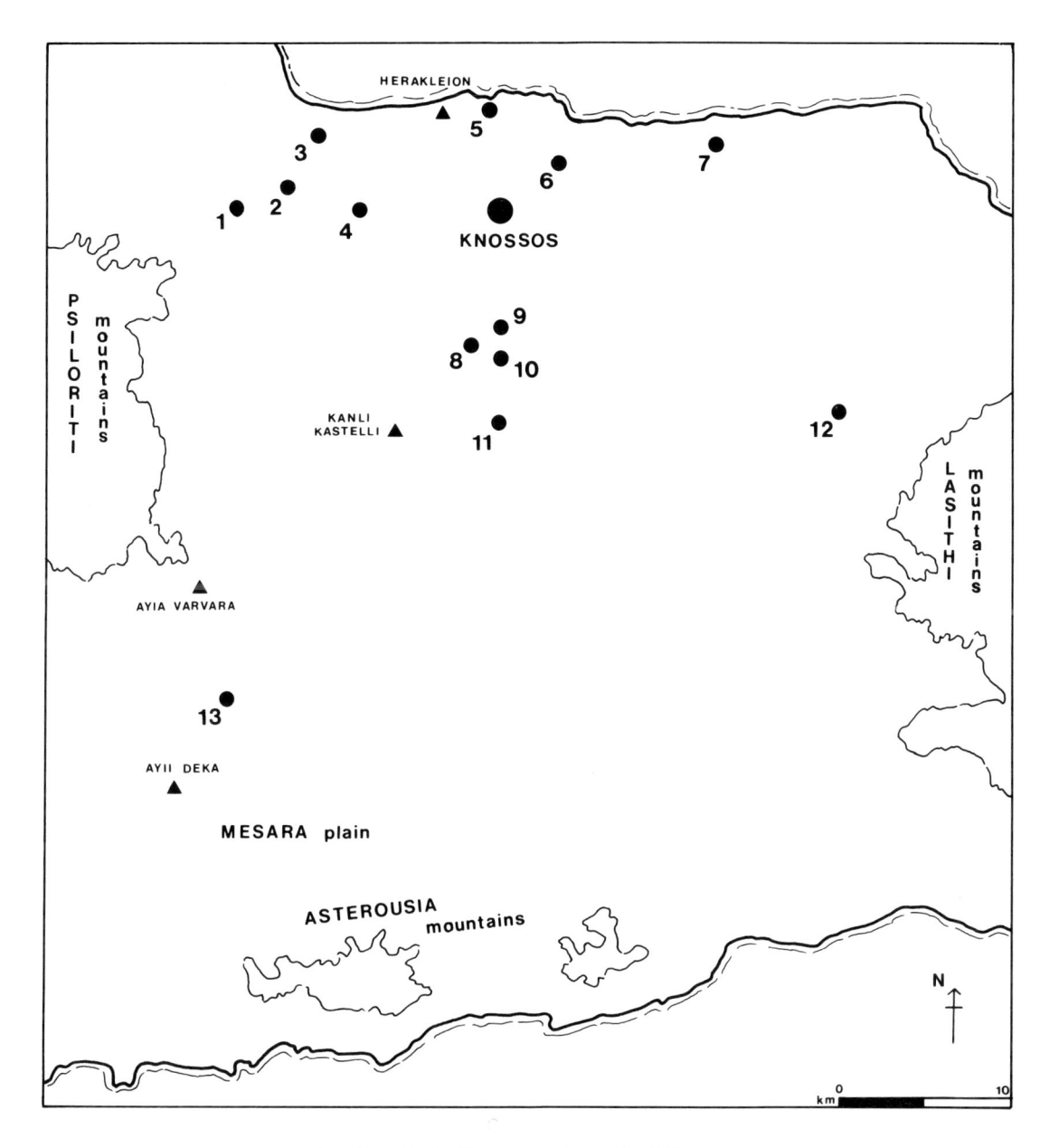

FIG. 1   Sites in the Knossos region, with 800 m contour

1 Tylissos
2 Kavrochori
3 Gazi
4 Giophyrakia
5 Poros
6 Prasa
7 Gournes
8 Mt. Iuktas
9 Archanes-Phourni
10 Archanes village
11 Vathypetro
12 Kastelli
13 Vorou

the powers at Knossos.[8] To the south the passes into the Mesara, such as that the modern road takes above the village of Ayia Varvara, make a low natural barrier that is easy to cross. These boundaries shape as a potential hinterland for Knossos the country between Psiloriti, the Mesara passes, the Lasithi mountains and the sea. (If it was the case that Knossos and Phaistos formed a large united region, the boundary would then be the south coast and include the Mesara plain and the Asterousia mountains, a quite different terrain from the low rolling hills around Knossos.)

Within the suggested north-coast hinterland the principal Old Palace period and Prepalatial sites other than Knossos make a surprisingly short list.

Tylissos **1**, an old settlement dating back to EM II, is a stage on the route from Knossos via Sklavokambos to Psiloriti and the Plain of Nida,[9] a district that was of considerable value (for Knossos, I presume) in the New Palace period, as the new excavations of Sakellarakis and Sakellaraki at Zominthos make clear. It will be interesting to see whether evidence is found that this district was already being exploited in the Old Palace period.

The shrine on Mt Iuktas **8** was 'probably the public open-air sanctuary of the Knossos area in the Old Palace period', Karetsou suggests.[10] The quality and quantity of the finds at this landmark indicate a special connexion with the Palace at Knossos. Around the end of the period another shrine, equally visible from Knossos, increased the sanctity of the mountain: the temple on its northern slopes at Archanes-Anemospilia.[11]

The rich cemetery nearby at Archanes-Phourni **9** had been in use since Prepalatial times and continued to receive burials through the Old Palace period (and later). Its pottery includes imports from the Mesara, as one might expect both from its situation on the route to the south and from the drawing power of its grandeur and importance. Tomb types show the influences of both the east Cretan and the south Cretan traditions of burial.[12]

In Archanes village **10** Middle Minoan remains have been reported. The probable major settlement would have been the Old Palace period predecessor of Archanes-Tourkoyeitonia. Other MM sites around Archanes that Sakellarakis and Sakellaraki report include Vitsila near Kanli Kastelli (Prophitis Ilias).[13] At Vathypetro **11** there is no evidence yet of an Old Palace period settlement preceding the LM I country house and other buildings.[14]

---

[8] The Venetians' banning of inhabitation in Lasithi (L.V. Watrous, *Lasithi: A History of Settlement on a Highland Plain in Crete* (*Hesperia* Suppl. 18; Princeton, 1982), 25) illustrates its alien nature.

[9] A. Vasilakis, 'Tylissos', in Myers *et al.* (n. 5 above), 272–5; G. Walberg, *Provincial Middle Minoan Pottery* (Mainz, 1983), 104–5.

[10] A. Karetsou, 'The peak sanctuary of Mt. Juktas', in R. Hägg and N. Marinatos (eds.), *Sanctuaries and Cults in the Aegean Bronze Age. Proceedings of the First International Symposium at the Swedish Institute in Athens ... 1980 (Skrifter ... Svenska Inst. i Athen* 4°, 28; Stockholm, 1981), 145; also B. Rutkowski, 'Minoan peak sanctuaries: the topography and architecture', *Aegaeum* 2 (1988), 81–2 (with refs.). A.A.D. Peatfield, 'Minoan peak sanctuaries: history and society', *Op. Ath.* 18 (1990), 125, reports use back to EM II.

[11] Y. Sakellarakis and E. Sakellaraki, 'Archanes-Anemospilia', in Myers *et al.* (n. 5 above), 51–3; eid., *Archanes* (Athens, 1991), 136–56.

[12] Eid., 'Archanes-Phourni', in Myers *et al.* (n. 5 above), 54–8; eid., (n. 11 above – 1991), 66–135.

[13] Eid., 'Archanes-Tourkoyeitonia', in Myers *et al.* (n. 5 above), 59–62; eid., (n. 11 above – 1991), 24–6.

[14] So J. Driessen kindly tells me. See also J. Driessen and Y. Sakellarakis, 'The Vathypetro-complex. Some observations on its architectural history and function', in R. Hägg (ed.), *The Function of the 'Minoan Villa': Proceedings of the Eighth International Symposium at the Swedish Institute in Athens (Skrifter ... Svenska Inst. i Athen,* 4°; Stockholm, in press); and discussion of Vathypetro at the 1992 Swedish Symposium.

To the northeast of Ayii Deka, Vorou **13** lies in the foothills on the south side of the Ayia Varvara pass into the Mesara plain. It is outside the immediate hinterland of Knossos, but the Knossian-type 'sheep bells' in the EM III/MM IA deposit outside Tholos Tomb A show Prepalatial links with the region north of the pass.[15] It is not clear whether or not these links continued into MM IB.

In the Pediada district southeast of Knossos, the settlement at Kastelli **12** was set where the western foothills of the Lasithi massif begin. Its pottery suggests that it may lie likewise on the edge of a Knossian cultural zone, or even just outside it: Demopoulou reports a Pediada style of pottery, influenced by — but different from — that of the Mallia workshops, and also different from the Knossian style.[16]

The pottery in the tombs at Gournes **7** defines an eastern boundary for a Knossian zone. It shows both Mallia-Lasithi elements, such as small baggy red ware jugs with fine grooved decoration on the body and trefoil spouts, and jugs with a painted motif of three solid circles that are exactly paralleled at Knossos.[17]

Other sites, if their use was not restricted to Prepalatial times, include:

Kavrochori-Keramoutsi **2** west of Herakleion, where Alexiou has reported a shrine deposit.[18] The pottery illustrated includes two eggcup goblets and may be all MM IA. (In these late Prepalatial deposits it is not always easy to distinguish MM IA from EM III but, luckily, that is not a problem that we must resolve here.)

Gazi **3**, where clay 'sheep bells' have been found.[19]

Giophyrakia-Tou Lirari to Papouri **4**, where Marinatos found MM IA (or EM III/MM IA) pottery that may come from a tomb (but no traces of the tomb).[20]

Poros **5**, the eastern suburb of Herakleion which has also produced sheep bells. An important chamber tomb, first used in MM III, shares architectural features with tombs that date back to the end of the Old Palace period at Knossos or straddle the transition to the New Palace period.[21]

Prasa nearby **6** seems to have been a substantial settlement with an Old Palace period phase, as well as Prepalatial and New Palace period phases.[22]

Settlements, Cemeteries and Shrines

We do not know enough of the Old Palace period town of Knossos to be able to make many conclusions from comparisons with other Old Palace period palatial settlements. Until more is excavated of Middle Minoan Knossos — the single most pressing need in Knossian studies — there

---

[15] S. Marinatos, 'Δύο πρώϊμοι μινωϊκοί τάφοι ἐκ Βοροῦ Μεσαρᾶς', *A.Delt.* 13 (1930–1), 137–70; Walberg (n. 9 above), 103–4, noting some later MM pottery.

[16] Demopoulou (n. 6 above), 31–3.

[17] A. Zois, Προβλήματα Χρονολογίας τῆς Μινωικῆς Κεραμεικῆς — Γοῦρνες, Τύλισος, Μάλια (Athens, 1969), pls. A and 9.6942, 6945 (red jugs); pls. A and 1–3 (juglets). For the parallel at Knossos: Momigliano (n. 7 above) – 1991), 169–70, fig. 4.16, and 173, pl. 23.

[18] S. Alexiou, 'Μικραὶ ἀνασκαφαὶ καὶ περισυλλογὴ ἀρχαίων εἰς Κρήτην', *PAE* 1966, 189–93, pl. 166b.

[19] C.E. Morris and A.A.D. Peatfield, 'Minoan sheep bells: form and function', in *Cretological VI, A'2* (Chania, 1990), 32.

[20] S. Marinatos, ''Ενάτη καὶ δεκάτη ἀρχαιολογικὴ περιφέρεια Κρήτης', *A.Delt.* 15 (1933–5), Parartema 49–83. Another deposit to the west of Herakleion is Ayios Myronas-Vryses, S. Alexiou, 'Μικραὶ ἀνασκαφαὶ καὶ περισυλλογὴ ἀρχαίων εἰς Κρήτην', *PAE* (1967), 210–11; Walberg (n. 9 above), 104.

[21] N. Platon, 'Nouvelle interprétation des idoles-cloches du minoen moyen 1', *RA* 6ᵉ série, 31–32 (Mélanges Charles Picard; 1948), 835–8, figs. 2–3; P. Muhly, Μινωικὸς Λαξευτὸς Τάφος στὸν Πόρο Ἡρακλείου (Athens, 1992), 144–8, 191.

[22] N. Platon, ''Ανασκαφὴ Μινωϊκῶν οἰκιῶν εἰς Πρασᾶ Ἡρακλείου', *PAE* 1951, 246–57.

is little to say about how the Palace and town worked,[23] and we have no means of assessing the present apparent uniqueness of Mallia in having both an Old Palace and a Quartier Mu with all the contents and functions of a palace, but without its architectural form.[24] (It is possible that a building, or group of buildings, equivalent to Quartier Mu lies buried at Knossos.) Warren's study of the Minoan roads suggests a network well established by or in MM IA within the town of Knossos, and developed further thereafter, with hints of radial continuations to other parts of Crete.[25] It would be valuable for defining a Knossian state to know better to what extent such a system may have existed outside Knossos in the Old Palace period. The road network within the town seems comparable to those at the other palatial settlements.

In habits of burial the hinterland of Knossos appears to lie between two traditions that were both venerable by the time of the Old Palaces, and are important markers of cultural regionalism: the round tholos tombs of the Mesara, and the rectangular house-like tombs of East Crete. The long-used cemetery of Archanes-Phourni appears to have been a point where the two traditions met.[26] (One must remember that some tholos tombs occur in eastern Crete. Likewise, the rectangular bone-enclosures attached to the Mesara tholos tombs may have a link with the east Cretan tradition, although the form is a natural one for builders to make.) The occurrence both of a curious rectangular tholos tomb on the hill of Gypsadhes at Knossos, in the Mesara tradition but with a difference, and of the house- (or shrine-) like Temple Tomb built not far away in the early stages of the New Palace period,[27] may corroborate the suggestion that it was at Knossos and Archanes that these eastern and southern burial practices merged.

A new tomb type that seems to have been specifically Knossian appeared at the end of the Old Palace period. It is not found in the regions to east and south: the rock-cut chamber tomb with multiple round or kidney-shaped chambers.[28] Its adoption may reflect differing social conditions since, it seems, burials in these tombs were on a much smaller scale than in the tholos tombs. Two possibilities, not mutually

---

[23] I have tried: see G. Cadogan, 'What happened at the Old Palace of Knossos?', in Hägg and Marinatos (n. 7 above), 71–4.

[24] J.-C. Poursat, *Guide de Malia au temps des premiers palais. Le Quartier Mu* (Athens, 1992), is a valuable new summary. See also his 'Town and palace at Malia in the protopalatial period', in Hägg and Marinatos (n. 7 above), 75–6, and 'La Ville minoenne de Malia: recherches et publications récentes', *RA* n.s. 1988, 61–82.

[25] In this volume.

[26] Cadogan (n. 4 above); J.S. Soles, *The Prepalatial Cemeteries at Mochlos and Gournia and the House Tombs of Bronze Age Crete* (*Hesperia* Suppl. 24; Princeton, 1992), 255.

[27] Lower Gypsadhes tholos tomb: Hood and Smyth (n. 1 above), 11, 57, no. 308; Temple Tomb: ibid., 11, 58–9, no. 323.

[28] Old Palace period multi-chamber and two-chamber (kidney-shaped) tombs in Mavro Spelio and Ailias cemeteries at Knossos (ibid. 11, 53–4, nos. 251, 257). At Mavro Spelio, Tombs I–III, V, VII, IX, XVII (E.J. Forsdyke, 'The Mavro Spelio Cemetery at Knossos', *BSA* 28 (1926–7), 243–96). Ailias awaits publication.

Kidney-shaped, Upper Gypsadhes (Hood and Smyth, n. 1 above, 11, 59 no. 331) Tomb XVIII assigned to MM IIIA or end of MM II (S. Hood, G. Huxley and N.K. Sandars, 'A Minoan cemetery on Upper Gypsades', *BSA* 53–4 (1958–9), 220–4). Its group of small pots (252, 254, fig. 31, pl. 53d.XVIII. 1–4) and three Vapheio cups (253–4, fig. 31, pl. 53c.XVIII. 10–12) fits well into the 'Knossos village, Trial KV group', which is equivalent to MM IIB (Cadogan *et al*, n. 2 above). So does the deposit in the pit of Mavro Spelio Tomb XVII (Forsdyke, above, 281), which includes a Mallia-Lasithi red ware jug with grooved decoration and trefoil spout (pl. 23.33) like those from Gournes (n. 17 above), Mallia and Myrtos-Pyrgos.

For the slightly later (MM III) Poros Tomb Pi 1967, see Muhly (n. 21 above), 146, who points out the similar Knossian-type MM III tombs in Kythera (J.N. Coldstream and G.L. Huxley, *Kythera: Excavations and Studies Conducted by the University of Pennsylvania Museum and the British School at Athens* (London, 1972), 220–7) which show that Kythera's links with Crete were not restricted to west Crete.

I. Pini, *Beiträge zur minoischen Gräberkunde* (Wiesbaden, 1968), 36–40, derives the type from Cyprus. See also Hood, Huxley and Sandars, above, 220, n. 9.

exclusive, are that we see here signs of the growth of a Knossian elite and/or of burial by family rather than by extended family or community, which had probably been the practice in the Mesara tholos tombs. (The eastern house tombs Soles sees as collective rather than communal.[29])

The placing of the mountain shrines on peaks where they are visible at great distances from each other may suggest a pan-Cretan network of these holy places and count against a notion of independent cultural regions. Stand on Mt Iuktas and look south to Kophinas in the Asterousia mountains (Phaistos region), as Alexandra Karetsou bade me do, and it is obvious that there was a link between the two shrines. The island-wide similarities of cult practice support the notion of interconnexion (although the at present uniquely large offering of phalli at Atsipades near Rethymno[30] may be a counter-argument). An alternative explanation would be to say, Yes, there was a single, overriding system of worship and, probably, of belief; but it may be that, as with Christianity in medieval western Europe, this was separate from political divisions and need not invalidate any case for different regions or states.

The general similarity in the plans (as far as we can see them) of the Old Palaces of Knossos, Mallia, Zakro and Phaistos is likewise an argument for a sharing of attitudes that was superior to any local divisions, and does not have to undermine the validity of such divisions. In Classical times every Greek city had an agora, but that did not hinder the cities' independence or their fighting each other.

Administration

The evidence of administration is so great at Phaistos, and so much less elsewhere except at Monastiraki, which is adding to the Phaistian picture, that it is hard to discern local patterns (although Weingarten suggests that the Hieroglyphic Deposits of Knossos and Mallia are a development of the system of Phaistos).[31] It is clear that on present evidence neither Phaistos nor Knossos matches Mallia, where much or all of the administrative business of the town was carried on outside the Old Palace building in the Quartier Mu group of buildings, which was also the artisans' centre. Another difference from the Lasithi region, and to some extent from the far east of Crete, is that in the Knossos region there was hardly any stamping of amphora handles to make seal impressions on them before the jars were fired,[32] although it is uncertain how much the practice was a part of a major administrative system. It may, rather, have been a matter of household management.[33] We may be

---

[29] Soles (n. 26 above), 179 (rightly correcting the excavator of Myrtos-Pyrgos), and 251, in a valuable discussion (114–258) of the house tombs, including the annexes of Mesara tholos tombs.

[30] E.B. French, 'Archaeology in Greece, 1989–90', *AR* 36 (1989–90), 77–8. A. Peatfield, 'Rural ritual in Bronze Age Crete: the peak sanctuary at Atsipadhes' (with comments), *Cambridge Archaeological Journal* 1 (1992), 59–87.

[31] J. Weingarten, 'Three upheavals in Minoan sealing administration: evidence for radical change', in T.G. Palaima (ed.), *Aegean Seals, Sealings and Administration: Proceedings of the NEH-Dickson Conference ... 1989* (Aegaeum 5; Liège, 1990), 106–7. Monastiraki: Kanta (n. 5 above).

[32] Cadogan (n. 4 above); id., 'Some Middle Minoan problems', in E.B. French and K.A. Wardle (eds.), *Problems in Greek Prehistory: Papers Presented at the Centenary Conference of the British School of Archaeology at Athens, Manchester, April 1986* (Bristol, 1988), 95–9. One example in the Knossos region is from Mt Iuktas, A. Karetsou, 'Τὸ ἱερὸ κορυφῆς Γιούχτα', *PAE* 1985, 295, pl. 142γ.

[33] As J. Weingarten suggests, in discussion of I. Pini, 'The Hieroglyphic Deposit and the Temple Repositories at Knossos', in Palaima (n. 31 above), 56.

sure that, if it had been a regular practice at Knossos, Sinclair Hood would have noticed it in studying the pottery from his excavations. It would be of value to examine petrographically examples found in the Knossos region to see if they might be imports. Finally, there is the possibility of regional variation in the Hieroglyphic scripts, and so perhaps in the language(s) and/or accounting practices of the different palatial centres.

Pottery

In late Prepalatial times the distribution of clay sheep bells is a sound Knossian regional denominator, with examples from Knossos, Archanes-Phourni, Archanes-Tourkoyeitonia, Tylissos and seven other sites. On the edge of the hinterland of Knossos they occur only at Vorou; farther away, they have been reported at Mallia. Morris and Peatfield point out that at Vorou the most common shape is the contemporary eggcup goblet, which is another characteristic of the Knossian region, and suggest that Vorou may have been in a buffer zone between north and south central Crete.[34]

In the Old Palace period the pottery of Knossos is quite different from that in west Crete, the Mallia-Lasithi region, and far eastern Crete, and from that found in the Mesara tholos tombs. This is a point to be taken on trust, which it would be inappropriate to argue at length at present. When the pottery of, principally, Archanes-Anemospilia and Phourni, Knossos, Mallia, Myrtos-Pyrgos, Palaikastro and Zakro is better known through publication, as well as that of west Crete, then, I trust, we shall comprehend that pottery is the best denominator of regional differences.

The pottery of Gournes, with parallels both at Knossos and in the Mallia-Lasithi region (where ceramic differences from Knossos are particularly strong in the Old Palace period), suggests that it lay on the boundary between the two regions.[35] When we view the Gournes pottery as a whole from MM IA through to MM II, or from Knossian-type eggcups to Mallia/Pyrgos III jugs and Chamaizi juglets, we may conclude that it was a frontier place for several centuries.[36] South of Gournes, Kastelli could have been in another buffer zone, both between Knossos and Mallia-Lasithi and, perhaps, between both of them and Phaistos with the Mesara. In turn that last region seems to have had a buffer zone — or outpost — at Monastiraki in the middle of the Amari valley, where west

---

[34] Morris and Peatfield (n. 19 above). For sheep bells at Archanes-Tourkoyeitonia, see also Sakellarakis and Sakellaraki (n. 11 above — 1991), 53, fig. 31, caption. Mesara-type double jugs occur in late Prepalatial deposits at Giophyrakia (Marinatos, n. 20 above, 50, fig. 3.4, 6), at Archanes-Phourni (Sakellarakis and Sakellaraki, n. 11 above — 1991, 124, fig. 103) and at Gournes (Zois, n. 17 above, pl. 24).

For the eggcup goblet and its relations see N. Momigliano, 'The development of the footed goblet ("egg-cup") from EM II to MM III at Knossos', in *Cretological VI, A'I* (Chania, 1990), 477–87. Eggcups outside the Knossos region include: Palaikastro (P. Warren, 'The first Minoan stone vases and Early Minoan chronology', *Kr.Chron.* 19 (1965), 26; R.M. Dawkins, 'Excavations at Palaikastro IV', *BSA* 11 (1904–5), 271); Myrtos-Pyrgos (unpublished); and Lerna in the Argolid (J.L. Caskey, 'Excavations at Lerna, 1955', *Hesperia* 25 (1956), 160, pl. 43c; C.W. Zerner, 'The Beginning of the Middle Helladic Period at Lerna' (Ph.D. dissertation, University of Cincinnati, 1978), 163–78; J.B. Rutter and C.W. Zerner, 'Early Hellado-Minoan contacts', in R. Hägg and N. Marinatos (eds.), *The Minoan Thalassocracy: Myth and Reality. Proceedings of the Third International Symposium at the Swedish Institute in Athens ... 1982* (Skrifter ... Svenska Inst. i Athen, 4°, 32; Stockholm, 1984), 75–83).

[35] Cadogan (n. 4 above); Zois (n. 17 above).

[36] Chamaizi juglets are a type-fossil of the Mallia MM II and (Myrtos-)Pyrgos III phases. They are more recent than the 'MM IA' often ascribed to the main phase at Chamaizi.

Cretan region and Phaistian traditions meet.[37] The western limits of a Knossian region will be hard to define until we know more pottery from sites west of Knossos.

It is also hard to separate the fine Old Palace period pottery — the so-called Kamares ware — of Knossos from its Phaistian equivalents until MacGillivray's publication of the pottery from Knossos allows us to make proper comparisons. I shall not attempt now to separate these fine styles or their associated coarser pottery, although the distinctions are there to be found, which will allow us equally to isolate imports and influences.[38] The apparent restriction of the production of lustrous, black-wash eggshell ware pottery to Knossos and Phaistos (or places of manufacture they controlled) puts the two palatial centres in a ceramically superior class to the rest of Crete, and marks the few pieces found beyond their regions as exports. Several pieces have been found at Palaikastro, probably in greater quantity than at Mallia-Lasithi sites, where they are rare,[39] which may suggest that they came from Knossos (the more likely source on geographical grounds) directly by boat, bypassing a possibly hostile and, in ceramic terms, defiantly un-Knossian Mallia-Lasithi region.

Defining the differences in pottery between Knossos and Phaistos will at once affect interpretations of the foreign relations of Middle Minoan Crete. There will be a chance that many of the exported pieces, in the Aegean and Mainland Greece and in the East Mediterranean, can be demonstrated to be from Knossos rather than Phaistos, such as the one-handled carinated (and barbotine) cup from Karmi in northern Cyprus.[40] But the total of exported pieces is small. It is poor statistics to attribute superiority to one palatial centre or the other on the basis of a larger or smaller handful of exports.[41] One may keep in mind that Knossos is better placed than Phaistos for links with the Aegean and Mainland Greece. For links with the Nile and the Syro-Palestinian coast the situation may have been more balanced since, through Kommos, Phaistos is well placed for journeys on the north wind to Libya and from there catching the coastal currents to the Nile Delta, Palestine and Syria.[42] Finally, the

---

[37] The pottery of Monastiraki has ties both with Phaistos (imported Phaistian pottery) and with the rest of western Crete ('blue ware'), Dr Kanta kindly tells me.

[38] Such as the Phaistian amphora Sinclair Hood has found at Knossos.

[39] Such as R.C. Bosanquet and R.M. Dawkins, *The Unpublished Objects from the Palaikastro Excavations 1902–1906* (BSA Suppl. Paper 1; London, 1923), 15–17, fig. 11 (stamped ware) and (probably) fig. 10. But the authors remark (p. 17): 'Of the Knossian eggshell ware, with its splendid polychrome effects, we found no evidence at all at Palaikastro.' L.H. Sackett and M.R. Popham, however, did ('Excavations at Palaikastro VI', *BSA* 60 (1965), 251).

It is hard not to detect Knossian influence in 'the lovely floral styles in alternating red and white of Palaikastro and Zakros' (J.A. MacGillivray, 'The foundation of the Old Palaces in Crete', in *Cretological VI, A'I* (Chania, 1990), 433). It is lacking in the Mallia-Lasithi region, which seems to have looked sometimes to Phaistos.

[40] Which 'could well be Knossian' (H.W. Catling and J.A. MacGillivray, 'An Early Cypriot III vase from the Palace at Knossos', *BSA* 78 (1983), 4).

[41] As memorably pointed out by A. Furumark, 'The settlement at Ialysos and Aegean prehistory c. 1550–1400 B.C.', *Op. Arch.* 6 (1950), 213–14, discussing Late Minoan/Late Helladic I–II relations.

[42] Evidence is exiguous for the role of Phaistos and its region in foreign relations in the Old Palace period: Aeginetan Red Burnished bowl sherds occur at Kommos in an MM IB context; other imports are in MM III contexts (P.P. Betancourt, *Kommos II. The Final Neolithic through Middle Minoan III Pottery* (Princeton, 1990), 192), although L.V. Watrous mentions two jug sherds 'probably from Cyprus' in an MM IB context ('Late Bronze Age Kommos: imported pottery as evidence for foreign contact', in J.M. and M.C. Shaw (eds.), *Proceedings of the Kommos Symposium held at the Royal York Hotel, Toronto on December 29 (1984), Scripta Mediterranea* 6 (1985), 7).

If, however, the administrative system of Phaistos was adopted, somehow, directly from the Near East, to be altered slightly in the systems of the Mallia and Knossos Hieroglyphic Deposits (Weingarten, n. 31 above), then relations were in an indefinable way closer than is suggested by the imports of pottery into the Phaistos region and the exports of Kamares ware (of which it has yet to be determined how much is from Phaistos).

likelihood that some exported MM pottery in the Near East is from the Mallia-Lasithi region and/or the Palaikastro-Zakro region[43] is a reminder that the production of pieces that were exported was not confined to Knossos and/or Phaistos. This may mean that their transmission was not restricted to those places either, and that — in some sense that is hard to define — the other MM palaces conducted their own foreign relations.[44]

Other finds

To set against such suggestions, the concentration of late Prepalatial and Old Palace period scarabs in the Mesara and around the Knossos region (Archanes-Phourni, Knossos and Gournes) may be another sign that north-central Crete and south-central Crete were different from the other regions and had, in foreign relations, a superior status. Or it may be that Knossos alone did (and the unique statuette of User — if it arrived within a few years of its being made; but its context is uncertain — may then reflect the fact). Similarly, it may — or may not — be significant that only Knossos among the palatial centres has yielded Middle Cycladic pottery in an Old Palace period context,[45] although such has been found also at Kommos.[46]

With other crafts, the evidence is still weak for identifying regional differences. For metalware there is evidence by default from the Mallia-Lasithi region, which alone has produced metal plate and 'shoe-socket' spearheads[47] — but the occurrences may reflect nothing more than the chances of use and preservation. Faience-making is one craft that probably had a Knossian bias, or was a Knossian monopoly. Almost all the plaques, box-fittings, small pots and pieces other than beads dateable to the Old Palace period or the beginning of the New Palace period come from Knossos.[48]

CONCLUSIONS

The lack of published excavation evidence from the hinterland of Knossos makes it more difficult to build a case for a Knossos cultural region in the Old Palace period, which might indicate in a material way a Knossos Old Palace period state, than for the Lasithi region or other parts of Crete. It is useful, then, to try to define such a region at Knossos both by the absence there of cultural traits seen in the other regions of Crete and equally by the presence of other traits that have not been found in those other

---

[43] Cadogan (n. 4 above); also 'Early Minoan and Middle Minoan chronology', *AJA* 87 (1983), 515–16. For a Mallia-Lasithi cup with internal handle from Kea see H.S. Georgiou, *Keos VI. Ayia Irini: Specialized Domestic and Industrial Pottery* (Mainz, 1986), 40, 49, no.187.

[44] General discussions of Minoan palatial trade and foreign relations: S. Alexiou, 'Ζητήματα τοῦ προϊστορικοῦ βίου: κρητομυκηναϊκὸν ἐμπόριον', *Arch.Eph.* 1953-4, part 3, 135–45, and 'Minoan palaces as centres of trade and manufacture', in Hägg and Marinatos (n. 7 above), 251–3; M.H. Wiener, 'The nature and control of Minoan foreign trade', in N.H. Gale (ed.), *Bronze Age Trade in the Mediterranean: Papers presented at the Conference held at Rewley House, Oxford, in December 1989* (SIMA 90; Jonsered, 1991), 325–50.

[45] M.S.F. Hood, 'Stratigraphic excavations at Knossos, 1957–61', in *Cretological I, A'*, 94; J.A. MacGillivray, 'Cycladic jars from Middle Minoan III contexts at Knossos', in Hägg and Marinatos (n. 34 above), 152.

[46] See n. 42 above.

[47] Cadogan (n. 4 above) and 'Pyrgos, Crete, 1970–7', *AR* 24 (1977–78), 74; B. Detournay, 'Armes', in B. Detournay, J.-C. Poursat and F. Vandenabeele, *Mallia. Le Quartier Mu II. Vases de pierre et de métal, vanneries, figurines et reliefs d'applique, éléments de parure et de décoration, armes, sceaux et empreintes* (Études Crétoises 26; Paris, 1980), 152–4, nos. 227–8.

[48] K.P. Foster, *Aegean Faience of the Bronze Age* (New Haven and London, 1979), 59–118.

regions, as I have tried to do in reviewing the evidence. This review can be only a preliminary sketch until more sites and more finds have been published, and we have a clearer idea of what is part of the contingency of archaeological deposition and what is sound evidence for regional variations.

In the meantime, I see the principal conclusions that we may draw as follows.

1. The geography of Crete allows us to envisage a territory for Knossos between the Psiloriti massif, the passes to the Mesara, the Lasithi massif and the sea — unless it was the case (and I find it unlikely) that the whole island was the territory of Knossos in the Old Palace period, as it probably was by Late Minoan I.
2. The cultural indicators, which include the pottery traditions, suggest that this region around Knossos was separate from the region(s) to the west and from the Mallia-Lasithi and Palaikastro-Zakro regions. Elements that may be specifically Knossian include the appearance of multi-chamber or kidney-shaped tombs dug into the hillside (while built house-tombs and tholos tombs continued to be used in the east and south of the island), the making of faience, and a leading, or *the* leading, role in Cretan Middle Bronze Age external relations. Signs of other cultural regions that are rare or do not occur in the Knossos region include shoe-socket spearheads, seal-impressed amphora handles and, in pottery, the Mallia-Lasithi repertoire, the red fabrics of Palaikastro-Zakro and the 'blue' wares of western Crete.
3. The relation of a Knossos region with Phaistos is hard to establish because of the disparity in the evidence. We know at present so much more of the pottery (and of the architecture and administration) of Phaistos than of Knossos that distinguishing in detail a Knossian pottery tradition from a Phaistian in the Old Palace period is a skill restricted to a few connoisseurs. (In the late Prepalatial period, the heyday of the so-called eggcups, it is slightly easier.) The pottery, however, from those Mesara tholos tombs that continued in use into Old Palace times, as well as from Phaistos, Kommos and sites found in the Mesara survey, suggests that Phaistos was probably a separate region from Knossos with a strong personality of its own — at least in ceramic terms.[49] The lesser incidence of Mesara-type tholos tombs in the Knossos region, and perhaps the superior evidence for foreign connexions, could support the view that the Knossos region was separate from that of Phaistos. Differences yet to be revealed in the pottery of Knossos and Phaistos are likely to strengthen the notion that the regions were separate.
4. A buffer zone in Pediada between the Knossos and Mallia regions, and also probably a Phaistos region, is likely. There may have been another such buffer zone to the south of Knossos, perhaps straddling the passes to the Mesara (maybe stretching even as far north as Archanes) between Knossos and Phaistos, as seems to have been the case in late Prepalatial times. (Earlier in the third millennium EM IIA fine painted bowls and light grey ware pots stand out at Knossos as imports from a different ceramic tradition in the Mesara.[50])
5. We need to look for more traits that may have been regional cultural denominators.
6. The situation in the Old Palace period appears markedly different from that in New Palace times,

---

[49] For the Old Palace period hinterland of Phaistos, see now L.V. Watrous *et al.*, 'A survey of the western Mesara plain in Crete: preliminary report of the 1984, 1986 and 1987 field seasons', *Hesperia* 62 (1993), 226.
G. Walberg ('Palatial and provincial workshops in the Middle Minoan period', in Hägg and Marinatos (n. 7 above), 281–5 esp. at p. 282, fig. 1) prefers a sole central Cretan region. Her other regions are western, east-central and eastern.
[50] See Wilson's paper in this volume.

and particularly from Late Minoan I. Then we may discern a considerable uniformity, evinced by the island-wide spread of (Knossian) metropolitan architecture and appurtenances that include Late Minoan IB pottery, and perhaps also of a Knossian administrative supremacy.[51] Add to this picture the decline in the New Palace period of Phaistos and Mallia from what they had been in Old Palace times,[52] and the evidence for destructions by fire from several sites outside the Knossian region at the end of the Old Palace period (such as Phaistos, Mallia, Vasiliki, Gournia and Myrtos-Pyrgos), and it is easy to conjure a history in which Knossos somehow emerged as Crete's major power only at the end of the Old Palace period. It could be that it had defeated the other centres in war, or it could have taken advantage of their being in a weakened state if they had suffered natural disasters.[53]

In the new era it seems that Knossos imposed a new pattern of society in Crete, through the founding of the country houses,[54] and probably also through an administrative control based on Linear A and sealings. If there was an independent Knossian region and other independent regions in the Old Palace period, which we can try to identify from their cultural remains, the group of events we loosely call the end of the Old Palace period is a transition like that from the Middle Ages to modern times.

---

[51] Weingarten (n. 31 above) sees an administrative hegemony of Chania, Knossos, Ayia Triada and Zakro in LM IB.

[52] Summaries by V. La Rosa, 'Ayia Triada', in Myers *et al.* (n. 5 above), 71–4, and 'Phaistos', ibid. 234–5. Mallia: Weingarten (n. 31 above), 109; Cadogan (n. 4 above).

[53] For war in early Crete, an idea that Sinclair has always been ready to envisage, see S. Alexiou, 'Τείχη καὶ ἀκροπόλεις στὴ μινωικὴ Κρήτη — ὁ μῦθος τῆς μινωικῆς εἰρήνης', *Kritologia* 8 (1979), 41–56.

[54] See papers in Hägg (n. 14 above), including G. Cadogan, 'The role of the Pyrgos country house in Minoan society', for possible Old Palace period predecessors of the country houses.

PLATE III Villa Ariadne, Knossos — Evans' Palm Trees (etching)

Chapter 5

Knossos in the New Palace Period (MM III–LM IB)

W.-D. NIEMEIER

RELATIVE AND ABSOLUTE CHRONOLOGY

According to the conventional chronology, the pottery period MM III, one apparently of relatively short duration,[1] marks the beginning of the Cretan New Palace period. As far as the relative chronology is concerned, Evans based his definition of MM III on a series of deposits from Knossos (cf. below) of which several had a reasonably tight stratigraphical position, though none formed part of a complete MM II–MM III–LM I sequence. Evans' general correctness in ascribing these deposits to MM III is confirmed not only by their pre-LM I contexts, but also through clear stylistic links now observable with Levi's 'third Protopalatial phase' at Phaistos (which might be better termed 'first Neopalatial phase'), which follows the MM IIB destruction there and precedes the LM I Palace.[2] As will be discussed below, at least some of these deposits are in fact later than Evans thought, and belong to the MM III/LM IA transition.

Evans' subdivision of MM III into two phases, MM IIIA and MM IIIB, still involves uncertainties and plays a part in controversial discussions. As G. Walberg has demonstrated, the stylistic features and the stratigraphical evidence put forward by Evans as criteria for the distinction of MM IIIA and MM IIIB are not convincing.[3] The pottery from the basements of the Early Town Section west of the Palace, which was illustrated by Evans as characteristic for MM IIIA,[4] is not in fact of homogeneous character, but contains types and decorations attributed elsewhere in his monumental work *The Palace*

It is a great pleasure for me to dedicate this contribution to Sinclair Hood, from whom I have learnt about Minoan Crete and whom I admire as a scholar and because of his humanity.

Special Abbreviation:

SMK = J.D.S. and H.W. Pendlebury, E. Eccles and M. Money-Coutts, *A Guide to the Stratigraphical Museum in the Palace at Knossos. Parts I–III* (London, 1933–5).

[1] P. Warren and V. Hankey, *Aegean Bronze Age Chronology* (Bristol, 1989), 60.
[2] Ibid. 54–6. For the reclassification of the 'third Protopalatial phase' as 'first Neopalatial phase', see F. Carinci, 'The "III fase protopalaziale" at Phaestos. Some observations', in R. Laffineur (ed.), *Transition: Le Monde Égéen du Bronze Moyen au Bronze Recent* (Aegaeum 3; Liège, 1989), 73–80.
[3] G. Walberg, *Middle Minoan III: A Time of Transition* (SIMA 97; Jonsered, 1992), 10–12.
[4] *PM II.i*, 369–71, fig. 206.

of Minos at Knossos to MM II or MM IIIB.[5] As S. Hood pointed out in 1966 after his stratigraphical excavations at the Royal Road at Knossos, 'The evidence is not altogether satisfactory for defining the character of these periods' (i.e. MM IIIA and B).[6] P.M. Warren and V. Hankey have argued that the recent excavations on the Acropolis slope on the southwestern outskirts of the city of Knossos do perhaps now offer evidence for a division between MM IIIA and B.[7] In the publication of that important excavation, H.W. Catling believed pottery deposits A and B represented MM IIIA, while C and D represented MM IIIB.[8] However, in a recent thorough investigation based upon a pottery deposit from his Stratigraphical Museum excavations, P. Warren has now convincingly dated deposits C and D to the MM III–LM IA transition.[9] In the Messara plain, which had close ceramic connexions with Knossos throughout Middle Minoan times,[10] no subdivision of MM III is recognisable. It forms a single ceramic period, followed by a short period marking the MM III/LM IA transition.[11] Thus the existence of two definable sub-phases, MM IIIA and B, at Knossos remains uncertain[12] and we can safely distinguish only pure MM III and the MM III–LM IA transition as distinct phases.

No clear stratigraphical LM IA–LM IB sequence has been found within the Palace at Knossos. In the city of Knossos, however, there are such sequences both from S. Hood's Royal Road excavations[13] and from Warren's near the Stratigraphical Museum.[14] These and sequences at other Cretan sites, as well as on Kythera and Kea, allow a clear definition of the periods in question.[15] The chronological succession from the pottery classified as LM IB to that classified as LM II has been recently confirmed by the stratigraphical evidence from Warren's excavations[16] and from Kommos.[17]

The absolute date of the start of the New Palace era is currently under discussion. The conventional date of *c*.1700 B.C. rests mainly on the alabaster lid with cartouche of the Hyksos ruler Khyan found near the North Lustral Basin in a pure MM IIIA level, according to Evans.[18] However, there are doubts about the context. None of the pottery associated with the Khyan lid has been published. As L.R. Palmer pointed out, D. Mackenzie described in his 1901 Pottery Notebook (under the heading 'Lot from N. Foundations — Area of Egyptian Lid') the contents of a single basket which

---

[5] G. Walberg, *Kamares: A Study of the Character of Palatial Middle Minoan Pottery* (Uppsala, 1976), 108.

[6] S. Hood, 'The Early and Middle Minoan periods at Knossos', *BICS* 13 (1966), 111.

[7] Warren and Hankey (n. 1 above), 57–60.

[8] H.W. and E.A. Catling, and D. Smyth, 'Knossos 1975: Middle Minoan III and Late Minoan I houses by the acropolis', *BSA* 74 (1979), 1–80.

[9] P.M. Warren, 'A new deposit from Knossos, c. 1600 B.C., and its wider relations', *BSA* 86 (1991), 335.

[10] Walberg (n. 5 above), 12 and *passim*.

[11] P.P. Betancourt, *Kommos II: The Final Neolithic Through Middle Minoan III Pottery* (Princeton, 1990), 37–48.

[12] V. Stürmer, *MM III: Studien zum Stilwandel der minoischen Keramik (Archaeologica Heidelbergensia* 1; Mainz, 1992), 19–21, admits that stratigraphical evidence for a subdivision of MM III is missing at Knossos but offers stylistic arguments for it. It is, however, hazardous to define a pottery phase only on stylistic grounds, without accompanying stratigraphical evidence.

[13] M.S.F. Hood, 'Archaeology in Greece, 1961–62', *AR* 8 (1961–62), 25–7; id., 'Stratigraphic excavations at Knossos, 1957–61', *Cretological I, A'*, 96–7.

[14] Warren (n. 9 above), 319.

[15] W.-D. Niemeier, 'Die Katastrophe von Thera und die spätminoische Chronologie', *JdI* 95 (1980), 5–18; Warren and Hankey (n. 1 above), 70–81.

[16] Warren and Hankey (n. 1 above), 81, with references.

[17] L.V. Watrous, *Kommos III: the Late Bronze Age Pottery* (Princeton, 1992), 119.

[18] *PM I*, 417–21, fig. 303; Warren and Hankey (n. 1 above), 136, pl. 14.A.

contained, together with fragments of stone vases, pottery ranging from Neolithic to Late Minoan.[19] Palmer concluded that the context was mixed and a typical sub-floor deposit. P. Warren, on the other hand, has argued that it was no mixed context but that the sherds from all strata were collected in one and the same basket.[20] Nobody doubts that the Khyan lid and the stone vase fragments belong together. However, a ewer reconstructed from these fragments shows a complicated technique of 'multiple assembly' not detectable before LM I, as demonstrated by L. Pomerance.[21] Thus the earliest possible date for the stratification of the Khyan lid appears to be LM I and it cannot serve as a chronological fixed point for the beginning of the New Palace period. The only other supposed piece of evidence for the absolute chronology of MM III under discussion is the Syro-Palestinian jug from tomb 879 at el-Lisht decorated with birds and dolphins, of which the latter are undoubtedly of Minoan inspiration.[22] The shape of this jug dates it to the first half of the Syro-Palestinian MB IIB,[23] i.e. to the second half of the 18th or the early 17th century B.C.[24] The closest parallel for the el-Lisht dolphins are on two burial pithoi from the cemetery of Pachyammos in eastern Crete, but of these one is usually dated to late MM III, the other to LM IA.[25] Therefore, and because of the absence of a clearly definable MM III phase in eastern Crete,[26] the el-Lisht jug too does not help us to ascertain the absolute date of MM III. We are thus left without any evidence at all that can be securely used to answer the question of absolute dating for the start of this period.[27] Of crucial importance for the absolute chronology of the phases MM III–LM IB is the date of the eruption of the Thera volcano. For those who, like the present author, trust the radiocarbon dates from the volcanic destruction level at Akrotiri on Thera, which is to be dated in Cretan terms to the later LM IA period,[28] the eruption occurred within the 17th century, probably in its second half.[29] This date

---

[19] L.R Palmer, 'The Linear B Palace at Knossos', in P. Aström, L.R. Palmer and L. Pomerance, *Studies in Aegean Chronology* (SIMA 25 pocketbook; Göteborg, 1984), 74–7.

[20] P.M. Warren, 'Absolute dating of the Aegean Late Bronze Age', *Archaeometry* 29 (1987), 205–11; id., 'The Thera eruption III: further arguments against an early date', *Archaeometry* 30 (1988), 176.

[21] L. Pomerance, 'A note on the carved stone ewers from the Khyan lid deposit', in P. Aström et al. (n. 19 above), 15–17; D. Levi, *Festòs e la Civiltà Minoica II.1* (Incunabula Graeca 77; Rome, 1981), 51. On the probable stratigraphic position of the Khyan lid, after the MM III destruction of the NW Lustral Basin, see J. Raison, *Le Palais du second millénaire à Knossos I: Le Quartier Nord* (Études Crétoises 28; Paris, 1988), 234, 238–9.

[22] B.J. Kemp and R.S. Merrillees, *Minoan Pottery in Second Millennium Egypt* (Mainz, 1980), 220–5, pls. 29–30; Warren and Hankey (n. 1 above), 135–6, pl. 13.

[23] J.M. Weinstein, review of Kemp and Merrillees 1980 (see n. 22 above), *Journal of the American Research Centre in Egypt* 19 (1982), 159–60 with n. 4.

[24] J.M. Weinstein, 'Egyptian relations with Palestine in the Middle Kingdom', *BASOR* 217 (1975), 10–11. Warren and Hankey (n. 1 above), 136, however, follow Bietak's chronology for MM IIB, which is too low: see W.G. Dever, 'Tell el-Dab'a and Levantine Middle Bronze Age chronology: a rejoinder to Manfred Bietak', *BASOR* 281 (1991), 73–9.

[25] R.B. Seager, *The Cemetery of Pachyammos, Crete* (University of Pennsylvania, The University Museum Anthropological Publications 7.1; Philadelphia, 1916), pls. viii–ix, xiv; Warren and Hankey (n. 1 above), 136, pl. 12.B–C.

[26] P.P. Betancourt, *The History of Minoan Pottery* (Princeton, 1985), 104.

[27] *Pace* Warren and Hankey (n. 1 above), 135–7. The MC III jug from Kommos mentioned there comes from a very late MM III context containing a transitional MM III/LM IA cup: see Betancourt (n. 11 above), 192.

[28] Niemeier (n. 15 above), 41–65; M. Marthari, 'The chronology of the last phases of occupation at Akrotiri in the light of the evidence from the West House pottery groups', in D.A. Hardy and A.C. Renfrew (eds.), *Thera and the Aegean World III.3: Chronology. Proceedings of the Third International Congress, Santorini Greece ... 1989* (London, 1990), 57–70; J.S. Soles and C. Davaras, 'Theran ash in Minoan Crete: new excavations on Mochlos', ibid. 89–95; P.P. Betancourt, P. Goldberg, R. Hope Simpson and C.J. Vitaliano, 'Excavations at Pseira: the evidence for the Thera eruption', ibid. 96–9; T. Marketou, 'Santorini Tephra from Rhodes and Kos: some chronological remarks based on stratigraphy', ibid. 100–13.

appears to be confirmed by the evidence of low growth or frost rings as well as sediments of volcanic sulphur in Greenland ice-cores. Though the association of these with the Thera eruption has been doubted, yet it becomes more and more probable, and would point to a date of 1628 B.C. for the eruption.[30] The start of LM IA is then to be dated around 1700 B.C.,[31] with that of MM III being placed to around 1800 B.C. or a little later.[32] With this higher chronology, the start of LM IB has to be raised to c.1620/10 B.C., with its end now falling at c.1520/10.[33] The traditional low chronology is with some revisions maintained by Warren, who puts the start of MM III at about 1700 B.C., that of LM IA shortly after 1600 B.C., with LM IB lying between c.1480 and c.1425 B.C.[34]

THE PALACE (FIG. 1)

According to Evans, the New Palace was rapidly erected in early MM III above the remains of the Old Palace, destroyed by an earthquake at the end of the MM IIB period.[35] However, the architectural history of the New Palace appears to have been more complicated than he believed and is difficult to reconstruct. The New Palace experienced several destructions, of which the more severe ones fell at the MM III–LM I transition, again within the late LM IA phase (cf. below) and yet again early in LM IIIA.[36] After each of them considerable parts of the Palace had to be restored or even reconstructed. Important light on this complicated architectural history has been shed in recent years by S. Mirié's study of the Throne Room area (based on Evans' excavation accounts and on the remains now visible), by J. Raison's work in the North-West Quarter, and by a selective programme of tests directed by Sinclair Hood.[37]

We start our 'tour' of the Palace from the west. The West Court is thought to have been extended over the houses to the north at the beginning of MM III, and over the two westernmost 'kouloures'

---

[29] See the different articles on the radiocarbon dates and the final discussion in Hardy and Renfrew (n. 28 above), and the very useful summary of the results by S.W. Manning, 'The Thera eruption: the third congress and the problem of the date', *Archaeometry* 32 (1990), 91–100.

[30] M.G. Baillie, 'Marking in marker dates: towards an archaeology with historical precision', *World Archaeology* 23 (1991), 233–43; S.W. Manning, 'Santorini, ice-cores and tree rings: resolution of the 1645 or 1628 debate?', *Nestor* 19 (1992), 2511–12; id., 'Thera, sulphur, and climatic anomalies', *OJA* 11 (1992), 245–53.

[31] P.P. Betancourt, 'Dating the Aegean Late Bronze Age with radiocarbon', *Archaeometry* 29 (1987), 45–9; S.W. Manning, 'The Bronze Age eruption of Thera: absolute dating, Aegean chronology and Mediterranean cultural relations', *JMA* 1 (1988), 56, table 10.

[32] W.-D. Niemeier, 'Erläuterungen zur absoluten Chronologie und zu den Kulturphasen in Zentralkreta', in J. Shäfer (ed.), *Amnisos. Nach den archäologischen, historischen und epigraphischen Zeugnissen des Altertums und der Neuzeit* (Forschungen des Archäologischen Instituts der Universität Heidelberg; Berlin, 1992), xxiii–xxiv, table on xxii.

[33] Niemeier, ibid. xxiv–xxvi.

[34] See, most recently, P.M. Warren, 'The Minoan civilisation of Crete and the volcano of Thera', *Journal of the Ancient Chronology Forum* 4 (1990–1), 29–39.

[35] *PM I*, 315; *II.i*, 287; *III*, 14 and 486. Also J.D.S. Pendlebury, *The Archaeology of Crete: an Introduction* (London, 1939), 148–52.

[36] M.R. Popham, *The Destruction of the Palace at Knossos. Pottery of the LM IIIA Period* (SIMA 12; Goteborg, 1970), 50–6; E. Hallager, *The Mycenaean Palace at Knossos: Evidence for a final Destruction in the IIIB Period* (Medelhavsmuseet, Memoir 1; Stockholm, 1977); S. Mirié, *Das Thronraumareal des Palastes von Knossos: Versuch einer Neuinterpretation seiner Enstehung und seiner Funktion* (Saarbrücker Beiträge zur Altertumskunde 26; Bonn, 1979), 38–44; W.-D. Niemeier, *Die Palaststilkeramik von Knossos: Stil, Chronologie und historischer Kontext* (Deutsches Arch. Inst., Arch. Forschungen 13; Berlin, 1985), 142–62.

[37] Mirié (n. 36 above); Raison (n. 21 above); H.W. Catling, 'Archaeology in Greece, 1973–74', *AR* 20 (1973–74), 34; id., 'Archaeology in Greece, 1987–88', *AR* 34 (1987–88), 68; C.F. Macdonald, 'Destruction and construction in the Palace at Knossos: LM IA–B', in Hardy and Renfrew (n. 28 above), 82–8.

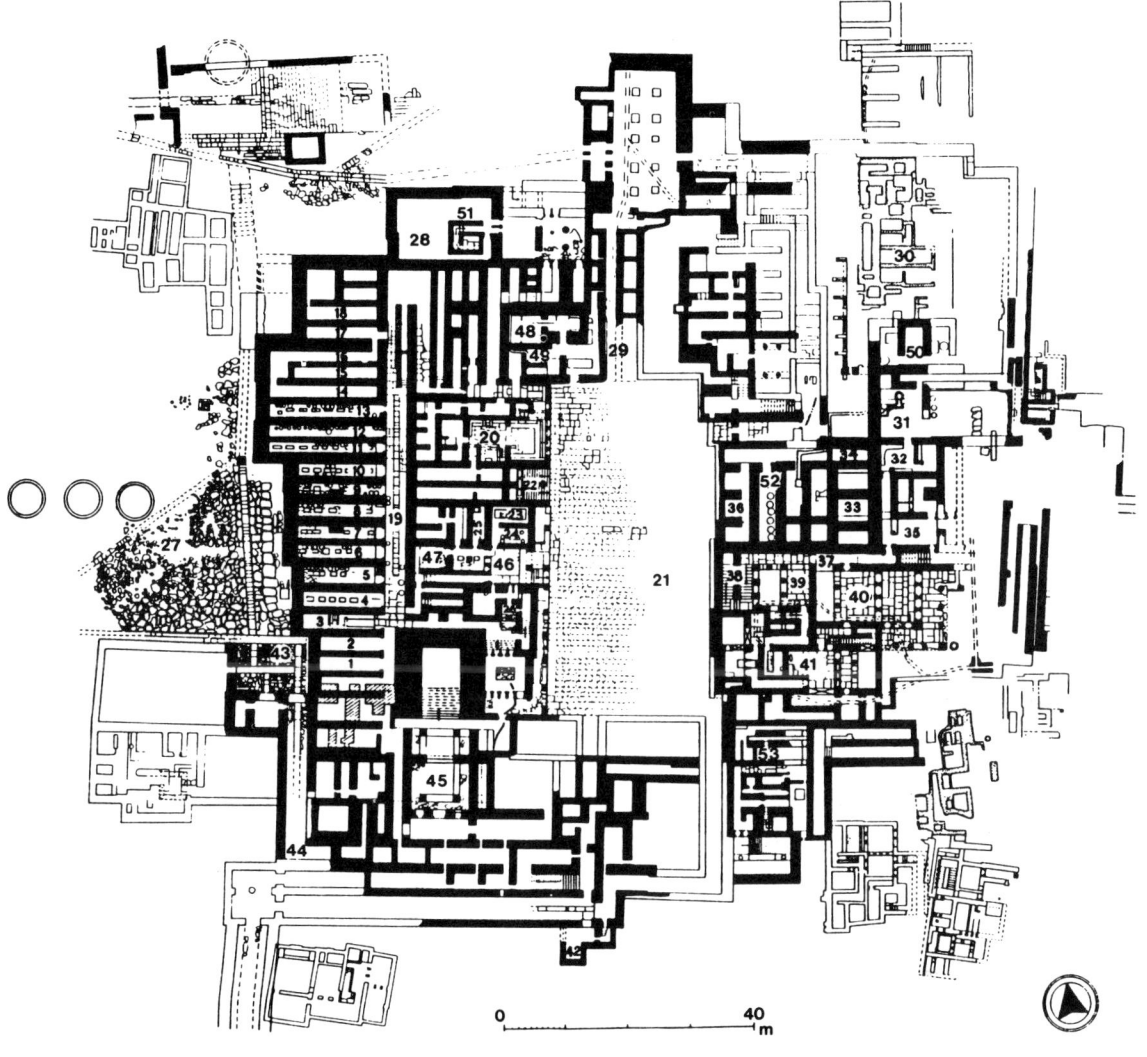

1-18	West Magazines	40	Hall of the Double Axes
19	Long Corridor and Kaselles	41	Queen's Megaron
20	Throne Room System	43	West Porch
21	Central Court	44	Corridor of the Procession
23	Temple Repositories	45	South Propylaeum
27	West Court and Kouloures	46	Room of the Column Bases
28	Khyan Lid Deposit	47	Pillar Crypts
29	North Entrance Passage	48	Early Keep
30	NE Quarter and Magazines	49	Room of the Knobbed Pithos
31	Area of the Stone Drain Heads	50	Magazines of the Great Pithoi
32	School Room	51	NW Lustral Basin
33	Loomweight Deposit	52	Room of the Medallion Pithoi
36	Corridor of the Bays	53	Magazine of the Lily Vases

FIG. 1 Plan of the New Palace at Knossos

(2 and 3), with the eastern one (1) being cleaned out and kept open until the end of MM III.[38] However, as Walberg has made us aware,[39] Evans reported the discovery in the easternmost 'kouloura' of fragments of plaster tripod offering tables with 'notched plume' or 'adder mark' decoration,[40] a motif which does not appear in pottery decoration before LM IB.[41] Moreover, LM pottery — in some cases specified as LM I — is reported from tests below the pavement of the West Court,[42] in the middle 'kouloura'[43] as well as in the wall stumps of rooms which had been levelled off when the pavement of the West Court in its present form was laid out.[44] Thus the 'kouloures' appear to have remained open later than MM III, and the paving of the West Court must be dated later than hitherto assumed, probably to LM I. The LM II–IIIA sherds found in two places in the northwest area of the West Court may have been deposited during later repairs.[45]

Evans had first supposed that the West Façade and the existing West Wing of the Palace were built in MM III. His evidence for this dating was the discovery of MM III pottery fragments in the lower level of the rubble masonry between the outer and the inner face of the gypsum slabs forming the lowermost part of the wall.[46] Later he changed his mind and thought that the west wall was built during MM IB and then underwent a series of alterations during MM III.[47] The soundings by Hood in the northwest angle of the Palace and the area of West Magazines 14–18 as well as in West Magazines A–C and 2 indicate that Evans' first suggestion was the more correct. According to Hood's results, the construction of the West Façade did not immediately follow the MM IIB destruction at the beginning of MM III, but dates from the very end of the MM III period.[48]

The West Porch, an impressive square portico with a huge central column leading on the left into the Corridor of the Procession, was dated by Evans to MM III and compared to the very similar West Porch of Pernier's 'First Palace' at Phaistos, dated by Evans to MM II.[49] In Evans' opinion the Knossian West Porch 'represents an amplified version of an original plan characteristic of the earlier part of the Middle Minoan Age, and of which good examples exist at Phaestos'.[50] However, Evans'

---

[38] *PM IV.i*, 61–6; Pendlebury (n. 35 above), 150.
[39] Walberg (n. 3 above), 116.
[40] *PM I*, 551; illustration of reconstructed offering table from 'kouloura I': *PM IV.i*, 180, fig. 142.
[41] A. Furumark, *Mycenaean Pottery: Analysis and Classification* (Stockholm, 1941), 158; Niemeier (n. 36 above), 109.
[42] *SMK*, B.I.27.
[43] *SMK*, B.I.20, 21
[44] *SMK*, B.I.8, 11.
[45] *SMK*, B.III.14, 18. LM IIIA sherd with water fowl: *PM IV.i*, 335, fig. 278; Pendlebury (n. 35 above), 247 with n. 7. See L.R. Palmer, *The Penultimate Palace at Knossos* (*Incunabula Graeca* 33; Rome, 1969), 113, who thinks that the entire West Court was laid out in LM III.
[46] A.J. Evans, 'The Palace at Knossos and its dependencies. Provisional report for the year 1905', *BSA* 11 (1904–5), 21. For the construction of the West wall, see J.W. Shaw, 'Minoan architecture: materials and techniques', *ASA* n.s. 33 (1971–3), 88–90, fig. 94.
[47] *PM I*, 128–31. This view is followed by J.C. Overbeck and Ch.K. McDonald, 'The date of the last palace at Knossos', *AJA* 80 (1976), 157–8.
[48] Catling (n. 37 above – 1973–74), 34.
[49] Evans (n. 46 above), 21; and *PM I*, 214–15, figs. 158–9; *II.ii*, 667–70. The pottery from tests below the West Porch stored in the Stratigraphical Museum at Knossos does not give any evidence for a dating of the construction since the latest elements reported are EM I (*SMK*, C.I.1–4), although Evans (*PM II.ii*, 670) reports late MM III pottery from beneath the West Porch. In any case there can be no doubt that the West Façade and the West Porch belong to the same building programme.
[50] *PM II.ii*, 424.

date of Pernier's 'First Palace' was too high. Its correct date is MM III[51] and it is contemporary with Levi's 'third Protopalatial phase', better defined as the first period of the New Palace period at Phaistos.[52] Thus the West Porches at Knossos and Phaistos are closer in date than Evans thought.

Evans supposed that the Corridor of the Procession was also built in MM III, but he correctly observed that the external remains, the wall-paintings and the pavement are Late Minoan.[53] This has been confirmed by the oval-mouthed amphoras, probably of Cycladic origin and with parallels in early LC I levels at Akrotiri on Thera, which were found below the red plaster and green schist slab floor and have been recently studied and illustrated by J.A. MacGillivray.[54] Of great interest in this connexion are the recent soundings in the southwest area of the Palace, to the east of the Corridor of the Procession. Here C. Macdonald was able to demonstrate that a substantial wall (Kappa), originally running against the east wall of the Corridor of the Procession and later cut off, was not built before the MM III/LM IA transition.[55] No MM III walls were identified in this area.

The stratigraphical sequence of three floor levels over a large part of the West Wing, as demonstrated by S. Mirié, is of great importance for the architectural history of this part of the Palace.[56] The lowest floor level, with 'iron-stone' paving, is succeeded, some 20–25 cms. above, by a middle floor level consisting often of lime plaster. Its existence is proved only in some areas; in other places the excavators have probably overlooked it.[57] The third floor level, with limestone paving, follows about 20–25 cms. above the middle one. A corresponding stratigraphy of floor levels exists in the Central Court.[58] Evidence for closer dating exists only for the lowest and uppermost floor levels. Kamares pottery was found below the lowest floor level in the area of the Stepped Porch[59] and apparently also below the lowest floor level in the Central Court.[60] Thus the lowest floor level is to be dated to the Old Palace Period, while the uppermost paving of the Central Court belongs to the early LM IIIA restoration of the Palace.[61]

Evidence for the architectural history of the West Magazines is mainly provided by soundings made in 1923 by D. Mackenzie in Magazines 5, 11, 12, and 13.[62] In Magazines 12 and 13 he discovered two successive pavements. Between the two pavements in Magazine 12 he found mainly MM III pottery but also some LM I fragments. A single sherd comes from an 'Ephyraean' goblet of LM II date.[63] MM III–LM IA pottery is also known from a 'kasella' in Magazine 4.[64] Thus the

---

[51] L. Banti, 'Cronologia e ceramica del palazzo minoico di Festòs', *ASA* n.s. 1–2 (1939–40), 9–39.
[52] Carinci (n. 2 above).
[53] *PM I*, 424; *SMK*, C.II.1–2, C.III.1–2.
[54] J.A. MacGillivray, 'Cycladic jars from Middle Minoan III contexts at Knossos', in R. Hägg and N. Marinatos (eds.), *The Minoan Thalassocracy: Myth and Reality. Proceedings of the Third International Symposium at the Swedish Institute in Athens ... 1982* (*Skrifter ... Svenska Inst. i Athen* 4°, 32; Stockholm, 1984), 155.
[55] Macdonald (n. 37 above), 84–5.
[56] Mirié (n. 36 above), 40–1, pl. 6.
[57] On this problem, see Mirié (n. 36 above), 41, with references to the original excavation records.
[58] Ibid. 38–9, pl. 5
[59] Ibid. 35–6.
[60] Ibid. 39.
[61] Popham (n. 36 above), 55–6.
[62] Overbeck and McDonald (n. 47 above), 159–60; Hallager (n. 36 above), 31–2.
[63] Popham (n. 36 above), 54, fig. 8.17 and pl. 34.c.

lower floor was laid not later than MM III/LM IA and Evans' MM III date for the construction of the West Magazines with the built floor cists and for the 'kaselles' in Magazines 4–18 and in the Long Corridor is confirmed.[65]

The cross walls in the Long Corridor in front of Magazine 3 and south of Magazine 17 were identified by Evans in the preliminary reports as later additions, since they were built over the pavement slabs of the Long Corridor.[66] In his final statement he changed his mind and dated them to MM III, thinking that their function was to keep the 'Enclave of the Kaselles', in which he saw a kind of 'Palace Treasury', under careful custody.[67] His earlier opinion, however, was the right one. The walls must be later, since the floor of the Long Corridor, on which they were built, is of LM IIIA date.[68] The few finds from the 'kaselles' do not support their identification by Evans as containers of precious relics.[69] The valuable objects probably fell into them during the destruction which preceded the laying of the LM IIIA pavement. The replacement of the 'kaselles' in the Magazines and Long Corridor by smaller and shallower cists must accordingly have taken place not, as Evans held, in MM IIIB or (Mackenzie's view) in LM IA, but in connexion with the laying of this LM IIIA floor.[70]

The southern part of the West Wing with the reconstructed South Propylaeum and the staircase to the 'Piano Nobile' is fraught with too many uncertainties to be discussed here.[71] The pottery found in a basement near the southwest angle of the Palace and classified by Evans as MM is undecorated and thus not datable more closely than between MM III and LM I.[72] The earlier East Façade of the West Wing is difficult to date.[73] Some evidence may be provided by the mason's mark in shape of a branch on the rounded corner of gypsum blocks immediately north of the Anteroom of the Throne Room.[74] Evans divided the mason's marks found at Knossos into three chronological groups.[75] The earliest signs, of Protopalatial date, tended to be rather large and deeply cut, while the latest ones were much smaller and very finely incised. An intermediate group was recognised by

---

[64] *PM I*, 457–8, fig. 328; M.R. Popham, 'Notes from Knossos, Part I', *BSA* 72 (1977), 191–2, pl. 28.a-e.; Warren and Hankey (n. 1 above), 74. The light-on-dark amphora (Popham, above, pl. 28.a-b) is most probably an import from the eastern Aegean: J.L. Davis, 'Minos and Dexithea: Crete and the Cyclades in the later Bronze Age', in J.L. Davis and J.F. Cherry (eds.), *Papers in Cycladic Prehistory* (Institute of Archaeology, University of California, Monograph 14; Los Angeles, 1979), 155 n. 7.

[65] *PM I*, 448–9.

[66] A.J. Evans, 'Knossos. Summary report of the excavations in 1900', *BSA* 6 (1899–1900), 20; id., 'The Palace of Knossos. Provisional report of the excavations for the year 1901', *BSA* 7 (1900–1), 41.

[67] *PM I*, 449–50.

[68] Hallager (n. 36 above), 35–8; J. Driessen, *An Early Destruction in the Mycenaean Palace at Knossos: A New Interpretation of the Excavation Field-Notes of the South-East Area of the West Wing* (Acta Archaeologica Lovaniensia, Monographiae 2; Leuven, 1990), 44–5.

[69] *PM I*, 451–2.

[70] Hallager (n. 36 above), 33–4. For Mackenzie's opinion, see ibid. 34; for Evans', *PM I*, 458–9. Overbeck and McDonald (n. 46 above), 160, follow Mackenzie's LM I date for the final floors. The evidence from the 13th Magazine, however, clearly points to a LM IIIA date for the construction of the latest floor with the smaller cists: see Palmer (n. 45 above), 65–7, pl. 4.

[71] S. Hiller, 'The South Propylaeum of the Palace at Knossos', in *Cretological IV, A'1* (Athens, 1980), 216–32.

[72] *PM I*, 554–6, fig. 403; Warren (n. 9 above), 334.

[73] *PM II.ii*, 798–803.

[74] *PM II.ii*, 799, fig. 521; *IV.ii*, 903, fig. 878.

[75] A.J. Evans, *The Prehistoric Tombs of Knossos* (Archaeologia 59; London, 1906), 166; S. Hood, 'Mason's marks in the palaces', in R. Hägg and N. Marinatos (eds.), *The Function of the Minoan Palaces. Proceedings of the Fourth International Symposium at the Swedish Institute in Athens ... 1984* (Skrifter ... Svenska Inst. i Athen 4°, 35; Stockholm, 1987), 205–10 with illustrations.

Evans on squared blocks in a series of important structures which he dated to the beginning of the MM III period, but which more probably belong to the MM III/LM IA transition (as will be argued below), viz. the West Bastion of the Northern Entrance Passage, the back wall of the Court of the Stone Spout and many walls in the Domestic Quarter. As S. Hood has suggested, a group of rather large signs, to which the branch sign from the Throne Room area belongs, may fall between Evans' first and second group.[76] Its date and thus the date of the earlier East Façade of the West Wing could be early MM III. According to Evans' description, the pottery from below the later façade appears to date from the MM III/LM IA transition.[77] The complex of rooms around the Room of the Column Bases was apparently rearranged in MM III.[78] This rearrangement probably went together with the earlier East Façade of the West Wing, since the mason's marks on the pillar of the East Pillar Room appear to belong to Hood's intermediate set between Evans' first and second groups.[79] This area formed one of the main sacred areas of the Palace, as indicated by the two Pillar Crypts but above all by the so-called Temple Repositories, two deep cists in which the well-known faience 'snake-goddesses' were found together with many other pieces of faience, small stone libation tables, fragments of stone hammers, pieces of gold, bronzes, four imported Cycladic jugs, clay sealings and a single Linear A tablet.[80] Most of the Minoan pottery published from the Temple Repositories is well within the MM III style, but there are also features which point forward to LM IA.[81] Thus the closing of the Temple Repositories is to be dated to the MM III/LM IA transition or in LM IA.

Evans saw the construction of the Throne Room complex further to the north as the result of a *tabula rasa*, with a wholesale invasion of new elements' in LM II.[82] As Mirié's careful study demonstrated, however, the origins of the Throne Room complex go back to the Old Palace period.[83] The recent excavations in the rooms behind the Throne Room appear to confirm Mirié's main results. Here three floor levels were found, to which, in the preliminary report, the excavators assign rough dates of MM II/III, MM III/LM IA and LM IIIA.[84] Their conclusion is that extensive changes took place in the restorations following the early LM IIIA destruction. The walls were rebuilt from the ground up, and alterations were made in the internal access routes and in the sizes of some rooms. One looks forward eagerly to the final publication of these excavations, which appear to reveal so much about the architectural history of this important part of the Palace.

We turn now to the North-West Quarter of the Palace, the area of the Early Keep. Here, Evans observes, 'the stratigraphy of this whole area ... was in many respects more complicated and difficult

---

[76] Hood (n. 75 above), 206.
[77] *PM* II.ii, 802–3 n. 1. Unfortunately, the pottery in question does not seem to have been kept.
[78] Driessen (n. 68 above), 106–7, fig. 10. For a partly different reconstruction, see E. Hallager, 'A harvest festival in the Minoan palaces?', in Hägg and Marinatos (n. 75 above), 170, fig. 1A.
[79] *PM* I, Suppl. pl. x.
[80] A.J. Evans, 'The Palace of Knossos. Provisional report for the year 1903', *BSA* 9 (1902–3), 38–94; *PM* I, 463–71, 495–523, 556–61. On the Cycladic vases, see MacGillivray (n. 54 above), 153–54. On the clay sealings and Linear A tablet, see the contributions to this volume by J. Weingarten and J.-P. Olivier.
[81] Betancourt (n. 26 above), 103–4; Warren and Hankey (n. 1 above), 73–4; Walberg (n. 3 above), 12–13.
[82] *PM* IV.ii, 902.
[83] Mirié (n. 36 above), 42–3.
[84] Catling (n. 37 above – 1987–88), 68.

to decipher than that of any other quarter of the palace'.[85] There are so many changes in the ideas of the excavators about this area that it is extremely difficult to get a clear picture of the stratigraphy.[86] Some of the best known frescoes from Knossos were found here — the miniature paintings of the Sacred Grove and Dance and the Grandstand Fresco as well as the so-called Saffron Gatherer (on these frescoes see below). In his preliminary report Evans attributed the fragments of the Saffron Gatherer and some miniatures to the highest floor level.[87] Only later did he place them on the floor beneath,[88] which in fact was not excavated until the year after.[89] Thus Evans' first statement is the correct one.[90] The latest floor in the Room of the Saffron Gatherer was dated by Evans to MM IIIB, but the level below this floor belongs to the third period in J. Raison's analysis of this area,[91] and the latest pottery preserved from this period is apparently of MM III–LM IA date.[92] The finds of Raison's fourth period, above the latest floor, comprise LM IIIA and LM IIIB pottery and Linear B tablets.[93]

Of special interest for the early history of the New Palace is the Room of the Knobbed Pithos. The base of the eponymous pithos was found on a rough stone floor in a burnt stratum together with MM III pottery and was originally ascribed to the first phase of the later Palace.[94] Only subsequently were an MM IIB mosaiko floor and an MM IIIA clay and plaster floor 'invented' above the pithos base, and the MM III pottery originally found with the pithos was 'repositioned' on that clay and plaster floor.[95] Apparently, one of the reasons for this change was Evans' stylistic dating of the knobbed pithos to MM II by comparison with similar pithoi in Magazine XXI at Phaistos, which he dated to MM II.[96] These pithoi, however, as D. Levi pointed out, belong to the Phaistos 'third Protopalatial phase' (which would be better named 'first Neopalatial phase'), and are thus to be dated to MM III.[97]

Evans thought that the North-West Lustral Basin, going back in its original elements to the earliest age of the Palace, was restored at the very beginning of the New Palace period and was destroyed in a local catastrophe during the earlier part of MM III.[98] According to Raison's reinvestigation of the area, the North-West Lustral Basin was more probably constructed in MM III and levelled at the very end of the MM III period.[99] Evans stated that the impressive bastions of the Northern Entrance Passage were constructed in early MM III.[100] However, the latest pottery elements from below the

---

[85] *PM III*, 17.
[86] See the recent thorough analysis in Raison (n. 21 above), 35–109.
[87] A.J. Evans, 'Knossos. Summary report of the excavation in 1901', *BSA* 6 (1899–1900), 44–5.
[88] *PM III*, 21–2.
[89] Mackenzie's day-book entry for 8 April 1901, quoted in L.R. Palmer and J. Boardman, *On the Knossos Tablets, I* (Oxford, 1963), 123.
[90] Raison (n. 21 above), 51–9.
[91] Ibid. 103–6.
[92] Parallels mentioned ibid. 104–5, nos. 617–19.
[93] Ibid. 106–9, for parallels for pottery mentioned in nos. 643–50.
[94] A.J. Evans, 'The Palace of Knossos. Provisional report for the year 1903', *BSA* 9 (1902–3), 25–7, fig. 13.
[95] *PM I*, 234–5, fig. 177; *III*, 23–5, fig. 12. Cf. L.R. Palmer and J. Raison, 'L'insula nord-ouest du palais de Knossos: position des sols et stratigraphie', *Minos* 14 (1973), 17–38, especially 23–4, 33, fig. 6 bis, and 36–7; Levi (n. 21 above), 54–7.
[96] *PM I*, 231–5.
[97] Levi (n. 21 above), 42–3; Carinci (n. 2 above).
[98] *PM I*, 405–11.
[99] Raison (n. 21 above), 230–8. Cf. especially the parallels for the pottery from the debris in the North-West Lustral Basin mentioned at p. 238 n. 443.
[100] *PM III*, 158–61.

bastions as well as from below the North Pillar Hall are apparently of MM III–LM IA date.[101] Consequently, the construction of the North Entrance system probably belongs to the MM III/LM IA transition and is thus later than Evans supposed.

The North-East Magazines containing a 'plentiful store of the ordinary pottery' of MM III were filled in, according to Evans, at the close of the Middle Minoan Age.[102] As Warren and Hankey argue, the date of this deposit may be slightly later, i.e. MM III/LM IA transition.[103] Above followed an LM IA level.[104] Further to the east, a level containing coarse pottery dated by Evans to MM III was found above the Old Palace period level of the Royal Pottery Stores.[105] Again, a transitional MM III/LM IA date appears possible.[106]

The original layout of the School Room area appears to be due to MM III building activities.[107] These were dated by Evans to early MM III, his MM IIIA. The rooms in question were constructed above the remains of the Stores of the Great Pithoi, dated by Evans to MM II.[108] As with the pithos in the Room of the Knobbed Pithos in the North-East Wing, this dating was based on stylistic comparison to the knobbed pithoi from Magazine XXI at Phaistos, which are in fact of MM III date.[109] Thus the building activities in the School Room area too cannot be early MM III but may have been executed in the MM III/LM IA transition.

The Loomweight Deposit in a deep basement just east of the East Corridor was dated to MM IIB by Evans.[110] S. Hood has argued that the naturalism of the well-known jar with the palms would be unique as early as this and has suggested an early MM III date for it.[111] More MM III elements in this deposit have been pointed out by P. Warren and V. Hankey as well as by G. Walberg.[112] According to the material preserved in the Stratigraphical Museum, the stratum in which the palm jar was found contained a mixture of MM II and MM III material[113] and appears to represent a filling for the construction of new substructure walls in MM III.[114] As D. Levi pointed out, the layers below the uppermost floor — dated by Evans to MM IIIB — most probably do not indicate the early MM III use suggested by Evans but rather represent a contemporary filling for the floor above,[115] on which stood tripod pots dated by Evans to the close of MM III.[116]

This room, the Room of the Tripod Vases, formed the most easterly compartment of the Royal

---

[101] Raison (n. 21 above), 176–8.
[102] *PM I*, 568–71.
[103] Warren and Hankey (n. 1 above), 61–2.
[104] Popham (n. 64 above), 193–4.
[105] *PM I*, 571–2.
[106] *PM I*, 360–84, especially 366 n. 2; *III*, 265–7.
[107] Warren and Hankey (n. 1 above), 61–2.
[108] *PM I*, 231–4; cf. plan on fig. 152, opposite 203.
[109] See nn. 94–7 above.
[110] *PM I*, 248–56.
[111] S. Hood, *The Minoans: Crete in the Bronze Age* (London, 1971), 43, 217, pl. 5; Betancourt (n. 26 above), 104, agrees with this dating.
[112] Warren and Hankey (n. 1 above), 52–4; Walberg (n. 3 above), 33 n. 42.
[113] *SMK*, M.III.2; Stürmer (n. 12 above), 9.
[114] *PM I*, fig. 187b opposite 250.
[115] Levi (n. 21 above), 50–1.
[116] *PM I*, 249.

Magazines, a unit of storerooms also comprising the Corridor of the Bays, the Magazine of the Medallion Pithoi, and the Area of the Stone Drain-Heads. Evans believed that this group of rooms was filled in at the same time to make the foundations for a rebuilt East Hall after the MM IIIB destruction of the Palace. According to him, 'the MM III vessels were here left on the floors, as of antiquated or of little account, at the time when the new structures were built above them'.[117] Unfortunately the eponymous vessels from the Room of the Tripod Vases have not been illustrated. Popham has published fragments of cups with spiral decoration in applied white-on-dark matt ground from this deposit.[118] Fragments from cups decorated with rippling listed by Mackenzie are no longer identifiable. Paralleled by MM III–LM IA deposits from the Unexplored Mansion and the Stratigraphical Museum excavation, this combination of ceramic features points to a date for this deposit during the MM III/LM IA transition instead of late MM III.[119] Since the floor of this room was imperfectly preserved, it is possible that these sherds were not found on the floor but came from below floor level, from the deep fill underneath.[120] The pottery from the Corridor of the Bays illustrated by Evans is too unusual for closer dating.[121] In the neighbouring Magazine of the Medallion Pithoi, Evans claimed to have found above a MM IIB 'mosaiko' floor four levels with three successive floors, all to be dated between MM IIIA and B.[122] As Levi pointed out,[123] the only element for a dating from this room is the 'medallion' pithos, dated by Evans to MM IIIB.[124] However, there is no real evidence for this date and, as Pendlebury showed, an LM I date appears more probable.[125] Medallion pithoi have been found in an LM IA context in the North-East House at Knossos,[126] as well as in the LM IB destruction level at Aghia Triadha.[127] In the West Magazines at Knossos, medallion pithoi remained in use until the final destruction of the Palace, since almost intact examples were found in the 5th and 10th Magazines.[128] Pendlebury considered it possible that only the Corridor of the Bays fell into disuse, whereas the Magazine of the Medallion Pithoi remained open to serve the needs of the supposed Great East Hall above. The stratification below the uppermost floor in the Magazine of the Medallion Pithoi is problematic, since fragments of medallion pithoi were found there too.[129] Moreover, in the entry in his 1913 notebook relating to test pit 47 below the uppermost floor of the Magazine of the Medallion Pithoi, Evans mentioned an LM II fragment (which according to the drawing in the notebook could as easily be LM IIIA).[130]

---

[117] Ibid. 301.
[118] Popham (n. 64 above), 192–3, 187, fig. 1A and pl. 29a.
[119] M.R. Popham et al., *The Minoan Unexplored Mansion at Knossos* (BSA Suppl. 17; London, 1984), 153–6, pls. 128.a-g, 132.a-c; Warren (n. 9 above), 319–40, 327 fig. 8: B, 328–9 figs. 9: H, J, K, M, N, and 10: J–L, N–Q.
[120] Popham (n. 64 above), 193.
[121] *PM I*, 566, fig. 412. For the find-place, see the plan on p. 323, fig. 236.
[122] Ibid. 319–22, fig. 233.
[123] Levi (n. 21 above), 53.
[124] *PM I*, 562–4.
[125] Pendlebury (n. 35 above), 204–5.
[126] *PM II.ii*, 418.
[127] F. Halbherr, E. Stefani and L. Banti, 'Haghia Triada nel periodo tardo palaziale', *ASA* n.s. 39 (1977), 141–2, 288.
[128] *PM I*, 563, fig. 409; *IV*, suppl. pl. lix.a; Hallager (n. 36 above), 30.
[129] *SMK*, M.I.2; Stürmer (n. 12 above), 14.
[130] Palmer (n. 45 above), 86, pl. 7. For the probable LM IIIA date of the fragment in question, see Popham (n. 36 above), pls. 42.d, 43.d.

Evans surmised that this sherd worked its way down from the second East Hall through the filling covering the medallion pithoi and on through a crack at the time of the conflagration. As L.R. Palmer showed, however, this is extremely unlikely.[131] Thus there must have been LM II–III repairs to the uppermost floor of the Magazine of the Medallion Pithoi, as in the West Magazines (cf. above).

The Royal Magazines had originally formed an annexe to the first floor of the Domestic Quarter and were only later separated by the blocking of the doorway between the Corridor of the Bays and the Middle East-West Corridor.[132] The reconstruction of the Domestic Quarter in its present plan after the MM IIB destruction was dated by Evans to MM IIIA.[133] An MM III/LM IA transitional date appears more probable, since pottery classified as MM III and LM I has been found in sub-floor tests below some rooms (Hall of the Double Axes, Queen's Megaron, Corridor of the Painted Pithos).[134] The sophisticated Old Palace drainage system continued in use, with new areas of the Domestic Quarter being incorporated into it.[135]

According to Evans a group of rooms south of the Domestic Quarter (Evans' 'South-East Insula') comprising the Magazine of the Lily Vases, the Magazine of the False-Spouted Pithoi and the South-East Bathroom was filled in in MM IIIB.[136] As has been demonstrated by P.P. Betancourt as well as by Warren and Hankey, an LM IA date for the pottery found in these rooms is more probable.[137]

It is a difficult task to get a clear picture of the development of the New Palace at Knossos from these confusing facts. Much more reinvestigation of the pottery stored in the Stratigraphical Museum is needed, as well as more soundings in other parts of the Palace, such as those which S. Hood directed in 1987. As it appears from the preceding survey, most parts of the New Palace as we see it today were not constructed immediately after the MM IIB destruction, i.e. at the beginning of the MM III period as Evans supposed, but some time later, at the end of MM III or even in the MM III/LM IA transition. Traces of an initial phase of the New Palace, to be dated within the opening years of MM III, appear to be formed by the earlier East Façade of the West Wing and the complex around the Room of the Column Bases in the same Wing; by the Room of the Knobbed Pithos and the North-West Lustral Basin in the North-West Quarter; and by the Magazines of the Great Pithoi and the Loomweight Deposit in the East Wing. The greater part of the West Wing, especially the West Façade and the West Magazines, were constructed in late MM III or during the MM III/LM IA transition.[138] The same appears to be true of the bastions of the Northern Entrance Passage, possibly the School Room area, the Royal Magazines, and the Domestic Quarter. Thus we appear to have two phases in the architectural history of the New Palace: a first one within MM III, succeeded by a

---

[131] L.R. Palmer, 'Knossos: the high relief frescoes', in F. Krinzinger et al., *Forschungen und Funde, Festschrift Bernhard Neutsch* (*Innsbrucker Beiträge zur Kulturwissenschaft 21*; Innsbruck, 1980), 329–30.

[132] *PM I*, 320–3, fig. 236. On this plan of the Royal Magazines, the blocking of the doorway is dated to LM IA, but Evans gives no evidence for this dating in the text.

[133] *PM I*, 327.

[134] Overbeck and McDonald (n. 47 above), 160–4, ill. 1.

[135] C.F. Macdonald and J. Driessen, 'The drainage system of the Domestic Quarter in the Palace at Knossos', *BSA* 83 (1988), 235–58.

[136] *PM I*, 573–84.

[137] Betancourt (n. 26 above), 104; Warren and Hankey (n. 1 above), 73. For the LM IA character of the clay bath from the South-East Bathroom, see Walberg (n. 3 above), 117.

[138] For the problem of distinguishing between ceramics of pure MM IIIB and MM III/LM IA transition, if fine decorated vases are lacking, (as in most of the deposits in question), see Warren (n. 9 above), 334.

second and extensive construction during the MM III/LM IA transition. This is comparable to the architectural history of the New Palace at Phaistos, where in phase III the structure was apparently a builders' yard, after which initial activity there came an interruption, to be followed by the full construction of the LM IA Palace.[139] Like phase III at Phaistos, the first phase of the New Palace at Knossos may have remained unfinished. This probable interruption at Knossos and Phaistos appears to have been due to a major earthquake destruction in Crete and the Cyclades, as has been most recently argued by Warren.[140]

Evans ascribed many of the *frescoes* from the Palace at Knossos to MM III.[141] For some time, however, scholars have grappled with the problems and difficulties of his dating.[142] The only fresco fragments which can be stratigraphically dated before the MM III/LM IA second phase of construction are the fragments of dados from a higher level in the Loomweight Basement, dated by Evans to MM IIB,[143] as well as the Spiral Fresco and a plaster relief fragment showing part of a bull's foot, dated by Evans to MM IIIA.[144] All were found stratified below the floor of the Magazine of the Tripod Vases, the construction of which is most probably to be dated to the MM III/LM IA transition (cf. above). The MM III/LM IA transition thus forms a *terminus ante quem* for these fresco fragments, which apparently formed part of the decoration of the first phase of the New Palace. Since they are filling material, they could have been transported from elsewhere in the Palace and need not be connected with the earlier East Hall, as Evans supposed.[145] In his revision of the chronology of the Knossos frescoes, Hawke Smith wants to make the High Reliefs, connected by Evans with his later East Hall,[146] contemporary with the supposedly MM IIIA Bull Relief mentioned above.[147] Since the Bull Relief was found below a floor which is probably MM IIIA/LM IA and the High Reliefs above a floor of the same period in the East Corridor and next to a blocking wall of LM IIIB date,[148] this suggestion must be rejected. On stylistic grounds, B. Kaiser dated the latest elements of the High Reliefs to LM IB.[149]

The Dolphin Fresco from the Domestic Quarter was dated by Evans to MM IIIB.[150] However, archaeological context and stylistic comparisons point to a much later date for this fresco, which apparently formed the decoration of a floor on the upper storey, probably in LM IIIA.[151]

As for the Bull Relief from the Northern Entrance Passage, Evans first placed it in MM IIIB after the earthquake, but later preferred MM IIIA.[152] Hawke Smith, following Evans, placed it at the

---

[139] Carinci (n. 2 above), 78–9.
[140] Warren (n. 9 above), 339–40.
[141] J. Evans, *Index to the Palace of Minos* (London, 1936), 52.
[142] C.F. Hawke Smith, 'The Knossos frescoes: a revised chronology', *BSA* 71 (1976), 65–76; S.A. Immerwahr, *Aegean Painting in the Bronze Age* (University Park, Pa., and London, 1990), 39, 84–5.
[143] *PM I*, 252, fig. 188.a-b.
[144] Ibid. 371, fig. 269 and 376, fig. 273.
[145] Ibid. 370.
[146] *PM III*, 495–6.
[147] Hawke Smith (n. 142 above), 66–8.
[148] *PM III*, 266; Popham (n. 36 above), 37.
[149] B. Kaiser, *Untersuchungen zum minoischen Relief* (Bonn, 1976), 291.
[150] *PM I*, 542–4, figs. 394–5; *III*, 377–8, 379, fig. 251.
[151] Hawke Smith (n. 142 above), 72–4; R.B. Koehl, 'A marinescape floor from the Palace at Knossos', *AJA* 90 (1986), 407–17.
[152] *PM II.i*, 356, and *III*, 189–90.

point of transition from MM IIIA to MM IIIB.[153] As has been explained above, the bastions of the Northern Entrance Passage were apparently constructed during the MM III/LM IA transition. If, as Evans thought, the Bull Relief adorned a 'loggia' on top of the Western Bastion, MM III/LM IA must form a *terminus post quem* for the attachment of the relief fresco. Kaiser dated it on stylistic grounds to LM II–IIIA.[154]

As I showed above, the frescoes in the area above the Early Keep were all found above the uppermost floors, which were laid in the MM III/LM IA transition and so give a *terminus post quem*. The *terminus ante quem* is formed by the LM IIIA–B contexts in which they were found. I agree for stylistic reasons with Hawke Smith's, Walberg's and Immerwahr's date of MM III–LM IA for the so-called 'Saffron Gatherer', which is really a blue monkey.[155] The miniature frescoes from the Room of the Spiral Cornice were dated by Evans to MM III.[156] In this dating, Evans gave great importance to the fragment of a miniature fresco from the lower cists of the 13th West Magazine, which — according to him — was found well stratified in an MM III context.[157] The cist in question, however, was not sealed in MM III, as was suggested by Evans, but in LM IIIA,[158] which thus forms the *terminus ante quem*. The most probable date for the miniature frescoes appears to be in LM I, possibly LM IB.[159] Thus the Saffron Gatherer appears to represent the only preserved fresco from the time of the MM III/LM IA second architectural phase of the New Palace.

Building activities in early LM IB in different parts of the Palace (the best evidence comes from the Domestic Quarter) appear to have followed an earthquake late in LM IA at about the time of the eruption of Thera.[160] LM IB pottery of the special Palatial tradition[161] has been found within the Palace only as strays in later deposits.[162] This is probably due to the fact that the Palace of Knossos escaped the LM IB burnt destructions[163] and it therefore does not indicate, as C. Macdonald thinks, that the Palace was not functioning as fully as before.[164]

THE TOWN AND THE CEMETERIES (FIG. 2)

The area of intensive settlement had already by MM I expanded to a size that was hardly surpassed at a later stage of the Bronze Age.[165] A new feature of the New Palace period appears to be the

---

[153] Hawke Smith (n. 142 above), 68.
[154] Kaiser (n. 149 above), 287–9.
[155] Hawke Smith (n. 142 above), 68–9; G. Walberg, *Tradition and Innovation: Essays in Minoan Art* (Mainz, 1986), 60–2; Immerwahr (n. 142 above), 41–2.
[156] *PM III*, 31–80.
[157] *PM I*, 527; *III*, 33.
[158] See n. 70 above.
[159] Hawke Smith (n. 142 above), 69; Immerwahr (n. 142 above), 63–6.
[160] Macdonald (n. 37 above), 85–8. For an LM IB date for the 'East Staircase' deposit, see Niemeier (n. 15 above), 8 with n. 38.
[161] For a definition of this term, see Betancourt (n. 26 above), 140.
[162] P.A. Mountjoy, 'The Marine Style pottery of LM IB/LH IIA: towards a corpus', *BSA* 79 (1984), 170–1.
[163] See J. Weingarten, this volume, who uses the same argument for explaining the lack of LM IB sealing deposits (and, one may add, Linear A tablets: see also J.-P. Olivier, this volume).
[164] Macdonald (n. 37 above), 88.
[165] S. Hood and D. Smyth, *Archaeological Survey of the Knossos Area* (2nd edn.; BSA Suppl. 14; London, 1981), 8–10.

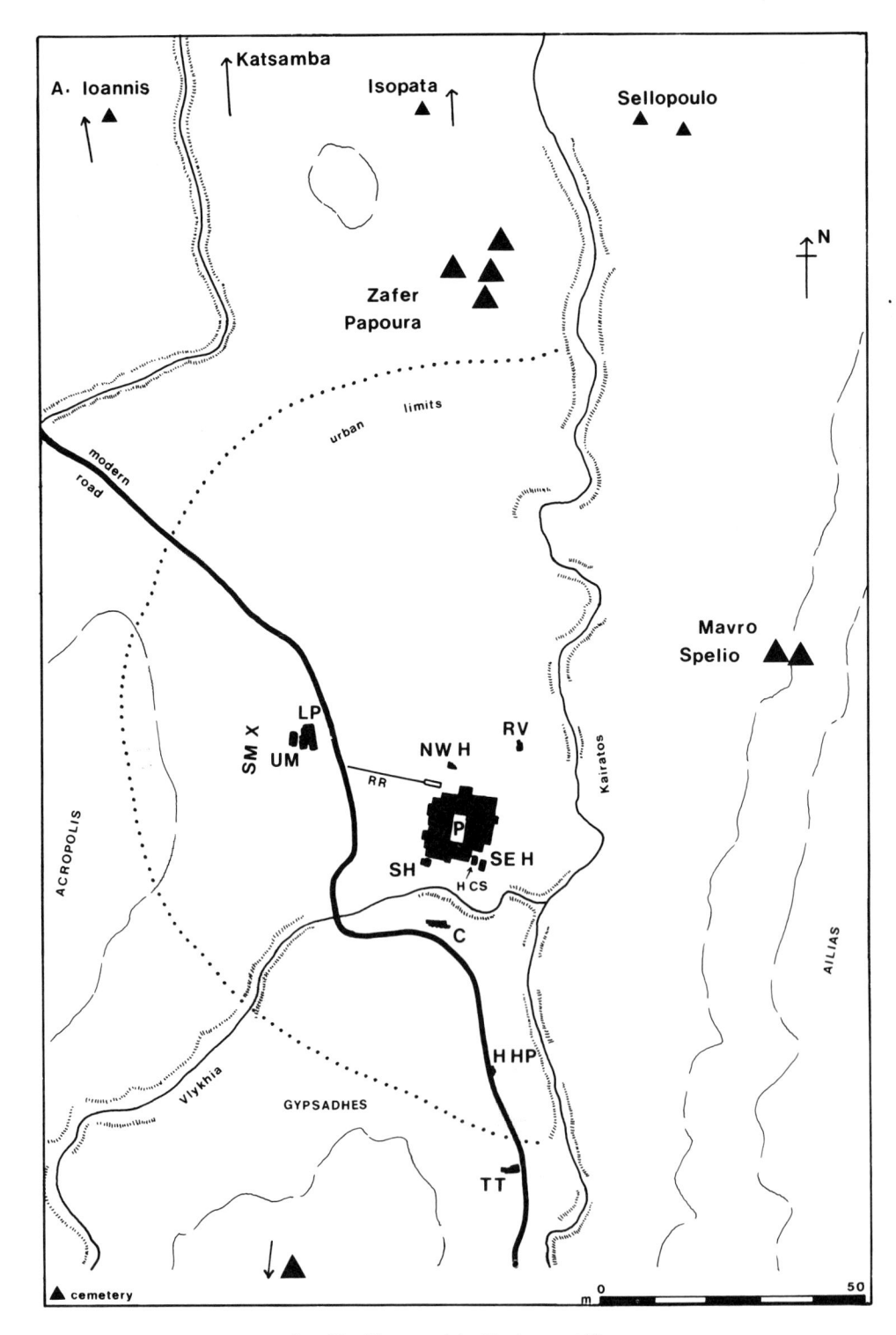

FIG. 2   The Town and its Environs at Knossos

'urban villas'[166] constructed around the Palace in MM III–LM IA — the Little Palace, the South House, the House of the Chancel Screen, the South-East House, the House of the High Priest[167] — which apparently served as the seats of high officials with religious functions.[168] The case of Quartier Mu at Mallia, an urban villa of the Old Palace period,[169] points to the possibility of Old Palace period predecessors. In the early New Palace period, at least one urban villa was also constructed at Amnisos, one of the two harbour towns of Knossos.[170]

Among the tombs of the New Palace period the most outstanding is the MM III Temple Tomb south of the Palace, connecting a rock-cut chamber tomb with splendid architectural features of palatial character.[171] There can be no doubt that this was a tomb for one or more leading members of the Palace society. The Royal Tomb of Isopata is another elite tomb possibly constructed in MM III.[172] As for the burials of the ordinary populace, some Old Palatial tombs continued in use,[173] while at the same time new chamber tomb cemeteries were started on nearby hillslopes at Mavro Spelio and Upper Gypsadhes.[174]

THE ROLE OF KNOSSOS IN CRETE AND THE AEGEAN

The Palace at Knossos is by far the largest palace of this period.[175] Was it a kind of *primum inter paria* or was it the political and administrative centre of the entire island, and did it also play the leading role in the domination of a large part of the Aegean area by Minoan Crete in this epoch?[176]

Key to FIG. 2

C	Caravanserai	RV	Royal Villa
H CS	House of the Chancel Screen	SE H	South-East House
H HP	House of the High Priest	SH	South House
LP	Little Palace	SM X	Stratigraphical Museum Excavations
NW H	North-West House	TT	Temple Tomb
RR	Royal Road	UM	Unexplored Mansion

---

[166] For a definition of this term, see P.P. Betancourt and N. Marinatos, 'The definition of the Minoan Villa', in R. Hägg (ed.), *The Function of the 'Minoan Villa'. Proceedings of the Eighth International Symposium at the Swedish Institute at Athens ... 1992* (Skrifter ... Svenska Inst. i Athen, 4°; Stockholm, in press).

[167] See the summary descriptions by J.W. Graham, *The Palaces of Crete* (2nd edn.; Princeton, 1987), 51–7.

[168] R. Hägg, 'Die Epiphanie im minoischen Ritual', *AM* 101 (1986), 48–55.

[169] For this interpretation, see W.-D. Niemeier, 'The origins of the Minoan "villa" system', in Hägg and Marinatos (n. 166 above).

[170] V. Stürmer, 'Areal A: die "Villa der Lilien"', in J. Schäfer (n. 32 above), 129–50. On Amnisos as the harbour of Knossos, see W.-D. Niemeier and J. Schäfer, 'Das Epineion', ibid. 345–48.

[171] *PM* IV.ii, 964–1002; I. Pini, *Beiträge zur minoischen Gräberkunde* (Wiesbaden, 1968), 38–40.

[172] Hood and Smyth (n. 165 above), 11, 34 no. 2 (with references).

[173] Ibid. 11.

[174] Pini (n. 171 above), 36–9; Hood and Smyth (n. 165 above), no. 331 (with references).

[175] Cf. the plans of the three major palaces (Knossos, Mallia, and Phaistos), illustrated by Graham (n. 167 above), pl. 7.

[176] Concerning evidence for this domination, see S. Hood, 'A Minoan empire in the Aegean in the 16th and 15th centuries B.C. ?', in R. Hägg and N. Marinatos (n. 54 above), 33–7; W.-D. Niemeier, 'Creta, Egeo e Mediterraneo agli inizi del Bronzo Tardo', in M. Marazzi, S. Tusa and L. Vagnetti (eds.), *Traffici micenei nel Mediterraneo* (Taranto, 1986), 245–59; M.H. Wiener, 'The isles of Crete?

The fact that the finest LM IB vases, those of the special Palatial tradition, were produced by Knossian workshops and exported all over the island cannot be taken to prove that Knossos was dominant in politics too, since we know nothing of the economic or social levels at which that pottery trade was conducted.[177] J.H. Betts has drawn attention to clay sealings found at various sites in Crete but impressed by the same gold rings of probably Knossian provenance, and he further cites the so-called ring matrix from Knossos with a seated goddess receiving an offering, a motive closely paralleled on a ring impression from Kato Zakro.[178] Betts postulated replica rings made at Knossos from such matrices, to be carried by officials when travelling to provincial towns. The picture they create seemed to him to be one of centralised bureaucracy at Knossos. As I. Pini has demonstrated, not only was the Zakro impression made by a significantly smaller ring, there are also clear differences in the motif.[179] There are other cases of such 'look-alikes', as J. Weingarten calls them, but usually at the same site.[180] The Zakro impression is interpreted by Weingarten not as evidence for a Knossian ring-owner exercising his authority in the heart of Zakro, but as evidence for document-sealing sent from one palace to the other. The impression of identical bull-leaping scenes on nodules from Aghia Triadha, Sklavokampos, Zakro and Gournia she sees as evidence for a network of tokens and documents travelling all over Crete. In this network Knossos appears to play an important role, but a less dramatic one than that suggested by Betts.

Many scholars see a conquest of Crete by Mycenaeans as the cause of the destructions at the end of the LM IB period.[181] The present author has a different view, ascribing these destructions to internecine conflicts between Knossos and the other palaces, in which Knossos got the upper hand.[182] This is not the place to repeat my arguments. But I would like to put one question: if a Mycenaean conquest is responsible for the LM IB destruction horizon, why did the invaders spare the most important palace of the island?

The Minoan thalassocracy revisited', in D.A. Hardy, C.G. Doumas, J.A. Sakellarakis, and P.M. Warren (eds.), *Thera and the Aegean World III, vol. 1: Archaeology. Proceedings of the Third International Congress, Santorini Greece ... 1989* (London, 1990), 128–60.

[177] M.R. Popham, 'Late Minoan pottery: a summary', *BSA* 62 (1967), 339–43.

[178] J.H. Betts, 'New light on Minoan bureaucracy', *Kadmos* 6 (1967), 15–28.

[179] I. Pini, 'Neue Beobachtungen zu den töneren Siegelabdrücken von Zakros', *AA* 1983, 570–1, fig. 10.

[180] J. Weingarten, 'Late Bronze Age trade within Crete', in N.H. Gale (ed.), *Bronze Age Trade in the Mediterranean: Papers presented at the Conference held at Rewley House, Oxford in December 1989* (SIMA 90; Jonsered, 1991), 308–10.

[181] e.g. Popham and Weingarten, this volume.

[182] W.-D. Niemeier, 'The character of the Knossian palace society in the second half of the fifteenth century B.C.: Mycenaean or Minoan?', in O. Krzyszkowska and L. Nixon (eds.), *Minoan Society: Proceedings of the Cambridge Colloquium 1981* (Bristol, 1983), 217–36; id. (n. 36 above), *passim*, especially 195–216.

Chapter 6

Late Minoan II to the End of the Bronze Age[1]

M.R. POPHAM

The editors have requested contributors to this volume to give emphasis to the part played by Knossos in their period surveys. The author found this difficult to do adequately within the space allotted for a period covering some 300 eventful years. So the rather unusual format has been adopted of giving a brief islandwide survey first, followed by four separate sections which concentrate on various aspects of the Knossian evidence during this period, ranging from pre-eminence to eclipse. The chapter ends with a Reading List.

INTRODUCTION

Around 1450 B.C., at the end of LM IB, it must have appeared that Minoan civilisation was in grave danger of being extinguished. Almost without exception its main centres, its villages and country villas had been burnt to the ground, and the island had experienced severe depopulation, while even Knossos, which suffered least, had not escaped injury. Minoan colonies abroad, whatever their status, be it as centres of control or trading posts or both, had been afflicted similarly; and this did, indeed, mark the end of Cretan power overseas.

Internal recovery, however, was largely achieved in LM II–IIIA1, though slowly and patchily, but with a fair prospect of progressive prosperity, which, however, was in the end thwarted. Paradoxically, this partial recovery was largely due to the very people who had been responsible for the devastation. As happened on other islands of the Aegean, a section of the Mycenaean conquerors stayed on and took control. On Crete they were established on fertile ground, both agriculturally and in inheriting Cretan traditional skills in administration (including literacy), technical expertise as

---

[1] I am grateful to the editors for giving me this opportunity to make a small offering of thanks to a friend from whom I learnt to excavate and to record in what was at the time a near revolution in digging techniques practised by the British School at Athens. Not only that, but Sinclair had trained up a team of expert Cretan workmen with a skilled vasemender as well, whose combined help I was able with gratitude to call upon when it became my turn to run a dig.

Without the constant help of the authorities of Herakleion Museum I would not have been able to illustrate my account of the pottery as I wanted. My thanks are also due to Mrs. A. Sakellariou for providing me with a photograph of the Cretan pyxis reproduced at PLATE 10.e.

metalworkers (including the manufacture of weaponry) and an artistic excellence which had set the fashion throughout the Aegean. Reorganisation of the shattered social structures and economy must have been gradual but it could build upon a pre-existing centralised administration and experience at Knossos, which had basically survived. The steps in that process can be but dimly perceived. An immediate change in table habits, at least at court, is apparent, as too are new burial practices in fresh cemeteries in which the first generation of its warrior class was interred. Initially efforts were directed towards re-establishing the main centres of control, with Mycenaean presence indicated near at home at Mallia, more distant at Phaistos and further afield at Chania in the west (FIG. 1), at all of which the new pottery fashions appear, followed by burials of Mycenaean character a generation later. By this time, close interactions between the island and the Mainland had been established, in which Cretan skills under their new patrons made the major contribution.

The degree and nature of this resurgence, centred at Knossos, become clear some seventy years later, in LM IIIA1, when a third generation of the invaders was reaching adulthood. Close control over much of the island was being exercised, in part through a centralised bureaucracy which recorded contributions in produce, flocks of animals, localised labour forces, manufactured goods and stores of military equipment and their owners, the last indicating the build-up of considerable power in weapons and chariotry (PLATE 7.c). Perhaps it was fear of this potential threat which led some other powerful state to extinguish the danger and to pillage and burn the Palace at Knossos along with its surrounding mansions. Whatever the cause and whoever the aggressors, Crete was then left to pursue its independent way, no longer an influential centre of technical and artistic excellence. It was free, too, of centralised control and it may be assumed that the various geographical regions, or provinces, existed independently under their local rulers. Not surprisingly, we know little of this unspectacular and uneventful stage in the island's history, which lasted well over a hundred years, through LM IIIA2 into IIIB.

It is not until well into the 13th century, and probably close to its end (late LM IIIB), that Crete again became involved in the international scene and made some impact abroad, but only to be caught up eventually in the unrest which affected the eastern Mediterranean as a whole and which ended in widespread and general destructions, in which the island was involved.

After its destruction in LM IIIA1 there are no signs that Knossos re-established any form of supremacy: on the contrary our present knowledge indicates that in the 13th century (LM IIIB) its inhabitants were still squatting in its old mansions, which had been partially cleared out and renovated, while the fringes of its ruined Palace were similarly reoccupied, apparently to serve some religious purpose, a relic of its one-time reputation in this field. This may, however, be just one manifestation of a much more general religious revival in times of trouble, when people turned for support to the heroes of the past and buildings they were thought to have inhabited.

Recent excavations strongly suggest that by now the capital of Crete had moved to Chania in the west, at least in the sense that it was the most flourishing town whose products, particularly its distinctive pottery, were reaching in fair quantity other regions of the island and were being exported over a large area stretching from Sardinia in the west to Cyprus in the east. These international contacts may, as some 'alien' pottery at Chania suggests, have attracted some settlers from the west, forerunners perhaps, of a greater movement of peoples from that region. Other areas of the island, too, seem to have become more outward-looking, in this case re-establishing long-broken contacts with the Dodecanese, where Cretan influence is again apparent.

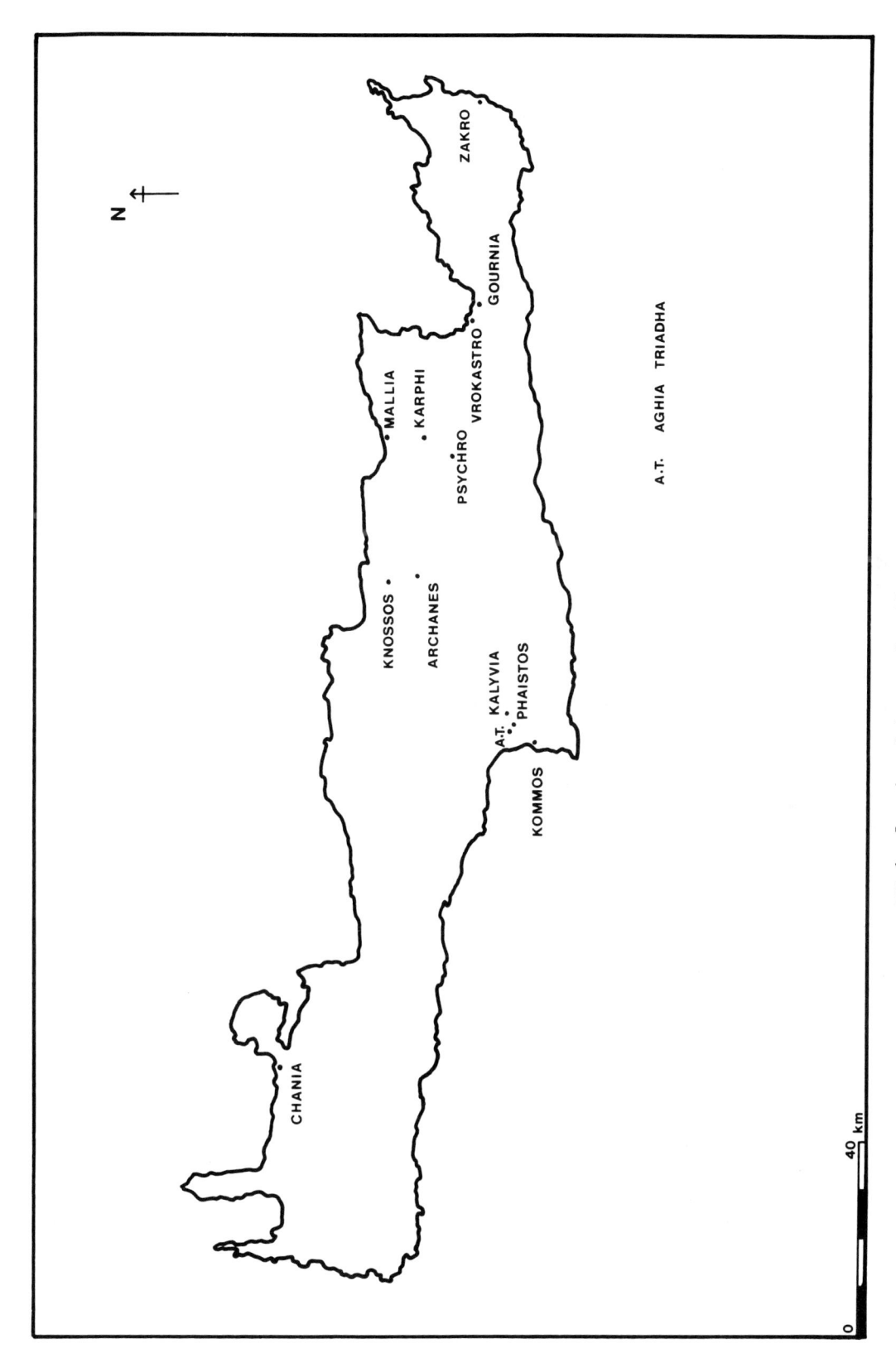

FIG. 1 Location of sites mentioned in the text

This resurgence ended around 1200 B.C., the end of LM IIIB, in destructions and the abandonment of poorly protected settlements, at a time when Mainland Greece, the Aegean islands and most of the Near East came similarly under attack. Egyptian records tell of the destructive force and widespread successes of invaders including a naval contingent manned by the 'Peoples of the Sea' which might well have overrun Crete in its progress eastwards. A few of these may have settled on the island, perhaps as chieftains of local communities, later to be buried with their new non-Aegean weaponry. Another group, possibly refugees from the Mainland, introduced pottery of Mycenaean type to the south coast at Aghia Triadha where a shrine was set up.

Chania was now no longer of any importance. Its inhabitants, after taking refuge from the dangers in neighbouring hillside caves, returned to form a sadly depleted settlement. Elsewhere the plains and coastlines were sparsely occupied except where the terrain offered some form of natural protection. Some peoples fled inland in LM IIIC to the mountains and their foothills to defensive sites such as Vrokastro and, more extremely, Karphi on the edge of the Lasithi mountain plain, where the offerings in the cave of Psychro complement the evidence of the Karphi shrine and places of worship elsewhere for continuing concern with religion and traditional religious symbolism.

Some respite from danger there must have been to allow contacts to be renewed with the Dodecanese and for outside influences and imports to reach the island. Further desertions are likely to be the result of further incursions, such as affected surviving towns on the Mainland and the Aegean islands.

The beginning of a new start is not discernible until the ill-named Subminoan stage, the beginning of the Iron Age, when Knossos, after a long gap, again emerges as an important, and possibly leading, centre.

THE MYCENAEANS AT KNOSSOS (FIG. 2)

Evans commented several times in *Palace of Minos* on what he perceived as drastic changes in the character of the last rulers in the Palace at Knossos: '... the last Palatial phase at Knossos represents a military and indeed militaristic aspect' (*PM IV.ii*, 785). At first, in company with other archaeologists who worked in Crete, he had regarded the destructions on the island as being all contemporary but, towards the end, he realised that this was not so. Knossos had survived the widespread disasters of *c.*1450 B.C. (LM IB), and indeed may have caused them: '... the appearance ... at Knossos of what there is every reason to suppose to have been a new and aggressive dynasty ... is marked ... by the eloquent cessation of the great rivals at Phaestos and Hagia Triada ...' (*PM IV.ii*, 786).

He was, no doubt, basing his conclusions on the evidence he had uncovered at Knossos, such as the warrior burials at Zafer Papoura, the fresco of shields along the Grand Staircase, a similar depiction on one of the Palace Style amphorae, and above all the Linear B records, which, though then undeciphered, could be seen from their ideograms and numerals clearly to include lists of the existing extensive armament of swords, chariots, cuirasses, and arrows (PLATE 7.c).

On his discovery of large deposits of tablets and their accompanying sealings, Evans commented 'the bureaucratic methods evidenced by the documents in the form of the linear script, B, introduced by the new dynasty, sufficiently declare the authoritative character of the government as regards internal matters' (*PM IV.ii*, 786), while the multiplicity of officials, signatures and countersignatures on these records 'point to a highly centralised and autocratic Government' (*PM IV.ii*, 885).

Basing his observations largely on the Palace Style vases and the latest frescoes within the Palace such as those in the Throne Room, itself 'an intrusive block', he observed, 'Lost is the free spirit ... the power of individual characterization and of instantaneous portraiture ... the strong sympathy with wild Nature ... A sacral and conventional style now prevails' (*PM II.ii*, 880).

Evans was perhaps overemphasising the degree of the changes. The Linear A archive at Aghia Triadha and deposits of sealings there and elsewhere in the 1450 destruction levels show that administrative control was no new feature, though the script certainly was and the extent of the control is likely to have been. Conventionalism and religious symbolism in art, too, were already present at that time, however prominent naturalism may have been. In particular he was certainly underestimating the earlier military background, which is implied by Cretan pre-eminence in sword design and manufacture, and in the Minoan domination, as he would have regarded it, of the Aegean and its islands.

However, certainly new was the overt expression and emphasis given to the aspect of militarism, to be seen, for instance, in the embellishment of swords and spearheads (PLATE 6.d–g), which proclaim the same pride in their possession and display as had been apparent in the weapons deposited in the Shaft Graves at Mycenae in an earlier era.

The characteristics highlighted by Evans appeared to archaeologists working on the Mainland to be in this and other aspects typically Mycenaean, and led Wace to propose that the Mainlanders had assumed control of Knossos, a theory accepted by Pendelbury though vehemently rejected by Evans. The resultant heated dispute was finally resolved, after Evans' death, by the decipherment of Linear B by Ventris as an early form of Greek, by which time the Knossos tablets had been supplemented by the archive found in the Palace at Pylos.

With this knowledge, it has become easier to recognise other features at Knossos which point to a Mycenaean influence and presence there after 1450 B.C. This evidence has been augmented by more recent findings. For instance, to military symbolism, such as the 'figure-of-eight' shield, can now be added the boar's tusk helmet, depicted prominently on a Palace Style jar and a kylix, and a single instance of a sword or dagger (PLATE 6.a and g). Again the number of warrior graves known has been significantly augmented by those discovered in the 'Hospital Cemetery' at Aghios Ioannis, at Sellopoulo and near the Temple Tomb. To their armament can now be added a 'bell helmet' with a covering of bronze (PLATE 6.b).

These additions to the known warrior burials have revealed another aspect of them which can be seen as representative of Mycenaean tastes, the so-called 'burials with bronzes'. An outstanding example of these was known to Evans, the Tomb of the Tripod Hearth (PLATE 7.d), as he called it, while two other burials in the Zafer Papoura cemetery, Tombs 36 and 99, had also contained a few bronze vessels. But, at the time, this find seemed to be a relatively isolated phenomenon. It can now be recognised as a feature at this stage at Knossos and elsewhere, with the discovery of two such burials at Sellopoulo and others at Archanes, while a long-known tomb at Kalyvia, near Phaistos, conforms to the same practice. Such ostentatious offerings of bronze vessels are characteristic of Mycenaean burials on the Mainland, beginning with the Shaft Graves at Mycenae and remaining a continuing feature of rich burials into the LH II and IIIA stages, especially well attested at Dendra but known over a wide area.

One of the archaeological criteria for the arrival of 'aliens' is the introduction of new tomb types with close parallels elsewhere. The appearance at this stage at Knossos and Phaistos of the typically

Mycenaean chamber tomb with its characteristic 'keyhole'-shaped long dromos or entrance passage (PLATE 7.a), is one such instance, made more significant in this case when it is found to occur in fresh burial grounds in new locations. It could well be that the appearance of stone-built tholos tombs at Knossos is another Mycenaean feature. More certainly so is the deposition, with warrior burials in particular, of squat alabastra in clay (PLATE 7.b), a type of vase which occurs for the first time at this stage in Crete, though current earlier on the Mainland.

Changes in burial practices with Mycenaean features are an important indicator. So, too, are new table habits with the same origin. The cup had been the traditional Cretan drinking vessel throughout the ages: it is now joined in equal numbers by the low-stemmed goblet, or kylix, a Mycenaean shape which at this period had adopted an unusual but characteristic type of decoration with a single motive, the so-called Ephyraean style (PLATE 8.a–b). Both shape and style are imitated at Knossos, but with an extended range of motives. These are considered in greater detail in the section dealing with the Knossos potters and their contribution, where attention is also given to another feature of Mycenaean tastes, the Palace Style jar (PLATES 6.a; 9.a–c), which became a prominent feature of house and tomb furniture at Knossos in the LM II to early LM IIIA stage, and was largely responsible for Evans' characterisation of its art.

It is easier to point to Mycenaean features in the initial LM II phase when they are innovations and when influences appear to be mostly in one direction, flowing from the Mainland to Crete. In the subsequent LM IIIA period, though still apparent and potent, they become less readily distinguishable as the two regions share mutual developments, in which the Cretan contribution again reasserted itself. This aspect is further explored in the section on interrelationships.

RELATIONS BETWEEN CRETE AND THE MAINLAND c.1450–1375

It was Furumark's contention that in the stage prior to the destruction at Knossos (LM II/LH IIB and early IIIA) interrelations between Crete and the Mainland were minimal, and this he interpreted as 'the calm before the storm', the beginning of the hostility which culminated in the Mycenaean attack on Knossos. He reached this conclusion under two disadvantages. Firstly, the stage in the development of LM pottery at the time when the Palace was destroyed had not been defined with any precision, so that, although he was the first to recognise that the LM IIIA style was already current, and that Cretan pottery of this stage had influenced that of the Mainland, he thought this took place after the destruction at Knossos. We can now see that this effect on Mycenaean pottery precedes that event. Secondly, he agreed with Evans that the changes apparent at Knossos in LM II were an internal development and not due to Mycenaean control of that centre. Later, however, he was to be among the first to accept the decipherment of Linear B as a form of Greek, which disproved this view.

More seriously, he had reached his conclusions solely on the basis of pottery, without taking into account aspects of interconnexions in other artefacts, particularly weaponry, bronze and stone vases, jewellery and signet rings, in which parallel features are strongly marked. This evidence, although already available, has become more obvious subsequently, especially with the publication in detail of two burials, Sellopoulo Tomb 4 at Knossos and Chamber Tomb 91 at Mycenae. The two contained swords of identical shape with their midribs incised with miniature running spirals so similar in execution that Catling has suggested that they are products of the same workshop. Also, two of the warriors in these burials wore necklaces of gold relief-beads of closely similar designs, a correspondence in practice and types which Evans had noted long before in his publication of similar warrior burials in the Zafer Papoura cemetery at Knossos. Other parallel features are apparent in their possession of gold signet rings which in both instances include ones depicting religious scenes.

Reference has already been made to other parallel features in the account above of Mycenaean aspects at Knossos, in particular the 'burials with bronzes' in which the bronze vessels deposited in both areas have a clear correspondence. Even in pottery, interrelations can now be perceived to have been much stronger than Furumark realised, for example in the adoption at Knossos of the 'Ephyraean' type of kylix, or goblet, and the fondness for large amphoras in the Palace Style. To these can also be added mutual imports of vases; the list of those known is not great (PLATES 10.e and 11.c), but they must have been enough to produce borrowings in shapes and style of decoration in both areas.

Less easy of transport but present in some Mainland burials are stone vases and even lamps of Cretan types and likely manufacture, as Warren pointed out some time ago. They were sufficiently prized to qualify as desirable grave goods there, as they were at Knossos in the same period.

One may suspect that there existed interconnexion in other objects which cannot at present be demonstrated. For instance, distinctly Minoan artistic features can be seen in the gold cups in the Royal Tomb at Dendra, where the offerings included weapons and jewellery of the types considered above. In this case, however, we do not have the contemporary Cretan counterparts with which to compare them.

Other instances of influences, which presuppose intercommunication, could similarly be proposed. Even the characteristic Mycenaean female figurines have been thought perhaps to have had their origin in Cretan prototypes at this time. Enough certain instances, however, have already been listed to demonstrate that relations between Crete and the Mainland (and especially the Argolid) had not become becalmed, as Furumark thought. On the contrary, they evidently continued to be close and productive. Nor are any storm clouds apparent, as far as I can see, to suggest imminent hostility between the two regions, though that remains one of the more likely causes for the destruction at Knossos around 1375 B.C. (late LM IIIA1).

KNOSSOS IN THE 13TH CENTURY (FIG. 2)

Postpalatial Knossos, understandably, received little attention in Evans' monumental *Palace of Minos*, for he sought courageously to present a survey of Minoan civilisation as a whole, centred on his excavations at Knossos, where the finds from the great destruction alone were enough to absorb all the energies of most archaeologists. Moreover, as a stage which he regarded as one of decadence, it

Key to FIG. 2

C	Caravanserai	RV	Royal Villa
H CS	House of the Chancel Screen	SE H	South-East House
H HP	House of the High Priest	SH	South House
LP	Little Palace	SM X	Stratigraphical Museum Excavations
NW H	North-West House	TT	Temple Tomb
RR	Royal Road	UM	Unexplored Mansion

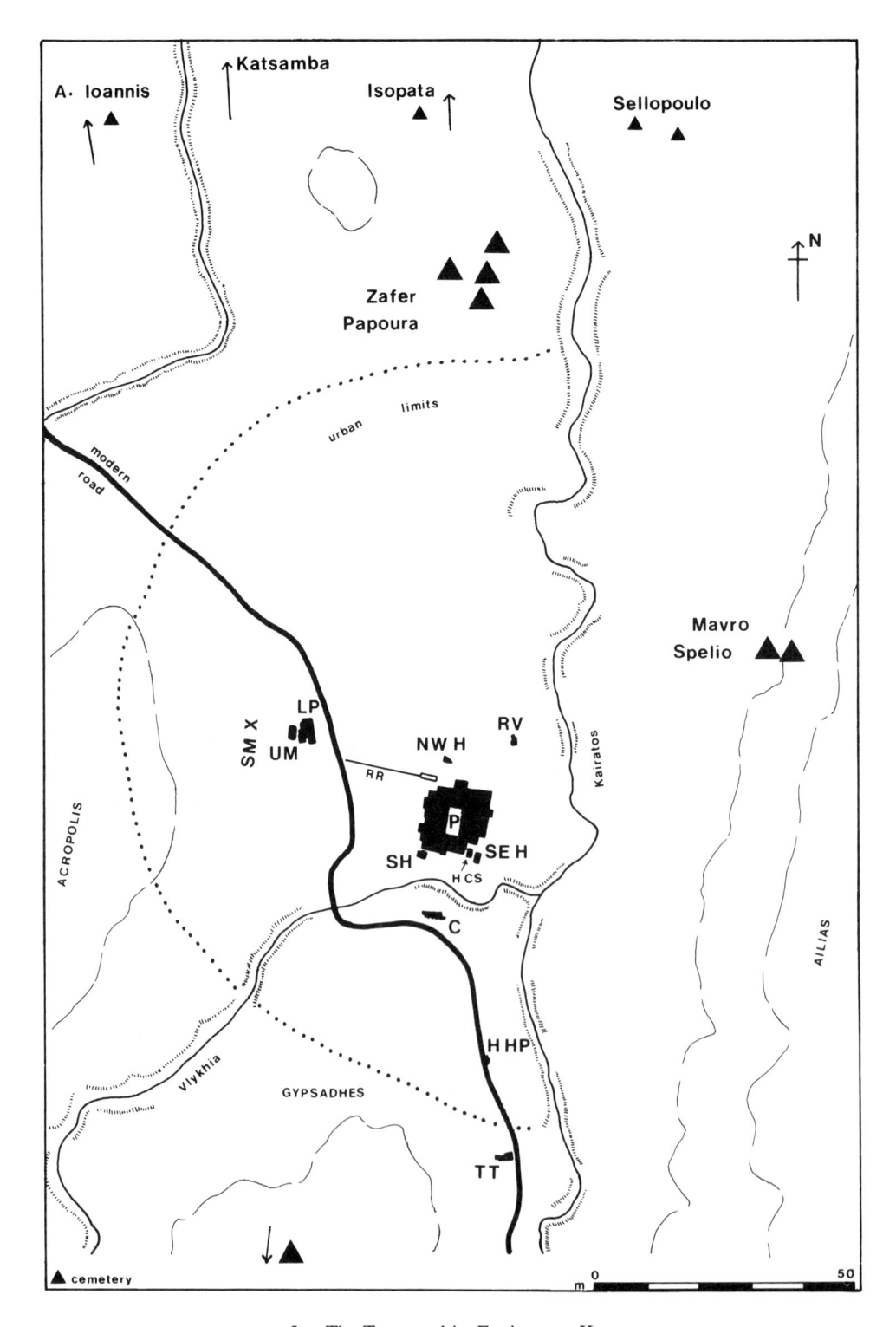

FIG. 2   The Town and its Environs at Knossos

had few attractions. Even so, it was by no means ignored; he considered aspects of the partial 'squatter' reoccupation of the Palace, as he interpreted it, as well as evidence from the Little Palace, particularly that with religious connections.

Moreover, he was impeded, though probably unaware of it, by the failure of his pottery expert, Mackenzie, on whom he greatly relied, to appreciate the character of the pottery in use at the time of the destruction beyond the presence of Palace Style vases and a few other features. At an early stage of the excavations this had led to a wrong ascription of the vases in the Royal Villa to 'the period of partial occupation' and a similar error was made, as I think current research will show, in the case of the Little Palace. Uncertainty on this same point is also apparent in the laudably early publication of the Zafer Papoura cemetery, though, with his acute sense of style, Evans had sensed that some 'debasement' had already occurred.

Definition of the LM IIIB pottery stage, too, was imprecise, perhaps largely because of the rather specialised nature of much of that found in the reoccupied regions of the Palace as well as to the small number of vases of this stage deposited in the cemeteries Evans had explored. This led, for instance, to a concentration on such features as the presence of the plain 'champagne cup' of the type which had been found in numbers in the Shrine of the Double Axes and its neighbourhood, with no apparent realisation that vases of this shape were equally at home much earlier in the LM IIIA stage following the destruction, and possibly introduced even before.

With our present better knowledge of the LM IIIB stage, what can we say of Knossos at that time?

Re-examination of the latest pottery found in the Palace building supports, in the author's opinion, Evans' view of its date when the partial reoccupation there came to an end, seemingly in an abandonment. Its distribution, too, confirms his and Mackenzie's conclusion that some large areas (the West Magazines and Throne Room complex) and other regions (parts of the East Quarter) were not cleared out and used by the reoccupiers, who appear to have lived mostly on the fringes of the building, probably largely for a religious purpose connected, at least in large part, with worship at the Shrine of the Double Axes. The vases of this stage are unusually restricted in range — stirrup jars, curious linked double amphoras, masses of 'champagne cups', while even the mugs are rhyta.

Such reoccupation, for which Evans' term 'squatter' is not quite inappropriate, has been paralleled at the recent excavation of the Unexplored Mansion and may now be suspected too in the case of the neighbouring Little Palace. Any reoccupation of the Royal Villa, North-West House, House of the High Priest and of the Caravanserai must have been minimal, while no pottery of this period was found in the Temple Tomb. So, too, with the somewhat more distant houses on Gypsadhes. Other buildings of this period must, of course, have existed; the so-called 'Machryteichos Kitchen' is an instance, if it is to be dated to this stage and not somewhat earlier. However, recent excavations along the Royal Road and near the Stratigraphical Museum have found surprisingly scant evidence of LM IIIB occupation, even making allowance for destruction by later builders.

Such a uniform picture is most unlikely to be wholly delusory, and it is reflected to some extent in other settlements in central Crete, such as Kommos, Aghia Triadha and Mallia. An apparent similar impoverishment and decrease in population is to be seen, too, in the known cemeteries at Knossos: at Zafer Papoura, for instance, the burials of this stage, though frequently looted, are poor in offerings, with only one weapon known, a knife, which has connexions, if not its origin, in Italy. Few burials can be ascribed to this period at Mavro Spelio and in the Upper Gypsadhes cemetery, and they are poorly furnished.

Where, we may reasonably ask (leaving the Palace aside for the sake of argument) is there any supporting evidence for the belief of some scholars that Knossos was, at this stage, the administrative centre of much of the island, exploiting its resources with a considerable well-armed militia to enforce its control? For such is the situation which would be implied if the Linear B Palace archives had belonged to this period.

Knossos may well have retained some prestige as an old religious centre and may even have retained some influence over neighbouring areas (as will be suggested in the consideration of the role of the Knossos potters), but it is difficult to see how its importance can have been any greater than this in the 13th century.

THE CONTRIBUTION OF THE KNOSSOS POTTERS

It was first in LM IB that a probably quite small group of talented potters established the pre-eminence of Knossian products throughout the island and caused a demand for their works overseas. They created new vase shapes and refined or modified others, while their range of decoration extended far beyond the marine scenes with which they are usually associated. The number of such vases that reached other districts of Crete was small, while their effect on local styles there (as distinct from those on the Mainland) was minimal. Even at Knossos few occur in deposits of this stage, when the great majority remain traditional in shape, technique and decoration, forming Furumark's sub-LM IA style.

Some at least of these potters appear to have survived the upheavals at the end of LM IB and to have worked on into the LM II period. Now, however, they had in part at least to meet the requirements of new patrons or masters with different tastes and preferences, a considerable challenge.

An example of this was the new shape of drinking vessel, the kylix (or stemmed goblet) introduced from the Mainland, where its form and system of decoration were already well established, the so-called Ephyraean goblet (PLATE 8.a–b). The shape was fairly faithfully imitated and its characteristic system of decoration with a single isolated motive adopted for the most part. However, the restricted range of motives used on their Mycenaean prototypes clearly did not satisfy the inclinations of the Knossian potters, who with great inventiveness and ingenuity added schemes of their own, sometimes too exuberantly but, at the best, with stunning effect.

Another demand was to be met by the large, purely decorative, amphora, usually referred to as the Palace Style jar (PLATES 6.a and 9.a–c). It was, of course, no innovation, and indeed is likely to have been a Cretan creation. Though, however, it had previously had only limited appeal on the island, yet the form had greatly attracted the Mycenaeans, perhaps in part because its size and bold decoration made it suitable for furnishing their great tholos tombs. This increased market again stimulated inventiveness, seen in a greatly expanded range of decoration, often in an ornate style appropriate to the size and function of the vase.

To our eyes the more restrained forms of decoration may be the most attractive, such as those which employ a kind of surface pattern, a fine example of which is the early, LM II vase (PLATE 9.a) with its tendrils of ivy leaves. As in other cases, it may be that greatest success was achieved in the subsequent early LM IIIA stage. Then a zonal decoration was employed to emphasise the monumental character of these jars, as, for instance, that on PLATE 9.b, which borrows its main spiral frieze from fresco painting.

This later, LM IIIA1 stage, though essentially a continuation of the LM II process, saw changes and development. The traditional painted drinking vessel, the cup, regains its previous pre-eminence, while decorated kylikes (though not plain ones) are rare. 'Quality control', as we may now call it, in potting greatly improves, accompanied by Knossian innovations both in a wide variety of designs and in shapes. Though generally different in character, the achievements of these potters could be held to match those of their predecessors in LM IB. Certainly their influence in Crete was much greater, in that their style spread to — one might almost say was imposed on — the rest of the island, where it supplanted previous traditions and formed the new basis for later local developments.

Though this early LM IIIA stage retained considerable continuity from LM II, we can perceive a move towards greater abstraction and the formalising of designs, features which were already present. Floral designs may be taken as an example of this.

These, which had especially attracted Cretan potters from the beginning of the Late Bronze Age, continued to be depicted in both naturalistic and more stylised versions, the latter type becoming increasingly dominant. This change in emphasis can be seen in the painting of the frieze of flowers on the LM II and early IIIA cups at PLATE 8.e and f. Successive depictions of the floral spray in particular show this process under way. We have most tantalisingly fragmentary vases of the earlier, more naturalistic LM II stage, though something of its character is apparent on the pyxis at PLATE 10.c. The theme had become more formalised by the time that the cup at PLATE 8.c was painted, on the borderline between LM II and LM IIIA, and is then depicted in a rather lifeless manner on the vase at PLATE 10.d, which belongs to the very end of the early LM IIIA stage or the beginning of the later phase, when naturalism was to die out.

This tendency towards formalism may account for an increasing popularity of abstract patterns, many seemingly derived from textile designs, which are painted in a rich variety of versions. Prominent among them are pendent festoons (such as those on the shoulder of the Palace Style jar illustrated, PLATE 9.b), composed of multiple pendent semicircles, or of tricurved arches, combined with a variety of fill ornament. Versions of the zigzag, too, are a favoured theme, often retaining a connexion with the iris bud motive; it, too, is to persist for a long time in an increasingly lifeless manner. Examples of these, starting in LM II and evolving in early LM IIIA, are shown in PLATES 9.d–f and 11.b–c.

Though subjects from marine life, especially the octopus and fish, more rarely the nautilus, continue to be depicted, albeit in a more formalised way (as in FIG. 3.a–c; PLATE 11.a and d), the Knossian potters turned in LM II to a new subject, birds, presumably borrowed from fresco scenes. Represented in flight or at rest, they usually appear in combination with flowers, more rarely associated with fish, as in the lively and somewhat flamboyant scene on the outstanding jug from Katsambas (PLATE 10.a). Few such intact vases have so far been recovered, but surely among them can be included the Palace Style vase found at Argos; its fill ornament alone proclaims its Cretan origin (PLATE 9.c).

Birds in a more miniature style decorate an LM II pyxis (PLATE 10.c), a vase type frequently associated with this theme, of which another, rather later example, with birds in full flight, was exported to Mycenae (PLATE 10.e). Though the paint of the former is poorly preserved, it clearly anticipates the sadly fragmentary, but outstanding LM IIIA1 cup from the Palace (PLATE 10.c). As in other fields, the subject was losing its interest by the time of the well-known alabastra from Phaistos painted at the end of the stage (compare PLATE 10.a and b), and thereafter appears little until its revival, outside Knossos, in the LM IIIC period.

FIG. 3 Pictorial sherds from LM Knossos. Scale 1:3

New shapes, too, appear at Knossos, particularly in LM IIIA1, markedly so in plain vases, where Mycenaean influences may be playing an important role. The same are likely to be responsible for new versions of the cup, now given a ring base, though the jug with cut-away neck (PLATE 11.a) may be the outcome of Knossian invention. So, too, the evolution of the amphoroid crater and its occasional pictorial representations which, like the fish on PLATE 11.d and the wild goats at FIG. 3.f–g, may have been the inspiration for a whole range of such Mycenaean vases which were to follow.

As we have seen, there were already signs that this initiative on the part of the Knossian potters was beginning to flag shortly before the destruction of Knossos; standards of manufacture were falling and some painting already displays declining interest in the established repertoire. These features are characteristic of the LM IIIA2 stage, and are yet more marked in LM IIIB, by which time the range of decoration at Knossos had become very restricted with little innovation, while traditional motives are simplified (PLATE 12.a) or, like the depictions of flowers and octopus, are symbolic, far removed from reality (PLATE 12.b–e). The contribution of the Knossian potters had already been largely made by establishing a model, which the various regions of the island at first closely imitated (PLATE 11.e–f) and then went on to produce their local versions, outstanding being that which evolved at Chania, sufficiently appreciated at Knossos to be imported in some quantity. However, there persisted in central Crete a degree of LM IIIB uniformity to which Knossian products may still have contributed. All was not stagnation, for the two-handled decorated bowl was introduced as well as a new shape of kylix of pleasing form and appropriately, if somewhat simply, decorated (PLATE 12.c and d respectively). Moreover, it is likely that it was at some centre in this region, though Knossos is not as yet indicated, that craters were being manufactured, which greatly extended their pictorial range beyond the customary octopus.

The role of Knossos in the final LM IIIC stage has still to be learnt. Few burials or extensive occupation deposits are known there from this phase. Initially change seems to have been slow, though later Knossos shared to some extent the innovations found in widely-spread regions of the Aegean and even further afield (PLATE 12.f). But for the major Cretan development — the evolution of the fringed style and the associated close manner of decoration as seen on PLATE 12.g — present evidence, admittedly sparse, points elsewhere, perhaps to east and south Crete, regions whose turn had then come to make their contribution to the final creative stage of Late Minoan pottery.

Further Reading

A.J. Evans' massive volumes of *The Palace of Minos at Knossos* (1921–35), though often cumbersome to use, remain vital reading on such matters as militarism, weaponry and pottery, despite their date and subsequent changes of classification and interpretation.

J.D.S. Pendlebury's *The Archaeology of Crete: an Introduction* (London, 1939), now sadly out of date, has not been adequately replaced and is still a useful summary of knowledge in 1939.

On more specific issues, the importance of the LM II/IIIA warrior burials at Knossos was emphasised by M.S.F. Hood and P. de Jong in their publication of further such burials — 'Late Minoan warrior-graves from Ayios Ioannis and the New Hospital site at Knossos', *BSA* 47 (1952), 243–77; and supplemented in M.S.F. Hood, 'Another warrior-grave at Ayios Ioannis near Knossos', *BSA* 51 (1956), 81–99. In the later publication of other warrior burials at Sellopoulo, the author and H.W. Catling reconsider the evidence of various aspects of such tombs, including the evidence for 'burials with bronzes' and such interrelationships with Mainland practices: 'Sellopoulo tombs 3 and 4, two Late Minoan graves near Knossos', *BSA* 69 (1974), 195–258.

Summaries of LM pottery will be found in P.P. Betancourt, *The History of Minoan Pottery* (Princeton, 1985) and the author's article 'Late Minoan pottery, a summary', *BSA* 62 (1967), 337–51. A. Kanta's *The Late Minoan III Period in Crete: A Survey of Sites, Pottery and their Distribution* (*SIMA* 58; Göteborg, 1970), is especially valuable for its gazetteer of sites and the wealth of illustrated material, much previously unpublished. More specific aspects are considered by the author in several articles: e.g. 'Some Late Minoan III pottery from Crete', *BSA* 60 (1965), 316–42; 'The Late Minoan goblet and kylix', *BSA* 64 (1969), 299–304; 'Late Minoan IIIB pottery from Knossos', *BSA* 65 (1970), 195–202. LM II pottery is discussed in some detail in connexion with the destruction deposits of that date in *The Unexplored Mansion at Knossos* (*BSA* Suppl. 17; London, 1984), 159–81. LM IIIA pottery is a basic constituent of the author's *The Destruction of the Palace at Knossos: Pottery of the Late Minoan IIIA Period* (*SIMA* 12; Göteborg, 1970). Palace Style vases are studied in detail by W.-D. Niemeier in *Die Palaststilkeramik von Knossos: Stil, Chronologie und historischer Kontext* (*Deutsches Arch. Inst., Arch. Forschungen* 13; Berlin, 1985).

Interrelationships between the Mainland and Crete are reviewed in a classic article by A. Furumark, 'The settlement at Ialysos and Aegean history c. 1550–1400 B.C.', *Op. Arch.* 6 (1950), especially 249–54. A basic revision of some of his opinions is given in the publication of the Sellopoulo tombs (see above). The export of stone vases is discussed by P.M. Warren in an article, 'Minoan stone vases as evidence for Minoan foreign connections in the Aegean Late Bronze Age', *PPS* 73 (1967), 37–56, which anticipated his overall account in *Minoan Stone Vases* (Cambridge, 1969).

My contributions have been written in the firm belief that Evans was correct in ascribing the end of the Palace at Knossos to a destruction dating around 1400 B.C. My studies of the pottery and my reading of the dig accounts which led up to the writing of the *Destruction of the Palace at Knossos* (see above) convinced me of this.

However, the reader should be aware that this dating has been challenged, principally by the late Professor L.R. Palmer, who maintained that the final destruction happened some 200 years later, around 1200 B.C., late in LM IIIB. The classic early and detailed account of this dispute will be found in *On the Knossos Tablets* (Oxford, 1963) by L.R. Palmer and J. Boardman, the latter of whom rigorously supports Evans' account and dating. The subsequent immense literature which has accumulated around this issue will be found listed in W.-D. Niemeier (see above) and also generally by J.-P. Olivier in this volume. The dispute still rumbles on, for many unresolved. To the author, apart from other aspects, the later dating would make nonsense of the archaeological picture at Knossos and in Crete overall, a view set forth in an article, 'The historical implications of the Linear B archive at Knossos dating to either c. 1400 B.C. or 1200 B.C.', *Cretan Studies* 1 (1988), 217–27.

PLATE IV   The Way to Silamos - Fig Tree   (etching)

Chapter 7

Urns with Lids:
The Visible Face of the Knossian 'Dark Age'[1]

J.N. COLDSTREAM

To those who have taken part in excavating the town of Knossos, whether in Sinclair Hood's[2] deep trenches in 1957 to 1961 by the Minoan Royal Road,[3] or in the area of the Minoan 'Unexplored Mansion' between 1967 and 1972,[4] or, most recently, in the plot behind the Stratigraphical Museum from 1978 to 1982,[5] a fairly regular stratigraphical pattern will be familiar. Not far below the modern surface the solid and stone-built houses of the Roman town will come to light and will often continue downwards for at least two metres, in several successive levels. Not much lower down, one may well encounter the latest Postpalatial LM III traces of Minoan Knossos. Sandwiched between these two main horizons are the much less substantial remains from the intervening millennium of the Iron Age, from the Subminoan (c.1100–970 B.C.) through the Protogeometric (c.970–810 B.C.), the Geometric (c.810–700 B.C.), the Orientalising (c.700–600 B.C.), the Archaic (c.600–480 B.C.), the Classical (c.480–325 B.C.) and the Hellenistic (c.325–36 B.C.) periods. From the Early Iron Age, with which

---

[1] I am grateful to the Managing Committee of the British School at Athens for permission to illustrate vases from the School's excavations in the North Cemetery of Knossos, in advance of the final publication. My thanks are also due to my wife, Mrs. Nicola Coldstream, who prepared the drawings; the final tracings are the work of Miss Susan Bird, Miss Emma Faull, Mrs. Davina Huxley and Mrs. Diana Wardle.

Abbreviations for the chronological phases of Knossian Protogeometric and Geometric pottery are those of J.K. Brock (n. 9 below), 214.

Measurements are in centimetres unless otherwise stated. H = height; DR = diameter of rim.

[2] It is a pleasure to offer these pages to Sinclair Hood, *doyen* among Minoan archaeologists, and Director of the British School at Athens during my tenure of the School's Macmillan Studentship. As Director of the Knossos excavations from 1957 to 1961 he taught me, like many others, how to dig. The tasks which he assigned to me during those years were all most instructive and rewarding: the sorting of massive deposits of post-Minoan pottery; the clearing of Early Iron Age tombs (none, alas, unplundered!); and the investigation of a site known as 'The Terracottas', in due course identified as the Sanctuary of Demeter.

[3] M.S.F. Hood, 'Archaeology in Greece, 1957', *AR* 4 (1957), 21–2; 'Archaeology in Greece, 1958', *AR* 5 (1958), 19–20; 'Archaeology in Greece, 1959', *AR* 6 (1959–60), 22–4; 'Archaeology in Greece, 1960–61', *AR* 7 (1960–61), 26–7; and 'Archaeology in Greece, 1961–62', *AR* 8 (1961–62), 25–9.

[4] L.H. Sackett *et al.*, *Knossos. From Greek City to Roman Colony. Excavations at the Unexplored Mansion II* (BSA Suppl. 21; London, 1992).

[5] P.M. Warren, 'Knossos: Stratigraphical Museum Excavations, 1978–80. Part I', *AR* 27 (1980–81), 73–92; id., 'Knossos: Stratigraphical Museum Excavations, 1978–82. Part II', *AR* 29 (1982–83), 63–87; and 'Knossos: Stratigraphical Museum Excavations, 1978–82. Part III', *AR* 31 (1984–85), 124–9.

this chapter deals, domestic traces are especially exiguous. Patches of earth floor or fragments of flimsy house walls may sometimes be recovered; but, by and large, our understanding of the Early Iron Age pattern of settlement depends more on isolated pockets of domestic pottery without any architecture, or on domestic deposits in wells.

If traces of the Early Iron Age settlement are somewhat elusive, the cemeteries are much more informative. Thanks to the local custom of using family chamber tombs cut into the rock, their contents are abundant and well preserved. The quality and variety of the tomb offerings demonstrate that Knossos continued to be the most important place in Crete, at least down to the end of the 7th century. We are given the impression that, even in the so-called 'Dark Age', Knossos was an unusually outward-looking place, always in touch with other Aegean centres and even with the Near East. Throughout the period of these tombs, Knossos was one of the leading communities in the Greek world, in the same category as Athens, Corinth, Argos and the cities of Euboea.

The distribution of these tombs, even when compared to the chief centres of the Greek Mainland, is exceptionally wide.[6] Groups of Early Iron Age tombs extend all the way from the inner suburbs of a rapidly expanding modern Herakleion as far inland as the rolling hill country well to the south of Knossos. Thanks to Sinclair Hood's *Archaeological Survey of the Knossos Area*, now in its second edition,[7] the history of the Knossian settlement and of its surrounding cemeteries is now exceptionally well documented over several millennia from Neolithic to Late Roman times. Our FIG. 1 is extrapolated from his *Survey*, showing the location of settlement deposits, cemeteries and sanctuaries through four successive phases of the Early Iron Age. For the most promising source of illumination during these periods, it is to the tombs that we should turn: especially to the tombs of the main North Cemetery, a large part of which was excavated in rescue operations by the British School at Athens between 1975 and 1980.[8]

Whenever a Knossian chamber tomb of the Early Iron Age is found unplundered, its floor may be covered with massed cremation urns crowned with their lids. Often the urns will not only crowd the chamber floor, but will need to have extra space made for them in niches hewn out of the dromos.[9] When the sequence of urns is continuous, they will betoken the steady use of the tomb by many successive generations of the same family. As the final homes of the cremated dead, they will have been made and decorated with unusual care. Small wonder, then, that the urn should have been the leading shape in the Knossian potter's repertoire, its ornament offering much scope for imaginative experiment on a large scale. It is the lids, however, which will have been more immediately visible to any Knossian reopening a family tomb for a new incumbent; by their lids, the urns of various forebears could be most easily recognised. In other places where urn cremation was regularly practised — for example, Athens in the Dark Age, and Thera during the 8th and 7th centuries — there was no regular method of covering the urns.[10] In Crete, at least from the 9th century B.C. onwards,

---

[6] J.N. Coldstream, 'Dorian Knossos and Aristotle's villages', in C. Nicolet (ed.), *Aux origines de l'Hellénisme : la Crète et la Grèce. Hommage à Henri van Effenterre* (Paris, 1986), 312 n. 4.

[7] S. Hood and D. Smyth, *Archaeological Survey of the Knossos Area* (2nd. edn.; *BSA* Suppl. 14; London, 1981).

[8] See n. 20 below.

[9] See J.K. Brock, *Fortetsa: Early Greek Tombs near Knossos* (*BSA* Suppl. 2; Cambridge, 1957), pl. 159, tomb II.

[10] Athenian urns, when covered, may be stopped by a large stone, or a bronze bowl, or a skyphos: see J.N. Coldstream, *Geometric Greece* (London, 1977), 31–2, figs. 3–4, and p. 81. For Thera: J. Boardman and D.C. Kurtz, *Greek Burial Customs* (London, 1971), 177 ff., fig. 33.

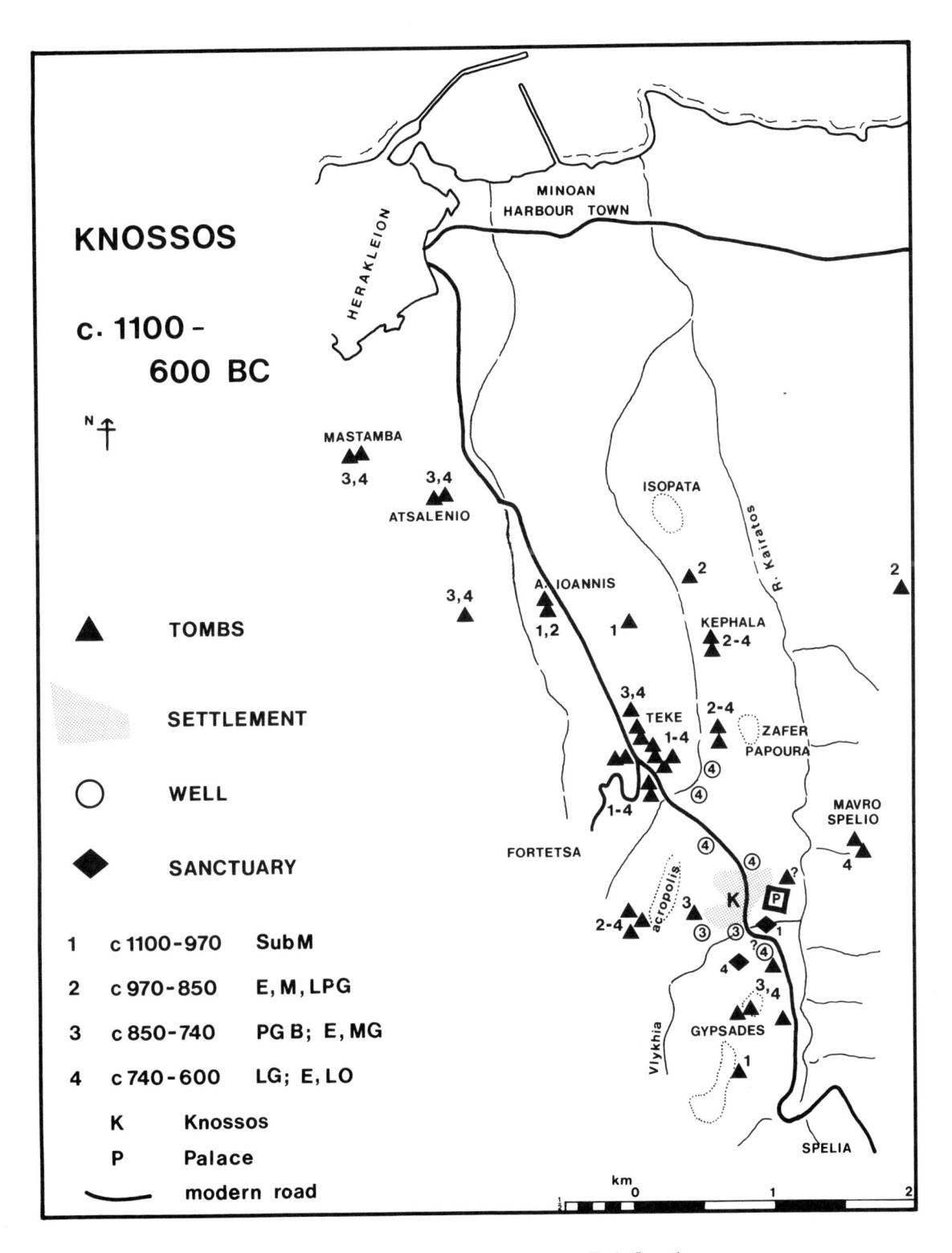

FIG. 1   Knossos: settlement pattern in the Early Iron Age

lids were often specially made to match the urns, decorated in an equally ornate style. Their forms reflect passing fashions, dictated sometimes by foreign connexions and sometimes by religious concerns. These lids, then, will form an important theme in this paper, as we follow the fortunes of Knossos through the Early Iron Age.

Both the construction of these rock-cut family chamber tombs and their reuse over many generations help to evoke one of the most settled societies of the Early Iron Age anywhere in the Aegean world, confident of the future, and also conservative of the past, the forms of the tombs being directly inherited from the LM III period. This is but one aspect of that unusually smooth continuity in the record of Knossos at the turn from the Bronze to the Iron Age and all through the so-called Dark Age. While the chief centres on the Greek Mainland seem to have become fragmented into small hamlets, Knossos is one of the few places in the Aegean to have preserved an urban nucleus from Minoan times — to judge from the many soundings in the central area where Subminoan (SM) pottery has been found directly above that of LM IIIC.[11] Religious continuity, too, is apparent in the persistence of a vegetation cult in the Spring Chamber by the Vlykhia stream,[12] the public sanctuary of the SM town; this shrine was eventually succeeded by the sanctuary of Demeter, a little way up the Gypsadhes hill, which was already receiving votives in the 8th century.[13] To some extent, however, these aspects of continuity at Knossos have been obscured by the massive overlay of later periods, down to Roman times. Of the Early Iron Age houses of Knossos, only exiguous traces of walls and floors have been recovered. In their domestic dwellings and religious cults the conservatism and continuity in Cretan tradition can now be much better documented in remoter and less encumbered places on the island — for example, in the settlements of the Kavousi region[14] and, for cult practices, in the great mountain sanctuary of Kato Symi.[15] For complete continuity in burials, however, the record of Knossos is unrivalled in Crete, in quality as in quantity.

Continuity, of course, does not exclude change. At some time near the transition between the Bronze and Iron Ages, Knossos must have passed under the control of Greeks speaking the Doric dialect. Although the first Dorians in Crete are archaeologically almost as elusive as on the Greek Mainland, there are two changes which could tentatively be connected with their coming to Knossos. The 'house' model from the Spring Chamber, enclosing the figure of a goddess, hints at a possible change in religious belief. Previous Minoan models of this type do not contain such figures.[16] Furthermore, unlike Minoan deities of vegetation, it seems that the goddess of this model is portrayed as residing in the Underworld; for the more explicit imagery of the 9th-century model in the Giamalakis collection,[17] apparently showing mortals upon its roof in the world above, suggests that

---

[11] Coldstream (n. 6 above), 314–17 n. 15, fig. 1.

[12] *PM II.i*, 128 ff.; J.N. Coldstream, 'A Protogeometric nature goddess from Knossos', *BICS* 31 (1984), 100 ff., and J.N. Coldstream *et al.*, *Knossos: the Sanctuary of Demeter* (BSA Suppl. 8; Oxford, 1973), 181 ff.

[13] Coldstream *et al.* (n. 12 above), 18–22 (pottery); 56–8, 89–90 (terracottas).

[14] Most recently, see G.C. Gesell, W.D.E. Coulson and L.P. Day, 'Excavations at Kavousi, Crete, 1988', *Hesperia* 60 (1991), 145–77.

[15] Most recently, see A. Lembesi, ''Ιερὸ Ἑρμῆ καὶ Ἀφροδίτης στη Σύμη Βιάννου', *PAE* 1987, 269–89; A. Lembesi and P. Muhly, 'The sanctuary of Hermes and Aphrodite at Syme, Crete', *National Geographic Research* 3 (1987), 102 ff.

[16] C. Mavriyannaki, 'Modellini fittili di costruzioni circolari dalla Creta minoica', *SMEA* 15 (1972), 161–70.

[17] Most recently, see I. Sakellarakis, ''Αρχαιολογικὴ ἔρευνα γιὰ μία ἀρχαιοκαπηλία τὸ 1949 στὴν Κρήτη', in *Φίλια Ἔπη εἰς Γεώργιον Ε. Μυλωνᾶν* 2 (Bibl. Arch. Et. 103; Athens, 1987), 37–70.

the goddesses in both models were envisaged as being in Hades during the winter months, like the Dorian Persephone. This hypothesis, which rests upon one[18] of several different interpretations of the Giamalakis model, would make the Dorian Sanctuary of Demeter the natural successor to the vegetation cult practised in the Spring Chamber. The coming of the Dorians may also have left its mark in the cemeteries. Even though the sequence of burials is continuous, in no single tomb does an SM burial follow directly after one of LM IIIC.[19] At the outset of the SM period, then, we have a sharp break, a caesura, in the use of individual tombs, which would be consistent with the arrival of newcomers taking over some of the local collective tombs no longer in use.

This break coincides with the beginning of the North Cemetery, a large part of which was cleared in rescue excavations by the British School between 1975 and 1980.[20] This was destined to become the main cemetery of Knossos throughout the Early Iron Age; whether it was entirely free of previous Minoan burials is a question on which differing views are possible. Of the various forms of the SM tombs there[21] — chamber tombs, shaft graves, and small caves opening off deep pits — none is alien to Knossos, each one having precedents in the LM III cemetery at Zafer Papoura.[22] What is new is the first sign of a change in burial rite. Whereas inhumation, as in LM III times, still remained the general rule,[23] the pit caves of the North Cemetery contained the earliest known cremations at Knossos: to judge from their gear, evidently the cremations of warriors.[24] The new rite can hardly have been introduced by Dorian newcomers, since precedents for it occur in eastern Crete well back in LM IIIC.[25]

The ashes of these cremated warriors were found loosely scattered over the tomb floor; but well within the SM period, some thought was given to housing cremated remains within a vessel. To begin with, the urn took the form of a coarse and heavy necked pithos some 40 cms. high (e.g. PLATE 13.a);[26] such pithoi might serve as urns through much of the PG period, although bell kraters and even bronze cauldrons could be used as rarer alternatives.[27] Clearly, orthodoxy in urn forms, at this stage, was not yet thought important.

---

[18] J.N. Coldstream, *Deities in Aegean Art before and after the Dark Age* (Bedford College, London, 1977), 10; id. (n. 12 above), 31 (1984), 100–1.; id., 'Some Minoan reflexions in Cretan Geometric art', in J.H. Betts, J.R. Green and J.T.H. Hooker (eds.), *Studies in Honour of T.B.L. Webster 2* (Bristol, 1988), 24.

[19] Coldstream (n. 6 above), 317.

[20] Preliminary reports: H.W. Catling, 'The Knossos area, 1974–1976', *AR* 23 (1976–77), 11–17, for the Teke group excavated in 1975–76; 'Knossos, 1978', *AR* 25 (1978–79) 43–58, for the main group excavated in 1978–9 on the site of the Medical Faculty of the University of Crete. Tombs on that site (KMF in Knossian records) are given in arabic numerals; those in the Teke group are designated by letters. The full publication will appear as *Knossos, the North Cemetery: Early Greek Tombs*, a forthcoming BSA Supplementary volume.

[21] Catling (n. 20 above — 1978–79), 45 ff.

[22] A.J. Evans, 'The prehistoric tombs of Knossos', *Archaeologia* 59 (1906), figs. 44, 51 (chambers), 79 (cave), 52–3 (shaft).

[23] As also in the SM burials in reused LM tombs in outlying areas of Knossos: Upper Gypsadhes, S. Hood, G. Huxley and N. Sandars, 'A Minoan cemetery on Upper Gypsades', *BSA* 53–4 (1958–9), 205–8, pls. 56–7, tombs VI and VII; and Aghios Ioannis, M.S.F. Hood and J.N. Coldstream, 'A Late Minoan tomb at Ayios Ioannis near Knossos', *BSA* 63 (1968), 209–12, pl. 52.

[24] Catling (n. 20 above — 1978–79), 46.

[25] e.g. the two LM IIIC pyxis-urns at Kritsa, see A. Kanta, *The Late Minoan III Period in Crete: A Survey of Sites, Pottery and their Distribution* (SIMA 58; Göteborg, 1980), 134, 138, fig. 54.4–5.

[26] References to pottery from the North Cemetery give the tomb number (see n. 20 above) followed by the catalogue number within the tomb. The coarse pithos-urn illustrated here is 258.58, EPG: H 42.2, DR 28. The earliest known urn cremation at Knossos is in a similar vessel found in tomb 2, well back in SM.

[27] e.g. Brock (n. 9 above), 18 and no. 159 (bell krater), no. 190 (bronze cauldron).

In Athens, meanwhile, urn cremation had been practised since the beginning of the Attic PG period, of which the earlier phases are contemporary with the later part of SM in Crete. The Attic urns took the form of large amphorae with finely painted circular decoration, neatly executed with compass and multiple brush, made specially for funerary use. In that orderly and 'rather regimented' society[28] there was even a distinction between the urns for men and women: neck-handled amphorae for men, belly-handled for women.

The impact of Athenian ceramic influence at a late stage of the Attic PG style defines the beginning of the Knossian PG period. In the North Cemetery, exports to Knossos of Attic PG pottery were much more plentiful than previous finds had led us to suppose. In the unplundered Teke tomb J, for example, Attic PG ware comprises approximately half of the total pottery finds, including a set of twenty-two drinking cups, three large skyphoi, an oinochoe and a small amphora.[29] In forming their own PG style under Attic influence, Knossian potters were characteristically eclectic. They quickly mastered the technique of compass-drawn concentric circles and imitated several Attic shapes, including the two types of Attic cremation amphora. These local amphorae, however, were never used as urns in the Knossian tombs; their funerary function there will be explored later. Instead, the local potters transformed their own urn, the coarse necked pithos, into a more elegant form with painted decoration, usually consisting of the fashionable Atticising circles (e.g. FIGS. 2 and 3).[30] Painted urns of this type continue at Knossos until the end of the 9th century, long after Athenian potters had converted to their rectilinear Geometric style.

Evidence for covering these early urns is understandably scanty since, even in intact tombs, constant reopening for later burials allowed very few of them to survive *in situ*. It seems, however, that the Knossians at first chose a local shape, the kalathos, to serve as lid; its concave profile (PLATE 13.b)[31] could effectively cover any rim diameter of urn. The bases of earlier PG kalathoi, designed as clay baskets rather than as urn lids, are rough and unpainted; even so, one of them was found on a small PG pyxis-urn in the Fortetsa group (no. 134), raising the possibility that earlier urns might have been protected by wicker baskets. But by the early 9th century one class of kalathos, smaller and shallower, was consciously designed as an urn lid; the base — or knob as it now became — now bears painted decoration, a Maltese cross or the like.[32]

The Knossians were slow to convert from inhumation to cremation, a process begun before the end of the 11th century but not complete until the middle of the 9th. Then it was that a new and lavishly decorated type of urn was evolved for the richer tombs, tall and straight-sided, and equipped for the first time with a lid carefully fitted over its vertical lip, and often echoing its ornament. Their style represents an astonishing break with the restraint of previous PG decoration; the novelty lies in the profusion of spirals, cables, arcs and other free-hand curvilinear ornament spreading all over the surface, unique for this time in the Aegean world, and derived partly from a resurgence of the Minoan spirit. These showy urns were made for approximately two generations (*c*.850–800 B.C.) correspond-

---

[28] V.R. Desborough, *The Greek Dark Ages* (London, 1972), 158.

[29] Catling (n. 20 above — 1976–77), 12–14, fig. 30.

[30] FIGS. 2 and 3 show the beginning and end of the main PG series at Knossos: first, 48.3 (H 34.8, DR *c*.22), is early EPG, displaying a very cautious use of only single circles; later, in LPG, comes O 37 (H 38.5, DR *c*.20).

[31] J 37: H 14.2, D 31.

[32] e.g. Brock (n. 9 above), no. 418 (PG).

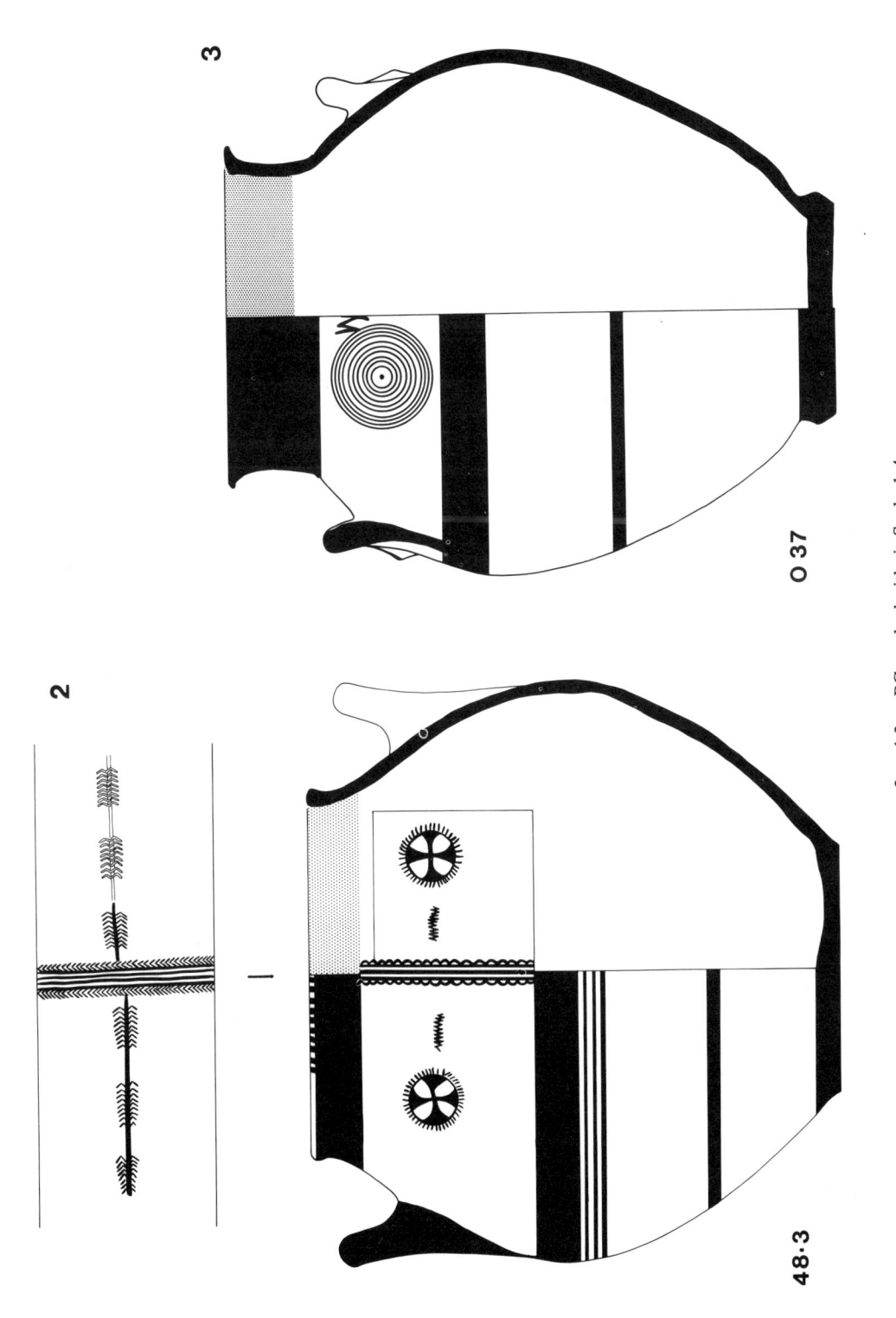

URNS WITH LIDS: THE VISIBLE FACE OF THE KNOSSIAN 'DARK AGE'

FIGS. 2 and 3   PG necked pithoi. Scale 1:4

ing to the PGB and EG phases, of which the former still preserves some PG elements, whereas EG more regularly borrows ideas from Attic Geometric and combines them with a heady mixture of local and Near Eastern motifs.

One painter of these straight-sided pithos-urns, working in the PGB phase, organised his spirals into schematic trees, upon which birds perch and open their throats in song. His most ambitious work, which also portrays fish under the handles and a majestic goddess of nature in each of the main fields,[33] is sadly fragmentary and lacks its lid. Happily lids survive for two other works from his hand, on which birds and trees fill the main fields (FIGS. 4 and 5; PLATE 13.c and d).[34] Their lids, tall, elegant, and as floridly decorated as their urns, are crowned by a conical finial knob, recalling skilled woodwork. This notion derives from a smaller and contemporary lidded vessel known to have been imported to Knossos, the Attic MG I pyxis.[35] Attic, too, is the origin of the idea behind the more elaborate knobs on the huge and much steeper lids for the EG straight-sided urns, knobs taking the form of miniature vessels;[36] but the Knossian potter, with his usual eclecticism, chose for his miniatures shapes which are not Attic, but local. A vast lid, for which the urn does not survive, has as its knob a miniature of the straight-sided urn (PLATE 14.a).[37] A local type of lekythos crowns the lid of the straight-sided urn in Teke G (PLATE 14.b),[38] an aristocratic tomb packed with urns and other vessels of exceptionally large size and unusually ornate decoration — clearly the tomb of a leading family for whom Knossian potters were commissioned to make exceptionally strenuous efforts.

These straight-sided urns with their towering lids, which must have been most conspicuous in their tombs, were clearly made for an elite. More modest cremations were still housed in the smaller and more conservative necked urns like those in FIG. 3, with PG concentric circle decoration. Admittedly, offerings for individual incumbents in chamber tombs cannot often be distinguished with confidence; but, more generally, the tombs containing the more ornate straight-sided urns tend also to be rich in metal offerings, the most constant index of wealth in the Early Iron Age. Concerning the tombs in which they occur, two points are of especial interest: they house the earliest cremations in their respective tombs, and the form of the tombs is often remarkably like that of the chamber tombs of LM III. Once again, we have a caesura in the use of tombs, less complete than at the transition from LM III to SM, but nevertheless suggestive of a new interest in the Minoan past. Around 850 B.C. nine of the Fortetsa tombs received their last incumbents, and then six more came into use.[39] Further north, the Aghios Ioannis group was abandoned altogether.[40] In the North Cemetery about thirty tombs were in use during the main PG sequence from the early 10th century until the middle of the 9th. Then, near the change from LPG to PGB, only ten continued to receive incumbents — although

---

[33] Coldstream (n. 12 above), 93 ff.
[34] PLATE 13.c and d; and FIG. 4 — 283.11 (urn) with 31 (lid): Coldstream (n. 12 above), 95 n. 31, pl. 8. FIG. 5 — 292.144 (urn) with 61 (lid): id. (n. 18 above — 1988), 26 n. 34, fig. 2.1.
[35] Cf. the Attic MG I pyxides, as in J.N. Coldstream, *Greek Geometric Pottery: A Survey of Ten Local Styles and Their Chronology* (London, 1968), pl. 3f–h. Two of these were found in the North Cemetery; also two MG I pointed pyxides with lids, also with finial knobs.
[36] Cf. ibid., pl. 4e; also the Attic krater in tomb 219, (n. 61 below).
[37] 107.138: H 30.5, D 23.5.
[38] Urn, G 6: H 58.5, DR 22.5. Lid, G 7: H 43, D 37. On the excavation of Teke G, see n. 45 below.
[39] Coldstream (n. 10 above), 99 ff. nn. 57–8.
[40] J. Boardman, 'Protogeometric graves at Agios Ioannis near Knossos (Knossos Survey 3)', *BSA* 55 (1960), 142 ff.

FIG. 4   PGB pithos 283.11. Scale 1:4

some others were reused at a much later period. At the same time, sixteen more tombs came into use, including some of the very richest. These include tombs 75 and 107, remarkable for the long dromoi with level floor, leading to well-cut chambers which are more spacious than what is needed for a succession of urn cremations.[41]

Furthermore, tomb 107 produced substantial parts of two LM III larnakes, one plain, the other with figured decoration of exceptional interest[42] including female figures, birds and trees; this could have supplied the inspiration for our PGB painter of trees when he was commissioned to make his straight-sided urn with the nature goddess for the same family tomb.[43] Some pieces of the figured larnax also

---

[41] Catling (n. 20 above — 1978–79), 50, fig. 23 (tomb 107).
[42] L. Morgan, 'A Minoan larnax from Knossos', *BSA* 82 (1987), 171–200.
[43] Coldstream (n. 12 above), 99 ff. n. 52.

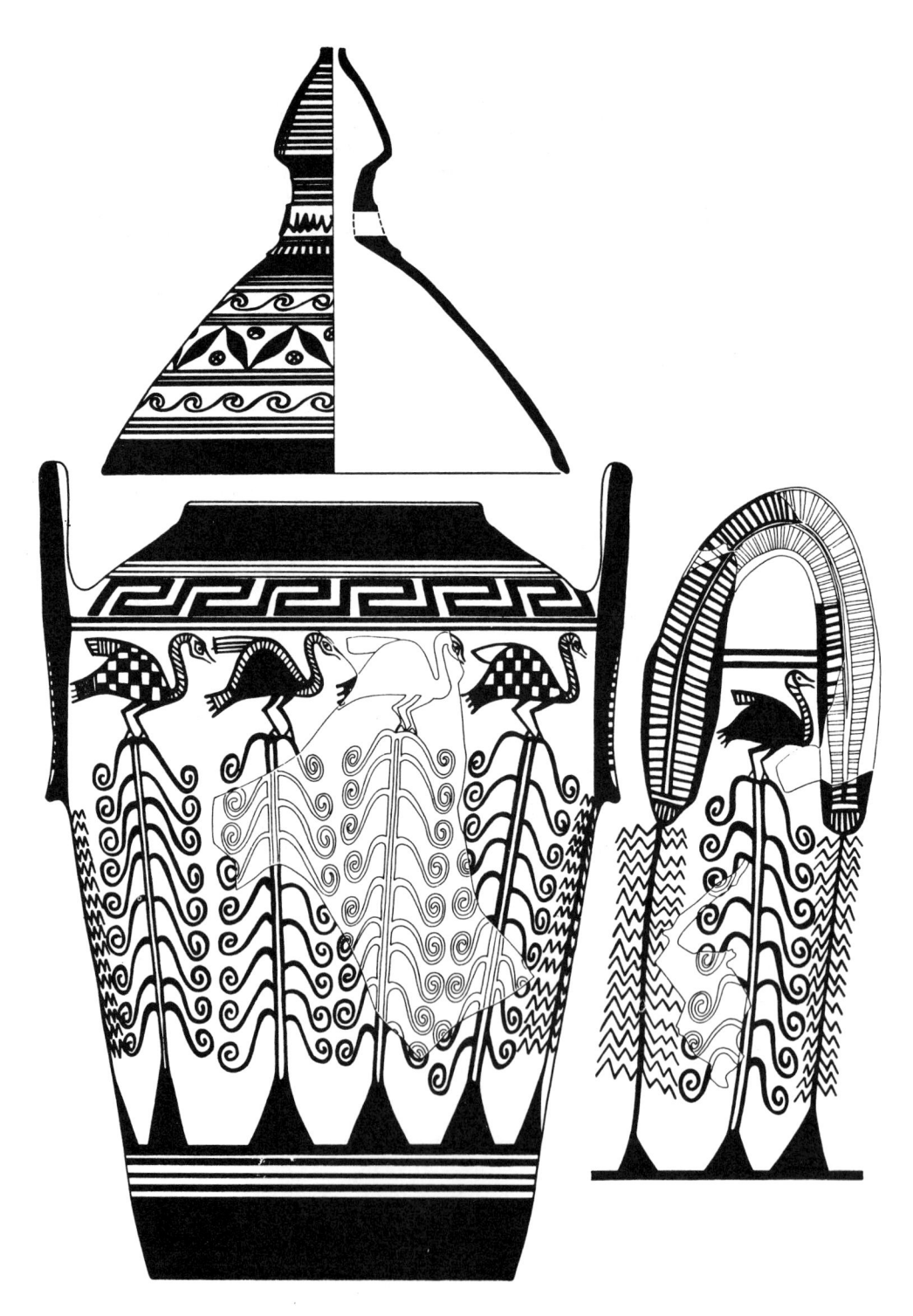

FIG. 5   PGB pithos 292.144, with lid 61. Scale 1:4

turned up in the dromos of the neighbouring tomb, no. 75. Both tombs were destined to receive more incumbents for at least six generations, well into the 7th century; in tomb 107, room had to be found for the later generations in niches and alcoves carved out of its long dromos.[44] The richest tombs in the Teke group, G and Q, also have Minoan affinities. From the chamber of G, excavated by Professor N. Platon,[45] came a fragmentary oval-mouthed jar of LM II (PLATE 14.c)[46] among a splendid corpus of late 9th-century pottery (including PLATE 14.a) and other finds. In Teke Q the dromos could not be fully cleared since it passed under a modern house; but at the stomion it is deep and level, and so must have been long. In a well-cut alcove opening off it the base of an LM III larnax was found *in situ*; in the rest of the tomb most of its long sides were recovered, decorated with papyrus flowers with spiral leaves.[47]

Altogether, remains of fifteen LM III larnakes were found in the North Cemetery excavations. Not all occurred in tombs of Minoan character: one, for example, came from a pit only one metre long, together with a smashed urn of the early 8th century.[48] The important point here is that none of the larnakes came to light in a context before the PGB phase of the later 9th century. The mystery of the larnakes offers a possible explanation for the caesura in the use of many tombs around 850 B.C. Then, at a time of rising prosperity, let us suppose that some leading Knossian families wished to associate themselves more closely with their Minoan predecessors, either by hewing out of the rock convincing imitations of LM III tombs and bringing in the larnakes from elsewhere, or by opening and reusing actual LM III tombs. Personally I prefer the second alternative,[49] even if some larnakes were found in tombs of obviously post-Minoan type, and even if the reusers often — though not always[50] — methodically cleared the chambers of the Minoan burials and their more movable goods. But if 75 and 107 were indeed reused LM III tombs, it follows that the SM warriors cremated in the pit caves were not inaugurating a wholly new cemetery but reviving the use of one already known. The idea of reusing LM III chamber tombs was not, of course, new in PGB; we know, for example, of LM tombs in the outlying burial grounds of Upper Gypsadhes and Aghios Ioannis receiving SM inhumations after an interval of disuse.[51] There, however, the reuse did not entail the clearance of earlier burials, as happened from PGB onwards. We seem to be witnessing two contrasting attitudes towards Minoan precedent: in the SM period, an effort to preserve existing customs, still with inhumation — perhaps in times of trouble and disturbance; later, the 9th-century users attempted a more conscious revival, completely clearing and taking over the Minoan tombs, spacious enough for many future generations of urn cremations.

The apogee of the ornate lid in the later 9th century coincides with one of the most exuberant phases of Knossian vase-painting, drawing on several sources of inspiration at the same time: the local PG tradition, neo-Minoan fantasy, free curvilinear motifs from oriental ivory and metalwork and,

---

[44] See n. 41 above.
[45] On the excavation of Teke G, see J.N. Coldstream, '"Bilingual" Geometric amphorae from the North Cemetery of Knossos', in ΕΙΛΑΠΙΝΗ. Τόμος Τιμητικὸς γιὰ τὸν Καθηγητὴ Νικόλαο Πλάτωνα (Herakleion, 1987), 336.
[46] G 37: H as restored 21.5.
[47] Catling (n. 20 above — 1976–77), 17, fig. 36.
[48] In tomb 85.
[49] For discussion, see Brock (n. 9 above), 4 ff.; Boardman (n. 40 above), 143.
[50] See n. 46 above.
[51] See n. 23 above.

to a lesser extent, the more austere rectilinear ornament of Attic Geometric. After 800 B.C. it was the Attic element that prevailed. It was possibly under Attic influence that a new, ovoid, type of urn was introduced, with a matching lid precisely fitting its inset lip. One of the earliest is in fact an Attic import,[52] even though the shape was only rarely used for Attic cremations in preference to the two traditional types of amphora. At all events, the ovoid urn was to become the normal form at Knossos for the next two centuries. An early lid for this class (FIG. 6)[53] still keeps the steep gradient and florid ornament of PGB and EG, but the motifs are now rectilinear and Attic, and the ribs below the finial are also of Attic origin.[54] In the Knossian MG phase both urn and lid settle down to a standardised form, still quite exuberantly decorated, but with the Attic meander much in evidence (PLATE 14.d).[55] The bulky urn often needs four handles to ease transport, while the lid became less steep and obtrusive, continuing the gentle gradient of the vessel's shoulder, and the finial is often replaced by a more practical knob with ribs below. No new impulse enlivens the monotonous and stereotyped ornament of most LG urns, on which the decorated area contracts: it often disappears altogether from the lids, which now have plain conical knobs (PLATE 15.a).[56] The old exuberance survives only in the output of the Bird Workshop[57] which, to judge from the quality and complexity of their decoration, produced urns for the elite; their lids sometimes sprout neat miniature vases on the knob which, like the oinochoe on FIG. 7,[58] are Attic in shape[59] as in notion.

The Attic connexion, so strong especially in the MG phase, cannot be explained merely through casual trade or even through local appreciation of Attic ceramic quality. In the North Cemetery alone, approximately one hundred Attic vessels were discovered, chiefly of the Attic LPG and MG phases. They form by far the largest group of imports, amounting to some three per cent of the total corpus. The range of shapes is unusually wide, including some which are rarely exported elsewhere, such as PG kraters and kalathoi[60] and MG pyxides. Of especial note, though for the most part very fragmentary, are fourteen finely decorated belly-handled amphorae, which in Athens would have been suitable as urns for female cremations. These form a continuous sequence from the 10th century until the early 8th, culminating in a vast MG II amphora over a metre high. This vessel, large enough to serve as a grave marker in Athens, was found in the extremely rich tomb 219 together with a lidded krater and a large flat pyxis, all three from the same Attic workshop, and possibly forming part of a gift exchange between leading families in Athens and Knossos.[61] As long as they were imported,

---

[52] Brock (n. 9 above), no. 454; Coldstream (n. 35 above), 240 n. 2.

[53] 100.53: H 25, D *c*.25.5.

[54] Cf. Coldstream (n. 35 above), pl. 3g.

[55] From an outlying tomb on Gypsadhes hill: J.N. Coldstream, P. Callaghan and J.H. Musgrave, 'Knossos: an Early Greek tomb on Lower Gypsadhes hill', *BSA* 76 (1981), 151, no. 58, pl. 21.

[56] Brock (n. 9 above), no. 824; Coldstream (n. 35 above), pl. 54f.

[57] Brock (n. 9 above), 149, under IVB; on the dating, Coldstream (n. 35 above), 246–9.

[58] 292.65: H 20.4, D 23.5.

[59] e.g. Brock (n. 9 above), no. 1047, neck-handled amphora on the lid.

[60] Attic PG kalathos: J.N. Coldstream, 'Knossos: an urban nucleus in the Dark Age?', in D. Musti *et al.* (eds.), *La Transizione dal Miceneo all' Alto Arcaismo; dal Palazzo alla Città. Atti del Convegno Internazionale, Roma ... 1988* (*Monografie Scientifiche, Serie Scienze Umane e Sociali*; Rome, 1991), 294, fig. 7.

[61] J.N. Coldstream, 'Gift exchange in the 8th century B.C.', in R. Hägg (ed.), *The Greek Renaissance of the 8th century BC: Tradition and Innovation. Proceedings of the Second International Symposium at the Swedish Institute in Athens ... 1981* (*Skrifter ... Svenska Inst. i Athen*, 4°, 30; Stockholm, 1983), 204 ff., figs. 1–5.

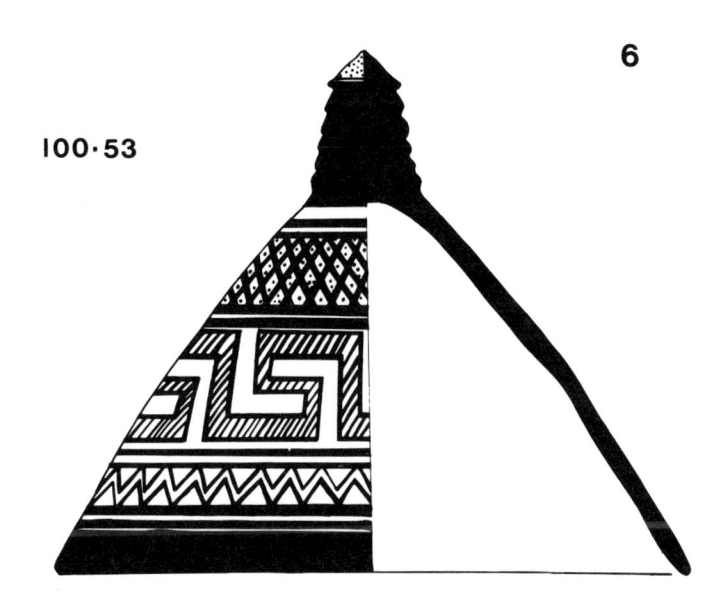

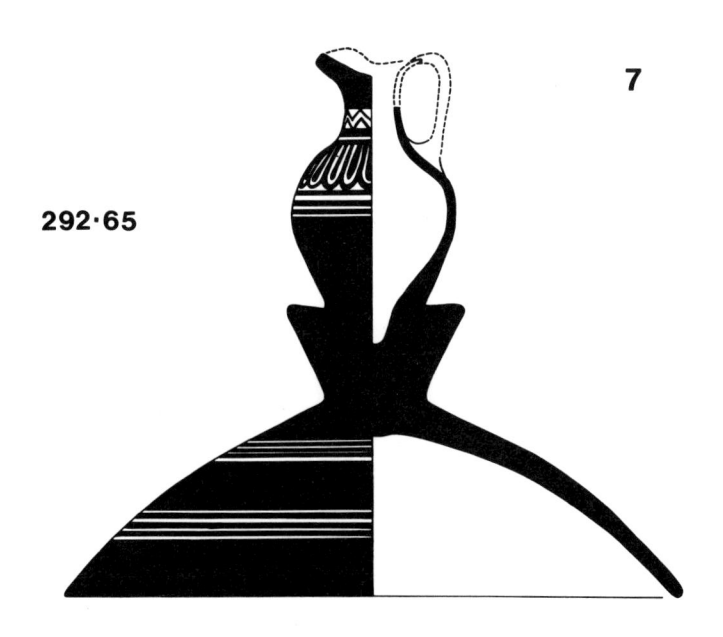

URNS WITH LIDS: THE VISIBLE FACE OF THE KNOSSIAN 'DARK AGE'   117

FIGS. 6 and 7   Conical lids. Scale 1:3

these amphorae gave rise to local imitations, on which Cretan fantasy was sometimes given full play.[62] If they never served the Knossians as urns, what was their funerary function? The Attic imports also include copious sets of drinking vessels: the PG set in Teke J has already been mentioned,[63] and there are also nine Attic MG I cups in Teke G. Similar sets, in local fabric and shapes, have been recovered from other intact tombs: from no. 285, for example, came a huge MPG bell krater in which six oinochoai and thirteen bell-skyphoi had been neatly stacked.[64] Knossos shared with Athens the habit of a funerary symposium at a cremation — with the difference that, whereas the Athenians often smashed their drinking vessels on the pyre,[65] the Knossians preferred to place their crockery intact within a tomb. The amphorae, then, whether Attic or local, will have contained the wine for these farewell parties. Their function thus invited fine decoration since, like the urns for the deceased, they will have been on show at the funeral. They were spectacular symbols of the bereaved family's wealth and status. If imported from Athens, they would also advertise the family's foreign connections, at a time when Knossos was a remarkably outward-looking place.

From the late 9th century onwards, contacts with the eastern Mediterranean were also becoming frequent. Pottery imports from that direction, which form about one per cent of the total aggregate in the North Cemetery, are usually slow-pouring shapes suitable for precious unguents. These begin with a few vessels from the Phoenician homeland and continue more abundantly with small Cypro-Phoenician juglets in Black-on-Red ware.[66] But the eastern prospectors came not only as visitors, but as residents too; for the local copies of these juglets are close and numerous enough to imply the establishment of an unguent factory at Knossos, staffed by eastern merchants employing local potters for the bottling of their produce.[67] Another category of oriental resident, one who had a more profound impact on the course of Cretan pictorial art, was the master-craftsman in metal: initially, the goldsmith detected by Boardman[68] as the first incumbent in the reused Minoan tholos tomb of Teke, near the northern edge of the North Cemetery; then, the bronzesmiths responsible for setting up the wholly oriental style and iconography of the first votive shields offered to the young Zeus in his cave sanctuary high up on the flank of Mount Ida.[69] Related to these shields, and echoing their shape, is a new class of lid for the urns, offering a more ornate alternative to the purpose-built lids as they tended to become increasingly plain (e.g. PLATE 15.a) and standardised. But before these clay 'shields' had become widely current, we have a strange lid of oriental character, ancestral to another form of Cretan Orientalising art, the coarse pithos with stamped relief figure decoration.

Tomb 100 in the North Cemetery was so thoroughly disturbed that nothing remained *in situ* except for some small finds; but their quality suggested a wealthy family, and from the copious pottery fragments 79 vessels could be distinguished. These are consistently of the 9th century, the latest being the EG lid (FIG. 6) with its poorly preserved urn. The only other traceable urns were three

---

[62] Coldstream (n. 45 above), 335 ff., pl. 20.
[63] Catling (n. 29 above).
[64] For similar sets, see Brock (n. 9 above), 161, under Small Kraters B(ii).
[65] e.g. the EG I Boot grave: R.S. Young, 'An Early Geometric grave near the Athenian Agora', *Hesperia* 18 (1949), 275-97; Coldstream (n. 10 above), 30.
[66] J.N. Coldstream, 'Cypriaca and Cretocypriaca from the North Cemetery of Knossos', *RDAC* 1984, 122-37.
[67] Ibid. 137.
[68] J. Boardman, 'The Khaniale Tekke tombs, II', *BSA* 62 (1967), 57-64.
[69] T.J. Dunbabin, *The Greeks and Their Eastern Neighbours* (*JHS* Suppl. 8; London, 1957), 40 ff.; Coldstream (n. 10 above), 287 ff.

fragmentary coarse pithoi like PLATE 13.a, one of which was provided with an extraordinary flat lid in the same coarse fabric (PLATE 15.b and c).[70] It bears eight passant sphinxes, executed with the same horseshoe-shaped stamp. Their helmets, straight wings and raised forepaws all have Near Eastern precedents, but their equine bodies and tails already suggest some artistic cross fertilization with the favourite quadruped of the Aegean Early Iron Age.

The domed lids, in spite of many transformations of shape during the 8th century, always maintain the appearance of shields with offset rims. Overt resemblance to the Idaean bronze votives is closest in the early stage (EG), when the dome resembles an umbilical boss or omphalos (FIG. 8).[71] Alternatively, the central boss may sometimes take the form of an animal's head.[72] Thereafter, mainly in MG, the domed top spreads out at the expense of the offset rim (FIG. 9; PLATE 16.a).[73] In contrast to the dark ground and rectilinear austerity in the decoration of the contemporary urns (as PLATE 14.d), the painters of these early 8th-century lids remained cheerfully free of any Atticising tendencies, usually applying free curvilinear motifs of PGB character, still on a light ground. This archaising manner continues on to many LG lids, so that during much of the 8th century an urn and its lid may be painted in two contemporary but totally different styles. During the course of LG, however, the fashion changes to a dark ground, with concentric zones of decoration in white paint (FIGS. 10–13; PLATE 16.b);[74] the intention, perhaps, was to simulate the appearance of engraving on bronze shields. One painter of these lids at the end of the 8th century revived the octopus from the Minoan repertoire for his central medallions (FIG. 14).[75] As one might expect, he reduced the creature to a strictly symmetrical, Geometric format.

Unlike the knobbed conical type, domed lids were not originally designed to cover urns; they have a life of their own. Their resemblance to the Idaean shields inclined Brock to suspect 'some religious purpose';[76] indeed, this and no other type of lid appears among the votives offered at Knossos to Demeter.[77] They are also common, however, in domestic contexts;[78] doubtless, a shield-like lid was thought no less protective of household goods than of human ashes. Even in the tombs they often outnumber the urns. They may sometimes occur in homogeneously painted sets, as in the Teke tholos tomb and in other tombs in the North Cemetery.[79] From tomb 134 came a set of MG miniature shield-lids with delightfully ebullient decoration (PLATE 16.c)[80] and without any appropriate vessels for them to cover.

---

[70] 100.27: D 34. H.W. Catling, 'Archaeology in Greece, 1982–83', AR 29 (1982–83), 52, fig. 94.
[71] N 8, EG: H 8.5, D 26.
[72] Brock (n. 9 above), 164, class F.
[73] FIG. 9 – 107.91, MG: H 7.4, D 23.6; PLATE 16.a – 292.123, EG: H 7.8, D 26.
[74] FIGS. 10–13 – 292.171, 190, 191, 240, all LG: Hs between 5.2 and 6.2, Ds between 21 and 22; PLATE 16.b – 163.2, LG: H 5, D 20.8.
[75] H 12: Coldstream (n. 18 above – 1988), 29, fig. 2.2.; others, S. Alexiou, 'Παραστάσεις πολύποδος ἐπὶ πρωτοελληνικῶν ἀγγείων ἐκ Κρήτης', Kr.Chron. 4 (1950), 294–318.
[76] Brock (n. 9 above), 165.
[77] Coldstream (n. 13 above), 21, nos. 23–7, pl. 10.
[78] J.N. Coldstream, 'A Geometric well at Knossos', BSA 55 (1960), 166–70; id., 'Knossos 1951–61: Protogeometric and Geometric pottery from the town', BSA 67 (1972), 78, 84 ff., 89 ff. Sackett et al. (n. 4 above), 81, 83.
[79] Teke tholos: R.W. Hutchinson and J. Boardman, 'The Khaniale Tekke tombs', BSA 49 (1954), 225, nos. 39–48. Also a set of domed lids from North Cemetery tomb 132; another, Brock (n. 9 above), pl. 46, from Tomb TFT.
[80] 134.18–19, 50, 54–5, 59, 62, 69, 72, all MG: Hs between 2.3 and 3.1, Ds between 9 and 10.

8

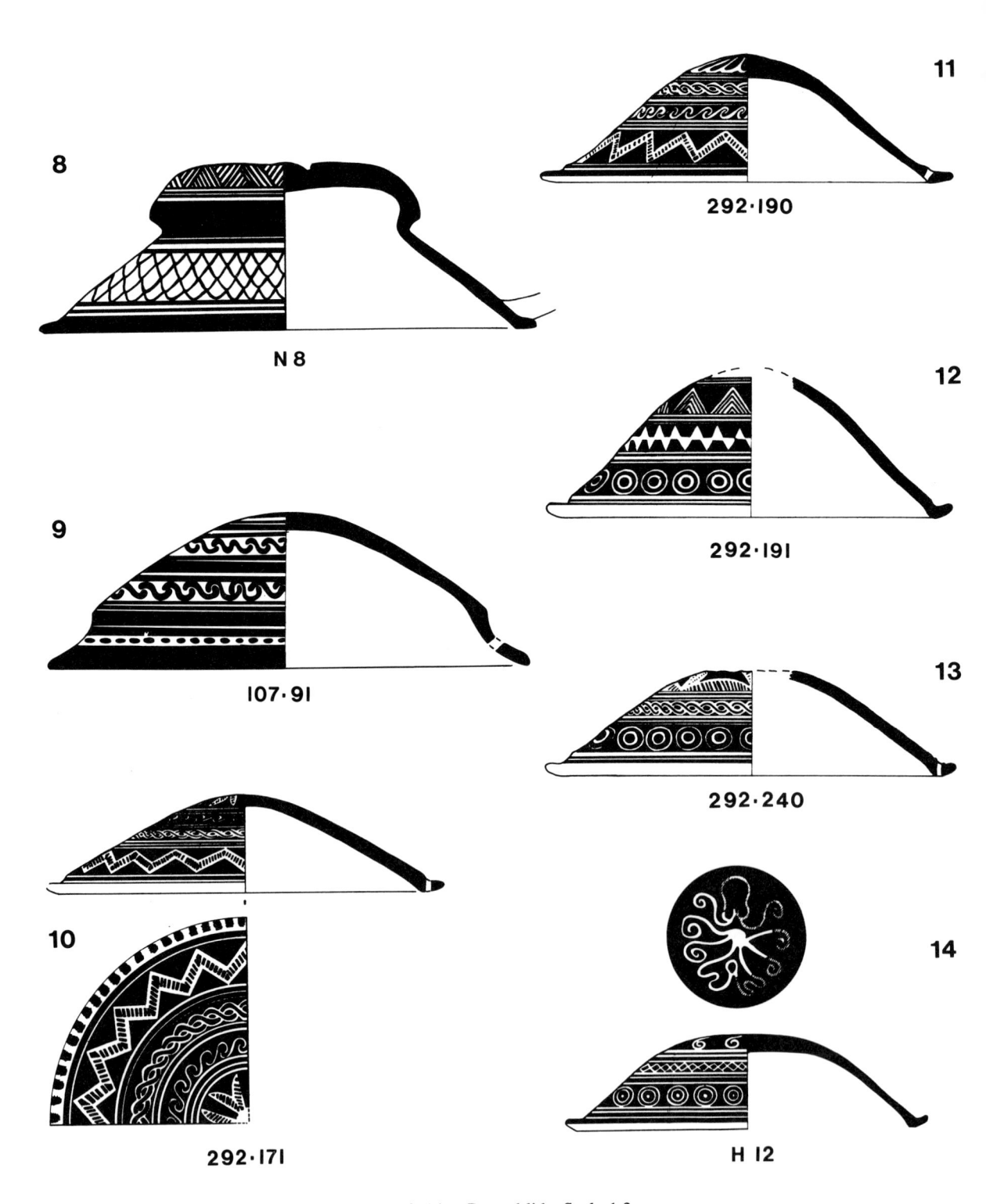

N 8

9

107·91

10

292·171

11

292·190

12

292·191

13

292·240

14

H 12

FIGS. 8–14   Domed lids. Scale 1:3

Domed lids thus perform a dual function, of protective care combined with ostentatious display. They were clearly symbols of protection, for the living as for the dead. Under whose protection? One possible link with the deity of the Idaean Cave, whose votives they resemble, appears on the lid Fortetsa 1414, with a boss in the form of an animal's head and a strange and rare figured scene perhaps representing Zeus brandishing a thunderbolt in front of a mantic tripod.[81] At the same time the ornate decoration was intended for display, in the household as well as in the tomb. The early omphaloid lids (FIG. 8; PLATE 16.a) are provided with a single loop handle attached to the rim, by which they could be hung on a wall. On the LG domed lids, without handles, the same purpose was served by pairs of suspension holes — and one should note that there are no corresponding holes on any of the urns.

The first two-thirds of the 7th century represent the final phase of the Knossian chamber tombs, now filling up to capacity to house the urns of a rapidly rising population.[82] The chief novelty lies in the bright polychromy of the elite urns, now painted with Orientalising designs in red, white and blue. Humbler cremations, meanwhile, were contained in plainer Subgeometric vessels, on which circle decoration predominates.[83] The polychrome urns often have purpose-built lids in the same colourful fabric, some of which have distinctive knobs in the form of miniature pyxides, miniature cauldrons with ring handles or animal heads.[84] Domed lids, with white decoration, also continue in fashion. One of the latest has a boss in the form of a human face, modelled in a fine Daedalic style of c.640–630 B.C.[85]

Thereafter, for reasons we do not yet fully understand, the use of the tombs came simultaneously to an abrupt end. To investigate why this happened would require another paper. Suffice it to remark that, for the late 7th century and the early 6th, we have virtually no material at Knossos from the settlement, from the cemeteries, or even from the sanctuary of Demeter, where one might expect the flow of votives to be continuous.[86] This curious phenomenon prompts the quotation marks enclosing the 'Dark Age' of my paper's title. For the early centuries of the Iron Age, the conventional 'Dark Age', abundant finds from the tombs supply us with ample documentation and go far to correct any impression that Knossos was then poor or isolated from her Aegean neighbours or even from the Near East. For us, at present, the true Dark Age of Knossos lies in the 6th century, when the archaeological record is almost mute. Was this an age of deep recession, or is it dark only because of our ignorance? This is one of the most intriguing mysteries which still await elucidation from future fieldwork at Knossos.

---

[81] Brock (n. 9 above), 122 ff., pl. 107.
[82] See, e.g., the Gypsadhes tomb, Coldstream, Callaghan and Musgrave (n. 55 above), 142 ff.
[83] Brock (n. 9 above), 150, class V, 'the poor man's burial urn'.
[84] Respectively Brock (n. 9 above), 164, classes G(ii)(a), G (ii)(b) and F.
[85] 107.127, unpublished.
[86] Coldstream (n. 6 above), 321; and (n. 60 above), 298. In the settlement, some pieces in a far from homogeneous, and very scrappy, well deposit appear to fall within the 6th century: J.N. Coldstream, 'Early Hellenic pottery', in Sackett et al. (n. 4 above), 75, 85 ff.

Chapter 8

On Knossos and her Neighbours
(7th Century to Mid–4th Century B.C.)

G. HUXLEY

A merit of facts, it has been said, is that they give us something to think about. Historical facts, however, about Archaic and Classical Knossos are scarce. This brief essay is an attempt to make bricks without straw, and without dropping any of them.

There are several reasons for the scarcity of facts. Firstly, Herodotus, Thucydides and Xenophon have little to say about Crete and the Cretans, because the island was peripheral to events in the Persian Wars and in the great Peloponnesian War and its aftermath. Secondly, our three principal informants about the nature of early Cretan society — Plato in the *Laws*, Aristotle in the *Politics* and Strabo, who took much from Ephorus — report upon Crete in general but give little detail concerning the characteristics of particular cities. Thirdly, no Cretan local history survives from antiquity, and the fragments of lost Cretan epichoric antiquaries show that the writers were likewise concerned with the entire island — some authors, such as Xenion,[1] wrote about particular cities of Crete, but the practice was usually to compose *Krētika* rather than, for instance, *Knōsiaka* or, say, *Phaistiaka*. The tradition of producing *Krētika* began at least as early as Charon of Lampsacus, who published a work in three books with that title late in the 5th century B.C.[2] The similarities believed to have existed between many Cretan cities in their social and political arrangements — in their having *kosmoi*, a Council, an Assembly, communal Messes and a subject population confined to each of their territories — enabled investigators to treat the polities of the isle as a consistent whole. The epigraphical evidence, however, suggests that the internal arrangements were not everywhere uniform, but when Aristotle discusses the Cretan constitution in *Politics* ii.10 he has the ninety or so cities in mind; similarly, in the lost Aristotelian *Polity of the Cretans* the island was treated in its entirety.[3] Historical events of Hellenistic times within particular Cretan cities are slightly more accessible, because Polybius was much concerned with their struggles, including those of Knossos.

A fourth reason why facts about the early history of Knossos are scarce is that few Archaic and

---

[1] F. Jacoby, *Die Fragmente der griechischen Historiker IIIB* (Leiden, 1950), 460.
[2] Ibid. *IIIA* (Leiden, 1940), 262 T1.
[3] *Heraclidis Lembi Excerpta Politiarum* ed. and trans. M.R. Dilts (*Greek, Roman, and Byzantine Monographs* 5; Durham, N.C., 1971), excerpts 14–15 (pp. 18–21).

Classical inscriptions have been found there. Fragments of Knossian laws exist,[4] but there is nothing to match the extensive public display of inscribed legislation at Gortyn. The 5th-century arbitration by Argos between Knossos and Tylissos offers evidence about boundaries, cults and warfare, but much remains obscure in the fragmentary texts from Argos and Tylissos recording the regulations.[5]

Because the literary and epigraphic evidence is slight, it is best to begin with a subject wherein some secure inferences are possible — historical geography. Understanding of the changes through time in the positions of settlements and cemeteries of Knossos has been increased most of all by the efforts of Sinclair Hood in surveying and listing, with David Smyth, the remains, both prehistoric and historic, in the neighbourhood of the Palace.[6] Their careful discussion of antiquities of the Iron Age and of Classical times, together with the evidence for temples, shrines and sanctuaries, has been immensely beneficial to students of the rise and early development of the Knossian *polis*. It is now clear that the main settlement of Archaic and Classical Knossos extended westwards and northwards from the neighbourhood of the Minoan Palace (FIG. 1). The limits of the city to the north may well be marked by the Teke cemetery and to the west by the Acropolis hill, upon which at least one temple stood. What is not clear is the process of formation of the Knossian *polis*. It can be supposed to have been already in existence in late Geometric times, but had incoming Dorians taken over a political unity and perpetuated it? Or was a Knossian state created anew by combination of villages into a *polis*, as in Aristotle's scheme in *Politics* I?[7] Iron Age and later finds in tombs come from places to the north of Teke and to the south of the Palace, but we should hesitate to infer that there were several villages in the neighbourhood of Knossos. Some of the isolated tombs may have belonged to farmhouses rather than to villages, and many of them may have been Bronze Age tombs reused in later times. To walk a distance to an existing tomb may have been preferable to the digging of a new one; so there may never have been a close connexion between cemeteries and settlements. Some Cretan communities, such as the Arkades, persisted in living in scattered settlements, but the arrangements in early historical Knossos may have been different. The Aristotelian model of a *polis* consisting of a *koinōnia* of several villages (*Politics* 1252b27) is not necessarily applicable to Knossian antiquities; but a possibility remains that there was an outlying *kōmē* on the lower Gypsadhes hill.[8]

That some kind of coalescence in due course came into effect is, nonetheless, clear, because in addition to the Dorian tribe Pamphyloi, two tribes, Aithaleis and Archēia, are attested;[9] the last may be connected with the god or hero Archos,[10] who is said in the regulations for Knossos and Tylissos

---

[4] *Inscriptiones Creticae I: tituli Cretae mediae praeter Gortynios* ed. M. Guarducci (Rome, 1935), viii, no. 2. Another Archaic text, possibly a law: *Ergon* 1972, 129–30, fig. 122.

[5] R. Meiggs and D. Lewis (eds.), *A Selection of Greek Historical Inscriptions to the End of the Fifth Century B.C.* (Oxford, 1969), no. 42; E. Schwyzer (ed.), *Dialectorum Graecarum exempla epigraphica potiora* (Leipzig, 1923), nos. 83 and 84.

[6] S. Hood and D. Smyth, *Archaeological Survey of the Knossos Area* (2nd edn.; BSA Suppl. 14; London, 1981).

[7] *Politics* 1252^{b}15–31, recently discussed by, among others, I. Morris, *Burial and Ancient Society: the Rise of the Greek City-State* (Cambridge, 1987), 7–10.

[8] J.N. Coldstream, P. Callaghan and J.H. Musgrave, 'Knossos: an early Greek tomb on Lower Gypsadhes Hill', *BSA* 76 (1981), 144. On the reuse of Bronze Age tombs remote from settlements, see J. Boardman, 'Protogeometric graves at Agios Ioannis near Knossos (Knossos Survey 3)', *BSA* 55 (1960), 143.

[9] *ICret* I (n. 4 above), viii, pp. 52–3.

[10] N.F. Jones, *Public Organisation in Ancient Greece: A Documentary Study* (Philadelphia, 1987), 226–7.

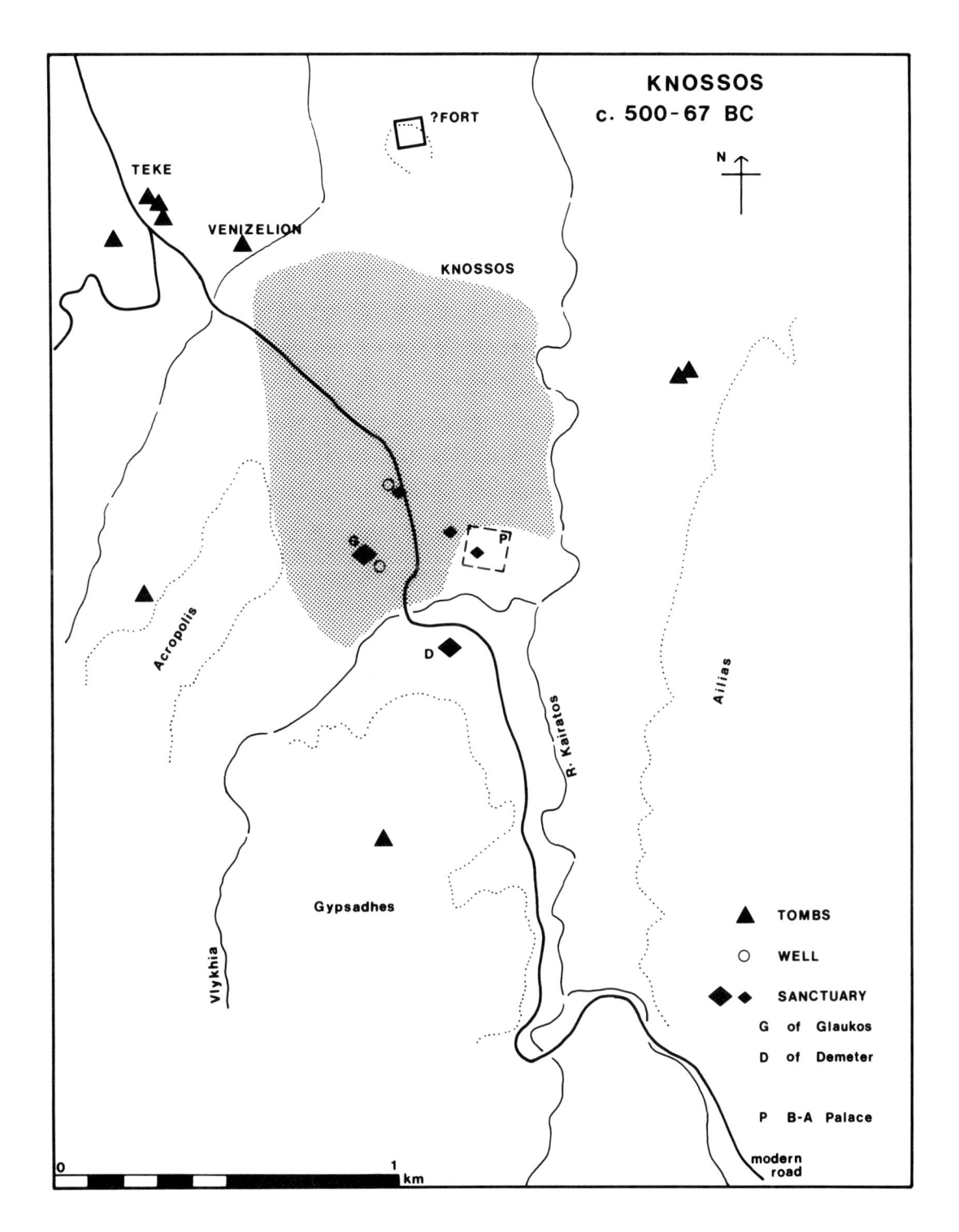

FIG. 1 Simplified plan of locations at Knossos

to have a precinct at Acharna.[11] At some time Dorian incomers had brought persons of non-Dorian stock into the tribal structure of the *polis*.

Originally a *basileus* would have ruled the Knossian *polis*, as in other Cretan states: Cretan kings, Aristotle says, were overthrown.[12] It is not known when the overthrow took place at Knossos, but in the third quarter of the 7th century at Axos Etearchos still had the title *basileus*.[13] In some cities such a person would have ruled over an extended tribal system in a group of villages constituting a *polis*. It is possible, but not provable, that such a systematic grouping existed already within the domains of Knossos too in about 700 B.C.

Territory controlled by Knossos extended far beyond the middle Kairatos valley and the neighbourhood of the Palace (FIG. 2). To the west lay Tylissos. The Argive regulations for that small city and Knossos refer to places on the boundary between the two. Neither party is to cut off territory or to take it all. Points on the boundary are defined as 'Swinemount' and 'Eagles' and 'the Artemision' and 'the river' (unnamed) and 'to Leukoporos and Agathoia, along the course of the rainwater'. If the river is the stream now called Platypérama, the largest watercourse between Knossos and Tylissos, then Knossian territory may well have extended to the sea in the 5th century between two nominally independent cities — Apollonia on the coast to the west and the harbour-town Herakleion to the east. East of Herakleion Amnisos with its river of the same name was a landfall for travellers to Knossos. How much land to the east of Amnisos was held by the Knossians at any particular time cannot be determined. There the fertile terrain intersected by watercourses leading northwards to the coast would have attracted farmers,[14] but encroachment upon the land of Chersonesos would have brought opposition from Lyttos (Lyktos), which relied upon a friendly Chersonesos for access to the sea. In the late 3rd or early 2nd century B.C. the Ephebes of Dreros swore friendship to Knossos and unceasing hatred towards Lyttos;[15] it may well be that as early as Archaic times Dreros and Knossos were allied in their enmity towards Lyttos.

Southwards from Knossos lay Lykastos. The place, now Kanli Kastelli, is mentioned in Homer,[16] but it may early have lost its independence to one of its neighbours. We know that by 184 B.C. Lykastos and its territory were Knossian, because it was in that year that the Gortynians cut off from Knossian territory the so-called Lykastion and gave it to the Rhaukians; at the same time the Diatonion (land around Astritsi?) was cut off from Knossos and given to the Lyttians.[17] Knossos needed to control the headwaters of streams flowing into her territory from south of Mount Iouktas; the Lykastion and the Diatonion may well have been incorporated within the territory of the Knossians already in Classical times.

---

[11] Meiggs and Lewis (n. 5 above), no. 42, B 35–6.
[12] *Politics* 1272^{a}8–9.
[13] Herodotus iv.154.1.
[14] Concerning the alluvial geology of the district, see L. Hempel, *Forschungen zur Physischen Geographie der Insel Kreta im Quartär: ein Beitrag zur Geoökologie des Mittelmeerraumes* (Abh. Akad. d. Wiss. in Göttingen, Math.-phys. Kl., 3. Folge, Nr. 42; Göttingen, 1991), 116–30.
[15] Schwyzer (n. 5 above), no. 193. C.D. Buck, *The Greek Dialects: Grammar, Selected Inscriptions, Glossary* (2nd edn.; Chicago, 1955), no. 120.
[16] *Iliad* ii.647.
[17] Polybius xxii.15.1. See also F.W. Walbank, *A Historical Commentary on Polybius iii* (Oxford, 1979), 201 for topographical discussion.

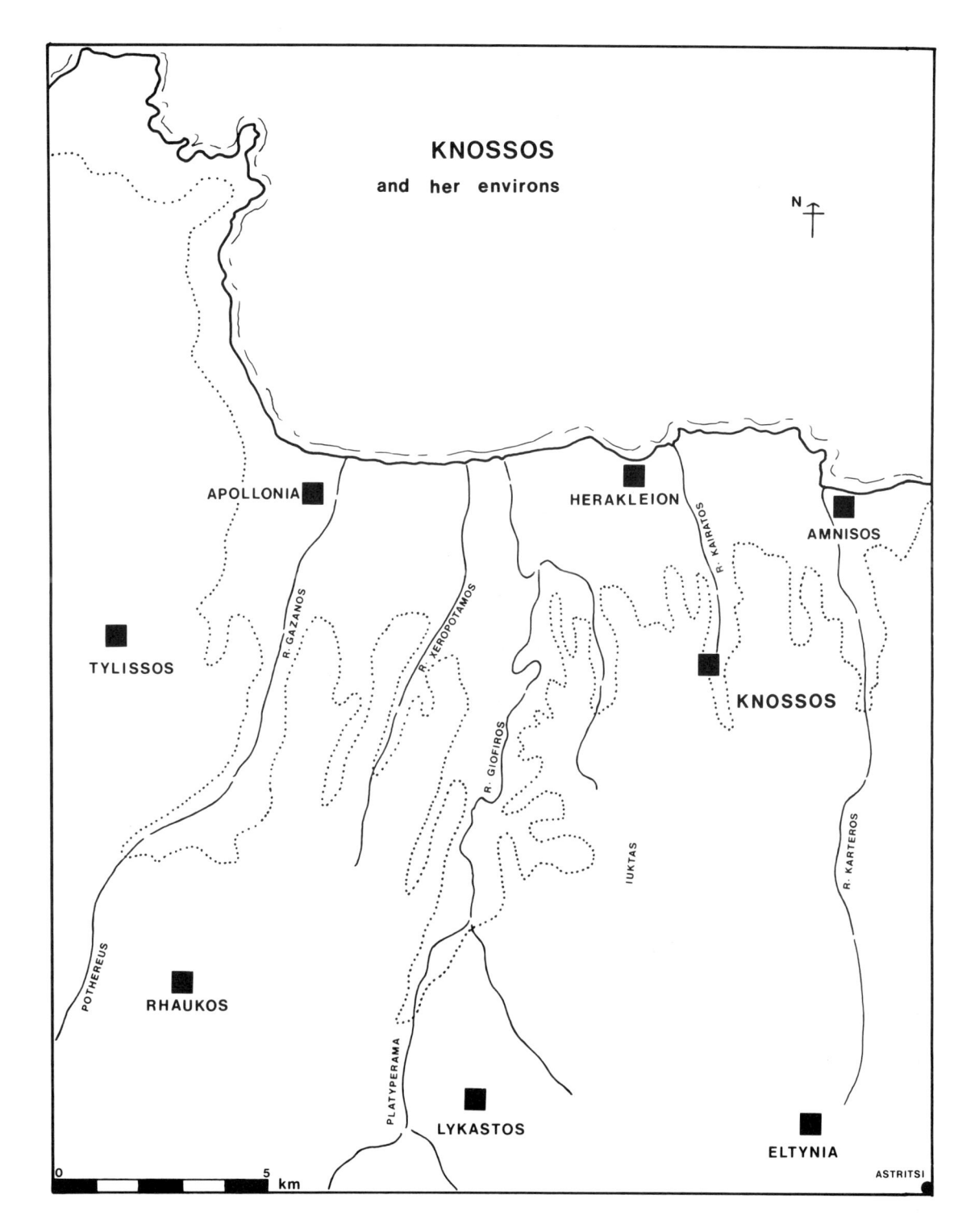

FIG. 2 Locations in the neighbourhood of the Knossos valley, mentioned in the text

From the point of view of the historical geographer Knossian domains at their greatest extent can be seen to accord with the customary division into *polis*, *khōra* and *eskhatiā*. The *polis* with its domain extended approximately from Teke and the Venizeleion to the Palace, and from the western slope of the Acropolis (Monastiriaki Kefala) to the Kairatos stream. The *khōra* worked for the landowning citizenry and for the state by the subordinate Mnoia and other subjects, called *perioikoi* by Aristotle,[18] would have included the middle Kairatos valley upstream from Knossos and much of the northern coastland between Amnisos and Chersonesos. The *eskhatiā* embraced high ground inland and remote from the *polis*, but suited to grazing by transhumant flocks in the care of herdsmen and women. However, not all of the *eskhatiā* would have been far from the *polis* proper: the rough slopes of Ailias to the east of the Kairatos stream can be classified as *eskhatiā*, as can the lofty places named on the boundary between Tylissian and Knossian territory. It is likely that bounds were also clearly defined within the territory of the Knossians, not only to delimit their individual allotments (*klēroi*) and the state and temple lands, but also to mark out bounds for the pasturage of animals. Such bounds, indeed, are indicated in a Lyttian inscription regulating rights of grazing.[19]

A significant and long-recognised fact of early Knossian history has been confirmed by recent excavations — the fewness of burials of the 6th century. There are signs of recession elsewhere in Crete late in the 7th century,[20] but at Knossos about 600 B.C. the decline seems to have become a catastrophe. At the Knossian shrine of Demeter finds of votives are not plentiful again until the temple was built, late in the 5th century.[21] The dearth of 6th-century material at Knossos calls for explanation. The city could have exhausted herself in rivalry with Lyttos (the more so if Lyttos was helped by her friends in Sparta),[22] but a military explanation of the catastrophe is insufficient; a plague following defeat is a possibility — we may recall that Epimenides of Crete, who, some said, was a Knossian, is supposed to have purified Athens and also to have composed *Katharmoi*.[23] Persistent failure of crops may also have afflicted Knossos. The collapse remains baffling, but there are signs of greater security, or of an early recovery, among the Eteocretans of eastern Crete at Palaikastro and Praisos. At Palaikastro a temple was built late in the 6th century, and there are fine architectural terracottas from Praisos.[24] The relative prosperity of eastern Crete brings to mind a passage in Herodotus, who wrote that there was plague and famine in Crete soon after the Trojan

---

[18] *Politics* 1272^{a}18.

[19] H. and M. van Effenterre, 'Nouvelles lois archaïques de Lyttos', *BCH* 109 (1985), 157–88, Text B, at p. 163. M. Bile, *Le dialecte crétois ancien : étude de langue des inscriptions; recueil des inscriptions postérieures aux IC* (Études Crétoises 27; Paris, 1988), no. 12B.

[20] J. Boardman, 'Crete', in J. Boardman and N.G.L. Hammond (eds.), *CAH III.3: The Expansion of the Greek World, Eighth to Sixth Centuries B.C.* (2nd edn.; Cambridge, 1982), 222–33, at pp. 230–2.

[21] J.N. Coldstream and R.A. Higgins, 'Conclusions: the cult of Demeter at Knossos', in J.N. Coldstream, *Knossos: The Sanctuary of Demeter* (BSA Suppl. 8; London, 1973), 182–3. For slight traces of 6th-century occupation in the neighbourhood of the Unexplored Mansion, see J.N. Coldstream, 'Early Hellenic pottery', in L.H. Sackett et al., *Knossos. From Greek City to Roman Colony: Excavations at the Unexplored Mansion II* (BSA Suppl. 21; London, 1992), 85–6.

[22] Pausanias iii.12.11 mentions a disputed tale of a war between Sparta and Knossos in the time of Epimenides. Archers from Lyttos were said to have been hired by Sparta in the Second Messenian War (Pausanias iv.19.4, with P. Perlman, 'One hundred-citied Crete and the Cretan ΠΟΛΙΤΕΙΑ', *CP* 87 (1992), 200).

[23] H. Diels and W. Kranz, *Die Fragmente der Vorsokratiker* I (9th edn.; Berlin, 1960), 3A2 (Knossos), 3A4 (Purification), 3A3 (Katharmoi).

[24] Boardman (n. 20 above), 232.

War; earlier still, Crete had suffered loss in the disastrous expedition of Minos to Sikania. Only the Praisians and the Polichnetai had not taken part in the expedition.[25] It is possible that Cretan storytellers retrojected into the heroic age of Minos and Idomeneus knowledge of a plague and great hunger of a more recent epoch, about a century and a half before the time of Herodotus' writing.

Such was the economic failure that skilled Cretans had to look for work elsewhere in the Greek world. Among the artists who went abroad were two Knossians, Chersiphron and his son Metagenes. They worked on the Ionic temple of Artemis at Ephesus and were said to have written a book about it.[26]

If Knossos was damaged by enemy action, then evidence for a military success in Crete at about the same time is pertinent. A find of armour at a shrine at Arkades can be dated late in the 7th century. Five helmets, eight corselets and sixteen *mitrai* were found. Inscriptions on some of the pieces name the dedicator who won the spoil in battle. The *polis* of the dedicators is not stated, but the use of inscribed omega with double circle points to Lyttos.[27] It may be that Lyttos in war with Knossos won Arkades and celebrated the victory by dedicating spoils in the newly acquired territory.

The land of Arkades was said to have suffered in a war of uncertain date — it was earlier than Theophrastus, who described its effects.[28] When the town of the Arkades was destroyed, cultivation of the land ceased. Springs and ponds then dried up, because without tillage water did not sink into the hardened earth. But when agriculture began again after six years, and the town had been refounded, the springs were replenished. The story shows how damaging war could be to an early Cretan *polis*. War, together with plague and famine, may have undone Knossos too, about 600 B.C.

At some time in the 480s Theron tyrant of Akragas gave relics alleged to have been the bones of Minos to the Cretans.[29] Theron may have hoped for Cretan help against the Carthaginians; in his respect for the Cretan veneration of the hero he would have recognised that there had been Cretan settlers among the founders of Gela, the mother-city of Akragas.[30] The destination of the bones, had they reached Crete, would have been Knossos, the home of Minos, but it seems that the relics did not arrive. The Cretans conveying them put in at Corcyra on their way back, where the unfriendly natives stole the bones and scattered them. The tale explained why Cretans were always hostile to visitors from Corcyra.[31]

Minos, however, was much in the thoughts of Cretans when, shortly before Xerxes' invasion of Greece, they enquired jointly at Delphi whether they should help fighting against the Persians.[32] The first priests of Apollo at Delphi had been of Knossian origin,[33] but a new priesthood had been installed after the First Sacred War.[34] In the early 5th century Crete could expect no special favour at Delphi. The Pythia's reply to the enquiry was sarcastically delivered in iambics, not in hexameters.

---

[25] Herodotus vii.169.2–170.2 and 171.1–2.
[26] Vitruvius, *De Arch.* vii.12 and 16 (pp. 157, 159 ed. V. Rose; Leipzig, 1899).
[27] Boardman (n. 20 above), 227.
[28] Pliny, *H.N.* xxxi.4.53 (vol. 5, p. 20 ed. C. Mayhoff; Leipzig, 1897). Seneca, *Q.Nat.* iii.2.5.
[29] Diodorus iv.79.4. H. van Effenterre, *La Crète et le monde grec de Platon à Polybe* (Paris, 1948, repr. 1968), 27.
[30] Thucydides vi.4.3.
[31] Ovid, *Ibis* 509–10 and Scholia.
[32] Herodotus vii.169.1.
[33] *Homeric Hymn* 3 to Apollo 393, 475.
[34] G. Forrest, 'The First Sacred War', *BCH* 80 (1956), 33–52.

Traces of the response are to be found in the text of Herodotus. 'You fools', said the Pythia, 'you resent all the tears Minos in his anger made you weep after you assisted Menelaos. The Greeks did not help in avenging his death at Kamikos, but you helped them to avenge the seizure by a foreigner of the woman from Sparta.'[35] When the response was brought home, the Cretans declined to join the Hellenic alliance. (It is true that Kleinias in Plato's *Laws* (707b4–6) claims a decisive part for Cretans at the battle of Salamis, but Herodotus says nothing about Cretan participants in the battle. If any Cretan volunteers fought there, they would not have gone with the official approval of the united Cretans.)

Persian power, however, was not ignored in Crete. Entimos of Gortyn in emulation of Themistocles went up to Artaxerxes and received gifts and honours from the King.[36] Hybrias the Cretan had the Persian court in mind when he boasted that the unarmed serfs of the Mnoia did obeisance to him as master and called him a great king.[37] The bridle ornament, almost certainly Achaemenian, found at the Knossian sanctuary of Demeter[38] is a reminder of possibilities of trade or gift-exchange with the empire and of winning booty in Persian service. The mother of Artemisia of Halicarnassus, who distinguished herself in the battle of Salamis, was a Cretan,[39] and by 480 Cretan ties with the Anatolian nobility entailed connexions with the imperial power, but details are lacking. Entimos cannot have gone to the King simply as a tourist.

Early in the 470s, at some time before the Dorians were admitted as new citizens to Himera, there was *stasis* at Knossos. The trouble, as we learn from Pindar,[40] caused Philanor's son, the young Ergoteles, who later distinguished himself as a long-distance runner, to leave Crete for the Sicilian city.[41] Many Cretans were renowned as runners, but the later career of Ergoteles is not our concern. The cause of the *stasis* is not known, but Aristotle mentions that *akosmia* was a frequent occasion of trouble in Cretan cities.[42] In competition for power, struggles between individuals and families over the office of *kosmos* would often have resulted in loss of face, or worse, for the defeated parties. Ergoteles was too young to have aspired to be a *kosmos* when he left Knossos; his elders may have emigrated, taking him with them.

Other causes of *stasis* can be identified. Friction between old and young, and between office-holders and ordinary citizens, is likely to have arisen in the assembly. Aristotle states that all citizens participated in the *ekklēsia* of a Cretan city; but the power of the citizens was limited in decision-making, since they had no right to modify proposals, only to vote for or against what seemed good to the elders and the *kosmoi*.[43] Another cause of friction would have arisen from landholding. Those

---

[35] Herodotus vii.169.2; H.W. Parke and D.E.W. Wormell, *The Delphic Oracle* ii: *The Oracular Responses* (Oxford, 1956), no. 93.

[36] Phainias in Athenaeus ii.48D–F, discussed by G. Zecchini, 'Entimo di Gortina (Athen. II. 48d–f) e le relazioni greco-persiane durante la Pentecontetia', *Ancient Society* 20 (1989), 5–13.

[37] *Poetae Melici Graeci* ed. D. L. Page (Oxford, 1962), 909. See also C.M. Bowra, *Greek Lyric Poetry from Alcman to Simonides* (2nd edn.; Oxford, 1961), 398–403.

[38] Coldstream (n. 21 above), 157–8, 185.

[39] Herodotus vii.99.2.

[40] *Olympian* xii.16.

[41] He would have settled there in 476 or soon afterwards: W.S. Barrett, 'Pindar's Twelfth *Olympian* and the fall of the Deinomenidai', *JHS* 93 (1973), 24.

[42] *Politics* 1272^{b}7–9, interpreted by A. Panagopoulos, Ἀριστοτέλης καί Κρήτη (Athens, 1987), 95–102.

[43] *Politics* 1272^{a}10–12.

whose demesnes were close to the *polis* and its assembly would have had political advantage over those whose *klēroi* were further away, at least at those times of the year when steady supervision of labourers on *klēroi* was necessary. Moreover, land held at a distance from the *polis* was more vulnerable to enemy attack, and losses suffered by owners of distant land would have diminished their economic power in competition with those living on 'home' territory. (Knossian raiding by land and sea, such as is mentioned in the regulations for Knossos and Tylissos, would have invited retaliation. It was to remove such disparities that Plato recommended the division of each *klēros* into two parts, one closer to the city, one further away, in as equitable a distribution as possible, with account being taken of the quality of the land: *Laws* 745c4–d4.)

The relations of Knossos with friendly neighbours in the mid-5th century seem to have been federal in character.[44] The text of the regulations for Knossos and Tylissos implies the adherence of other cities to the arrangements about booty agreed by the Knossians and the Argives, and there seems to be a reference to a federal assembly (*plēthos*) of the contracting states.[45] Also envisaged is the possibility of the presence of Argive forces in Crete. Within the federal arrangements special care is taken to secure benefits for Tylissos, the weaker and smaller neighbour of Knossos. It seems also that Delphic Apollo approved the agreements, since Knossos and Tylissos were required to send the best of their plunder jointly to Pytho. Other members of the federation are not named: it is not likely that Lyttos was among them, since Lyttians were friends of Sparta's ancient enemy Argos, but, as suggested above, Dreros and Knossos may already have been allied against Lyttos.

In Plato's *Laws* the Cretan speaker is a Knossian, Kleinias, and we are told that it is the Knossians who have been entrusted by the greater part of Crete with the founding of a new city.[46] Plato regards Knossos as being eminent in the island;[47] that the city did not lack respect abroad is also clear from the grant by Mausolus of political privileges to Knossians.[48] But it is not certain that Plato visited Crete before forming a favourable opinion of Knossos. There is apt local scenery in the mention of shady cypress groves beside the path from Knossos to the Idaean Cave; beneath the trees the old men — Kleinias, Megillos the Spartan and the Athenian stranger — could rest on their pilgrimage, but local scenery is not proof of autopsy.[49] Plato may well have heard about Crete from an informant in the Academy.

In the *Laws* the joint refoundation of the new Magnesia under the direction of Knossos points also to a federal arrangement; in this matter, too, Plato may have had a local informant. Ephorus also, as Strabo's use of him shows, was well informed about Cretan customs, but the source of his knowledge

---

[44] The incipient federalism may have continued the early Syncretism mentioned by Plutarch *De Frat. Amore* 490B; it anticipates, but did not necessarily develop into, the Hellenistic Cretan *Koinon*. Concerning the *Koinon* and its antecedents see G. Busolt, *Griechische Staatskunde* ii (3rd edn.; Munich, 1926), 740–1; V. Ehrenberg, *The Greek State* (2nd edn.; London, 1969), 129; R.F. Willetts, *Aristocratic Society in Ancient Crete* (London, 1955), 225–34.

[45] Meiggs and Lewis (n. 5 above), no. 42, A8, A14–15.

[46] *Laws* 703c2–5.

[47] *Laws* 752e4–5.

[48] S. Hornblower, *Mausolus* (Oxford, 1982), 75, text M7 (= J. Crampa, *Labraunda: Swedish Excavations and Researches* III.2: *The Greek Inscriptions* (Stockholm, 1972), no. 40).

[49] For a judicious discussion of the problem see G.R. Morrow, *Plato's Cretan City: A Historical Interpretation of the* Laws (Princeton, 1960), 25–8.

is not known.⁵⁰ Aristotle, too, provides an instructive, but general, account of the Cretan polity, but details peculiar to historical Knossos are not included.

When Aristotle wrote about Crete in the *Politics* a foreign war had 'recently' crossed over into the island.⁵¹ The result had been to reveal the weakness of Cretan laws and customs. Almost certainly Aristotle refers to the disruption caused when Knossians brought in Phalaikos and his Phocians from Cape Maleia in 346 to help them in a war against Lyttos. The city was taken and the Lyttians were expelled. However, a Spartan force under Archidamos, originally intended to help Taras against the Leukanians, was invited to Crete by the dispossessed Lyttians, who were reinstalled in their city.⁵² After the short-lived Knossian success the threat of external intervention in Crete persisted. In some respects Archaic Crete lasted into the 4th century, the Persian Wars having marked no innovation in social and political organisation, and Crete was moreover not exposed to the disruptive effects of Attic democratic imperialism. However, separate development in secure insularity was brought to an end by Phalaikos, who, driven from Lyttos, immediately besieged Kydonia, where he was slain.⁵³ The island was demonstrably open to attack from now on, and such federal authority as existed could not concert a joint defence. If Diodorus is to be believed, King Agis of Sparta, equipped with Persian funds and ships and assisted by mercenaries rescued after the Battle of Issus, was able to compel most of the cities of Crete to take the side of Darius.⁵⁴

There are no statistics for the population of Archaic and Classical Knossos, but an indication of the city's size, or needs, in relation to other Cretan places is given by the record of corn supplied to Greek states by Cyrene during the hunger of 330 to 326 B.C.⁵⁵ Altogether the Knossians received 10,900 *medimnoi* in two batches. Slightly smaller amounts were sent to Kydonia (10,000) and Gortyn (10,000). For comparison, Hyrtakina received 5,000 *medimnoi* and Elyros (if the name is correctly read on the stone) 3,000. Lyttos is absent, perhaps owing to its ties with Sparta, the enemy of Alexander. The figures suggest that Knossos was among the most populous cities of Crete at the time.

Foreign armies brought an additional threat, the danger of an uprising among the serfs of the countryside; rural unrest might lead to loss of income in kind at the *syssitia*, upon which the life of the state relied. Yet long after 346 Knossian life had a steady continuity, most impressively seen in two cults. First, in a shrine of a Knossian hero, whole pots, illustrating four centuries of ceramic evolution, were found above a floor. Older votives were respected when new ones were installed, from the 5th century B.C. to the Roman conquest. It has been suggested that the hero was Glaukos son of Minos;⁵⁶ and if the festival associated with the ceremonies was the Theodaisia, then the god Dionysus may also have been worshipped in the shrine — he had as one of his epithets Theodaisios.⁵⁷ Secondly, the worship of Demeter on the Gypsadhes hill may well have begun at the time of the Dorian settlement. Her rites continued in the open until the construction of the Classical temple late in the 5th century. Thereafter the cult of the goddess in and around the temple endured for at least six centuries; not even the arrival of Campanian colonists at Knossos in 36 B.C. brought

---

⁵⁰ Strabo x.4.16–22 (Ephorus: *F.Gr. Hist.*, n. 1 above, 70 F 149).
⁵¹ *Politics* 1272ᵇ20.
⁵² Diodorus xvi.62.3–4.
⁵³ Diodorus xvi.63.2–4.
⁵⁴ Diodorus xvii.48.2.
⁵⁵ M.N. Tod (ed.), *A Selection of Greek Historical Inscriptions* ii: *From 403 to 323 B.C.* (Oxford, 1948), no. 196.
⁵⁶ P.J. Callaghan, 'KRS 1976: excavations at a shrine of Glaukos, Knossos', *BSA* 73 (1978), 1–29, at p. 25.
⁵⁷ Hesych. v. Θεοδαίσιος, and see R. Pfeiffer, *Callimachus* i (Oxford, 1949), on Fr.43,86 (a Cretan and Boeotian context).

the sequence of dedications to an end.[58] Archaic and Classical Crete had been remarkable for its political conservatism until foreign invasions brought disruption; but even in times of turmoil religion still firmly linked the life of the Knossian *polis* with the remote past.

---

[58] Coldstream (n. 21 above), 186.

Additional note: the following works, drawn to my attention by the editors, may also be found to be helpful: A. Strataridaki, 'The historians of ancient Crete: a study in regional historiography', *Kr.Chron.* 28-29 (1988-9), 137-93; A. Panagopoulos, 'Βασικὴ βιβλιογραφία τῆς Δωρικῆς Κρήτης', *Cretan Studies* 2 (1990), 163-96.

Chapter 9

Archaic, Classical and Hellenistic Knossos — A Historical Summary[1]

P.J. CALLAGHAN

In the early 5th century B.C. there was *stasis* at Knossos. Ergoteles, who won the men's footrace at Olympia in 472 B.C., had earlier been expelled from the city.[2] The known history of the settlement after the mysterious 6th century B.C. break does not extend very much further back than these events and it may be significant that a shrine concerned with initiation practices was also established in the southern part of the city at about this time.[3] The evidence from pottery may in fact be defective here. There was little change in many forms between the later 7th and the later 6th century B.C. and since Archaic material may often be found out of context in the better preserved Classical and Hellenistic layers it is impossible to date much of it closely. In other words much of the so-called lacuna may be a result of our inability to date the pottery closely.

Around the middle of the 5th century B.C. Argos, Tylissos and Knossos became allies. Two closely related inscriptions have been found relating to these events, one in Tylissos and one in Argos.[4] Apart from various ritual and hospitable acts which need not concern us here, two general themes should be noted. The first concerns the joint Knossian and Tylissian exploitation of the territory of the Acharnaeans, part of which was already in Knossian possession. Joint exploitation of tributary territory is not unusual in Crete,[5] and the main problem concerns the position of the land involved.

Special Abbreviation:
ICret = *Inscriptiones Creticae* ed. M. Guarducci (Rome, 1935–1950)
   ICret I: tituli Cretae mediae praeter Gortynios
   ICret II: tituli Cretae occidentalis
   ICret III: tituli Cretae orientalis
   ICret IV: tituli Gortynii

[1] This paper is reprinted, with slight alterations, from L.H. Sackett *et al.*, *Knossos. From Greek City to Roman Colony: Excavations at the Unexplored Mansion II* (*BSA* Suppl. 21; London, 1992), 133–6. Permission to reprint was kindly granted by the author P.J. Callaghan, L.H. Sackett and the Managing Committee of the British School at Athens.
[2] Pausanias vi.4.11; Pindar, *Olympics* xii; *ICret* I, viii, p. 47.
[3] P. Callaghan, 'KRS 1976: Excavations at a shrine of Glaukos, Knossos', *BSA* 73 (1978), 1–30.
[4] M.N. Tod (ed.), *A Selection of Greek Historical Inscriptions* (Oxford, 1933), 59 ff., no. 33; R. Meiggs and D. Lewis (eds.), *A Selection of Greek Historical Inscriptions to the End of the Fifth Century* B.C. (Oxford, 1969), 99ff., no. 42.
[5] e.g., see *ICret* III, vi, no. 7.A–B; and further on the fate of Rhaukos below.

Most modern commentators identify Acharna with modern Archanes, although the first mention of the latter belongs to the later medieval period. Rigsby rightly points out that the territory should lie in the Herakleion valley, although he still accepts the Acharna/Archanes equation.[6] I would prefer to place the site of Acharna somewhere in the vicinity of Tylissos, a position that would make more sense of Tylissos' clear subsidiary position *vis à vis* Knossos in the inscriptions.

The second set of provisions concerns the distribution of spoils which are envisaged as being taken on *future* campaigns. This includes the possibility of victories at sea and of the Knossia itself being invaded. Quite probably no specific enemy is contemplated and these are general provisions to cover every possible future course of events. Conversely, the engagement of Argos may indicate that Crete had been drawn into a wider arena and that Sparta and her allies are the shadowy enemy lurking in the background. In this case Lyttos with its claims to Laconian origins may well be involved.[7]

In 346 B.C. Phocian mercenaries, working in alliance with the Knossians, captured Lyttos. Diodorus states that the original inhabitants were expelled and only regained possession of their city and territory after receiving aid from the Spartans.[8] Archaeology, however, tells a different story. Among the debris of a later sack at Lyttos were found the remains of Archaic pithoi, which must therefore have survived intact the events related here.[9] If there was no wholesale destruction of the *asty* it seems to me far more likely that the Lyttians were reduced to tributary status and received a garrison, a situation broadly similar to that at Acharna but in stark contrast to the wars of extirpation waged in the Hellenistic period and related below.

That political prominence was achieved more through both the establishment of a network of alliances and the holding of smaller places in a tributary status than through wholesale destructions is amply illustrated by the treaty between Miletus and several Cretan cities dated to the period 260–240 B.C.[10] The Cretan states are organised in three groups (FIG. 1). Phaistos was allied with the neighbouring Matala and Polyrrhenia in the far west. Gortys headed a group that comprised the neighbouring small-scale communities of the Ariaioi and the Hyrtaioi and the two larger neighbouring powerful cities of Arkades and Lyttos. Thus this network was a purely regional one.

In contrast Knossos headed a far larger group of cities that must have made it the most powerful Cretan city of the period. More important, perhaps, is the distribution of the allied states. We find that the immediate hinterland of Knossos was controlled by a network of alliances: Apollonia, Tylissos, Rhaukos, Eltynia and Herakleion all followed the Knossian banner. To the east Lyttos could be neutralised or at least contained by the many allied states in a broad band of territory stretching from Chersonesos to Istron. All of the cities in this area were part of the alliance. Against Arkades stood Priansos, while in the far east Itanos and Praisos could be used to counterbalance the influence of Hierapytna. Just west of the Herakleion valley the powerful states of Axos and Eleutherna formed part of the Knossian federation. Their influence would have neutralised that of Rethymnon and Lappa. In the west of the island Kydonia and Phalasarna adhered to the alliance and formed a powerful pro-Knossian block there.

---

[6] K.J. Rigsby, 'Cnossus and Capua', *Trans. Amer. Philol. Ass.* 106 (1976), 327–8.
[7] I owe this thought to Dr. N. Sekunda.
[8] Diodorus xvi.62.3 ff.
[9] A. Lembesi, 'Lyttos', *A.Delt.* 26 B'2 (1971), 494–6, pls. 512–13.
[10] *ICret* I, viii, no. 6.

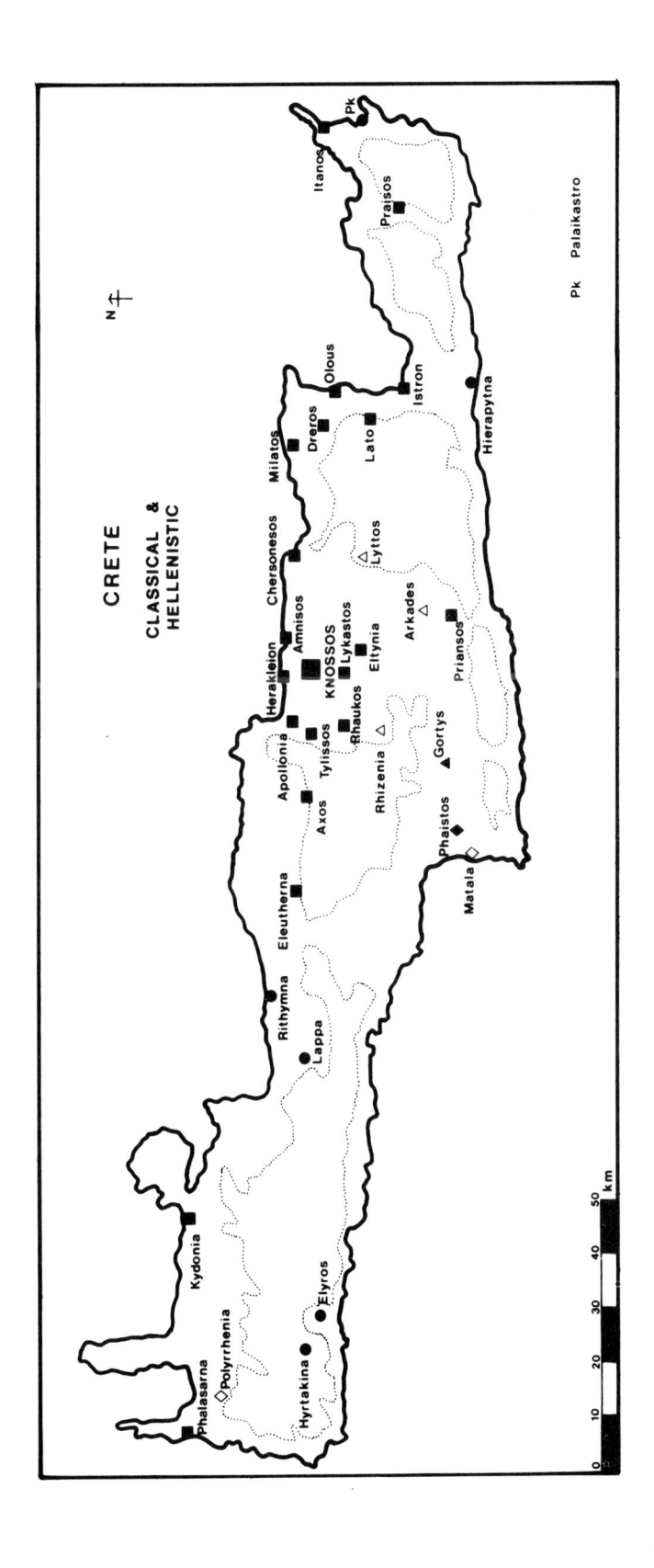

FIG. 1 Location of sites in Crete mentioned in the text

In other words, Knossos seems to have maintained a position of predominance throughout the whole island and it is this, rather than the number of its adherents, that distinguished it from the more parochial Gortys.

An interesting feature of this treaty is the absence of Tritonion, Lykastos, Rhizenia and Pannona from the list of allied states. This may imply that the first two had already been swallowed up in the Knossia and the others by Gortys. Tradition states that Lykastos at least was razed to the ground on its capture,[11] thus perhaps providing the first evidence for the alternative and increasingly applied Hellenistic strategy of territorial expansion by the major powers at the expense of lower order settlements in the hierarchy.

In the Lyttian War of 221–219 B.C. it is said that the whole of Crete followed Gortys and Knossos against Lyttos. If this is so then the web of alliances we noted above must have been extended considerably in the intervening generation.[12] Foreign powers also intervened in this struggle as the opposing factions called in their external allies.[13]

In 220 B.C. Knossos managed to surprise a Lyttos whose defences had been depleted by the absence of its field army. The city was thoroughly sacked, an event which has left a clear impression in the archaeological record. The women and children were carried away to Knossos and the returning Lyttian troops were forced to leave their devastated homeland and seek shelter with the sympathetic population of Lappa.[14] Already, however, the previously monolithic alliance had been broken up by the defection of many important cities and the Gortynian state was itself paralysed by *stasis* over the question.[15] Knossos may originally have intended to subsume the conquered territory within its own borders, but in the event this proved impossible and it is likely that Lyttos was soon resettled. It was certainly a force to be reckoned with as early as 184 B.C.

In 184 B.C. Knossos suffered what must have been a disastrous defeat at the hands of the Gortynians, probably allied with the Rhaukians and Lyttians. It was deprived of Tritonion and Lykastos, which were given to the two allied cities. Gortys itself may well have kept additional territory not mentioned in the sources.[16] The Gortynian policy appears to have been to strengthen Knossos' immediate neighbours in a sort of policy of encirclement, but in the event Roman diplomatic intervention forced a return to the *status quo ante bellum*.

The next major event was the fall of Apollonia to the Kydonians in 171 B.C.[17] The territory of the stricken city was seized by the Knossians, who held it until it was awarded to Gortys by Egyptian arbitration about 166 B.C. The two cities then took advantage of a new-found harmony of purpose to extend their holding further in the Herakleion Valley. They sacked the powerful city of Rhaukos and divided its territory.[18] The new border ran right through the city, past the Prytaneion and then in what seems to have been a southwesterly direction into the flanks of the Ida massif. It is fairly obvious that the city of Rhaukos thus ceased to exist as a functioning urban settlement. Of some

---

[11] Strabo x.479.14.
[12] Polybius iv.53.3–54; *ICret* I, viii, pp. 48–9.
[13] Polybius iv.55.1 ff.
[14] Polybius iv.54.
[15] *ICret* IV, p. 21.
[16] Polybius xxii.15.1 ff.
[17] *ICret* IV, no. 181.
[18] *ICret* IV, no. 182; Polybius xxx.23.1.

interest is the fact that Knossian territory extended all the way into the mountains; it is possible that Tylissos had already fallen to Knossian arms by this time. It makes its last appearance in history in a treaty between Eumenes II and many Cretan cities in 183 B.C.,[19] and the ensuing silence as well as the known Knossian hold on territory north of the city of Rhaukos in 165 B.C. both suggest that Knossos was the aggressor and victor.

Thus it would seem that, in a relatively rapid process, most of the middle-order settlements of the Herakleion valley were wiped out in the early part of the 2nd century B.C. and the spoils divided between Knossos and Gortys. The suppression of the urban centres themselves suggests an intensification of the strategy of exploitation current in the earlier periods and implies the rise of vast territorial units here that find parallels in other parts of Crete.[20] The extension of Gortynian power north of the spine of the island and into territory that had been under Knossian influence during the 3rd century B.C. implies a diminution of the latter's influence at the same time as its absolute power was growing.

Nor was the former pre-eminence of Knossos in the upper valley the only point of attrition. We have seen that in 260–240 B.C. she also controlled a vast belt of territory to the east stretching from Chersonesos to Istron. In the course of the 2nd century B.C. most of this land fell under the influence of Lyttos, thus creating a strong competitor on Knossos' right flank. There is good evidence[21] that much of this Lyttian expansion was carried out in the face of strong Knossian opposition. By the 1st century B.C. the hapless Knossians may have found themselves between the hammer and the anvil whenever Lyttos and Gortys cared to unite.[22]

The later 2nd and early 1st centuries B.C. were taken up by a series of wars between Knossos and Gortys.[23] At times the Knossians were successful but a note in Vitruvius suggests that a new border between the two states ran along the river Pothereus (probably the modern Gazanos), which implies that the Gortynians may have been able to take the area including the former territory of Tylissos and to establish a corridor of land stretching from the north to the south coast.[24]

Evidence for Knossian diplomatic activity outside the island during the Classical and Hellenistic periods is relatively sparse. Her capture of Lyttos in 346 B.C. brought her into conflict with Sparta and in the following year the Knossians were awarded a wreath by the Athenians.[25] Generally anti-Macedonian during the Hellenistic period, Knossos supported Rhodes against Demetrius Poliorketes in 305 B.C.[26] and seems to have adhered to a pro-Aetolian policy with remarkable fidelity.[27] She

---

[19] W. Dittenberger, *Sylloge Inscriptionum Graecarum* ii (3rd edn.; Leipzig, 1917), no. 627.

[20] For example the suppression of Milatos by Lyttos in the 2nd century B.C. (Strabo x.479.14); and the fall of Praisos to Hierapytna c.150 B.C. (*ICret* III, nos. 9–10 and commentary on pp. 103 ff.).

[21] The Drerian oath is very pro-Knossian and anti-Lyttian (H. van Effenterre, 'A propos du Serment des Drériens', *BCH* 61 (1937), 327–32) and seems to represent the fears of the Drerians that their city might be taken over by the neighbouring Lyttos. They turned to Knossos for help, as they had probably done in the 3rd century B.C.

[22] As they may well have done to attack Lato, where a Gortynian sling bullet has been found (*ICret* IV, p. 22).

[23] R.F. Willetts, *Aristocratic Society in Ancient Crete* (London, 1955), 240.

[24] Vitruvius, *De Arch.* i.4.10. None of the rivers in the Herakleion valley literally lies between Knossos and Gortys. They all flow south–north. Vitruvius does not specifically say that the Pothereus formed the border, but his wording implies that it did.

[25] *Inscriptiones Graecae* (Berlin, 1927) ii–iii³.1443, col. II, 121 f.

[26] Diodorus xx.88.9.

[27] Willetts (n. 23 above), *passim*.

had to submit to the hegemony of Philip V in 217/16 B.C.[28] but was soon actively anti-Macedonian once more.[29] The Aetolian connexion was a well-established one. Recent excavations at Kallion in Aetolia have uncovered a sealing with the official crest of the Knossians in a house inhabited by prominent statesmen of the Aetolian League.[30] Since Kallion was destroyed by the Gauls during the first half of the 3rd century B.C. this is also a relatively early date for such interaction.

The treaty with Pergamon in 183 B.C. may have been primarily to allow Eumenes II access to a pool of mercenary soldiers,[31] and other treaties with Rhodes may have been concerned with similar rights of access.[32] The Knossian (and general Cretan) penchant for either mercenary service or piracy in the many wars that wracked the Hellenistic world probably brought them into contact with many rulers and states[33] and it is unlikely that the relative isolation of the Archaic and Classical periods could have been maintained. Nevertheless, Knossos, along with most of the rest of the island, managed to remain free of any subjugation from the outside until the brutal Roman conquest by Metellus in 67 B.C.

I have sought to show in this short summary that the rise of a great territorial state in the Knossia was a feature of the Hellenistic period. It is one of the more confusing aspects of Cretan history that the concomitant rise of other great states at Lyttos and Gortys might very well have led to a fall in the relative influence of Knossos at the same time as its absolute power increased.

---

[28] Polybius vii.11.9.
[29] *ICret* I, no. 49.
[30] P. Panos, 'Τὰ Σφραγίσματα τῆς Ἀιτωλικῆς Καλλιπόλεως' (Athens, 1985), no. 88.
[31] Dittenberger (n. 19 above), no. 627.
[32] For Cretan mercenary activity cf. G.T. Griffith, *The Mercenaries of the Hellenistic World* (Cambridge, 1935), *passim*.
[33] Ibid.; H.A. Ormerod, *Piracy in the Ancient World: An Essay in Mediterranean History* (Liverpool, 1924), *passim*, and [Editors' note: P. Brulé, *La Piraterie crétoise hellénistique*, (Centre de recherches d'histoire ancienne 27, Annales Litt. de l'Univ. de Besançon 223; Paris, 1978), *passim*].

Chapter 10

Roman Knossos and the Colonia Julia Nobilis Cnossus

S. PATON

In 67 B.C. the Roman conquest of Crete by Q. Caecilius Metellus was accomplished. The campaign had been a brutal one, exacerbated by fierce political rivalry among the Roman generals, particularly between Metellus and Pompey. The Cretan resistance was led with considerable skill by the Knossian Lasthenes who had, in 71, inflicted a humiliating defeat on a Roman fleet under the command of M. Antonius. By the end of the war Lasthenes was sufficiently celebrated for Pompey to find it worth his while to prevent Metellus from including him in his triumph,[1] and when Metellus took Knossos by siege he caused the house of Lasthenes to be burnt and his property to be destroyed.[2]

Metellus 'gave laws to the island'[3] (once, in the days of its independence, renowned for giving laws to others); he celebrated his triumph — without Lasthenes — and was awarded the title of Creticus by a grateful Senate. The island was incorporated in the Roman province of Crete-and-Cyrene. Of its principal cities Gortyna, not Knossos, was chosen as the capital, partly no doubt because of the spirited role that Knossos had played in the resistance, and partly because the position of Gortyna was more suitable — it lay on a central route across the island and possessed, at Matala, one of the few natural harbours on the south coast, through which communication could be kept up with Cyrene's port of Apollonia. The voyage across the Libyan sea took two days and nights,[4] and the governors, or at any rate members of their staff, must have had to make the crossing many times during the course of their tours of duty.

Little is known of affairs at Knossos during the next twenty years or so; presumably it returned

---

Special Abbreviation:
ICret = *Inscriptiones Creticae* ed. M. Guarducci (Rome, 1935–1950) —

   ICret I: tituli Cretae mediae praeter Gortynios
   ICret II: tituli Cretae occidentalis
   ICret III: tituli Cretae orientalis
   ICret IV: tituli Gortynii

KS = S. Hood and D. Smyth, *Archaeological Survey of the Knossos Area* (2nd edn.; *BSA* Suppl. 14; London, 1981).

[1] Cassius Dio xxxvi.19.
[2] Appian, *Sicelica* (frag.) 6.5.
[3] Livy, *Epitomae* xcix.
[4] Strabo x.4.5.

fairly quickly to a state of prosperity. Strabo, who had family connexions there through his Knossian grandmother, implies that its territory was diminished from former times,[5] but the siege by Metellus does not appear to have caused widespread damage — the fact that the destruction of Lasthenes' property is particularly mentioned suggests that it was exceptional, and no sign of violent disruption at this period has so far been detected in the archaeological record. But the convulsions in the Roman world following Caesar's assassination, and the consequent struggle for supremacy between Mark Antony and Caesar's heir Octavian, brought Crete and the affairs of its cities once more to prominence. By the end of the civil wars Knossos had undergone great changes; it had lost a valuable part of its territory to Capua and had gained a Roman colony — not just the only colony in Crete, but, until the time of Hadrian, apparently the only one in the province.[6]

Although the colony existed early in the reign of Augustus the date of its foundation is not securely known, and the *Res Gestae* of Augustus does not include Crete-and-Cyrene in the list of provinces in which he founded colonies. A possible explanation for this may be looked for in the anomalous status of Crete during the period between the assassination in 44 B.C. and the settlement after Actium in 31. In the days of uncertainty following the Ides of March, the Senate passed a resolution conferring the status of law on all Caesar's *acta*. It also assigned the governorship of Crete to Brutus, to follow his praetorship. Caesar's will was handed over to the surviving consul, Mark Antony, who issued spurious decrees supposedly based on Caesar's intentions, among them one which declared that, after the governorship of Brutus, Crete should no longer be a province and its cities should be free. The inconsistency was pointed out, bitterly, by Cicero: since the appointment of Brutus followed Caesar's death Caesar could have made no provision that depended on it. But nothing could be done; the province of Crete was lost — 'provinciam Cretam perdidistis'.[7] Caesar had been a keen founder of colonies; if his arrangements for the future, which now had the force of law, had included a plan to found a colony at Knossos this plan would have been very difficult to implement, since the status of a new colony sent out to a country which had suddenly ceased to be a Roman province would be legally uneasy, to say the least of it.

After Philippi in 42 Crete became part of Mark Antony's domain in the East; it was therefore under Roman rule, but not of a very orthodox kind. In 37/6 B.C. Antony gave territory in Crete to Cleopatra[8] but we do not know what part of the island was disposed of in this way. Several governors are known from this period; one was L. Lollius, in about 38 B.C., and another, probably in 37/6, was Crassus, who appears to have been in favour of Cleopatra's influence — his coins bear the image of a crocodile, reflecting the Ptolemaic interest. It is not known for certain who this Crassus was; the most likely candidate is M. Licinius Crassus, grandson of the consul of 70, who supported Antony but prudently changed sides before Actium.[9] At Knossos coins were issued by a series of Greek magistrates,[10] also presumably firmly attached to the cause of Mark Antony and Cleopatra;

---

[5] Strabo x.4.7.
[6] R.G. Goodchild, *Tabula Imperii Romani*, Sheet H.1.34, Cyrene (London, 1954), 5.
[7] *Philippics* ii.38.
[8] Cassius Dio xlix.32.5.
[9] Ibid., li.4.3. If his mother was the daughter of Metellus Creticus he may have inherited a considerable *clientela* in Crete (*Inscriptiones Latinae Selectae*, ed. H. Dessau (Berlin, 1955), no. 881). Her tomb is a famous landmark on the Via Appia.
[10] Anne E. Chapman, 'Some first century B.C. bronze coins of Knossos', *Num.Chron.* 8, 7th ser. (1968), 13–26.

one of these magistrates was, apparently, Antony's Cretan agent Kydas, who had been denounced as a scoundrel by Cicero some ten years earlier — 'portentum insulae, hominem audacissimum et perditissimum'. Cicero had asserted, in 43 B.C., that Antony's judiciary law was framed for this man's benefit — 'Cretensis iudex, isque nequissimus'.[11]

But Mark Antony was not the only contender for supremacy to offer bits of Crete as reward to his supporters. In Sicily, in 36, Octavian's soldiers threatened to mutiny; they knew their bargaining position to be strong since war with Antony was imminent and they would be needed for it. Octavian placated them by buying land for them from Capua, and to Capua, in compensation, he promised land at Knossos[12] — land that would not be his to give unless he won the war. These settlements were made, Dio says, not long afterwards — presumably after Actium in 31 — and Capua's share of the Knossian territory turned out to be extremely valuable, bringing an income of 1,200,000 sestertii a year.[13] And it must have been after Actium, and probably after the settlement of the provinces early in 27 B.C., that the Colonia Julia Nobilis Cnossus was established, its omission from the *Res Gestae* being perhaps because, in founding it, Augustus was merely carrying out the intentions of his adoptive father, Caesar.

From the Augustan period on through the first century the life of the colony seems to have followed fairly orthodox lines. Those of the magistrates and holders of the various priesthoods who are known to us almost all have Latin names, and several of them seem to have Italian connexions.[14] The territory belonging to Capua lay further up the valley to the south and was administered separately, the revenue being dealt with by an *arcuarius Cretae* at Capua.[15] In A.D. 84 a boundary dispute between this Capuan land and a citizen of the colony, a descendant of one of the first colonists, was settled by the Imperial procurator in Crete, P. Messius Campanus.[16] There is evidence of strong links between Campania and Crete during the Roman period, shown by inscriptions in the first century[17] and by the presence of Campanian pottery in the first, second and third centuries;[18] whether these links came about because the original colonists who settled at Knossos were from Campania or whether they reflect a more general pattern throughout the island it is not yet possible to say. The colony honoured M. Nonius Balbus, patron of Crete, in a dedication at Herculaneum,[19] and in the Augustan period M. Sonteius Casina was honoured in an inscription for the care he had taken of the affairs of three wards whose name, like that of the procurator of A.D. 84, was Campanus; M. Sonteius Casina had been aedile and duovir of the colony at Knossos, but the inscription was set

---

[11] *Philippics* v.5.14.
[12] Cassius Dio xlix.14.5.
[13] Velleius Paterculus ii.81.2.
[14] I.F. Sanders, *Roman Crete: An Archaeological Survey and Gazetteer of Late Hellenistic, Roman and Early Byzantine Crete* (Warminster, 1982), 14.
[15] *Inscr. Lat. Sel.* (n. 9 above), no. 6317.
[16] K.J. Rigsby, 'Cnossus and Capua', *Trans. Amer. Philol. Ass.* 106 (1976), 313–30.
[17] *ICret* IV, nos. 295 and 314.
[18] J.W. Hayes, 'The Villa Dionysos excavations, Knossos: the pottery', *BSA* 78 (1983), 97–169. L.H. Sackett *et al.*, *Knossos. From Greek City to Roman Colony: Excavations at the Unexplored Mansion II* (BSA Suppl. 21; London, 1992), 147 ff. (the Roman pottery). P.M. Warren, 'Knossos: Stratigraphical Museum Excavations 1978–82, Part IV', *AR* 34 (1987–88), 86–104.
[19] Sanders (n. 14 above), 14; *CIL* x.1433.

up at Gortyna.[20] No example has been found at Knossos of the distinctive Campanian sepulchral stelae, on which the dead person and his family are shown carved in high relief within a shrine or aedicula;[21] if the colonists came from Campania it might be supposed that they would have brought their burial customs with them.

The civic centre of the colony was sited not directly over the centre of the Minoan city but slightly to the north of it (FIG. 1). The ruins of the great Minoan Palace must have been an impressive site in the first century — it is possible that the Romans thought it was haunted. The Elder Pliny gave a vivid account of its bewildering intricacy in his description of the Cretan labyrinth.[22] There is plenty of evidence that the Romans were deeply interested in the past of Knossos and in its legends. Knossian coins of Augustus bear the labyrinth as the city's symbol; the complex manoeuvres of the Troy Game, a cavalry exercise performed at Rome by boys of aristocratic family under Caesar[23] and many times under Augustus,[24] were likened by both Pliny and Virgil[25] to the Knossian labyrinth. The game was a reminder of the Trojan ancestry of the Julian family, since it was supposed to have been invented by Aeneas' son Ascanius; as Virgil pointed out, the family had Cretan ancestors as well.[26] Catullus and Ovid wrote about the Minotaur and Theseus and Ariadne. Few Romans, however, can have taken this enthusiasm to such lengths as the Emperor Galba, who displayed in his hall a family tree demonstrating his descent, through his mother's family, from Pasiphae, wife of King Minos.[27]

For knowledge of the Roman city we are dependent on the descriptions of travellers and on the archaeological record, which would probably have been extremely meagre had it been concerned with Roman remains alone. The paramount importance of Minoan Knossos to the Aegean Bronze Age has led to intense archaeological investigation of the whole area in major excavation, in rescue work and in survey. Although little of this research has been specifically addressed to the problems of the Roman period our knowledge of the life of the colony, though fragmentary and from this particular point of view more or less random, is almost entirely an incidental benefit from the splendour of its predecessor. The major source of information on the remains of Roman Knossos is the *Archaeological Survey of the Knossos Area*, published by Sinclair Hood and David Smyth in 1981. There can be few Roman cities, not investigated for their own sake, of which as much detail is known as is recorded about Roman Knossos in the *Survey*.

Roman ruins at Knossos were described by many travellers through the ages. The earliest account we have is that of Buondelmonti in the fifteenth century, who saw the so-called Tomb of Caiaphas and discovered a fine mosaic.[28] In the sixteenth century Onorio Belli noted the remains of the theatre

---

[20] *ICret* IV, no. 295; cf. A. Chaniotis and G. Preuss, 'Neue Fragmente des Preisedikts von Diokletian und weitere Lateinische Inschriften aus Kreta', *Zeitschr. Pap. u. Epig.* 80 (1990), 198 (I owe this reference to Dr. Ch. Kritzas).
[21] M. Frederiksen, *Campania*, edited with additions by N. Purcell (London, 1984), 287 ff.
[22] *HN* xxxvi.19.85.
[23] Suetonius, *Caesar* xxxix.2.
[24] Id., *Augustus* xliii.2.
[25] *Aeneid* v.588–91.
[26] *Aeneid* iii.108.
[27] Suetonius, *Galba* ii.
[28] Cristofero Buondelmonti, *Descriptio Insule Crete et Liber Insularum*, ed. Marie-Anne Spitael (Herakleion, 1981), ch. xi.

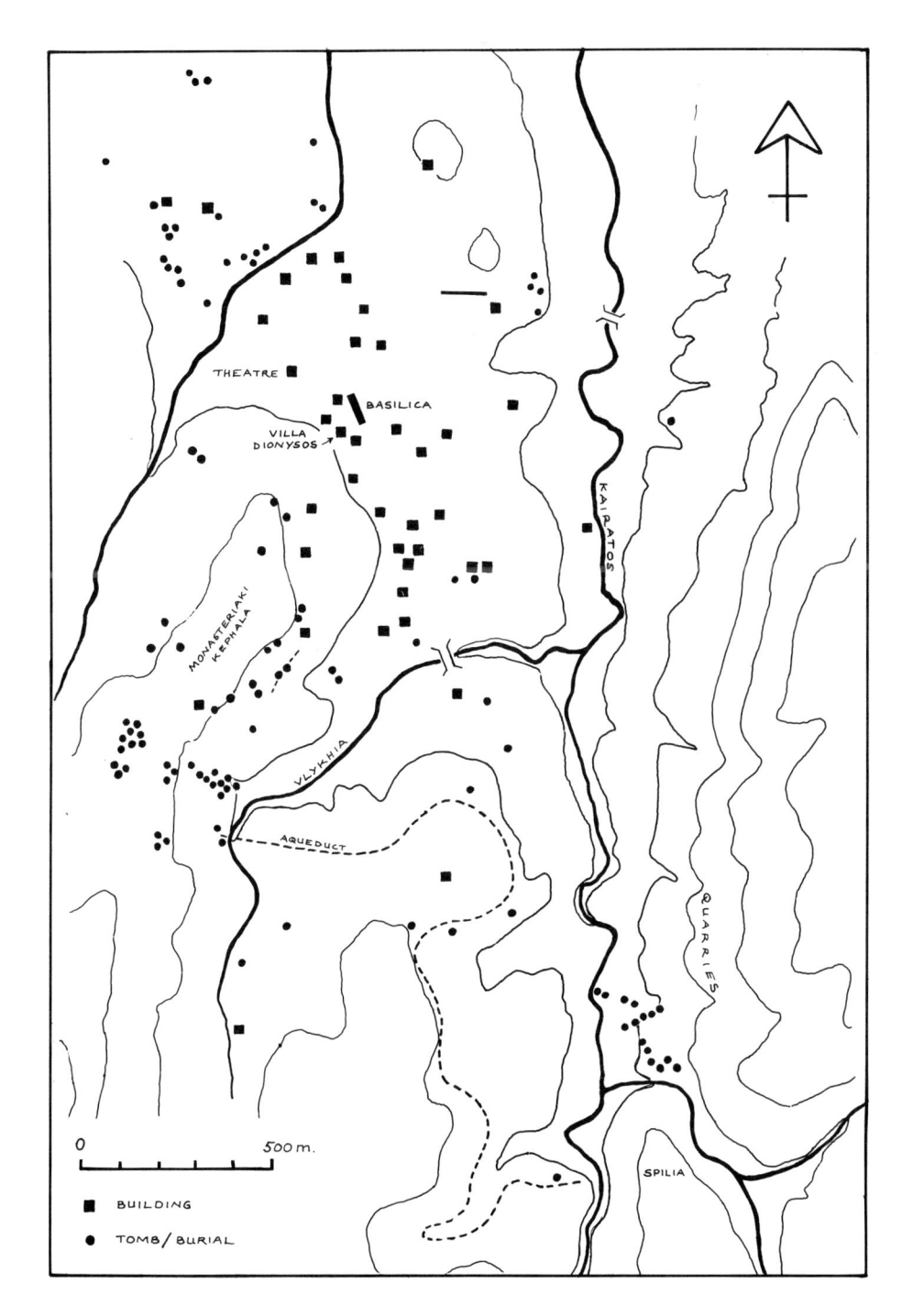

FIG. 1 Plan of locations at Knossos

and made a plan of the basilica;[29] descriptions of the site by later visitors include those of Cornaro, of Pococke in the eighteenth century and of Pashley and Spratt in the nineteenth.[30] Halbherr did some excavation in the forum area in the 1880s,[31] and Roman remains throughout Knossos were found and recorded on many occasions by Sir Arthur Evans and R.W. Hutchinson. The coins of Knossos were first published by Svoronos in 1890[32] and the inscriptions by Margherita Guarducci in 1935.[33] General accounts of the city in the Roman period are to be found in the introduction to the *Survey* and in Ian Sanders' *Roman Crete*,[34] while recent excavations, chiefly of residential areas to the west of the Palace of Minos, have added greatly to our detailed knowledge. The pottery sequence has been analysed in two major publications, that of the Villa Dionysos by J.W. Hayes[35] and that from the Roman levels above the Unexplored Mansion by L.H. Sackett, in a full excavation report which also includes important studies of the lamps, coins, plaster sculptures and other finds in bone, metal and terracotta.[36]

Although we know roughly the limits of the Roman city — between the hill of Monasteriaki Kephala on the west and the Kairatos valley on the east, with the Vlykhia to the south and the northern limit along the old line of the stream bed south of the Venizeleion Hospital (FIG. 1) — we know almost nothing of its plan. Roads were built and looked after; a coin of Tiberius was found beneath the surface of the Roman road on the site of the Royal Road excavations,[37] and an inscription found in 1975 at Pentevi records the repair, in the reign of Nero, of a road which may have been the main route to the port of Herakleion.[38] Stretches of Roman road have also been observed from time to time following the line of what is now the main road southwards to Archanes, through the modern village in the direction of the Roman bridge over the Vlykhia.[39] Further north the modern road veers to the west; the line must differ here from the ancient one since it cuts right through the Roman theatre. The Roman route may have continued due northwards, passing the forum area on its eastward side, though the existence of a western road to the coast on a line close to that of the modern road is indicated by the presence of cemeteries in the area of the Venizeleion Hospital, and of graves found near the Fortetsa turning. Sections of minor streets have been observed at several points in the southern part of the city, mostly following older lines; the northern part, where formal planning is more to be expected, is still largely unexplored and its orientation unknown.

For the earliest phase in the Roman period, between the conquest of 67 B.C. and the foundation of the colony, not much evidence has survived. In the southern part of the town several sites which

---

[29] E. Falkener, *A Description of Some Important Theatres and Other Remains in Crete, from a MS History of Candia by Onorio Belli in 1586* (London, 1854).

[30] Andrea Cornaro, *Historia Candiana* (unpublished MS in Italian, early 17th century, quoted by Pashley (infra) 205), fol. 2; Richard Pococke, *A Description of the East, and Some Other Countries*, ii (London, 1745); Robert Pashley, *Travels in Crete*, i (London, 1837); T.A.B. Spratt, *Travels and Researches in Crete*, i (London, 1865).

[31] F. Halbherr, 'Researches in Crete', *The Antiquary* 28 (1893), 110–12.

[32] J.N. Svoronos, *Numismatique de la Crète ancienne* (Paris, 1890).

[33] *ICret* I (Rome, 1935).

[34] Sanders (n. 14 above).

[35] Hayes (n. 18 above).

[36] Sackett (n. 18 above).

[37] R.H.J. Ashton, 'Knossos Royal Road South 1971 and 1972 excavations: the Coins', *BSA* 84 (1989), 49 ff.

[38] *A.Delt.* 30.B'2 (1975), 341; H.W. Catling, 'Archaeology in Greece, 1983–84', *AR* 30 (1983–84), 61.

[39] Information from Dr. C.F. Macdonald; the bridge is *KS* no. 204.

had been in use during the Hellenistic period were abandoned at this time; one of them was a house with a wine press,[40] another was the shrine of the hero Glaukos,[41] whose cult was perhaps frowned upon by the Roman authorities, military initiation rituals being suitable for the well-to-do young men of Rome but not for those of conquered countries. On a hillside to the southwest of the town an isolated Roman farmhouse was excavated in 1975, which had been built, occupied and abandoned all within the period between 67 B.C. and the foundation of the colony — scarcely more than a generation. A small group of tile graves nearby was slightly later in date, and the area was soon in use as a cemetery.[42] This impression of discontinuity is not, however, borne out by other excavations in the western part of the town. On the site of the Stratigraphical Museum Extension the arrival of the colony was archaeologically unnoticeable,[43] and in the Roman levels excavated on the site of the Unexplored Mansion a Hellenistic street continued in use through the greater part of the Roman period, and the property lines of the various houses seem to have remained more or less the same into the second century, in spite of rebuilding necessitated probably by earthquakes.[44]

Unlike the shrine of Glaukos, the sanctuary of Demeter, on the lower slopes of Gypsadhes south of the city, continued in use during the period in which the colony was established and on into the middle of the second century, although the ceremonies in the Roman period seem to have been more convivial than spiritual.[45] Demeter's followers included members of the Knossian aristocracy; a statue of Kore which probably came from here was set up in the first or second century by a lady called Nonia Ancharia.[46] She must have belonged to the same family as Ancharius Priscus, who was powerful enough, in the reign of Tiberius, to prosecute the provincial governor Caesius Cordus for extortion.[47] Several inscriptions refer to the imperial cult at Knossos though we do not know where its temple stood; M. Sonteius Casina was a priest of Augustus as well as being duovir and a conscientious guardian, and an unnamed priest of Vespasian is known from a tombstone.[48] Isis may also have been worshipped; an inscription of the first century A.D. with the letters ISID was found on a hillside to the north of the city, near the remains of a building, perhaps a temple.[49] Another building which may have been a temple[50] was noted near the eastern end of the great concrete wall, the Makryteichos, from which the lower village of Knossos takes its name,[51] and a fourth, a little to the southeast of the forum area, was thought to be a temple but may perhaps be the remains of baths.[52]

---

[40] *KS* no. 200.
[41] *KS* no. 197; P.J. Callaghan, 'Excavations at a shrine of Glaukos, Knossos', *BSA* 73 (1978), 1 ff.
[42] *KS* no. 177. P. Callaghan, H.W. Catling, E.A. Catling and D. Smyth, 'Knossos 1975: Minoan *paralipomena* and post-Minoan remains', *BSA* 76 (1981), 83–108.
[43] Warren (n. 18 above), 88.
[44] Sackett (n. 18 above), 18.
[45] J.N. Coldstream *et al.*, *Knossos: The Sanctuary of Demeter* (*BSA* Suppl. 8; London, 1973).
[46] *ICret* I, viii, no. 21, p. 73.
[47] Tacitus, *Annals* iii.70.
[48] Sanders (n. 14 above), 38; *ICret* I, viii, no. 54.
[49] *KS* no. 76
[50] *KS* no. 85.
[51] *KS* no. 86.
[52] *KS* no. 121; D.G. Hogarth, 'Knossos: II. Early town and cemeteries', *BSA* 6 (1899–1900), 81, pl. xii; *PM II.ii*, plan opp. 547; cf. C.A. Ralegh Radford, 'Report on Roman Remains at Knossos', 1937 (unpublished).

In the first century Knossos seems to have been plagued by earthquakes. The Unexplored Mansion site shows signs of at least two in the reign of Augustus, with a third in the middle of the century, while the story of Dictys Cretensis records another in the thirteenth year of Nero (66–7). The fullest picture of life in the city comes from the period after this, through the second century until the end of the Antonine period, when another major earthquake may have occurred. At this time Knossos, like most of the Roman world, seems to have enjoyed great prosperity. Pottery, lamps, metalwork, mosaics, fine stucco-work, painting, and olive oil and winemaking were among the industries. The wine may have been exported; Cretan wine reached Ostia,[53] though Juvenal had a low opinion of it.[54] And it is in the later second century that we have a first glimpse of the Christian community at Knossos, led by its stern Bishop Pinytos, who snubbed the Bishop of Corinth for writing to recommend that his flock should attempt austerities which they already practised as a matter of course.[55]

The houses of this period were most enthusiastically decorated. Mosaics have been uncovered on many sites at Knossos, some of them very fine.[56] Walls with painted plaster imitating coloured marble have been found in the late first-century house on the site of the Stratigraphical Museum Extension and on the site of the Unexplored Mansion in the second-century House of the Diamond Frescoes, which also had decorative architectural mouldings of stucco. The Villa Dionysos, further to the north, was a peristyle building with magnificent mosaics representing the god and his companions (PLATE 17); several of its large rooms were lined with panelling of imported coloured marble set in elaborate stucco mouldings, while others were painted to imitate this effect.[57] This building lies to the north of what appears to have been the main residential area, close to the theatre and the western side of the forum; its position and the size and formality of its rooms suggest that it was designed not as a private house but for some official purpose. It may have been a collegiate building, the headquarters of a guild; the *vinarii* of Knossos might be suitable tenants for an establishment such as this with the vinescrolls and Dionysiac imagery of its mosaics. Amongst the pottery in the deep fill that buried it after its destruction there were found fragments of more than fifty different types of wine amphorae, from all over the Roman world.[58] Like the House of the Diamond Frescoes, the Villa Dionysos was destroyed, probably by an earthquake, towards the end of the second century.

It is for this period, between the middle of the first century and the end of the second, that we also have most information about the citizens of the Colonia Julia Nobilis from their tombs. The main cemeteries lay in the hillsides round the city, to the north in the area of the Venizeleion Hospital, to the southwest on the hills of Monasteriaki Kephala and Bairia, and to the south towards Spilia. Many simple tile graves have been found, but the most typical tomb was a rectangular chamber cut in the rock, with a short entrance passage at one side and loculi with stone-cut beds for the dead on the

---

[53] Cretan amphorae at Ostia: C. Panella, 'Anfore', in A. Carandini *et al.*, *Ostia* III.ii, *le Terme del Nuotatore* (*Studi Misc.* 21; Rome, 1973), 477.

[54] Juvenal, *Satire* xiv.270.

[55] Eusebius, *Hist. Eccl.* iv.23.7.

[56] *KS* nos. 91, 92, 94 (possibly wall or vault mosaics), 100, 112, 114, 115, 117, 119, 128, 130, 131, 135, 195, 234.

[57] *KS* no. 114. The Villa Dionysos was excavated partly by R.W. Hutchinson and C.A. Ralegh Radford in 1935–7 and partly by Michael Gough in 1957–71.

[58] J.W. Hayes (n. 18 above), 140–1.

other three, and niches for lamps and grave offerings. Most of these tombs have been disturbed, in antiquity or in more recent times. Two tombs of this kind were excavated in 1970 in the area to the southwest of the city; both had been disturbed but the remaining contents, including lamps, glass vessels and two terracotta actors' masks, enabled the excavator to date their period of use to the second half of the first century into the first half of the second century.[59] A clay theatrical mask was also found in 1968 in one of a group of four tombs further to the south.[60]

One unpillaged tomb in the southwestern cemetery, excavated in 1978, gave a vivid picture of the luxury and sophistication available to Knossian citizens of this time.[61] It contained jewellery, terracottas (including another mask) and a fine collection of elaborate and delicate glass vessels, many of them probably imported from Italy. There were also the bronze fittings and the lock for a wooden casket; the metal bindings and attachments of boxes such as this have been found elsewhere at Knossos, including remains of two *arcae* (so far unpublished) from the Villa Dionysos, and several lockplates, latches and other attachments found in a Hadrianic context at the Unexplored Mansion site, where a locksmith may have been at work.[62]

The rock-cut tombs of the Spilia cemetery have also produced rich finds of this period including jewellery, coins, lamps and glass,[63] though theatrical masks are not so far reported from this area; they seem to be confined to the burials on the southern slopes of Monasteriaki Kephala and Bairia. Built tombs of the Roman period seem to have been more common to the north of the city (though one was found near the Sanctuary of Demeter) and perhaps to be of later date; the so-called Tomb of Caiaphas, described by early travellers but destroyed in about 1880, was probably a great concrete-built mausoleum, perhaps of the fourth or fifth century.[64] Several built Roman tombs were found in the North Cemetery excavations of 1978,[65] where one tomb of the early fifth century turned out to have been constructed from the dismantled pieces of a Roman Corinthian portico of mid-second-century date (FIGS. 2 and 3). The blocks of the portico were of Pentelic marble and had apparently been shipped from Attica to Crete in building-kit form, since instructions for assembly were inscribed on their undersides.[66] It is not clear why a building of the form of a temple should have been standing in this cemetery; it may perhaps have been a heroon.

Public works of the Roman period include an aqueduct bringing water to the city from the south, of which many stretches have been recorded along the eastern slopes of Lower Gypsadhes.[67] Concrete supports mark the point where it crossed the Vlykhia[68] and it probably continued along the contour, round the eastern side of Monasteriaki Kephala; a possible further stretch was found

---

[59] *KS* no. 170. K.A. Wardle, 'Two notes from Knossos', *BSA* 67 (1972), 271–83.
[60] *KS* no. 157. P.M. Fraser, 'Archaeology in Greece, 1968–69', *AR* 15 (1968–69), 33.
[61] *KS* no. 186. J. Carington Smith, 'A Roman chamber tomb on the south-east slopes of Monasteriaki Kephala, Knossos', *BSA* 77 (1982), 255–93.
[62] K. Branigan, 'Metal objects and metallurgical debris', in Sackett (n. 18 above), 375.
[63] *KS* no. 361. H.W. Catling, 'Archaeology in Greece, 1983–84', *AR* 30 (1983–84), 61 (excavation by A. Lembessi); id., 'The Knossos area, 1974–76', *AR* 30 (1983–84), 22–3 (excavation by A. Karetsou).
[64] *KS* no. 57.
[65] H.W. Catling, 'Knossos, 1978', *AR* 25 (1978–79), 52, 56–7.
[66] S. Paton, 'A Roman Corinthian building at Knossos', *BSA* 86 (1991), 297–318.
[67] *KS* nos. 318, 346–53.
[68] *KS* no. 160.

FIG. 2 Roman Corinthian building from the North Cemetery, reconstruction from front

FIG. 3 Roman Corinthian building from the North Cemetery, reconstruction from side

above the tombs excavated in 1978.[69] If the aqueduct was built after these tombs went out of use in the mid-second-century the city must have had to wait a long time for this desirable amenity, and possibly also for others that depended on it, such as public baths. The large number of wells and cisterns found in all the residential parts of the Roman city may reflect this state of affairs — the Villa Dionysos alone, although situated so near the monumental centre, had two wells of its own.

Apart from the Villa Dionysos the most conspicuous relic of Roman Knossos nowadays is the mass of concrete masonry rising out of the field on the other side of the road to the east, which is all that now remains of what was long ago identified as the Roman Civil Basilica.[70] It was a vast structure, 105 m long by 32 m wide with a hall at one end measuring 27 m by 64 m, and was drawn in the late sixteenth century by Onorio Belli;[71] his plan was reproduced by Ian Sanders in *Roman Crete* with an excellent discussion of this complex and puzzling building.[72] Trial trenches were dug in the area in 1937[73] but no evidence for its date was recovered, and very thorough stone-robbing of the area has obliterated the details of its design. Although brick-faced concrete was in use in other Roman cities in Crete it does not appear to have been fashionable at Knossos, where large concrete structures seem usually to have been faced with coursed stone (perhaps because suitable stone was easily available; several stone quarries of the Roman period have been recorded on Mt. Ailias, east of the Kairatos valley[74]); their architectural features have consequently been very vulnerable to stone-robbers through the ages. The theatre, or amphitheatre, had been greatly damaged even by the late sixteenth century when Belli saw it, and was finally destroyed when the road from Herakleion to Archanes was built in the 1880s.[75] Parts of its foundations have occasionally been briefly visible in recent times; they were made of exceptionally strong and durable white concrete,[76] but nothing is yet known of its size or orientation. The presence of theatrical masks in three chamber tombs whose period of use was between about A.D. 50 and 150 suggests that Knossos had a theatre at that time — that is, perhaps before it had an aqueduct — but this is by no means certain.

Although the public buildings of the colony have been little investigated so far, and those that have remained above ground have been disfigured by stone-robbing, there is reason to believe that in their day the monuments of Knossos did not fall behind those of other cities of the eastern Empire. Many of them were decorated with imported marble, in architectural elements such as the fine Proconnesian capitals of the Villa Dionysos and its columns of *fior di pesco* from Euboea and the elegant Pentelic of the Corinthian building from the North Cemetery, and also in minor pieces, such as floor tiles and veneer panelling. The most popular variety was *breccia di settebasi* from Skyros, but *marmor thessalicum*, *marmor synnadicum* from Phrygia, *africano* from Teos and the yellow marble of Numidia have also been found. Above all, the citizens seem to have had a love of sculpture; although Roman statues were much in demand during the Venetian period for shipping home to Italy a large

---

[69] *KS* no. 168; see above, n. 52.
[70] *KS* no. 112.
[71] Falkener (n. 29 above).
[72] Sanders (n. 14 above), 67–9 , pl. 25.
[73] Ralegh Radford (n. 52 above).
[74] *KS* nos. 264, 266–7.
[75] *KS* no. 110.
[76] Personal observation, April 1993 — during work on street lighting.

number have survived to be unearthed during the past century.[77] The finest of these, and the best known, is the cuirassed statue of Hadrian, found in 1935 buried in a pit in the Villa Dionysos and now standing in the garden of the Villa Ariadne (PLATE 18). Instead of Athene, he has the goddess Roma on his breastplate, with Romulus and Remus and the wolf — perhaps in deference to the status of Knossos as a Roman citizen colony. Another version of this statue, possibly a copy, is in the Herakleion Museum; its legs were found, together with fragments of other statues, in an area rich in Roman finds a little to the north of the theatre.[78] Private portraiture was also esteemed, as can be seen from the head of a young man found in a building in the field south of the Villa Dionysos[79] and in the remarkable series of plaster heads from the House of the Diamond Frescoes.

Since our knowledge of Roman Knossos comes mostly from the areas where Roman remains overlay those of the Bronze Age, the part we know least about is the centre of the city and its public buildings, which were situated not directly over the Minoan city but some distance to the north. It is here that we should expect to find the city's monuments and information about its formal planning and its civic life; the techniques of geophysical survey might do much to enlighten us on these points.[80] The new excavations in the field north of the Villa Ariadne[81] have already, in one season, begun to reveal the monumental character of buildings in this region, particularly in the Severan period and the third century, of which, apart from pottery deposits, we have so far known very little. Although several sites have shown signs of damage by earthquake towards the end of the Antonine era evidence is now beginning to appear that the colony quickly recovered its former state of vigour and prosperity. It is greatly to be hoped that these investigations will continue, since there is much to be learnt about this central part of the city and about the development of its monuments throughout the Roman period.

---

[77] e.g. *KS* nos. 76, 93, 97, 99, 109, 112–14, 129–31, 136, 197.
[78] *KS* no. 99.
[79] *KS* no. 130. G.B. Waywell, 'A Roman portrait bust from Knossos', *BSA* 68 (1973), 295–6.
[80] E.B. French, 'Archaeology in Greece, 1991–92', *AR* 38 (1991–92), 59–60.
[81] Knossos 2000. The project is a joint operation by the British School at Athens and the University of Birmingham, under the direction of Dr. K.A. Wardle.

PLATE V Makryteichos, Knossos - Communications (etching)

Chapter 11

The Inscribed Documents at Bronze Age Knossos[1]

J.-P. OLIVIER

An account of Cretan Bronze Age writing or scripts based on a single site, even if that site is the 'capital' of the island, can only be an incomplete exercise, for the written material which has come down to us is distributed very unequally in both time and space. This would be true whatever site was chosen, and indeed is particularly true at Knossos, where for the Hieroglyphic script we have 102 documents found mostly in a single part of the Palace (and covering a very brief period), for Linear A 35 documents spread out over the whole site (and spanning the whole known lifetime of this script), and for Linear B about 3,500, practically all of them in the Palace (but practically all involving serious problems of dating). Moreover, the scripts survive at Knossos in greatly unequal proportions: one third of the Hieroglyphic material but only a single related seal out of 136,[2] about 3% of the Linear A and practically the whole body of Cretan Linear B. It would thus be not only illusory but downright misleading to use Knossos as the base for a simple history of writing in Bronze Age Crete, let alone for an account of its origins and development.[3]

I must content myself, then, with reporting, as it were, on the state of play. The first section will deal with editions, the character and number of the documents, and their provenances and dates of discovery. In the second section I shall examine the chronology of each category of document. In the third, I shall summarise the present trends in research.

EDITIONS, CHARACTER AND NUMBER OF THE DOCUMENTS,
PROVENANCES AND DATES OF DISCOVERY

I) Editions of texts[4]

a) **Hieroglyphic**:
A.J. Evans, *Scripta Minoa: The Written Documents of Minoan Crete with Special Reference to the Archives of Knossos.* Volume I. *The Hieroglyphic and Primitive Linear Classes* (Oxford, 1909) [*SM* I].

---

[1] I should like to express my gratitude to Mrs. Helen Hughes-Brock for her English translation of the French text.
[2] Of some sixty seals whose provenance is given simply as 'Crete' it is clear that a number must come from Knossos — but which?
[3] For a short introduction to the subject see J.-P. Olivier, 'Cretan writing in the second millennium B.C.', *World Archaeology* 17.3 (1986), 377–89.
[4] For Hieroglyphic and Linear B, A.J. Evans, *Scripta Minoa* I (Oxford, 1909) and II (Oxford, 1952; edited by J.L. Myres) are the 'historic' editions which for one reason or another must still be consulted. (Note that there are no such editions for Linear A. To find

J.-P. Olivier and L. Godart, *Corpus Hieroglyphicarum Inscriptionum Cretae* (to be published in Rome, 1994) [*CHIC*].

b) **Linear A**:

L. Godart and J.-P. Olivier, *Recueil des inscriptions en linéaire A*. Volume I. *Tablettes éditées avant 1970* (Paris, 1976) [*GORILA* I].

L. Godart and J.-P. Olivier, *Recueil des inscriptions en linéaire A*. Volume II. *Nodules, scellés et rondelles édités avant 1970* (Paris, 1979) [*GORILA* II].

L. Godart and J.-P. Olivier, *Recueil des inscriptions en linéaire A*. Volume IV. *Autres documents* (Paris, 1982) [*GORILA* IV].

L. Godart and J.-P. Olivier, *Recueil des inscriptions en linéaire A*. Volume V. *Addenda, corrigenda, concordances, index et planches des signes* (Paris, 1985) [*GORILA* V].

N.B. 1) For the roundels (**Wc**) of vol. II, see now E. Hallager, 'The Knossos roundels', *BSA* 82 (1987), 55–70.

2) For the unpublished fragment of tablet found in the South-West House in 1992 [**KN 49**],[5] see below, *passim*.

3) For the unpublished inscription painted on a terracotta figurine found at Poros, a suburb of Herakleion, in 1992 [**PO Zg 1**],[6] see below, *passim*.

c) **Linear B**:

1) Tablets from Palace archives:

A.J. Evans, *Scripta Minoa: The Written Documents of Minoan Crete with Special Reference to the Archives of Knossos*. Volume II. *The Archives of Knossos: Clay Tablets Inscribed in Linear Script B* [Edited from notes and supplemented by J.L. Myres] (Oxford, 1952) [*SM* II].

J. Chadwick, L. Godart, J.T. Killen, J.-P. Olivier, A. Sacconi and I.A. Sakellarakis, *Corpus of Mycenaean Inscriptions from Knossos*. Volume I (1–1063) (Cambridge and Rome, 1986) [*CoMIK* I].

J. Chadwick, L. Godart, J.T. Killen, J.-P. Olivier, A. Sacconi and I.A. Sakellarakis, *Corpus of Mycenaean Inscriptions from Knossos*. Volume II (1064–4495) (Cambridge and Rome, 1990) [*CoMIK* II].

[*CoMIK* III (5000–7999) planned for 1994; *CoMIK* IV (8000–9947) for 1998].

J.T. Killen and J.-P. Olivier, *The Knossos Tablets: A Transliteration* (5th edn.; Salamanca, 1989) [*KT*^{5}].

2) Vase with painted inscription:

A. Sacconi, *Corpus delle iscrizioni vascolari in lineare B* (Rome, 1974), 178.[7]

II) Character and number of the documents

a) **Hieroglyphic**:

Ha (clay 'crescents'):[8] **29** (N.B.: some have seal impressions; the Hieroglyphic inscriptions among these are listed under **I**) [**#001–#029**].[9]

---

the various first editions of the documents one has to consult GORILA — see text). Please also note that the section that here deals with the editions of the Texts contains the abbreviations by which they will be referred to elsewhere in this chapter.

[5] My thanks are due to C. Macdonald, who found it, for allowing me to make use here of what is probably the earliest specimen of Linear A from Knossos.

[6] I shall publish this in collaboration with N. Demopoulou and G. Rethemiotakis and am grateful to them for permission to use it here.

[7] **KN Z 1716** (the signs on **KN Z 1715**, p. 177, are simply an imitation of writing and not, strictly speaking, an inscription).

[8] = 'Graffito inscriptions on clay sealings' in SM I, ii.8.1, 163–6.

[9] *CHIC*: its catalogue numbers (see above, section I,a) are prefixed by #.

He (clay 'medallions' — FIG. 1 'label'):[10] **18** [= #030–#047].
Hg (clay bar with three sides): **1** [= #048].
Hh (clay bars with four sides): **19** [= #049–#067].
Hi (clay tablets): **2** [= #068–#069].
I (seal impressions on clay): **32** (NB: some occur on 'crescents' with incised inscriptions, listed under **Ha**) [#123–#125, #134, #139–#147, #156–#170, #176–#179].
S (steatite seal — FIG. 1): **1** [= #203].[11]

TOTAL: **102** documents.

b) **Linear A**:
Tablets: **6** [= **1** — FIG. 1, **2, 22, 28, 32** (?), **49** (South-West House, 1992, unpublished)].
Wb (clay sealing): **1** [= **33**].[12]
Wc (clay roundels): **6** [= **3, 26** (?), **29, 30, 42, 43**].
Za (inscriptions on stone vases): **4** [= **10, 17, 18, 19**].
Zb (inscriptions incised on clay vases): **11** [= **4, 5, 20, 27**,[13] **34, 35, <36>, <37>, <38>, <39>, 40**].
Zc (inscriptions painted on clay vases): **2** [= **6, 7**].
Ze (inscription on a stone architectural element): **1** [= **16**].
Zf (inscriptions on metal — FIG. 1): **2** [= **13, 31**].
Zg (inscriptions on miscellaneous objects): **2** [= **<21>** and **PO Zg 1** (Poros, Herakleion, 1992, unpublished)].

TOTAL: **35** documents.

c) **Linear B** (FIG. 2):
Tablets: *ca.* **3,400**.[14]
Wb (labels for baskets of tablets): **35**.
Wm (nodules *with* string-hole but *no* sealing): **11**.
Wn (nodules *with* sealing but *no* string-hole): **2**.
Ws (nodules *with* both sealing *and* string-hole): **16**.
Z (vase with painted inscription): **1**.

TOTAL: *ca.* **3,500** documents.

---

[10] = 'Graffito Inscriptions on Clay Labels' in SM I, ii.8.2, 166–9.

[11] It would be strange if some of the known seals did not come from Knossos, particularly from tombs, but no information whatsoever survives. See n. 2 above.

[12] Not unpublished, as claimed in GORILA II, p. lvi: see *PM II.ii*, 419–20, where Evans even proposes a date, MM III.

[13] Vase not seen by the authors of GORILA. Found in the 1980s by J.A. MacGillivray in the study collection of the Herakleion Museum (inventory number HM 5194).

[14] This figure is approximate but it is not arbitrary. A quarter of a century ago I arrived at a total of 4,358: J.-P. Olivier, *Les scribes de Cnossos* (*Incunabula Graeca* 17; Rome, 1967), 19. Now I make it 3,333, adding up the items published under separate numbers between 1 and 8838 in *KT*^{5}, since:
  1. some 400 joins and quasi-joins of fragments have been made in the last 25 years among items bearing numbers under 9000;
  2. there remain many joins and even more quasi-joins — 200 at the very least — to be discovered among items numbered above 9000;
  3. 64 numbers are not tablets (**Wb, Wm, Wn** and **Ws**);
  4. of the 3,000 or so new small fragments rediscovered in the Herakleion Museum in 1984 probably all but about 100 belong to previously known pieces;
  3,400 is thus a fair estimate of the total.

HIEROGLYPHIC

seal

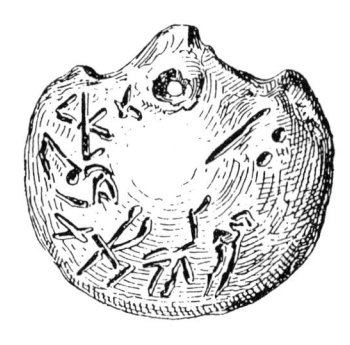

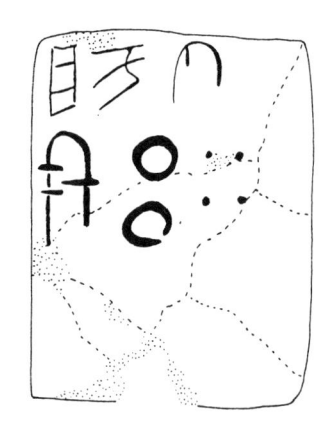

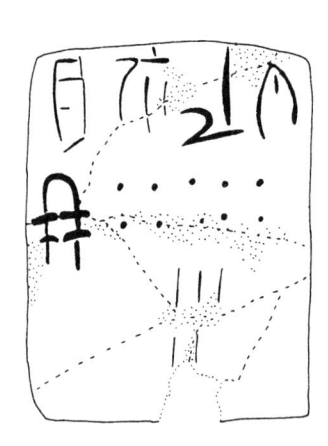

'label'

LINEAR A

tablet

ring

FIG. 1 Hieroglyphic and Linear A scripts.
Hieroglyphic: seal (steatite: AM 1938.929/*CHIC* 203); 'medallion label' (clay: *CHIC* 39).
Linear A: tablet (clay: KN 1 a and b); ring (gold: KN Zf 13). Scale 1:1, except ring at 4:1, seal at 2.5:1.

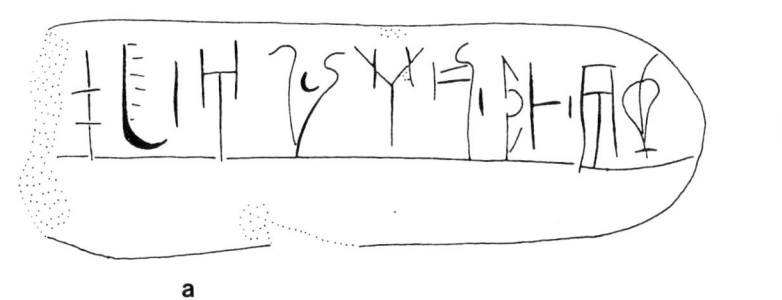

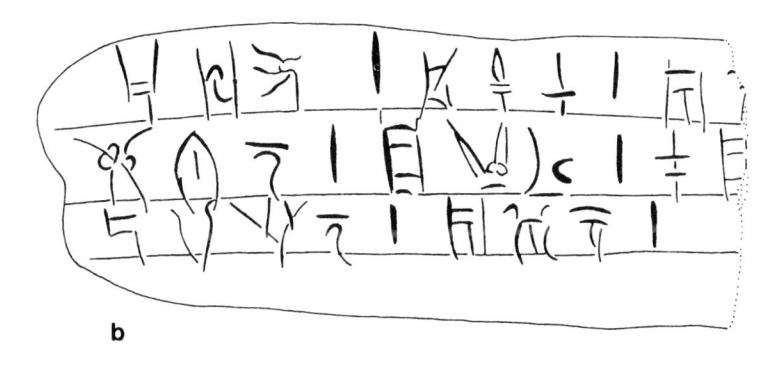

FIG. 2 Linear B script. Tablets (clay):
a KN 114 verso — Room of the Chariot Tablets; b V 503 — West Magazine VIII (Scribe 115). Scale 1:1

III) Provenances and dates of discovery

a) Hieroglyphic:[15]
#001–#069, #123, #124, #139–#147, #156–#168, #176, #178: Palace, Hieroglyphic Deposit (1900).
#125 (KN I (1/1) 03 / CMS II.8 84): Little Palace (1905–1910).
#134 (KN I (1/2) 01 / CMS II.8 56) and **#178 (KN I (1/?) 03 / CMS II.8 57)**: Palace, Kamares Pit Area (1901?).
#177 (KN I (1/?) 02 / CMS II.8 120): Palace, East Temple Repository (?) (1903).
#203 (KN S (2/2) 01 / SM I P. 49): 'Hellenika, Knossos' (before 1909).
#169, #170, #179: ? (?)

b) Linear A:[16]
KN 1: Palace, Temple Repositories (1903).

---

[15] Rather than furnish an incorrect plan, I refer the reader to J. Driessen, *An Early Destruction in the Mycenaean Palace at Knossos: A New Interpretation of the Excavation Field-Notes of the South-East Area of the West Wing* (Acta Archaeologica Lovaniensia, Monographiae 2; Leuven, 1990), 49, fig. 7.

[16] Ibid. 123, fig. 16. Evans' 'Sketch Plan of Palace and Surroundings' (PM II.i, 140, fig. 71) is still useful insofar as it has not been superseded.

KN 2: Palace, Corridor by S.E. Insula (1902 ?).
KN 22: ? (?) [with Linear B tablets not published by Evans].
KN 28: Palace, Corridor by S.E. Insula (1902 ?).
KN 32 (?): from Giamalakis Collection.[17]
KN 49: South-West House (1992); unpublished.
KN Wb 33: North-East House (19---).
KN Wc 3: Palace, East Temple Repository (1903).
KN Wc 26 (?): former Erlenmeyer Collection (*CMS* X 120); now Martin-Shøyen Collection, Oslo.
KN Wc 29: Palace, East Temple Repository (1903).
KN Wc 30: Palace, East Temple Repository (1903).
KN Wc 42: ? (?).[18]
KN Wc 43: ? (?).[19]
KN Za 10: House of the Frescoes (1923).
KN Za 17: Lower Town (1926).
KN Za 18: 'Villa Ariadne' (before 1937).
KN Za 19: 'In a field north of the Palace' (before 1935).
KN Zb 4: Palace, South-East Rubbish Heap (1902).
KN Zb 5: Palace, South-West Basement (1901).
KN Zb 20: Gypsadhes Hill (1957).
KN Zb 27: Palace, Temple Repositories (1903).
KN Zb 34: Palace, West Magazine III (1878).
KN Zb 35: Palace, West Magazine X (1901)
KN Zb <36>: Palace, West Magazine IX (1901).
KN Zb <37>: Palace, West Magazine IX (1901).
KN Zb <38>: Palace, West Magazines (1901).
KN Zb <39>: Palace, West Magazines (1901).
KN Zb 40: Unexplored Mansion (1972).
KN Zc 6: Palace, Basement of Monolithic Pillars (1902).
KN Zc 7: Palace, Basement of Monolithic Pillars (1902).
KN Ze 16: Tholos tomb on Kephala ridge (1938).
KN Zf 13: Mavro Spelio, Tomb IX, E 1 (1927).
KN Zf 31: Mavro Spelio, Tomb IX, B 2 (1927).
KN Zg <21>: Gypsadhes Hill (1957).
PO Zg 1: Poros, Herakleion (1992); unpublished.

c) **Linear B**:
1) Evans' excavations[20] (mostly between 1900 and 1910):
A: Clay Chest.
B: South-West Area.

---

[17] With a batch of 15 tablets in Linear B from Knossos, but the batch may have been put together by the collector.

[18] Roundel first published by E.L. Bennett, Jr., 'Some Minoan texts in the Heraklion Museum', in E. Grumach (ed.), *Minoica: Festschrift zum 80. Geburtstag von Johannes Sundwall* (Berlin, 1958), 38, as Hieroglyphic; omitted from *GORILA* II; number assigned by Hallager (p. 158 above), 62.

[19] See n. 18 above.

[20] Following my *Scribes de Cnossos* (n. 14 above), 20–4. Plan unchanged — i.e. equally erroneous — but in visually more pleasing form in K.-E. Sjöquist and P. Åström, *Knossos: Keepers and Kneaders* (*SIMA* 82 pocketbook; Göteborg, 1991), 8.

B1: S.W. Corner.
B2: Near S.W. Door.
B3: By S.W. Door (above terrace).
B4: Area beyond W. Wall.
B5: W. Area: Near S.W. Entrance.
C: Room of Chariot Tablets.
D: Court of Altar.
E1: Room of Column Bases.
E1 bis: Near N. Entrance to Room of Column Bases.
E2: E. Pillar Room.
E3: N. of Room of Column Bases.
E4: Passage on E. Side of Room of Chariot Tablets.
E5: Corridor of House Tablets and near Entrance to E. Pillar Room.
E6: Room of Niche.
F1: West Magazine II.
F2: West Magazine III.
F3: West Magazine IV.
F4: West Magazine V.
F5: West Magazine VI.
F6: West Magazine VII.
F7 a: West Magazine VIII: S.E. Corner.
F7: West Magazine VIII.
F8: West Magazine IX.
F9: West Magazine X.
F10: West Magazine XI.
F11: West Magazine XII.
F12: West Magazine XIII.
F13: West Magazine XIV.
F14: West Magazine XV.
F15: Corridor of Stone Jambs.
F16: Near Door of West Magazine VII.
F17: Near Door of West Magazine VIII.
F18: North End of Long Corridor (from West Magazine IX to West Magazine XII).
F19: N.W. Passage (Long Corridor flanking West Magazine XIII).
F20: N. Half Long Gallery near Stairs.
F21: West Magazine XVIII.
G1: Gallery of Jewel Fresco.
G2: Room East of Gallery of Jewel Fresco.
G3: Small Room to the East of Gallery of Jewel Fresco.
H1: Antechamber to Throne Room.
H2: Bath Room.
H3: Corridor of Stone Basin.
H4: South of Corridor of Stone Basin.
H5: Under blocked Doorway of Room W. of Throne.
H6: Under blocked Door of Room behind Throne.
I1: Room of Flower Gatherer.
I2: Spiral Cornice Room.

I3: Area of Bull Relief.
I3 bis: S. of Bull Relief Area.
I4: Area of Bügelkannes: under N. Wall.
I5: North Threshing Floor.
I6: East of Chamber of Hieroglyph Inscr.
J1: East–West Corridor.
J2: Hall of Colonnades.
J2 bis: South Doorway of Hall of Colonnades.
J3: Corridor of Sword Tablets.
J4: Queen's Megaron.
J5: Court of the Distaffs.
K: S.E. Front.
K1: Room of Clay Signet.
K2: Bean Room.
K3: Area south of Signet Room, S.E. Front.
L: Arsenal.
M: Little Palace.

2) Excavations after Evans:
North of Royal Road, immediately west of Armoury Area (1957–9; S. Hood; **8144–8150**).
North of Royal Road, immediately west of Armoury Area (1960; S. Hood; **8170–8171**).
North of Royal Road, close to Armoury (1961; S. Hood; **8210–8215**).
Near the Little Palace (1965; surface; **8711**).
Unexplored Mansion (1968, 1972; M.R. Popham; **8833**).
Northern Entrance (1987; A.A.D. Peatfield; **8838**).

CHRONOLOGY OF THE DOCUMENTS

a) **Hieroglyphic**:
Palace, Hieroglyphic Deposit: MM II (A.J. Evans; P. Yule);[21] MM III (A.J. Evans; I. Pini).[22]
Little Palace: ?
Palace, Kamares Pit Area: ?
Palace, East Temple Repository (?): MM III B.[23]
'Hellenika, Knossos': surface find or from clandestine excavations.

Commentary: the earliest attested Hieroglyphic is from Mallia, Quartier Mu (MM II),[24] the latest is from Petras, Siteia district (LM I, unpublished). Thus the dates from Knossos, even if still in need of clarification, are not out of line with those from the rest of Crete.

---

[21] *PM I*, 272; P. Yule, 'On the date of the "Hieroglyphic Deposit" at Knossos', *Kadmos* 17 (1978), 1–7; id., *Early Cretan Seals: A Study of Chronology* (Marburger Studien zur Vor- und Frühgeschichte 4; Mainz, 1980), 215–19.
[22] *SM I*, 21; I. Pini, 'The Hieroglyphic Deposit and the Temple Repositories at Knossos', in T.G. Palaima (ed.), *Aegean Seals, Sealings and Administration: Proceedings of the NEH-Dickson Conference ... 1989* (Aegaeum 5; Liège, 1990), 37–44, pls. 3–7.
[23] If coming from the same deposit as Linear A **KN 1**, **Wc 3**, **Wc 29** and **Wc 30** (cf. below).
[24] J.-Cl. Poursat, *Fouilles exécutées à Mallia. Le Quartier Mu. I: Introduction générale* (Études Crétoises 23; Paris, 1978), 25.

b) **Linear A**:[25]
KN 49: MM II ?
KN 1, Wc 3, Wc 29, Wc 30, Zb 5, Zb 27: MM IIIB.
KN 2, 28: MM IIIB ?
Wb 33: MM III.[26]
Zc 6, Zc 7: MM III ?
Zf 13: MM III-LM IA.
Zb 20, Zg <21>: LM IA.
Zf 31: LM IA ?
Za 10: LM I.
Zb 40: LM II ?
PO Zg 1: LM IIIA1.

N.B. The remaining 16 documents 'cannot be dated precisely, either because their context is unclear ..., or because they have no context at all'.[27]

Commentary: since the finding of the two new (unpublished) documents in 1992, **KN 49** and **PO Zg 1**, Knossos can now claim not only some of the earliest Linear A known (contemporary with the MM II finds from Phaistos:[28] 21 tablets, 4 sealings and 10 roundels),[29] but also what is in absolute terms the latest specimen.[30] This latest inscription, painted on the skirt of a clay figurine, is dated both by its archaeological context and by the style of the figurine. This puts its date beyond dispute and makes it, moreover, practically contemporary with the 'great' destruction of Knossos (according to the traditional high dating) and thus a quite exceptional proof that Linear A was still being used, for non-archival purposes, some seventy-five years after the Mycenaeans came to power.

c) **Linear B**:
There is no question here of putting forward any single date for the 3,400 or so tablets from Knossos. The old controversy about their dating (beginning of LM IIIA2 versus second half of the 13th century)[31] appeared to have died down,[32] but recently has been not only revived but revived with new complications. Whereas thirty years ago the two schools of thought agreed that the Knossos

---

[25] I refer the reader to the article by F. Vandenabeele, 'La chronologie des documents en linéaire A', *BCH* 109 (1985), 9–11. This was the source used for the dates put forward in *GORILA* V.
[26] See n. 12 above.
[27] Vandenabeele (n. 25 above), 10–11.
[28] Ibid. 12–15 and 18–20.
[29] Until **KN 49** is published we cannot be entirely sure that it really is in Linear A. It is a small fragment, less than 4 cm², and bears only a single sign that can be identified (and that not with absolute certainty). The tablet fragment itself, however, is of a type so far known exclusively for Linear A.
[30] Previously this honour went to the jar from the Unexplored Mansion, **KN Zb 40** (LM II?). (The pair of signs cut on the door-jamb of the tholos tomb on the Kephala ridge, **KN Ze 16**, *could* be LM II but could equally well be earlier. There is also the thorny epigraphical problem that they *could* be Linear B. They are best excluded from discussion for the present.)
[31] L.R. Palmer and J. Boardman, *On the Knossos Tablets* (Oxford, 1963).
[32] M.R. Popham, 'The historical implications of the Linear B archive at Knossos dating to either c. 1400 BC or 1200 BC', *Cretan Studies* 1 (1988), 217–27.

tablets were all more or less contemporary[33] ('unity of the archives' was the phrase used) the question now is: *how many* destructions by fire were responsible for baking them?[34]

The two principal events which have led to the re-examination and reframing of the problem are the following.

1. The raising of the date of the tablets from the Room of the Chariot Tablets. Driessen, using an assemblage of arguments, none of which would carry conviction by itself but which put together do seem persuasive, has demonstrated that the tablets found in the Room of the Chariot Tablets are two or three generations earlier than those of the 'main bulk' of the archives.[35] If the main bulk are put at the 'traditional' date at the beginning of LM IIIA2, *c*.1375 B.C., then the documents from the Room of the Chariot Tablets must go back to LM II, i.e. before 1400 B.C., and thus become, for us, the earliest Linear B tablets from Knossos. That makes them the first written manifestation of the economic and political activity of the Mycenaeans in Crete, at a moment when Minoan influence was still much more felt than it was some generations later.[36]

2. The down-dating of the tablets by scribe 115 (and of some others ...). I shall do no more than summarise this point here, having expounded it fully elsewhere.[37] The hand of a scribe known at Knossos to whom I assigned the number 115 in 1967[38] has been recognised on two of the three tablets found at Chania in 1990.[39] The two teams[40] who published the Chania tablets did of course notice the extraordinary resemblance of the writing to that of scribe 115 at Knossos, but they stopped short of identifying them as one and the same, first because the tablets came from Chania, not Knossos, secondly because three signs on the larger of the two Chania tablets did not occur in the repertoire of scribe 115. I have been able to show without a shadow of doubt that these three signs (which are consecutive, because they form the beginning of a complete word of four signs) were written not by the principal scribe of the large Chania tablet but by a *different* individual scribe, who corrected the first man's text. From now on, therefore, palaeographically speaking, we no longer have reason to doubt — or rather, we have every reason to believe — that scribe 115, who wrote some forty tablets at Knossos, has left us two tablets at Chania as well.

As for the archival argument, it is well known that, at certain times at least, the Mycenaean administration at Knossos was dealing with ploughing oxen,[41] flocks and herds of sheep, goats, swine and cattle,[42] and chariots,[43] which were at *ku-do-ni-ja*, the ancient Κυδωνία, i.e. modern Chania.

---

[33] On the few exceptions see Olivier (n. 14 above), 110–21.

[34] J. Driessen, 'Le palais de Cnossos au MR II-III : combien de destructions ?', in A. Farnoux and J. Driessen, 'La Crète mycénienne' (BCH Suppl., to be published in 1994).

[35] Driessen (n. 15 above).

[36] Ibid. 130.

[37] J.-P. Olivier, 'KN 115 = KH 115. Un même scribe à Knossos et à La Canée au MR IIIB: du soupçon à la certitude', *BCH* 117 (1993), 19–33.

[38] Olivier (n. 14 above), 57–8.

[39] The third tablet is useless for palaeographical study. Only one sign on it can still be read with certainty.

[40] L. Godart and Y. Tzedakis, 'Les nouveaux textes en linéaire B de La Canée', *Rivista di Filologia e di Istruzione Classica* 119.2 (1991), 129–49; E. Hallager, M. Vlasakis and B.P. Hallager, 'New Linear B tablets from Khania', *Kadmos* 31 (1992), 61–87.

[41] **KN Ce 59**.3b: tablet from the Room of the Chariot Tablets.

[42] **KN Co 904**: tablet from the Northern Entrance.

Better still, scribe 115, who worked in a 'department' which dealt with the textile industry, had administrative relations with Chania. It was he, in fact, who had registered the amounts of wool (probably destined for the finishing of textiles) on the back of tablets written by scribe 113, and this scribe 113 at Knossos is known to us only as dealing with wool and cloth in western Crete. On these cloth tablets, the joint work of 113 and 115, the name of Chania, *ku-do-ni-ja*, occurs twice.[44]

Finally, since scribe 115 was in some way or other partly in charge of cloth production at Chania, there is nothing historically improbable about his making a journey there.[45] The chances of our coming upon two tablets written just while he happened to be there were slim, to be sure, but one does strike lucky sometimes.

The point here is that the Chania tablets are categorically dated by the excavators to the end of LM IIIB1, i.e. c.1250 B.C.[46] Of course, for those who date the main body of the Knossos archives to LM IIIB,[47] this is simply an argument in their favour.[48] The problem is for those who date the archives, with the great destruction, to the start of LM IIIA2, c.1375 B.C. As for those who prefer the middle of LM IIIA2, c.1330 B.C., they may well be the agents of some compromise solution.[49] Others more competent than I will have to be the judges of that.

For my own purposes the only certainty is that scribe 115 at Knossos and the principal scribe at Chania are one and the same man and that the dates of the destruction levels at Knossos and Chania which yielded tablets in his hand will have to be harmonised somehow.[50]

If, however, harmonising these dates means lowering the date of scribe 115's tablets, then those of at least scribe 103 must come down too, since 103, the writer of some 250 tablets,[51] was working in the same textile 'department' as 115. Once we start involving 103, we are embroiled with at least ten other scribes who worked alongside him in two 'departments' in the West Wing — *at least* ten, because scribe 119 is attested both in Magazine VIII of the West Magazines (whence come at least seven of 115's tablets) and also in the East–West Corridor of the East Wing (whence come the rest of 119's tablets and all the tablets, about 500 of them, written by his close collaborator 117) and we thus have ten scribes and 1,000 tablets which must follow in the wake of 115.[52]

---

[43] **KN Sd 4404**: tablet from the Arsenal.

[44] **KN Lc 481** and **Lc 7377**.

[45] We need hardly remind ourselves that fragile, heavy tablets of unbaked clay will not have been carried around outside the administrative centres where they were written.

[46] Hallager, Vlasakis and Hallager (n. 40 above), 67–70.

[47] Thus, following Palmer (n. 31 above), E. Hallager, *The Mycenaean Palace at Knossos: Evidence for Final Destruction in the IIIB Period* (*Medelhavsmuseet memoir* 1; Stockholm, 1977); W.-D. Niemeier, 'Mycenaean Knossos and the age of Linear B', *SMEA* 23 (1982), 219–87; id., *Die Palaststilkeramik von Knossos: Stil, Chronologie und historischer Kontext* (Deutsches Arch. Inst., Arch. Forschungen 13; Berlin, 1985).

[48] One appreciates all the more the scholarly rigour of Hallager and his collaborators (n. 40 above), who, face to face with real palaeographical difficulties but unable to see a solution, did not attempt to bypass them.

[49] M.S.F. Hood, 'The date of the Linear B tablets from Knossos', *Antiquity* 35 (1961), 4–7; id., '"Last Palace" and "Reoccupation" at Knossos', *Kadmos* 4 (1965), 16–44; C. Hawke Smith, 'The Knossos tablets: a reconsideration', *Kadmos* 14 (1975), 125–32; J. Raison, 'Chronologie des premières attestations du grec en Grèce', in *Étrennes de septantaine: travaux de linguistique et de grammaire comparée offerts à Michel Lejeune par un groupe de ses élèves* (*Études et commentaires* 91; Paris, 1978), 209–16.

[50] Without sensationalising — the large Chania tablet gives a list of personnel and does so in exactly the same form as that employed on 115's tablets at Knossos, so that we cannot seek an easy way out by looking for different, or successive, administrative situations.

[51] Olivier (n. 14 above), 125–6.

[52] That is not even the 'maximum' hypothesis. I will not let myself be caught by that old demon, the 'unity of the archives'.

As we have seen, things are moving at both ends of the time-scale as regards the old problem of the date of the Linear B tablets from Knossos. The problem at the upper end is clearly the lesser, since pushing back the 500–odd tablets from the Room of the Chariot Tablets[53] (which comprise altogether fewer than 1,500 signs or 5% of the extant material)[54] affects the 'main bulk' of the archives less drastically than bringing down by more than a century 1,000 documents (with over 8,000 signs or at least 25% of the extant material). Here we are shaking the whole chronological and historical edifice.

It goes without saying that the conjunction of these two movements sends toppling the old idea of the 'unity of the archives' and is going to force us to start asking again a number of very serious questions.

PRESENT AND FUTURE LINES OF RESEARCH

In the field of Cretan writing discoveries in the last few years have been coming thick and fast.[55]

1. 1989: the first Linear B tablet comes to light at Chania (excavators date it to LM IIIB but it comes from a disturbed context).[56]
2. 1990: date of the destruction of the Room of the Chariot Tablets is pushed back to LM II.
3. 1990: three more Linear B tablets are found at Chania, this time on a LM IIIB1 floor (and the possibility is aired that one or even two of them may be in the hand of the Knossian scribe 115).
4. 1990: two vases with painted inscriptions in Linear B are discovered in Quartier Nu at Mallia (LM IIIB; the first Linear B writing found at this site).[57]
5. 1990: a fragment of a four-sided bar comes to light during a survey at Mallia, pointing to the presence of a third Hieroglyphic archive deposit there.[58]
6. 1991: the first two items from Minoan archives (MM II) on Samothrace are published (the most northerly evidence for Minoan accounting; a roundel with no inscription — but of a type specifically used in Linear A archives — bears an impression from a Hieroglyphic seal!).[59]
7. 1991: a roundel with a Hieroglyphic inscription is discovered at Petras near Siteia in the very

---

I share Driessen's view (n. 34 above), though he and I use different vocabulary, that all the links between 'geographical' groupings of tablets need to be re-examined from scratch under the triple spotlights of archaeology, palaeography and archive studies. Nonetheless, one must bear in mind the fact that all these re-examinations will have their limits, because in the final reckoning we could find ourselves faced with twenty (or more ...) groupings of more than ten tablets each with *no* links among themselves and the 'unity of the archives' would become an 'atomisation'.

[53] Already suspected of being 'misfits': see Olivier (n. 14 above), 116, 121 and 128; J. Chadwick, 'The organization of the Mycenaean archives', in A. Bartoněk (ed.), *Studia Mycenaea: Proceedings of the Mycenaean Symposium, Brno, April 1966* (Brno, 1968), 11–21.

[54] That is, documents whose historical (but not necessarily archaeological) existence we had to assume in any case.

[55] The list which follows reads almost like a series of newspaper headlines with news flashes from far and wide. The 'stories' which affect Knossos have been cited above. Some of the others are still wholly or partly unpublished.

[56] E. Hallager, M. Vlasakis and B.P. Hallager, 'The first Linear B tablet(s) from Khania', *Kadmos* 29 (1990), 24–34.

[57] A. Farnoux and J. Driessen, 'Inscriptions peintes en linéaire B à Malia', *BCH* 115 (1991), 71–97.

[58] S. Müller and J.-P. Olivier, 'Prospection à Malia : deux documents hiéroglyphiques', *BCH* 115 (1991), 65–70.

[59] D. Matsas, 'Samothrace and the northeastern Aegean: the Minoan connection', *Studia Troica* 1 (1991), 159–79.

destruction level where a Linear A tablet was found the year before (the latest Hieroglyphic known: LM I).[60]
8. 1992: Linear A at Knossos is pushed back to MM II (thus 'becoming' as early as at Phaistos).
9. 1992: Linear A discovered at Poros in Herakleion brings the use of Linear A for non-archival purposes down to LM IIIA1.
10. 1992: the presence of the Knossos scribe 115 at Chania becomes a certainty.

All these events, directly or indirectly, affect research on the documents of Knossos.

- We have already seen that points 2 and 10 call in question the notion of the 'unity of the archives'. Each deposit of tablets will have to be carefully (re)studied *as a deposit in itself* before we start comparing it with other deposits. (For this we are going to need a new study of the 'Handlist' of Evans' Linear B tablets and of all the 'Knossian' archive documents in the Ashmolean Museum, so as to arrive at a closer understanding of the locations where the Knossos tablets were in use).[61]
- Point 10 means that we must reopen the files on the date of the final destruction of the Palace at Knossos (LM IIIB?). No need to say more!
- Point 6 implies that the use of the roundels and 'noduli' was more complicated that we could have imagined — and the excavation is still in progress.[62]
- Point 7 means that we must now reinvestigate very carefully a number of traces of Linear A which had been previously suspected in the Hieroglyphic Deposit at Knossos.

Of course the *magna opera* already underway will continue nonetheless: the publication of *CoMIK* III and the completion of *CoMIK* IV; the compilation of KT^6 (the sixth — and last? — edition of the Knossos Tablets in transliteration); finally, in conjunction with these two, the search for new joins on which J.L. Melena has been successfully engaged for some years (the joins growing ever more numerous as the fragments grow tinier!).

With all this in progress, one can begin to dream of possibilities for the future. Now that the corpora of the three Cretan scripts are practically completed, we shall at least be able to start a thorough-going comparative palaeographical study of the three. That, however, is not the easiest of the tasks ahead, nor the most urgent.

For the Hieroglyphic script *CHIC* will make it possible to study not only the script as a whole but also the inscriptions on seals and seal impressions on the one hand and the archives and other documents on the other (not to mention comparing these two bodies of evidence). Since about a third of the Hieroglyphic material comes from Knossos, the role of the 'capital' (at least as far as the archive documents and the seal impressions are concerned) will be of the foremost importance.

As for Linear A, although it is still poorly represented as regards numbers of documents, the 1992

---

[60] Excavations directed by Metaxia Tsipopoulou, whom I thank for furnishing the information.
[61] In this matter my *Scribes de Cnossos* (n. 14 above) was based on *On the Knossos Tablets* (n. 31 above). After the drawings for *CoMIK* IV have been completed (probably in 1994), I envisage a second edition, but it will have to wait until the information in the 'Handlist' has been gone through in the closest detail and recompiled.
[62] On these see J. Weingarten in this volume.

discoveries at the top and bottom ends of the chronological scale enlarge the horizons significantly and give hope of still further finds. At the same time the quality and diversity of the Knossian documentation (the archives apart) provide us with some of the background indispensable to any approach to the material.

As for Linear B, it reigned alone at Knossos and over Knossos, and from there over the whole of Crete,[63] for the whole of our century — and that belief was not to the benefit of scholarship.[64] Now the Knossian situation has been blown apart by the double explosion caused in 1990 by the evidence about the date of the Room of the Chariot tablets and the discovery of the new tablets at Chania. Any serious study of Knossos, be it general or particular, limited to Knossos or embracing the Mainland, be it historical, economic, prosopographical, pinacological or what you will, will have to wait until the dust has settled and some kind of balance and consensus about the chronology has emerged.

---

[63] But we must not forget the existence of Mainland Linear B, which outdoes Cretan Linear B in number of signs.

[64] I omit here intentionally the jars with painted inscriptions. These are the work not of scribes but of illiterate painters copying from models (which themselves are interesting in that they reflect a different graphic tradition from that of the tablets). The jars were crucial in the days before we had any tablets from outside Knossos. Now they can go back to playing what should always have been their proper role, that of purveyors of fairly simple information about pottery workshops.

Chapter 12

Sealings and Sealed Documents at Bronze Age Knossos[1]

J. WEINGARTEN

Sealings are the impressions of engraved gems or metal rings pressed into moist clay in order to authenticate or secure something of value. In the Cretan climate, sealings will only be preserved if the clay has been baked hard; in practice, this means either the occasional impressions on pithoi, jar handles or loomweights made before the ceramic is fired or those sealings accidentally preserved because of a destruction fire. Since seal impressions on vases or small finds are rare, and burnt destructions unfortunately few, there are long periods during which seals were produced yet with little or no information on how they were actually used. Sealstones on the other hand (though not metal rings) are almost indestructible; they can be handed down from generation to generation before burial; they also pass inadvertently through archaeological levels, slipping through the crevices to confuse chronology and our view of glyptic progress. The discrepancy between the durability of seals and the fragility of sealings means that we inevitably have uncertainties, unbalanced evidence and interesting disputes among glyptic scholars.

PREPALATIAL KNOSSOS

At first sight it must seem surprising that no Prepalatial sealstones have been found in or around Knossos, but this gap simply reflects the lack of excavated early tombs in the area (almost all Prepalatial seals on Crete come from funerary contexts). In fact, we must wait until well into the Middle Minoan age before we find dated seals in the Knossos cemeteries. It is not difficult, however, to imagine what these early seals will have looked like — probably much like the EM II seals in Phourni Tholos E at Archanes, some eight kilometres to the south: carved buttons and cylinders of ivory, steatite and schist.[2] As is often the case with early Cretan seals, their shapes are more varied and interesting than their strictly rectilinear or geometric engraved devices.

Special Abbreviations:
CHIC = J.-P. Olivier and L. Godart, *Corpus Hieroglyphicarum Inscriptionum Cretae* (to be published in Rome, 1994).
GORILA = L. Godart and J.-P. Olivier, *Recueil des inscriptions en linéaire A*, 5 vols. (Paris).
See also J.-P. Olivier, this volume.

[1] I am grateful to Professor Dr. I. Pini of the CMS for the photographs used in PLATES 19–20, 22.a, 23, 24.b, and to the Ashmolean Museum for PLATE 22.b. I would also warmly thank Dr E. Hallager for his suggestions on designing FIG. 1.
[2] EM II: J.A. Sakellarakis, 'Gruppen minoischer Siegel der Vorpalastzeit aus datierten geschlossenen Funden', *Jahrbuch des Römisch-Germanischen Zentralmuseums Mainz:* 27 (1980), 1–12, fig. 4. Late EM I seals have been reported in southern Crete from the lower level of Tholos II at Lenda = *CMS* II.1, 195–200, 202–3 (pottery evidence is not yet published); no seals were found in the Subneolithic level.

FLAT-BASED CLASSES

A			
B			
s	a	a	a
I	II	III	IV *

HANGING-NODULE CLASSES

A

B

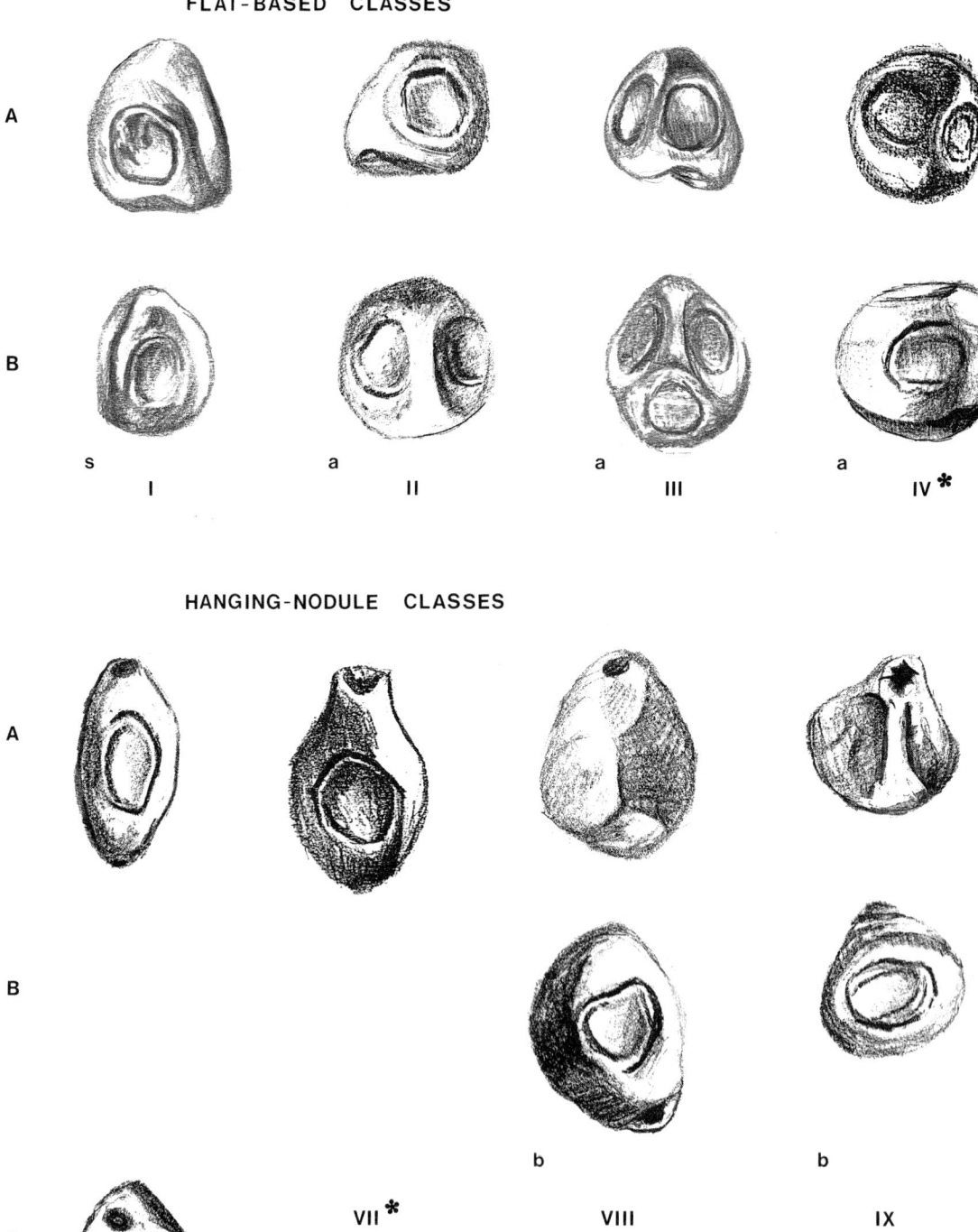

C

p
VI *   VII *   VIII b   IX b

FIG. 1 Neopalatial Minoan Sealing shapes (not to scale)

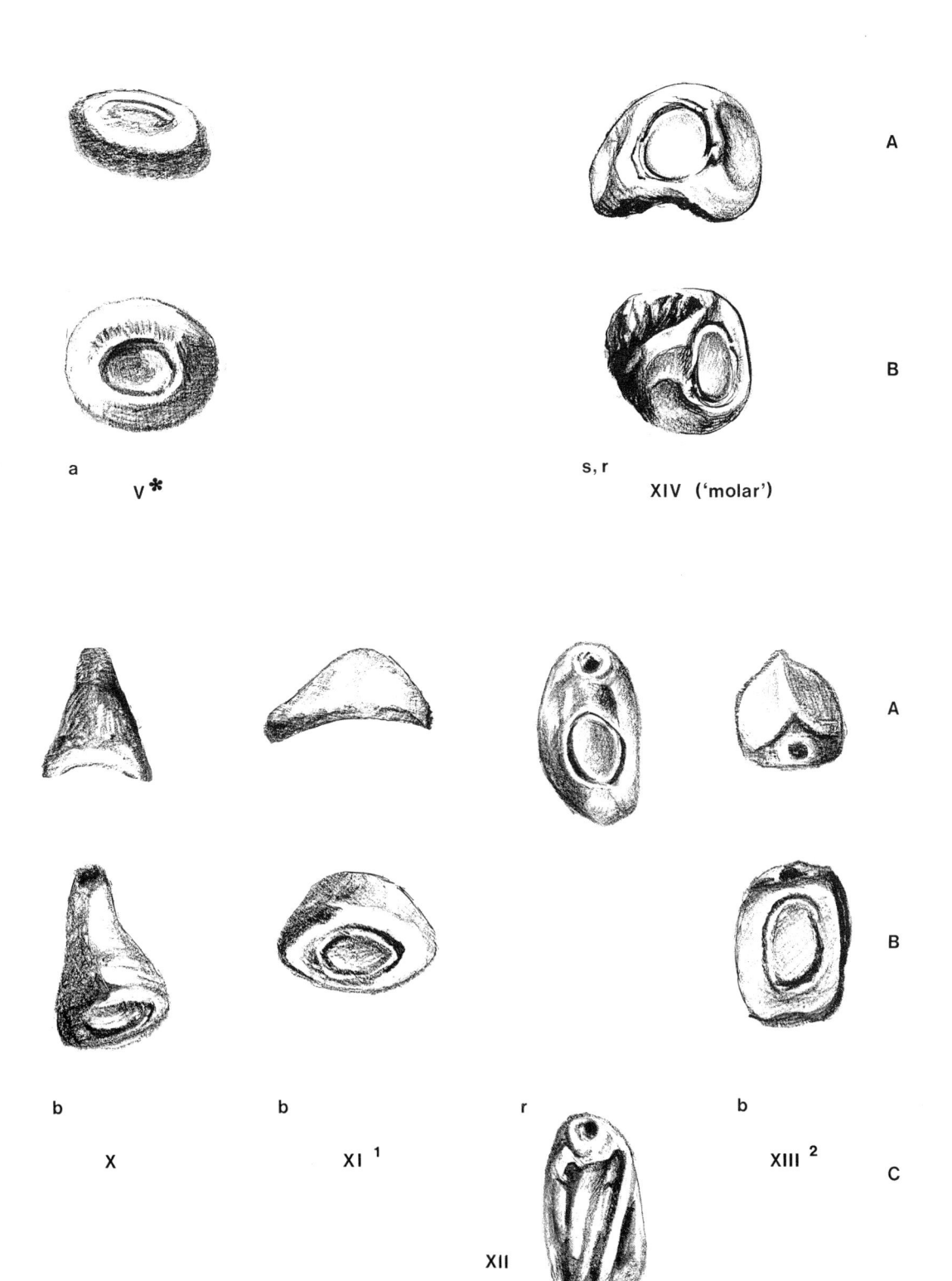

a

v *

s, r

XIV ('molar')

A

B

A

B

b

X

b

XI ¹

r

XII

b

XIII ²

A

B

C

Although no seals as early as this come from Knossos itself, the presence of similar ivory and soft-stone seals can be inferred from two seal impressions in clay found just outside the EM IIA West Court House, in a suitably burnt destruction.[3] These two sealings, among the earliest evidence for the *use* of seals on Crete,[4] encapsulate the kind of problem we shall constantly face in the study of seals and sealings.

1. SMV 865 (a smooth clay dome fashioned around a wooden object). The clay of this sealing strikes some pottery experts as non-local.[5] Could it in fact represent a sealed container brought to Knossos from elsewhere? Its seal impression — four concentric circles, central dot and an outer border of raised dots — is strongly reminiscent of stamped concentric circles on EC/EH II 'frying pans' as well as impressed pithoi and hearth bands from Lerna, Kea and Tiryns (*CMS* V, 122, 451–5, 539–50), but it also finds parallels closer to home at Lenda and Platanos (*CMS* II.1, 220, 270, 279, 334). The visual identification of the clay of such tiny artefacts can be treacherous and, as often happens, the seal design points unhelpfully in several directions at once.

2. SMV 866. This broken sealing also bears a device better known on 'frying pans' than on contemporary seals — a tight, continuous spiral filled with finely-drawn cross-stripes. The cross-stripes, however, which enhance the sense of rotating movement, are not known on EC/EH pottery or on contemporary seals; the closest glyptic parallel is a filled-in spiral on an MM IIB sealing from Phaistos (*CMS* II.5, 183, itself probably stamped by an 'heirloom' seal). While the seal-design might be judged precocious, it is just as likely that motifs on seals, sealings(!) and pottery are not as synchronous as we would wish.

The West Court seal impressions mean that we can be quite sure that engraved seals were used as early as EM IIA for truly sphragistic purposes (that is, as seals) and were not specially reserved

---

Key to FIG. 1

A	characteristic aspect		C	additional characteristics
B	view of impression from			p profile
	a	above		r reverse
	b	below	*	shape known in Protopalatial deposits also
	s	side		
1	most common nodulus shape		2	*OJA* 7 (1988) = Class VI/B

MINOAN NEOPALATIAL SEALING SHAPES (not to scale)

---

[3] With EM IIA pottery: D.E. Wilson, 'The Early Minoan IIA West Court House at Knossos' (Ph.D. dissertation, University of Cincinnati, 1984), 210–11.

[4] For a discussion of early seal use, illustrated by Prepalatial sealings from western Crete (EM III/MM IA Khamalevri; EM II/III Chania, Greek-Swedish Excavations; seals impressed on small finds and pottery), see M. Vlasakis and E. Hallager, 'Evidence for seal-use in prepalatial western Crete', in J.-C. Poursat and W. Müller (eds.), *Sceaux minoens et mycéniens : chronologie, fonction et interprétation* (*CMS* Beiheft 5; forthcoming). To their catalogue now add a nodulus from Mallia: M. Hue and O. Pelon, 'La Salle à piliers du palais de Malia et ses antécédents', *BCH* 116 (1992), 31–3, figs. 33–4.

[5] D.E. Wilson, pers. comm, and this volume, p. 41 n. 123.

for the decoration of an occasional pot or just worn as personal ornaments or amulets. It seems evident that they already possessed some communication value but, as we shall see, the difficulty lies in interpreting the level of that communication.

The next preserved sealing at Knossos, a jar-stopper stamped by two ivory seals, comes from the floor of a house (dated EM III or a little later) near the South Front of the Palace.[6] While the function of a jar-stopper is quite straightforward, the real question is: why was it marked with seal impressions at all? Our answer to this depends very much upon our understanding of the Prepalatial economy, a conundrum that makes the South Front stopper a worthy document in this offering to its excavator, Sinclair Hood.

Unlike the sealings from the West Court House (and the great majority of Minoan sealings to come), the stopper was stamped by two *different* seal impressions, though whether these were produced by the two ends of a single, (probably) ivory cylinder[7] or by two different seals is uncertain. One impression shows a simple geometric design, the other three lions walking nose-to-tail around a central motif (FIG. 2). The lions belong to the EM III–MM IA Parading Lions Group, a glyptic style group identified by Yule.[8]

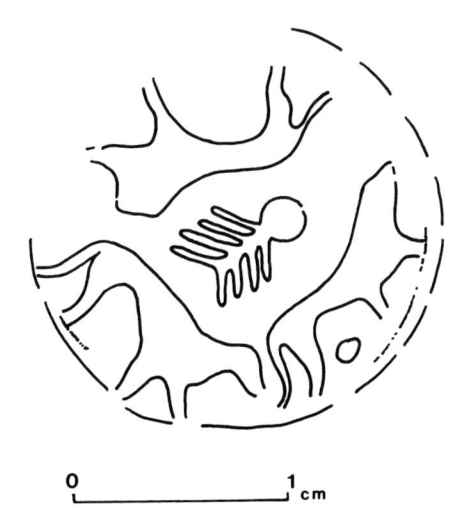

FIG. 2 Seal impressions on EM III jar stopper

---

[6] M.S.F. Hood and V.E.G. Kenna, 'An Early Minoan III sealing from Knossos', in *Antichità Cretesi: Studi in onore di Doro Levi I* (*Cronache di Archaeologia* 12–13 (1973–4)), 103–6. Hood suggested that the pottery, though pre-polychrome, was more characteristic of the beginning of MM IA than of EM III; defined as EM III in G. Cadogan *et al.*, 'Early Minoan and Middle Minoan pottery groups at Knossos', *BSA* 88 (1993), 21–8.

[7] Hood and Kenna (n. 6 above), 105–6.

[8] P. Yule, *Early Cretan Seals: A Study of Chronology* (Marburger Studien zur Vor- und Frühgeschichte 4; Mainz, 1981), 208–9. A second jar-stopper at Knossos (no provenance; reproduced in I. Pini, 'The Hieroglyphic Deposit and the Temple Repositories at Knossos', in T.G. Palaima (ed.), *Aegean Seals, Sealings and Administration: Proceedings of the NEH-Dickson Conference ... 1989* (*Aegaeum* 5; Liège, 1990), pl. ivc = Table 1, 10) is stamped by an ivory seal of the related Border/Leaf Complex (Yule, above, 209–10). It is also dated EM III/MM IA(?) on stylistic grounds.

It is a pity that we cannot know who stamped this jar-stopper, or why. It might have been a fairly trivial act meant to guard the contents of the jar against pilfering servants, a private precaution (the stopper was found in a house) of no wider significance. However, if the impressions were intended to identify the owner or origin of the jar outside his immediate household, or if *two* seal-owners were jointly involved, the sealing takes on a public purpose. The distinction is important: household sealings are by definition local and isolated, and usually sporadic, while seal impressions meant for extramural communication have wider economic ramifications. If jars were in fact being marked for exchange or tax purposes (two obvious possibilities) this implies an emerging administrative system at Knossos before the foundation of the Palace.

Pini has suggested just such early administrative use of seals at Knossos, arguing from thirteen sealings almost certainly impressed by seals manufactured no later than MM I (TABLE I; to which we can now add the two West Court nodules).[9] The problem is that the date of manufacture of a seal does not necessarily date the sealing. As we know both from Near Eastern and from later Minoan evidence, seals may be reused surprisingly long after their original manufacture.[10] Of the thirteen sealings, only the South Front jar-stopper is from a secure Prepalatial context, so it is a matter of opinion when the other seals were actually impressed on the surviving clay documents. In the absence of well-stratified evidence, we might consider a pragmatic test of administrative purpose: *what had the sealings sealed?*[11] Here Pini's list (TABLE I) is equivocal:

– four possible jar-stoppers (impossible to choose between household or external use);
– one Class VII pear-shaped nodule (FIG. 1), a sealing type used in Palatial administration from MM IIB onwards; but note that this nodule was found in the LM IIIA(!) Arsenal Deposit;
– and five noduli.

Noduli (sing. nodulus) are clay nodules marked with seal impressions just like sealings, but without string-holes or any other means of attachment to objects; that is, they never could have sealed anything. Such 'sealings that do not seal', when found in Palatial contexts, have been interpreted as dockets (handed out in return for occasional work, to be later exchanged for rations or other payment);[12] as such, they had an administrative function. On the other hand, these early noduli could have served still less sophisticated purposes, for example as *laisser passer* or private receipts (like IOUs). Such simple documents are practical in a society already too populous for entirely face-to-face

---

[9] Pini (n. 8 above), 34–7, and the discussion, 56–60.

[10] At Quartier Mu at Mallia, securely dated to MM IIB, 21% of sealings were stamped by seals undoubtedly of Prepalatial (EM–MM I) manufacture: see J.-C. Poursat, response to Pini (n. 8 above), 55.

[11] Except for direct-object sealings (e.g. vase-stoppers or sack-sealings) the shapes of Minoan scalings were neither arbitrary nor individual but followed set, usually local, conventions. Such conventions often enable us to deduce the date, function and probable origin of the sealing. See J. Weingarten, 'The sealing structures of Minoan Crete: MM II Phaistos to the destruction of the Palace of Knossos. Part I: The evidence until the LM IB destructions', *OJA* 5 (1986), 282, fig. 1; ead., 'Part II: The evidence from Knossos until the destruction of the Palace', *OJA* 7 (1988), 15; ead., 'Late Bronze Age trade within Crete: the evidence of seals and sealings', in N.H. Gale (ed.), *Bronze Age Trade in the Mediterranean: Papers presented at the Conference held at Rewley House, Oxford ... 1989* (SIMA 90; Jonsered, 1991), 303–24.

[12] J. Weingarten, 'Some unusual Minoan clay nodules', *Kadmos* 25 (1986), 1–21, and following addenda: 'I. Some unusual clay nodules' in 'Seal-use at LM IB Ayia Triada I', *Kadmos* 26 (1987), 38–43; and 'II. More unusual Minoan clay nodules', *Kadmos* 29 (1990), 16–23.

contacts but where literate instruments are limited or lacking. Thus it is not surprising that we find noduli on Prepalatial sites.[13] Since the use of noduli only makes sense outside the immediate household, these documents surely testify to an extended role for seals (at least for authentication), though not yet necessarily to any administrative structures. Until more evidence comes to light, it seems safest to distinguish Prepalatial economic organisation (in which sealings undoubtedly played some role) from any kind of formal administration, which probably did not exist before the foundation of the Palace.[14]

THE FIRST PALACE PERIOD AT KNOSSOS

With the rise of the Palace there was an undoubted need for formal administrative systems. The necessity of feeding and clothing Palace dependants required records of income and disbursements which, in turn, meant controlling the movement of goods in and out of workshops and storerooms. It is not certain (though we assume, perhaps wrongly) that written records existed from the beginning of the First Palaces but, even if they were absent, sealings could have served as basic storeroom documents: in addition to physically securing doors and containers, broken sealings could be collected, counted, and the seal impressions controlled, in a simple but effective bookkeeping system.[15] Such use of storeroom sealings was widespread throughout the ancient Near East. The system can also be reconstructed in its entirety in Crete at MM IIB Phaistos, where the diagnostic sealing types were found in their thousands.[16] At Protopalatial Knossos, however, despite at least two major burnt destructions, there is nothing at all comparable;[17] instead of new types of sealings connected with storerooms, the limited evidence points rather to a continuing use of noduli with only occasional actual sealings. Admittedly, the stratified evidence is minimal:

– three noduli, all stamped by the same seal (a standing quadruped, perhaps a goat; PLATE 19.a) found in an MM IB level near the South-West Palace angle;[18]
– one nodulus and one (basket?) sealing, together with a fragment of a Linear A tablet, in an MM IIA

---

[13] Vlasakis and Hallager (n. 4 above); it is rather more startling to find them still being used at Knossos at the end of the New Palace Period: Weingarten (n. 12 above). It must be emphasised that the noduli on Pini's list could be either Pre- or Protopalatial documents, in the latter case simply stamped by earlier seals (on two noduli from the SE Pillar Basements, HM 405/6, see n. 26 below).

[14] This useful distinction was proposed by Ann Blasingham in the discussion following Pini's paper (n. 8 above), 59.

[15] P. Ferioli and E. Fiandra, 'The use of clay sealings in administrative functions from the 5th to the 1st millennium B.C. in the Orient, Nubia, Egypt and the Aegean: similarities and differences', in Palaima (n. 8 above), 221–32.

[16] E. Fiandra, 'A che cosa servivano le cretule di Festòs', *Cretological II, A'* 383–95. Fiandra was able to make a detailed analysis of 1544 of the more than 6,500 sealings (stamped by 327 different seals). She discovered that about 10% had secured various kinds of identifiable goods, such as jars or rush matting, while about 90% had sealed either flaring wooden pommels or small wooden cylindrical pegs; these pommels and pegs were identified as having sealed doors, boxes or chests. See also M.H. Wiencke, 'Clay sealings from Shechem, the Sudan, and the Aegean', *JNES* 35 (1976), 127–30.

[17] I have been able to identify only a *single* peg sealing (T 325, without provenance or date) among the boxes of Knossos sealings in the Herakleion Museum.

[18] I am grateful to Dr C. Macdonald and to the Managing Committee of the British School at Athens for permission to discuss these noduli (HM 1100a–c). N.B.: the associated pottery should be classed as MM IB (C. Macdonald, pers. comm.) and not MM IIA (Weingarten, n. 12 above — addendum II, A–14); see the joint study of early Knossos pottery (Cadogan et al., n. 6 above).

workshop under the later South-West House.[19] The seal impression had flaked off the basket-sealing but the nodulus preserved the impression of a remarkable gem: a central human hand (= *CHIC* 30? [= P–9/10?]) against a background of *en rapport* asymmetric interlacing. Although it does not constitute an inscription (i.e. at least two signs) it is tempting to regard this unique seal impression as the earliest evidence for the use of Hieroglyphic seals at Knossos.

Such an interpretation would render the scrap of Linear A tablet in the workshop even more puzzling, but that tablet in any case is bound to upset ideas on scribal progress: all other evidence points to the exclusive use of a Hieroglyphic script at Knossos (and at Mallia)[20] at a time when proto-Linear A was already in use at Phaistos.[21] Certainly the skewed distribution of Hieroglyphic inscribed seals and sealings suggests a north/south scribal divide during the First Palace Period:

1) finds of Hieroglyphic seals are almost entirely limited to northern and eastern Crete;
2) impressions from Hieroglyphic seals are restricted to the two northern Palaces.[22]

At Mallia the evidence from Quartier Mu securely establishes the administrative use of the Hieroglyphic script and inscribed seals in MM IIB.[23] Dating at Knossos is much less satisfactory but there are some indications that Hieroglyphic seals were being used for administrative purposes at least as early as that. For example, three of the six sealings from the early South-East Pillar Room (TABLE II; PLATES 19.b, 20.a and b), although not closely dated,[24] were stamped by seals engraved with two and three Hieroglyphic signs.[25] Continuity (and a somewhat leisurely pace of administrative

---

[19] C. Macdonald, 'Excavations south west of the Palace at Knossos', forthcoming. N.B.: in this period, the South-West House was adjacent to, but not part of, the Palace; it is, in fact, remarkable that the only Protopalatial sealings *in* the Palace are those of the Hieroglyphic Deposit (see n. 29 below).

[20] Knossos MM IIIB (n. 28 below): *PM I*, 271–85; Mallia MM IIB: J.-C. Poursat, 'Sceaux et empreintes de sceaux', in B. Detournay, J.-C. Poursat and F. Vandenabeele, *Fouilles exécutées à Mallia. Le Quartier Mu II: Vases de pierre et de métal, vannerie, figurines et reliefs d'applique* (Études Crétoises 26; Paris, 1980), 157–229.

[21] Equivalent to MM IIB: P. Warren and V. Hankey, *Aegean Bronze Age Chronology* (Bristol, 1989), 48, Table 2.4. The heterogeneous documents in Room 25 at Phaistos (7 two-sided bars, 4 tablets, a mini-tablet, 2 irregular shapes, etc.) suggest a lack of scribal standardisation. The tablets were written in proto-Linear A but the script on the bars is problematic: originally published as Hieroglyphics (G. Pugliese Carratelli, 'Nuove epigrafi minoiche di Festo', *ASA* n.s. 19–20 (1957–8), 363–88) and now re-published as Linear A (*GORILA* I PH 7–28). Although we cannot read the texts, we can follow the gist through ideograms (also on roundels): MEN, vases, WINE?, FIGS and GRAIN — sufficiently diverse concerns to prove a developed scribal administration of goods and personnel.

[22] *CHIC* (Rome, 1994 — forthcoming). A single possible exception among 327 seal-types at Phaistos (*CMS* II.5, 239), if not naturalistic in intent, may be taken to 'prove the rule'.

[23] See n. 20 above.

[24] MM IA, but not stratigraphically sealed: S. Andreou, 'Pottery Groups of the Old Palace Period in Crete' (Ph.D. dissertation, University of Cincinnati, 1978), 30. *PM I*, 146, 196, dated the deposit to early MM I on the basis of two 'Hieroglyphic A' seal impressions which Evans believed earlier than Protopalatial 'Hieroglyphic B'. The A to B progression has been invalidated by the subsequent discovery of large numbers of 'Hieroglyphic A' seals being manufactured in the MM IIB Mallia Stoneworking Atelier: see Yule (n. 8 above), 170–1. 'Hieroglyphic A' defines a *style* based on a technique of crudely incising or gouging signs and pictographs into soft stone, most commonly steatite three-sided prisms.

[25] TABLE 2: **Td**, **Tf**, and possibly **Te** (one sign on either side). The Double Axe and Sepia signs on **Td** and perhaps **Te** may be read as A-SA (*CHIC*, 03–08), a very common two-sign Hieroglyphic formula (possibly abbreviating the full formula of *CHIC*, 03–08–08–30–70). Cf. A-SA on roundels at Mallia (**Wc** '5'), Gournia (**Wc** 1), and Samothrace (D. Matsas, 'Samothrace and the Northeastern Aegean: the Minoan connection', *Studia Troica* I (1991), 168, 170, figs. 15 and 16). It is tempting to interpret A-SA on seals as representing the 'temple' in Hieroglyphic administration (see n. 34 below).

innovation) is also attested by the presence of two noduli.[26] Some sphragistic progress, however, is indicated with the appearance of a new type of sealing, Class VI (FIG. 1; PLATE 19.b), which hung from a cord at either end. Class VI, the first in a long line of Minoan hanging nodules (which tells us nothing about the objects sealed),[27] was certainly later used for administrative purposes in Palaces and villas.

There is a quantum jump from such scattered sealings to the proliferation of records in the Hieroglyphic Deposit. For the first time at Knossos we can witness (rather than imagine) meticulous record-keeping by skilled administrators. Though beset with difficulties of dating (no ceramic evidence)[28] and of the definition of the deposit itself[29] and, of course, with the script undeciphered, the Hieroglyphic Deposit nonetheless signals a full-scale literate bureaucracy at work in the First Palace:

1. Scribes were writing on clay in a fluent, near-cursive Hieroglyphic script that argues habitual practice.
2. Scribes were efficient: three- and four-sided bars and medallion-shaped 'labels' (FIG. 3.a)[30] were densely covered with script, usually on all available faces.
3. The new crescent-shaped sealings (PLATE 21; diagnostic of the Hieroglyphic deposits) may have been created with scribal requirements in mind: this most spacious of Minoan sealing shapes accommodates whole groups of incised signs.[31] Such inscriptions attest a close scribal interest in sealing activities.

    Expanded literacy is also witnessed (albeit negatively) by the appearance of a second new sealing type, the flat-based nodules (Class IV, V; FIG. 1): fairly flat cakes of clay pressed down over leather strips; these strips have been interpreted as the traces of leather or parchment documents.[32] Very similar document-sealings are quite common in all later Minoan sealing deposits.
4. Three- and four-sided prisms engraved with Hieroglyphic signs are in common use. Whatever the undeciphered texts of the Hieroglyphic seals declared — whether names or titles or ornamental

---

[26] Pini (n. 8 above), judges one of the noduli, **T2** (and the object sealing, **Tc**) to be of Prepalatial date, thus splitting the two noduli as well as the 'deposit' into separate periods.

[27] Possible functions for Class VI nodules: (1) as box or chest sealings (J. Weingarten, 'Seal-use at LM IB Ayia Triada', *Kadmos* 26 (1987), 1–43); or (2) as document sealings (E. Hallager, in discussion in Palaima, n. 8 above, 119–20).

[28] MM IIB: most scholars have accepted this date, following Yule (n. 8 above), 215–19. MM III: J.J. Reich, 'The date of the Hieroglyphic Deposit at Knossos', *AJA* 74 (1970), 406–8. MM II and III: Pini (n. 8 above), 37–46, divides the sealings into two periods: MM II crescents and MM III document-sealings (Class IV–V), plus 'advanced' seal-motifs.

[29] The main deposit (not *in situ*) was excavated at the north end of the Long Gallery but, as M.A.V. Gill pointed out ('The Knossos sealings: provenance and identification', *BSA* 60 (1965), 66), documents were also picked up elsewhere. At least some of the strays were recorded in Mackenzie's day-books as coming from Magazines IV, XII and XIII. His descriptions leave no doubt that these were inscribed crescents — though we do not know *which* crescents — so it was hardly unreasonable of Evans to have associated them with the nearby Long Gallery crescents.

[30] Medallions (flat clay discs, pinched and pierced at the top) are known only from the Mallia and Knossos Hieroglyphic Deposits; see n. 40 below.

[31] As many as eleven signs on a single crescent. Ideograms (GRAIN, WINE, OLIVES), with or without additional sign-groups, indicate the commodity-based nature of many transactions; but see n. 37 below.

[32] I. Pini, 'Neue Beobachtungen zu den tönernen Siegelabdrücken von Zakros', *AA* 1983, 559–72; J. Weingarten, 'The use of the Zakro sealings', *Kadmos* 22 (1983), 8–13.

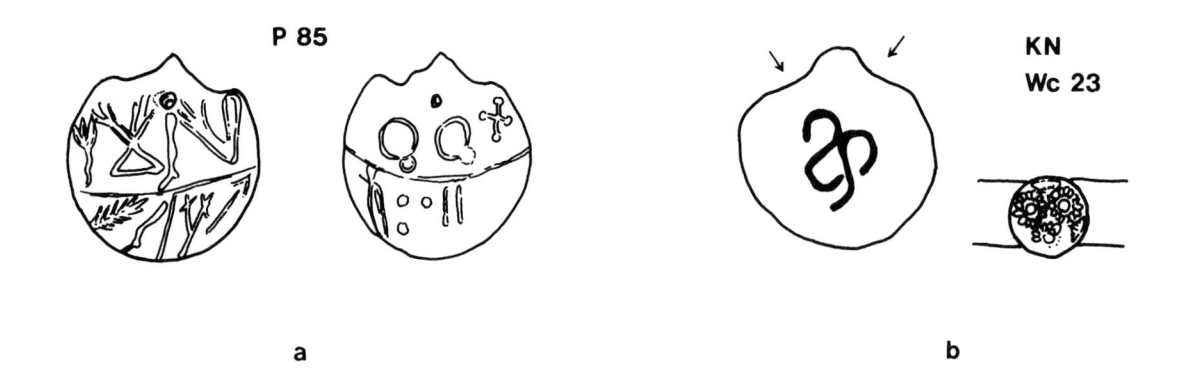

FIG. 3 a Medallion from Hieroglyphic Deposit; b Roundel from Temple Repositories

marks of ownership — Palatial administration was to some extent dependent on their employment.[33] About one third of the seal inscriptions included one of the two most common Hieroglyphic formulae, TROWEL+ARROW or TROWEL+EYE. As Olivier has convincingly proposed, TROWEL+ARROW and TROWEL+EYE must represent two venerable Minoan institutions, perhaps temple and palace.[34] Since (as far as sealings can tell us) the TROWEL+ARROW and TROWEL+EYE seals functioned in precisely the same way as other Hieroglyphic seals, it seems reasonable to accept that they all served some similar, probably official, purpose.

Sphragistic procedures have also become noticeably more complex. Multiple stamping (first seen on the South Front stopper) is now a regular administrative habit: just under half (48.4%) of intact sealings were stamped by two, three or even four *different* seals. When one of the multiple impressions is from a Hieroglyphic seal, it is customarily interpreted as an official 'countermark' (controller stamp) for the activity.[35] Countermarking may well have existed, but the explanation does not illuminate those transactions (the majority indeed) where all seals are Hieroglyphic, or none is,

---

[33] Almost half the documents were stamped by Hieroglyphic seals. On inscribed seals, see J.-P. Olivier, 'The relationship between inscriptions on Hieroglyphic seals and those written on archival documents', in Palaima (n. 8 above), 11–23; id., 'Les Sceaux avec des signes hiéroglyphiques. Que lire? Une question de définition', in W.-D. Niemeier (ed.), *Studien zur minoischen und helladischen Glyptik: Beiträge zum 2. Marburger Siegel Symposium ... 1978* (CMS Beiheft 1; Berlin, 1981), 105–16.

[34] Olivier (n. 33 above, in Palaima, n. 8 above), 17–18. However, both formulae sometimes appear on the same seal and even on the same seal face. While an individual can, of course, hold both religious and secular titles, one does not expect such contradictory *institutions* to be named on the same seal, at least not on seals that are used within palatial administration. I am more inclined to interpret TROWEL:ARROW and TROWEL:EYE as two main branches of the royal administration, perhaps one as the royal estate, and the other, the Treasury or Stores. On a suggestion for the 'Temple', see n. 25 above.

[35] J.-C. Poursat, 'Fonction et usage des sceaux en Crète à l'époque des premiers palais: quelques remarques', in W. Müller (ed.), *Fragen und Probleme der Bronzezeitlichen Ägäischen Glyptik, Beiträge zum 3. Internationalen Marburger Siegel-Symposium ... 1985* (*CMS* Beiheft 3; Berlin, 1989), 222.

or only a single seal impression appears. Whatever the underlying rationale for multiple stamping — and this is still quite obscure — the habit was limited to Knossos (see also below, at the MM IIIB Temple Repositories) and to LM IB Zakro.[36] Elsewhere in Crete single stamping was the norm.

In a multiple sealing system there are necessary interrelationships between the different sealing partners: at the very least, all partners to the transaction must be present to impress their seals while the clay is still wet. If they were all attending at the Palace, one would expect to find a kind of concentrated sealing authority, with relatively few seals responsible for a disproportionately large number of sealings (as at MM IIB Phaistos, where 13% of seal-owners stamped 70% of the sealings). Such a pattern is best explained by resident seal-owners repeatedly sealing and unsealing on the spot. That is the *intensive* model of seal use. However, the rate of seal use in the Hieroglyphic Deposit was remarkably low: only two seals appear even twice in our records, a little bump in an otherwise flat landscape of completely individual transactions. This *non-intensive* pattern of seal use may reflect external seal-owners each sending one or two sealed objects to the Palace from elsewhere. Thus, the bureaucratic activity reflected in the records of the Hieroglyphic Deposit has nothing in common with day-to-day storeroom activities as expressed by the sealing system at Phaistos. Rather, it appears that the Knossos Hieroglyphic administrative system was not directly concerned with Palatial storeroom accounting but rather with some specialised bureaucratic operation addressed from the hinterland to the centre.[37] One is tempted to think local tax records, but this is quite speculative.

NEOPALATIAL KNOSSOS

The MM IIIB/LMIa Temple Repositories[38]

The administrative debris swept into the cists of the Temple Repositories is our only evidence for Neopalatial bureaucratic procedures at Knossos prior to the Mycenaean take-over. However fragmentary this evidence, it is striking that the sealings and written documents reflect administrative structures more akin to those of MM IIB Phaistos (and to future LM IB deposits elsewhere) than to the recent Hieroglyphic past of Knossos itself.

Most significantly, scribes have abandoned the Hieroglyphic script and are now writing in Linear A.[39] Sir Arthur Evans thought that the script had changed as a result of dynastic revolution — but

---

[36] J. Weingarten, 'The multiple sealing system of Minoan Crete and its possible antecedents in Anatolia', *OJA* 11 (1992), 25–37.

[37] We can only be fairly sure that the sealings did not secure large or bulky containers (despite inscribed commodity ideograms; see n. 32 above) because the visible cord impressions show them too fine to have tied the pithoi or sacks in which such commodities would have been shipped or stored.

[38] MM IIIB: A.J. Evans, 'The Palace of Knossos', *BSA* 9 (1902–3), 44. G. Walberg classes the pottery as later MM III, perhaps 'transitional' to LM IA: *Middle Minoan III: A Time of Transition* (SIMA 97; Jonsered, 1992), 12–13, 30. Some glyptic scholars argue that at least some of the seals should be dated to LM IA: Pini (n. 8 above), 46–53; J.G. Younger, 'Bronze Age Aegean seals in their middle period (ca. 1725–1550 B.C.)', in R. Laffineur (ed.), *Transition : Le Monde égéen du Bronze Moyen au Bronze Récent* (Aegaeum 3; Liège, 1989), 59. See now M. Panagiotaki, 'The Temple Repositories of Knossos: new information from the unpublished notes of Sir Arthur Evans', *BSA* 88 (1993), 49–91.

[39] Hieroglyphic and Linear A documents are found together in the MM IIIB Mallia 'Hieroglyphic Deposit', indicating a possible period of overlap at that site (O. Pelon, 'L'Épée à l'acrobate et la chronologie maliote II', *BCH* 107 (1983), 703). Linear A (at 11 sites) is much more widespread than was the Hieroglyphic script. On Linear A accounting practices marking centres of intensive regional exploitation see T.G. Palaima, 'Preliminary comparative textual evidence for palatial control of economic activity in Minoan and Mycenaean Crete', in R. Hägg and N. Marinatos (eds.), *The Function of the Minoan Palaces. Proceedings of the Fourth*

does a new dynast sweep away a bureaucratic structure along with redundant bureaucrats? It is remarkable that Knossos officials were no longer equipped with inscribed seals. Why were these seals, so characteristic of Hieroglyphic administration, not 'translated' into Linear A? What other civilisation had — and used — inscribed seals, then stopped, without as explanation either a change in political control or a decline in literacy?

Accompanying the switch in script, medallions — the typical Hieroglyphic 'mini-documents' — also disappear. Knossos scribes now issue roundels (FIG. 3.b), a laconic type of Linear A document already known at MM IIB Phaistos.[40] Roundels are flat clay discs, usually with a very brief inscription written on one side and one or more seal impressions on the rim. Hallager has convincingly interpreted roundels as receipts, the recipient of goods acknowledging units of 'debt' by marking the edge of the roundel with the equivalent number of seal impressions.[41] Roundels are, strangely enough, the Minoans' closest approach to the sealed written documents known from the Near East, but they appear to be documents written for a functionally illiterate bureaucracy. That may be why, on roundels, each seal impression equals one unit — so the scribe cannot cheat the seal-owner regarding numbers — and why, too, the vast majority of roundels are inscribed with simple ideograms, which even the barely literate could understand. It is a simple system that allows the functionally illiterate to transact Palatial business with confidence. If seal-owning officials were now themselves generally illiterate, the demise of inscribed seals becomes more understandable.

In addition to roundels, Knossos bureaucrats still had to hand the traditional sub-literate noduli. Indeed, it may not be coincidence that the Temple Repositories witness a tremendous proliferation of noduli, now the *most* common (54.3%) form of sealed document.[42] The use of noduli was by no means restricted to marginal seal-owners: on the contrary, some of the most active seal-owners (those who may reasonably be thought of as sealing leaders) stamped noduli exclusively and no true sealings at all. At the same time another administrative strand led to a great increase in the use of flat-based clay *document* sealings (38.5%). We know nothing about the actual leather documents, which have vanished without further trace, but because (1) the sealings were found within the Palace, and (2) the seal-owners who stamped them were entirely distinct from those who stamped noduli, it does seem likely that these were bureaucratic instruments of some specialised kind. Of course, the responsible officials whose seals they bore need not have been capable of either reading or writing these documents. In the time-honoured manner the contents could have been dictated to scribes and read aloud.[43]

International Symposium at the Swedish Institute in Athens ... 1984, (Skrifter ... Svenska Inst. i Athen, 4°, 35; Stockholm, 1987), 301–06.

[40] E. Hallager, 'The Knossos roundels', *BSA* 82 (1987), 55–70. It is quite uncertain whether roundels replaced medallions *in function*. Although the shape of some roundels in the Temple Repositories resembles medallions (and the one comes in when the other goes out), a key difference is that medallions were never stamped by seals, an obligatory procedure for roundels (see n. 30 above). Also, medallions were almost always pierced, as if for hanging, whereas roundels never were.

[41] E. Hallager, 'Roundels among sealings in Minoan administration: a comprehensive analysis of function', in Palaima (n. 8 above), 121–48.

[42] J. Weingarten, 'Old and new elements in the seals and sealings of the Temple Repository, Knossos', in Laffineur (n. 38 above), 42–4; ead. (n. 11 above — Part II), **A19 – A29**.

[43] Even in Egypt, a society that placed an exceptionally high value on literacy, only an estimated 0.3–1% of the population could read and write: see J. Baines and C.J. Eyre, 'Four notes on literacy', *Göttinger Miszellen: Beiträge zur ägyptologischen Diskussion* 61 (1983), 67. The ability to read and the ability to write are of course not the same, and in ancient societies the number who could read, at least for economic purposes, is likely to have been much higher than the number of writers.

The career of the most active seal-owner represented in the Temple Repositories highlights a number of concurrent sphragistic trends. He stamped only noduli and no true sealings but nonetheless dominated sealing activity. Responsible for 22.7% of all sealed documents (in an intensive model of seal use) he was very probably an in-house official sealing these noduli on the spot.[44] Further description of his activities, however, is anything but straightforward.

1. Strictly speaking, he was not an individual at all, but a sealing *pair*, the sum of two different seals (sea shells + long-horned goat; PLATES 22 and 23) always used together. In a similar manner, other pairs of seals jointly stamped nearly half (47%) of all sealings in the Temple Repositories. So the habit of multiple sealing, already common in the Hieroglyphic Deposit, continued apace in MM IIIB (though without the refinement of Hieroglyphic seals).

2. Whether multiple sealing partners represented one actual person or two is unknown. In the case of the two seals of the sealing 'leader', there is some evidence that these seals participated in a larger corporate identity: the long-horned goat breaks down, in fact, into *two* seals, different versions of the same scene.
- A + A (PLATES 22.a+23.a). The sea-shells are paired with a goat with glyptic fillers, of which a rectangular 'manger' is the most prominent (*PM I*, fig. 518b);
- A + B (PLATES 22.b+23.b). The sea-shells are paired with a goat with shorter horns and without the manger (*PM I*, fig. 518a). We have dubbed such variants 'look-alikes' because they look so much alike that they must have been made intentionally similar in order to assert some similar authority.[45] The question naturally arises, who used these look-alikes and why? Since the variants could hardly have been distinguished in the rough-and-tumble of normal sealing practice, it seems reasonable to assume that they shared in a common glyptic identity. One tempting explanation is that look-alikes allowed the prerogatives of a seal to be multiplied without recourse to written titles or instructions.[46] It might then be more than coincidence that a growing use of look-alikes in Palatial administration follows on the loss of inscribed seals.

LM IB Knossos?

Because Knossos escaped the worst of the LM IB burnt destructions, leaving no sealing deposits, it is impossible to make direct comparisons with the major LM IB deposits elsewhere. If we extrapolate trends from the Temple Repositories into LM I, we can imagine (in a fuzzy way) that the sealing administration of Knossos might have been something like that of LM IB Zakro, especially in their very common habit of multiple sealing and the explosion in the use of look-alike rings and gems.[47]

---

[44] The three most active seal-owners (two of whom stamped only noduli) together accounted for 53.3% of sealed documents.

[45] We no longer maintain that the sea-shells seal also exists in two versions (as in Weingarten, n. 42 above, 41–2; it now appears that the system of look-alikes in the Temple Repositories was only asymmetric, loc. cit.). The 'look-alike' phenomenon was already known in a small way at MM IIB Phaistos (Weingarten n. 36 above, 32), but it was at Knossos and at LM IB Zakro that look-alikes played a major role in sealing administration. Zakro look-alikes: Weingarten (n. 11 above — Part I), 289–93, and Pini (n. 32 above), 563–72; and at Knossos: Weingarten (n. 42 above), 40–2.

[46] Note a possible parallel in the use of look-alike seals at proto-literate archaic Uruk: M.A. Brandes, *Siegelabrollungen aus den archaischen Bauschichten in Uruk-Warka* (Wiesbaden, 1979), 93–100. (I am grateful to Dr. J. Aruz for bringing this reference to my attention).

[47] Weingarten (n. 36 above). Such characteristics help us occasionally to spot LM IB sealings exported from Knossos to other

Nothing remotely like such a system survives into the final destruction deposits of Mycenaean Knossos.

MYCENAEAN KNOSSOS: THE FINAL DESTRUCTION DEPOSITS

The major political upheaval signalled by the change from Minoan Linear A to the Mycenaean Greek of Linear B had fundamental administrative consequences. There was a noticeable tightening up of administrative controls in an economy subjected to more intensive scribal scrutiny. Former Minoan centres now reported upwards to Knossos,[48] a hierarchical shift that resulted in a stream of detailed information reaching Palatial officials. Palaima has described how Mycenaean scribes were closely monitoring a proliferation of central and locally based officials,[49] whose concerns went well beyond collecting due income and auditing the distribution of goods, to an active intervention in the details of local economic life and craft production.[50]

At the same time sealings actually decreased in frequency and shifted to a strongly *non-intensive* pattern of seal use. Over 60% of sealings were stamped by seal-owners who left just one, two or three sealings each. This probably reflects non-resident seal-owners each sending a few sealed items to Knossos.[51] These sealings were found scattered over many rooms, magazines, halls and corridors in the Palace, as well as in external buildings; it looks as if the sealed objects arriving at Knossos were dispersed in storerooms and workshops throughout the building complex. Since sealings were often found mixed up with Linear B tablets, it is likely that scribes were keeping track of at least some of the traffic in sealed goods. Scribes also occasionally wrote Linear B transaction notes on sealings;[52] when they scrawled ideograms right over the seal impressions, it looks as if their inscriptions literally took precedence over the obscured seal impressions. One has the feeling that Mycenaean scribes have assumed some management functions, perhaps at the expense of the former seal-owning class.

Mycenaean administration rejected a number of traditional Minoan documents and sealing practices too. It dropped the long-lived (MM IIB–LM IB) roundel. One wonders if this simple receipt was abandoned because seal-owners no longer personally took goods from Palace stores but now had to pass through channels under the direct control of scribes. Flat-based document-sealings also disappeared.[53]

---

sites (Weingarten, n. 11 above), our only glimpse of a network of sealing activities radiating outwards from Knossos to the east and south of the island.

[48] Reoccupied Minoan sites, such as Amnisos, Kydonia, Stavromenos(?), Phaistos (and Aghia Triadha), *ku-ta-to*, and *se-to-i-ja*, were incorporated into the Mycenaean administrative system as second-order centres: J. Bennet, 'The structure of the Linear B administration at Knossos', *AJA* 89 (1985), 231–49.

[49] T.G. Palaima, 'Origin, development, transition and transformation: the purposes and technique of administration in Minoan and Mycenaean society', in Palaima (n. 8 above), 96–8: by persons holding the title of *e-qe-ta*, *ko-re-te*, *po-ro-ko-re-te*, or *qa-si-re-u*, or having the status of 'collector'. On the functions of these titles, see M. Lindgren, *The People of Pylos: Prosopographical and Methodological Studies in the Pylos Archives. II: The Use of Personal Designations and Their Interpretations* (*Boreas* 3:II; Uppsala, 1973), *passim*.

[50] New Linear B tablet formats and scribal techniques helped bureaucrats to process much larger amounts of data. See W.C. Brice, 'Notes on Linear A. V: the legibility of the account tablets', *Kadmos* 30 (1991), 42–8; Palaima (n. 49 above), 98, 102.

[51] Weingarten (n. 11 above — Part II), 11–13.

[52] J.-P. Olivier, 'La série **Ws** de Cnossos', *Minos* 9 (1968), 173–83.

[53] We have only two document-sealings from Mycenaean Knossos, both from the Room of the Chariot Tablets (Weingarten, n. 11 above — Part II, 10–11), where it has been argued that there was an earlier destruction: J. Driessen, 'Le palais de Cnossos au MR II–III : combien de destructions ?', in A. Farnoux and J. Driessen (eds.), *La Crète mycénienne* (*BCH* Suppl.; forthcoming). Cf. the

Such nodules appeared early (at Knossos as early as anywhere) and thereafter were found in every Minoan sealing deposit. Whatever the purpose of these putative sealed documents, they were not required by the Mycenaeans. Sealings were now virtually restricted to two types of nodules (FIG. 1):

1. hanging nodules of Class VI (with Linear B inscriptions on VI/A);
2. direct-object sealings (XIII), simple balls of clay pressed down directly on to the cords which bound the sealed objects. These cords were often sturdy enough to have secured fairly heavy or bulky goods, including the basic commodities upon which the Palace depended.

Multiple stamping completely died out. This distinctively Knossian sealing habit (dating back at least to the Hieroglyphic Deposit) may have had its roots in local economic or kin-based units, entities that either no longer existed or no longer counted in an altered social order.

The Linear B personnel tablets of the **As** series record approximately three times as many men with non-Greek names as with Greek names.[54] Given this numerical inferiority, it was probably unavoidable that the Mycenaeans had to rely on pre-existing Minoan administrative units, but higher ranks seem to be almost exclusively Greek: compare the personal names of so-called 'shepherds' with those of collectors (who held an ill defined but important position in the Mycenaean economic system). The Mycenaeans may nonetheless have taken over more than the physical structures of government.[55] There is some evidence that they retained an important Minoan office. Appropriately, the evidence for this rests upon seals and sealings.

In the realm of sealings there was only one Mycenaean innovation, a curious type of combination nodule, which hung from cords but was *also* pressed against either a wooden or wickerwork object (FIG. 1; PLATE 24a: Class XII).[56] In the Near East such combination nodules were associated with archives, where they sealed boxes or baskets filled with tablets. If they were used for the same purpose at Knossos, that would be evidence for a very specific administrative import.[57] It would also follow that the few seal-owners who stamped such nodules (TABLE III) must have been resident

---

clear LM II fire destruction of the Unexplored Mansion, with only a single sealing (Class VI; a surface find) and no tablets. See J.H. Betts, 'The sealstones and sealing', in M.R. Popham *et al.*, *The Minoan Unexplored Mansion at Knossos* (BSA Suppl. 17; Oxford, 1984), 196, pl. 190d.

[54] L. Baumbach, 'An examination of the personal names in the Knossos tablets as evidence for the social structure of Crete in the Late Minoan II period', in O. Krzyszkowska and L. Nixon (eds.), *Minoan Society: Proceedings of the Cambridge Colloquium 1981* (Bristol, 1983), 3–10.

[55]
	non-Greek names	Greek names
Shepherds	75	92
Collectors	0	28

Extracted from P.H. Ilievski, 'Observations on the personal names from the Knossos D Tablets', in J.-P. Olivier (ed.), *Mykenaïka: Actes du IXe Colloque international sur les textes mycéniens et égéens ... 1990* (BCH suppl. 25; Paris, 1992), 331. See also Bennet (n. 48 above).

[56] Weingarten (n. 11 above — Part II), 6–8, fig. 3. Class XII is not confined to Knossos: one example is known from LM IIIA1 Chania and six from Pylos (ibid. 7; and ead., 'The sealing bureaucracy of Mycenaean Knossos: the identification of some officials and their seals', in Farnoux and Driessen (n. 53 above).

[57] I am indebted to Dr E. Fiandra for information on the Near Eastern use of such nodules; see also Ferioli and Fiandra (n. 15 above), 225 n. 15. The evidence for their similar purpose in Mycenaean administration is presented in Weingarten (n. 56 above). See also K.R. Veenhof, 'Cuneiform archives, an introduction', in K.R. Veenhof (ed.), *Cuneiform Archives and Libraries: 30° Rencontre assyriologique Internationale ... 1983* (Nederlands Hist. Arch. Inst. te Istanbul, Uitgaven 57; Leiden, 1986), 16 n. 69.

bureaucrats, because boxes of unbaked bookkeeping tablets were unlikely to have been transported from outside the Palace. If so, they would be the only seal-owners at Knossos demonstrably working as resident officials within the Palace.

One ring-owner stamped seven of the nineteen combination nodules, by far the most of anyone (TABLE III). If we are right, he should have been a particularly active resident official. His ring, as it happens, is a famous one: the goddess approached by a priestess with rhyton offering (PLATE 24.b, top). This is the same design which appears again, most intriguingly, in intaglio, on the so-called clay matrix (PLATE 24.b, centre) from the Room of the Clay Signet.[58] Not only that, but, almost unique in our records, it is a ring with a history behind it.

Three generations earlier, someone at Knossos used a ring like that to authenticate a document sent to Zakro (PLATE 24.b, bottom). The sealing from this document was found in House A, but, as I have argued elsewhere, the clay of this sealing strongly suggests that it originated in Knossos.[59] Now, the act of sending a document from Knossos to the east does not make him particularly important, but his use of a metal ring certainly must betoken some status. So the question arises, how was this ring handed down from Minoan to Mycenaean times? Did a descendent of the ring-owner survive the Mycenaean take-over to emerge as an official at Mycenaean Knossos? Or did some Mycenaean seize, or receive, this ring as booty, and just happen to serve in the Palace at the time of our records?

Before tackling these questions we must first take into account a surprising difference between the Minoan and Mycenaean rings. Our photograph (PLATE 24b), which shows the ring impressions and the matrix (photographically reversed) to scale, clearly demonstrates that the Zakro impression (bottom) was impressed by a significantly smaller ring; in addition, one can see that the arms of the Zakro seated goddess are posed quite differently from those on the Knossos ring and matrix.[60] Therefore the original rings were not identical and could not have been made from a single mould. Instead, there were at least two rings with subtle differences between them. We would describe these rings as 'look-alikes', that is, rings which look so much alike that they must have been made intentionally similar in order to exercise some similar authority. The question remains, was it the chance survival of a single ring, or did the Mycenaeans purposely employ a look-alike ring in an administrative manner?

Given that the goddess ring was stamped on combination nodules far more often than any other seal at Knossos, we may accept (1) that this ring-owner regularly sealed baskets of tablets and, consequently, had some responsibility regarding their contents, and (2) that he must also have been a resident official in the Palace. If (as a working hypothesis) the look-alike goddess ring was chosen on purpose, we would expect to find other officials equipped with look-alike versions of the same ring. Would this, then, plausibly explain the existence of a ring-matrix for this ring — and only for this ring? In short, it is proposed that the function of the clay matrix was to produce look-alike replica rings for various officials of the same rank or function. In support, we may call upon evidence from Pylos, where officials were running a sealing bureaucracy very much like that of Mycenaean Knossos: in the Pylian archives, one ring of a group of look-alike gold rings had stamped precisely the Class XII form of combination

---

[58] Despite Evans' dating the matrix to a level 'not later than LM I' (*PM II.ii*, 768), both entries in Mackenzie's day-book of 24 and 25 April 1901 and the new excavation results reported by N. Momigliano and S. Hood, ('Excavations of 1987 on the South Front of the Palace at Knossos', *BSA* 89 (1994), in press), demonstrate that the matrix was found in a context later than LM II.

[59] Weingarten (n. 11 above), 308.

[60] Pini (n. 32 above), 570–1, pl. 10. Evans (*PM II.ii*, 769 n. 1) had noted this discrepancy but did not take the matter further.

nodule.[61] It does look as if a customary Minoan office had been taken over by the Mycenaean bureaucracy. Perhaps, in a sense, the inherited look-alike goddess ring *was* war booty, for the structures of administration are no less the spoils of war than any other resources of the island.

With the fall of the Palace the history of sealings at Knossos comes to an end.[62] Scattered sealings are still found at Chania in LM IIIB (and may some day turn up near Knossos too). Indeed, as long as inscribed stirrup jars were being produced and traded we should not be surprised to discover sealings on any of the same sites.[63] Nonetheless, it does look as if the use of seals fell back to pre-administrative levels, perhaps not quite local and isolated, but, on current evidence, sporadic and no longer integrated into a larger bureaucratic organisation.

TABLE I

Knossos sealings in the Herakleion Museum impressed by seals not later than MM I*

	KSPI	Sealing Type	Seal Shape	Seal Design
1	T2	nodulus	plate seal	Pini pl. IIIA
2	?	nodulus?**	conoid or stamp cylinder	pl. IIID
3	?	nodulus	plate seal	
4	?	nodulus	conoid or stamp cylinder	pl. IIIC
5	Vb	VII	bar or cube	pl. IIIE,F
6	Ta	stopper?	?	pl. IVA,B
7	T?	stopper?	plate seal?	
8	Tc	lid? (cloth?)	conoid or stamp cylinder	pl. IIIB
9		stopper	" "	Hood & Kenna fig. 1
10		stopper	" "	Pini pl. IVC
11		lump	plate seal	pl. IVD
12		nodulus	?	pl. IVE
13		?	plate seal	Ash. Museum no number

Pini: n. 8 above.   Hood and Kenna: n. 6 above.
KSPI: M.A.V. Gill, 'The Knossos sealings: provenance and identification', BSA 60 (1965), 58–98.
*   Rather than a nodulus, this may be a rare example of a seal cut in relief (cf. J. Aruz, 'The "Aegean" pottery-impression from Troy IIB', *Kadmos* 25 (1986), 164–7).
** Extracted from Pini (n. 8 above), 34 — to which is added the types of objects sealed.

---

[61] Evidence for look-alike rings at Pylos in Weingarten (n. 56 above), where it is proposed that these rings belonged to the former Minoan office of *qa-si-re-u*.

[62] The date of the destruction of the Palace is, of course, hotly disputed. I follow the early LM IIIA2 date proposed by M.R. Popham (*The Destruction of the Palace at Knossos: Pottery of the LM IIIA Period* (SIMA 12; Göteborg, 1970); see also id., 'The historical implications of the Linear B archive at Knossos dating to either c. 1400 B.C. or 1200 B.C.', *Cretan Studies* 1 (1988), 217–27) rather than the LM IIIB destruction date argued by E. Hallager, *The Mycenaean Palace at Knossos: Evidence for Final Destruction in the IIIB Period* (Medelhavsmuseet memoir 1; Stockholm, 1977), and by W.-D. Niemeier, 'Mycenaean Knossos and the Age of Linear B', *SMEA* 23 (1982), 219–87, and *Die Palaststilkeramik von Knossos: Stil, Chronologie und historischer Kontext* (Deutsches Arch. Inst., Arch. Forschungen 13; Berlin, 1985).

[63] Sealings at Chania (with Linear B tablets): E. Hallager, M. Vlasakis and B.P. Hallager, 'New Linear B tablets from Khania', *Kadmos* 31 (1992), 61–87. Inscribed stirrup jars: E. Hallager, 'The inscribed stirrup jars: implications for Late Minoan IIIB Crete', *AJA* 91 (1987), 171–90.

TABLE II

Sealings from the South-East Pillar Room

KSPI	Sealing Type	Seal Shape	Seal Design
T1	direct object sack? (leather thongs)	disc	reversed C-spirals, filling triangles, cf. H2 (=P53); Z 134.*
Tc	direct object lid? (cloth?)	conoid or stamp cylinder	Pini (n. 8) pl. IIIB
T2	nodulus, pyramidal	plate seal	" " pl. IIIA
	cf. nodulus shape **Pe** from Knossos Hieroglyphic Deposit		
Te**	nodulus thick oval	discs?	a) double axe b) 'barley corn'
Td	Class VI	prism	hieroglyphics (P 16; read by *CHIC* as H 3–8 = A-SA)
Tf	fragment	?	hieroglyphics (P 15; read by *CHIC* as H 3–1–43)

* Parallels drawn by Evans, *Scripta Minoa* I, 146–7.
** *PM IV.ii*, fig. 617: attributed to Hieroglyphic Deposit (corrected by Gill n. 29 above, 66, 85); seal impressions may be the hieroglyphic signs A and SA (n. 25 above; cf. **Td**).

TABLE III

*Combination Nodules (Class XII) at Mycenaean Knossos**

KSPI		Provenance	Seal Design
R 12	1	Landing on Grand Staircase	Opposed quadrupeds
R 51	1	Lower E–W Corridor	Goddess with rhyton**
R 54	6	Door S Hall of Colonnades	" " "
R 61	1	" " "	Man milking cow
R 88	2	" " "	Collared bitch
R 94	2	Wooden Staircase B	Quatrefoil
R 105	1	Queen's Megaron	Three dolphins**
N 12	1	Room of Chariot Tablets	Effaced***
J 3	1	North Entrance Passage	Sailing ship
Va	1	Arsenal Deposit	Three water fowl
Vd	2	" "	Contorted lion
Total:	19		

* Compiled from Weingarten, *OJA* 7 (1988), Appendix III–VI.
** Probable ring impression.
*** Inscribed, **Ws** 8493.

Chapter 13

The Minoan Roads of Knossos[1]

P.M. WARREN

MINOAN ROUTES AND ROADS

Similarities of expression across the sites of Minoan civilisation, such as ashlar masonry, the general form of Minoan 'villas' or the Linear A writing system, and the exchange of sophisticated goods such as Marine Style pottery, all required good systems of land communication. Research in recent years has much enriched our knowledge of Minoan routes and roads both from the theoretical viewpoint[2] and practically. At the outset of Minoan studies a remarkable amount was achieved by Evans, whose way-stations and forts in east Crete have been reinvestigated in the excellent work of the Greek roads research team.[3] Evans also brought to light evidence for a great north–south transit route across the

---

Special Abbreviation:
KS = S. Hood and D. Smyth, *Archaeological Survey of the Knossos Area*, (2nd edn.; *BSA* Suppl. 14; London, 1981).

[1] Sinclair Hood gave me my first opportunity to take part in Minoan fieldwork, as a member of his excavation team in his final Royal Road season at Knossos in 1961. Thereafter he was my teacher on our travels in the 1960s and has been a guide and friend ever since. This article is written as a small token of thanks and appreciation, in the hope that the subject may interest one who has set standards of fieldwork and scholarship which we *epigonoi* can only try to maintain.

[2] S. Chryssoulaki, 'L'urbanisme minoen. A. Le réseau routier urbain', in P. Darcque and R. Treuil (eds.), *L'habitat égéen préhistorique* (*BCH* Suppl. 19; Paris, 1990), 371–80.

[3] A.J. Evans and J.L. Myres, 'A Mycenaean military road in Crete', *The Academy* 1204 (June 1, 1895), 469–70; A.J. Evans, 'Explorations in Eastern Crete II. A town of castles', *The Academy* 1259 (June 20, 1896), 512–13; id., 'Explorations in Eastern Crete III. Mycenaean Dicta', *The Academy* 1261 (July 4, 1896), 17–18; id., 'Explorations in Eastern Crete IV. Above the Libyan Sea', *The Academy* 1263 (July 18, 1896), 53–4. A.C. Frothingham, Jr., 'Archaeological News: Krete', *AJA* 1st series 10 (1895), 399–403; 1st series 11 (1896), 454–67. J.D.S. Pendlebury, *The Archaeology of Crete: An Introduction* (London, 1939), 7–16. J.C. McEnroe, 'Minoan House and Town Arrangement' (Ph.D. dissertation, University of Toronto, 1979, *non vidi*), mentioned in J.W. Shaw, (n. 38 below — 1982), 193 n. 84. Greek Roads Research Team: Y. Tzedakis, S. Chryssoulaki, S. Voutsaki, Y. Venieri and L. Kyriopoulou, and, with his always excellent photographs, St. Alexandrou. For their work, see Y. Tzedakis, S. Chryssoulaki and L. Kyriopoulou, ''Ο δρόμος στή Μινωϊκή Κρήτη', *Cretological VI, A'2* (Chania, 1990), 403–14; Y. Tzedakis, L. Kyriopoulou and S. Chryssoulaki, 'Μινωϊκοί δρόμοι και οδικοί σταθμοί στήν Ανατολική Κρήτη', *6th International Colloquium on Aegean Prehistory ... Athens, 1987* (to appear); Y. Tzedakis, S. Chryssoulaki, S. Voutsaki and Y. Venieri, 'Les routes minoennes : rapport préliminaire — Défense de la circulation ou circulation de la défense?', *BCH* 113 (1989), 43–75.

island from and to Knossos.[4] The roads research team have also revealed Minoan roads in western Crete.[5] Within urban areas the road network of Mallia has been studied by H. van Effenterre and S. Damiani Indelicato[6] and that of Zakros by L. Platon.[7] Current excavations at Palaikastro are extending knowledge of the town's roads.[8] At Akrotiri on Thera C. Palyvou has examined the relationship of road lines to architecture.[9]

For Knossos R.W. Hutchinson's review of Minoan town planning in 1950 referred to roads,[10] the evidence of the Royal Road and the Stepped Portico–Viaduct system having been set out by Evans in 1928.[11] All the data were summarised by Sinclair Hood in his and D. Smyth's *Archaeological Survey of the Knossos Area*.[12] Recent discoveries and the opportunity to describe and illustrate for the first time some older discoveries now merit a new review.

THE CITY NETWORK

The evidence now permits definition of the main or arterial lines and some of the inner lines and circulation of the city's road network (*le réseau routier urbain* of S. Chryssoulaki) (FIG. 1). There are still unknowns in relation to the surviving remains and without doubt further roads will be found. What we do observe is a remarkable confirmation as well as an expansion of the system found and described by Evans. Overall a dual function is clear, servicing and interrelating the various parts of the city and the Palace, and connecting the Minoan capital to the outside world through arterial routes to destinations north, south, west and, probably, east (PLATE 25).

1. The Royal Road

Excavated in 1904 and 1905, this best known of Minoan roads[13] appears to have been the main east–west artery of the city (FIG. 1; PLATES 25–7). Towards its eastern end it bifurcates, the main east–west line terminating inside the Theatral Area,[14] while a branch runs southeast behind this building to end at the northwest corner of the Palace (PLATE 27). From this branch two further roads lead off, first a stepped way ascending southwards towards the West Court of the Palace and second,

---

[4] *PM II.i*, 60–92.

[5] Tzedakis, Chryssoulaki and Kyriopoulou (n. 3 above), 410–14; Tzedakis, Chryssoulaki, Voutsaki and Venieri (n. 3 above), 45, 50, 57 and n. 43, figs. 1–2, 11–13.

[6] H. van Effenterre, *Le Palais de Mallia et la cité minoenne: étude de synthèse* (*Incunabula Graeca* 76; Rome, 1980), 257–65. S. Damiani Indelicato, *Piazza pubblica e palazzo nella Creta minoica* (Rome, 1982), 27–41 (chiefly in relation to orientation of the Palace).

[7] L. Platon, 'L'urbanisme minoen. B. Espace intérieur et espace extérieur dans la ville minoenne', in Darcque and Treuil (n. 2 above), 381–93.

[8] J.A. MacGillivray and J.M. Driessen, 'Minoan settlement at Palaikastro', in Darcque and Treuil (n. 2 above), 395–412; J.A. MacGillivray, L.H. Sackett, J.M. Driessen and S. Hemingway, 'Excavations at Palaikastro, 1991', *BSA* 87 (1992), 122, fig. 1.

[9] C. Palyvou, 'Notes on the town plan of Late Cycladic Akrotiri, Thera', *BSA* 81 (1986), 179–94.

[10] R.W. Hutchinson, 'Prehistoric town planning in Crete', *The Town Planning Review* 21.3 (October 1950), 210.

[11] *PM II*, passim.

[12] *KS*.

[13] A.J. Evans, 'The Palace of Knossos', *BSA* 10 (1903–4), 45–54; id., 'The Palace of Knossos and its dependencies', *BSA* 11 (1904–5), 1–3; *PM II.ii*, 572–90.

[14] *PM II.ii*, 579, fig. 362. See also pp. 201–2 below and nn. 45–7 below, for the early stages of the road in the Theatral Area.

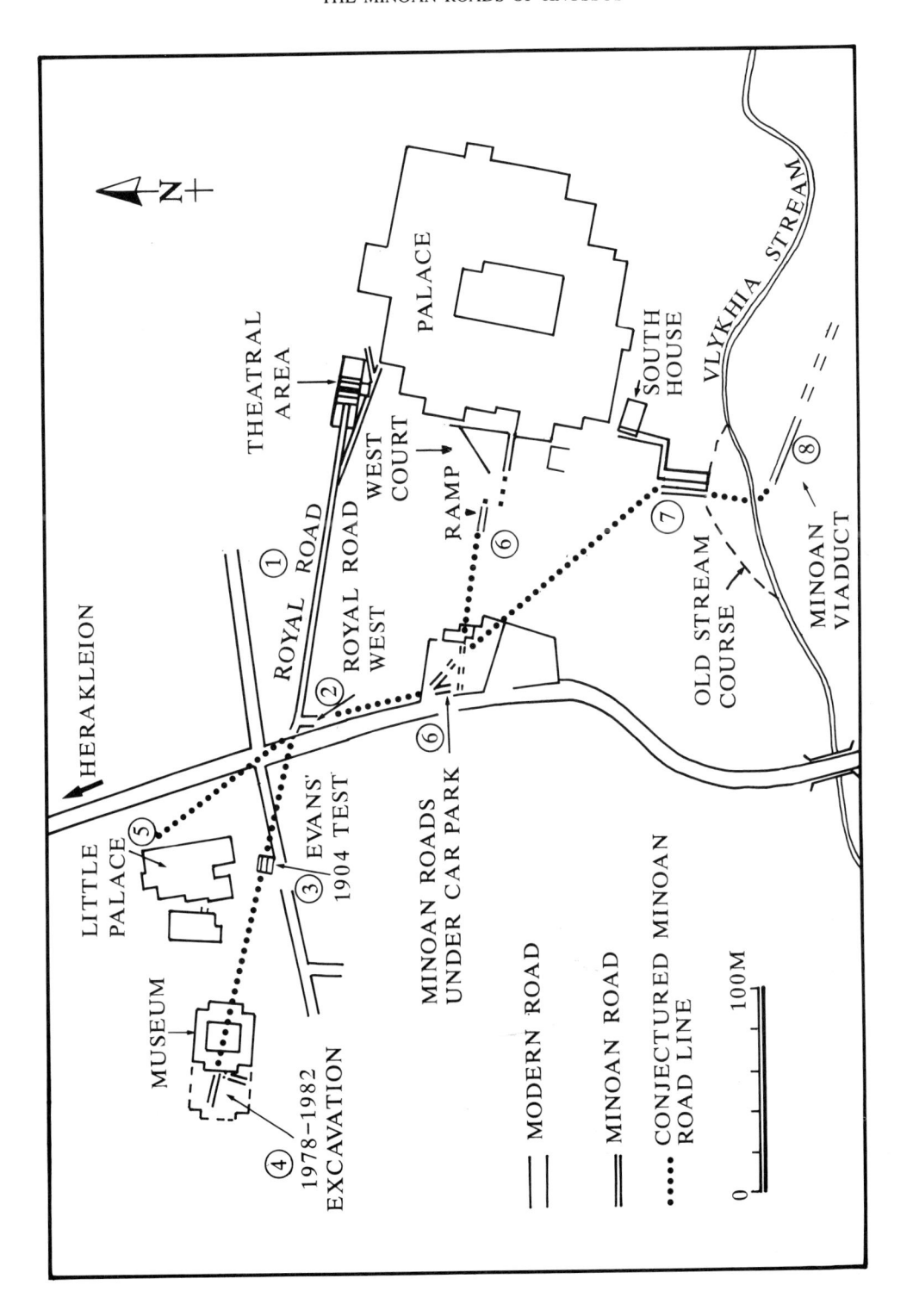

FIG. 1 The Minoan roads of Knossos

beside the southeast corner of the Theatral Area, a narrower paved course leading off northeast towards the north entrance of the Palace (FIG. 1).

From its terminal point (in its later history) at the foot of the steps inside the Theatral Area about 160 metres[15] of the Royal Road are exposed westwards. After this the road appeared to continue at least 60 metres further west (no. 3 below) and we shall have reason to see that it probably extended much further still (no. 4 below). Along the first 160 metres the total width of the road is about 3.80 m., comprising two side wings each of 1.20 m. and the central section 1.40 m. in width.[16] This section consisted of two lines of rectangular slabs of varying length up to 2.80 m., but each 0.70 m. wide (PLATE 26). Evans refers to a stone drainage channel running along at least part of the south side of the road.[17]

Both sides of the road were lined with buildings. On the north these included the Arsenal or Armoury, with its stores of bronze-headed arrows and Linear B tablets referring to those and other military equipment, while west of this was a building with an ivory workshop (*KS* nos. 213, 214, with refs.). On the south side the constructions directly lining the road seem to have been platforms and a possible long grandstand.[18]

2. Royal Road West

Excavations on the south side of the Royal Road in 1971–3 brought to light at the western end a north–south road of exactly the same form and construction as the Royal Road and making a T-junction with it.[19] This new road (FIGS. 1 and 2; PLATES 28 and 29), 3.42 m. below the modern surface, ran from the Royal Road 12.90 m. southwards (actually slightly east of south, about 175°) to the south limit of the excavation, and must have continued further south. The main section, although not well preserved, again comprised two lines of slabs totalling 1.40 m. in width; it was flanked on the east by a drain of irregular flat cobbling 0.58 m. wide and on the west by a much larger cobbled area, 2.90 m. in width. The total width was 4.88 m., making the arrangement here substantially wider than that of the Royal Road itself at 3.80 m. On both sides the cobbling ran up to a flanking wall; the eastern was in fact the west wall of a substantial building; it gave no evidence of interior division and may perhaps have been a large platform or grandstand running eastwards.

Royal Road West provided important dating evidence, discussed in the section on dating below. But it went out of use at the MM IIIB–LM IA transition, since it was covered by a thick fill of this date. Over this fill at the point of junction with the Royal Road was built a staircase 3.20 m. wide, rising up from the Royal Road (FIG. 2; PLATES 28, above, and 29, right). This staircase could well have given access to a rebuilt platform on the east. It is also probable that a column rose in the centre

---

[15] Ibid. 572 states 'about 170 metres'. As measured for *KS* the distance is about 160 metres. If the remains east of the Theatral Area steps are included the distance is at least 170 metres.
[16] Ibid. 574, fig. 359.
[17] Ibid. 576.
[18] P.M. Warren, 'Knossos. Excavations in the area of the Royal Road', *A.Delt.* 28 B'2 (1973), 575; id., 'Knossos 1973. Royal Road excavations and study season', *A.Delt.* 29 B'2 (1973–4), 903. The 'bastion' on the south side of the Theatral Area forms the climax of these structures as one moved eastward: see *PM* II.ii, 582 and figs. 362–5.
[19] P.M. Warren, 'Knossos. Royal Road South excavations', *A.Delt.* 27 B'2 (1972), 628 and pl. 588e; H.W. Catling, 'Archaeology in Greece, 1971–72', *AR* 18 (1971–72), 21, fig. 35.

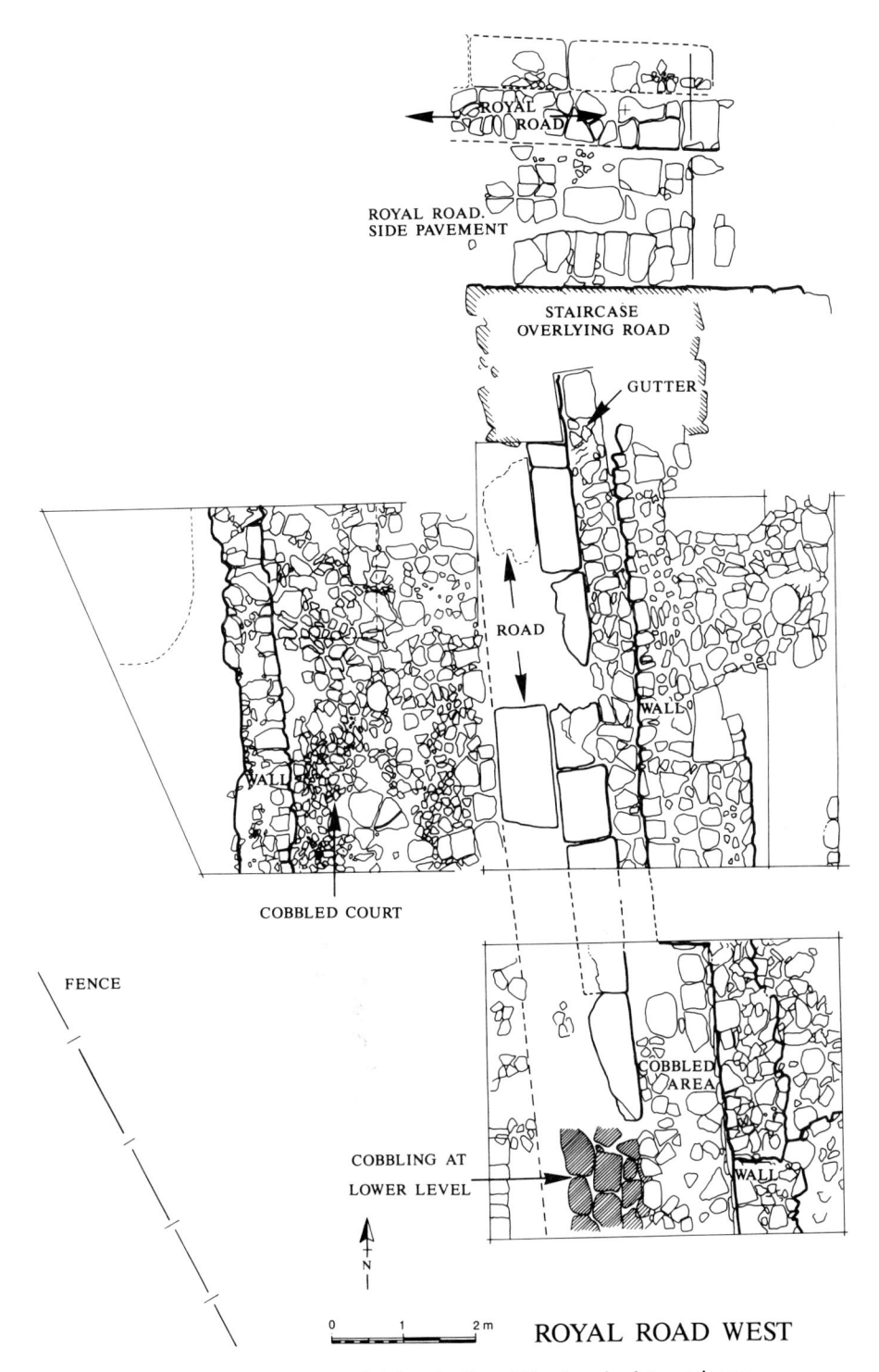

FIG. 2 Royal Road West, joining the Royal Road under later staircase

of the stairway, since a large stone column base was found built into a later wall only 1.72 m. to the west (PLATE 32, right). The whole arrangement recalls the Grandstand Fresco from the Palace.[20]

The western exposed end of the Royal Road seems to have served as a larger junction in the city network rather than simply as the terminus of Royal Road West (see below, nos. 3–5).

3. West Extension of the Royal Road (FIG. 1; PLATE 25)

When Evans was uncovering the Royal Road in 1904 he decided to test the hillside up to the west, beyond the modern main road. Here, on an 'exact prolongation' of the Royal Road line and about 60 m. west of the exposed west end, his test pit found at 4.55 m. depth what he described as similar paving to that of the Royal Road.[21] He concluded that the road ran at least this far west of the Theatral Area, some 230 m. in all. Work the following year indicated that at its preserved west end the Royal Road turned more to the northwest than was previously supposed, in the direction of the about-to-be-discovered Little Palace. This northwesterly bend does not, however, negate the 1904 evidence, as we shall shortly see. It may be that there was a bifurcation or more complex junction here (similar to the adjacent modern position with the north–south main road crossing the east–west side road which leads up west to Knossos village and down east to Makryteichos). Thus the north–south line was provided by Royal Road West up to the south side of the Royal Road; the route would then have continued north with a dog-leg, that is a left turn on to the Royal Road for a few metres and then a bend right leading up northwest towards the Little Palace (see no. 5 below). The east–west road was straight, along the line of the Royal Road, ascending westwards.

4. Further west extension of the Royal Road

That the Royal Road ran much further west on the same line as the long section from the Theatral Area finds support in a discovery of the 1978–82 excavations immediately west of the Stratigraphical Museum (FIGS. 1 and 3; PLATE 25). Here a Minoan road, about 1.7 to 2.2 m. wide, was found to run approximately 21.4 m. east–west across the site without finishing at either end (FIG. 3; PLATE 31).[22] The road ascends 1.20 m. westwards on its preserved length (a rise of 1 in 17.8 or 5.6%) and had a surface of irregular paving or earth and small pebbles. It served buildings on each side, their doors opening on to the road. This road appears to be right on line with the main line of the Royal Road down to the east, surveyed by D. Smyth, and may thus represent its westward course, though no longer with the double line of central slabs. The distance from the preserved western end of the Stratigraphical Museum site road to the Theatral Area is about 346 metres. This appears to be long by Minoan standards[23] and simply emphasises the arterial function of the road within the Minoan city.

---

[20] *PM III*, 47, fig. 28, pl. xvi. See also n. 18 above.
[21] Evans (n. 13 above — 1903–4), 49 n. 1.
[22] P.M. Warren, 'Knossos: Stratigraphical Museum excavations, 1978–80. Part I', *AR* 27 (1980–81), 92, fig. 64.
[23] At Mallia if we take as all one the road from Quartier Mu winding southeast past Delta, then turning east to run out of the city beyond Zeta, the length is about 376 metres (from van Effenterre, n. 6 above, fig. 366). At Palaikastro the main preserved road from Blocks K/L with a turn eastward west of Block N and on east to beyond Block Chi is about 313 metres. The north–south road on the west side of Gournia appears to have a maximum preserved length of about 136 metres.

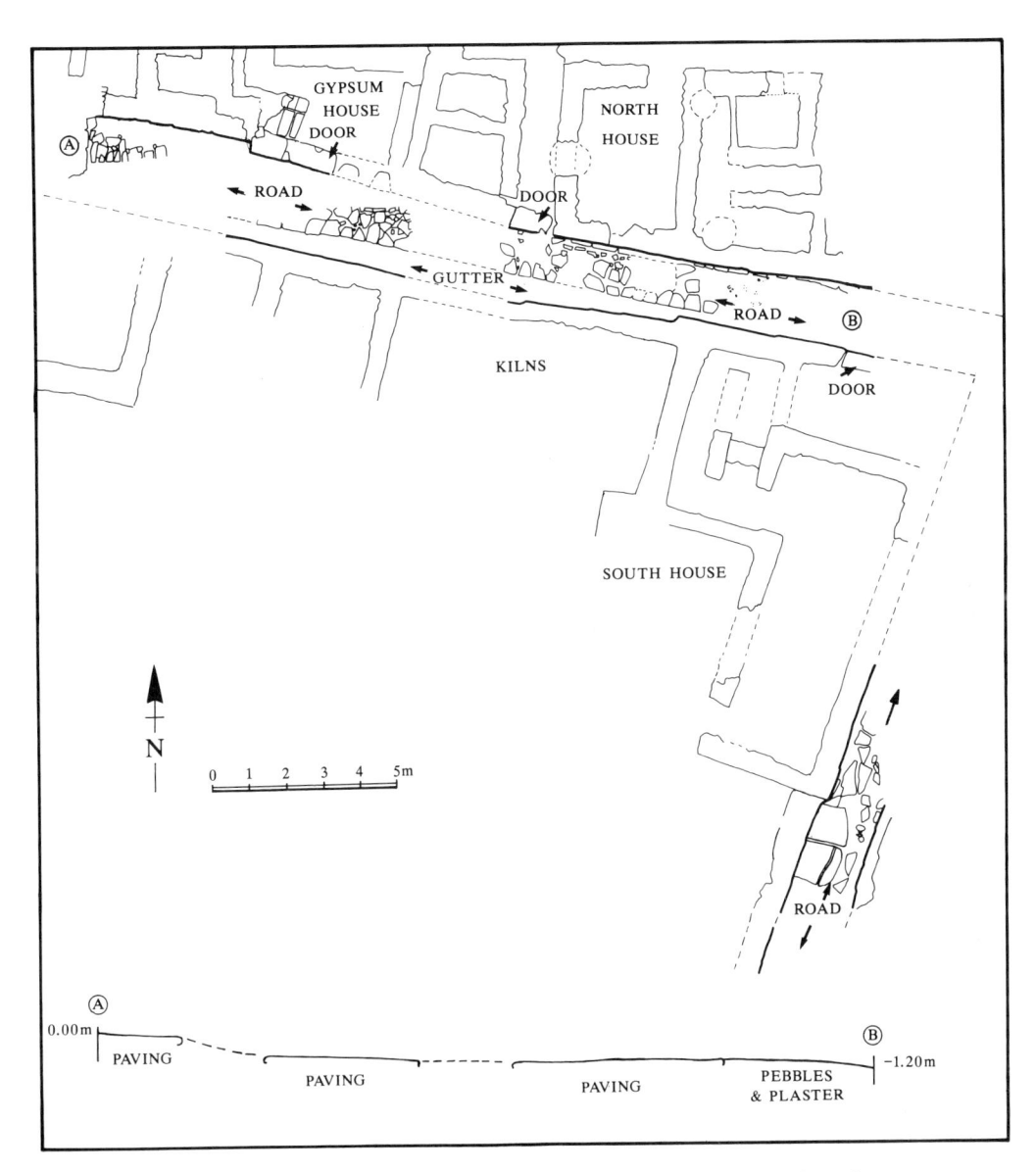

FIG. 3 Stratigraphical Museum site, with east-west and north-south roads

The Stratigraphical Museum site also revealed a second road, up to 1.68 m. wide, more finely paved with large though still irregular slabs. This ran at right angles to the east–west road, south from it (FIG. 3; PLATE 32, left). Its preserved north end in fact lay about 7.75 m. short of what will have been its T-junction with the east–west road, just under the Stratigraphical Museum, though the building bordering the road on its west was uncovered (FIG. 3: South House).

5. Road at the northeast corner of the Little Palace (FIG. 1; PLATE 25)

Outside the northeast corner of the Little Palace Evans uncovered a section of paved road, seemingly towards 19 metres long and running northwest. Although he suggested[24] that this followed the assumed line of a southeast to northwest route running up from the Stepped Portico southwest of the Palace (see no. 7 below) and also that it continued the line of the Royal Road after it had turned northwest at its preserved end (see no. 3 above), the proposal poses problems. Evans thought this piece of road to be 'apparently of later work' (*PM II.i*, 153), while later it is labelled 'Early Paved Way' (*PM II.ii*, fig. 318). On this figure (by Christian Doll, the architect) the road is shown only in conjectural form (dashed outline) as a fragmentary line of single blocks about 1.15 m. wide, while earlier in the volume it is described as 'a central line of pavement with two side wings' (*PM II.i*, 155), a description which could be thought comparable with the Royal Road. These possibly discrepant accounts and illustrations, when added to the distance factor (a gap of 60 metres between this point and the bend at the west end of the Royal Road), leave some uncertainty as to whether the paved section beside the Little Palace really was the continuation of a main north–south road. Obviously there must have been a main route from the city to the harbour town at modern Poros in the eastern suburbs of Herakleion, and Evans did find traces of a Minoan north–south road 900 metres north of Knossos on the west side of the modern main road.[25] But whether that continues the Little Palace paved way is an open question.

6. Roads under the car and coach park west of the Palace (FIGS. 1, 4 and 5; PLATE 25)

Discoveries made by R.W. Hutchinson in 1937 are central to our subject and are best described by quotation.

Knossos. The Curator obtained permission from the Government to sink trial pits in the space between the entrance to the Palace site and the Herakleion-Arkhanes road, where it had been proposed to lay out a car park. The area turned out to be mainly, if not entirely, covered by Minoan paving, similar to that of the West Court of the Palace of Minos, and crossed by three processional ways of poros paving slabs, one running roughly parallel to the modern road, a second running in a west-east direction towards the ramp that leads into the West Court, and the third leading towards the South House and the Stepped Portico. The paving rests on an Early Minoan stratum, and appears to be contemporary with the earliest Palace. Foundations of the Protogeometric and Roman periods were found above it.[26]

Some Trial pits which I opened in 1937 disclosed three similar lines of double slab paving as the Royal Road, one leading toward the ramp that ascends to the West Court, a second in the direction of the bridge-head over the Vlychia ravine by the Caravanserai, and third running parallel to the modern road and almost on the same line, evidently part of the great North–south road connecting the Minoan port of Herakleion with that of Komo on the South coast (exactly as Sir Arthur had prophesied these would be found).[27]

---

[24] *PM II.i*, 153, 155 and fig. 71 (showing the assumed SE-NW line); *II.ii*, fig. 318 (showing 'Early Paved Way' in conjectural form).
[25] *PM II.i, and ii*, 154 and plan opp. 547; *KS* no. 69.
[26] G.M. Young, 'Archaeology in Greece, 1936–1937', *JHS* 57 (1937), 137.
[27] Hutchinson (n. 10 above), 210.

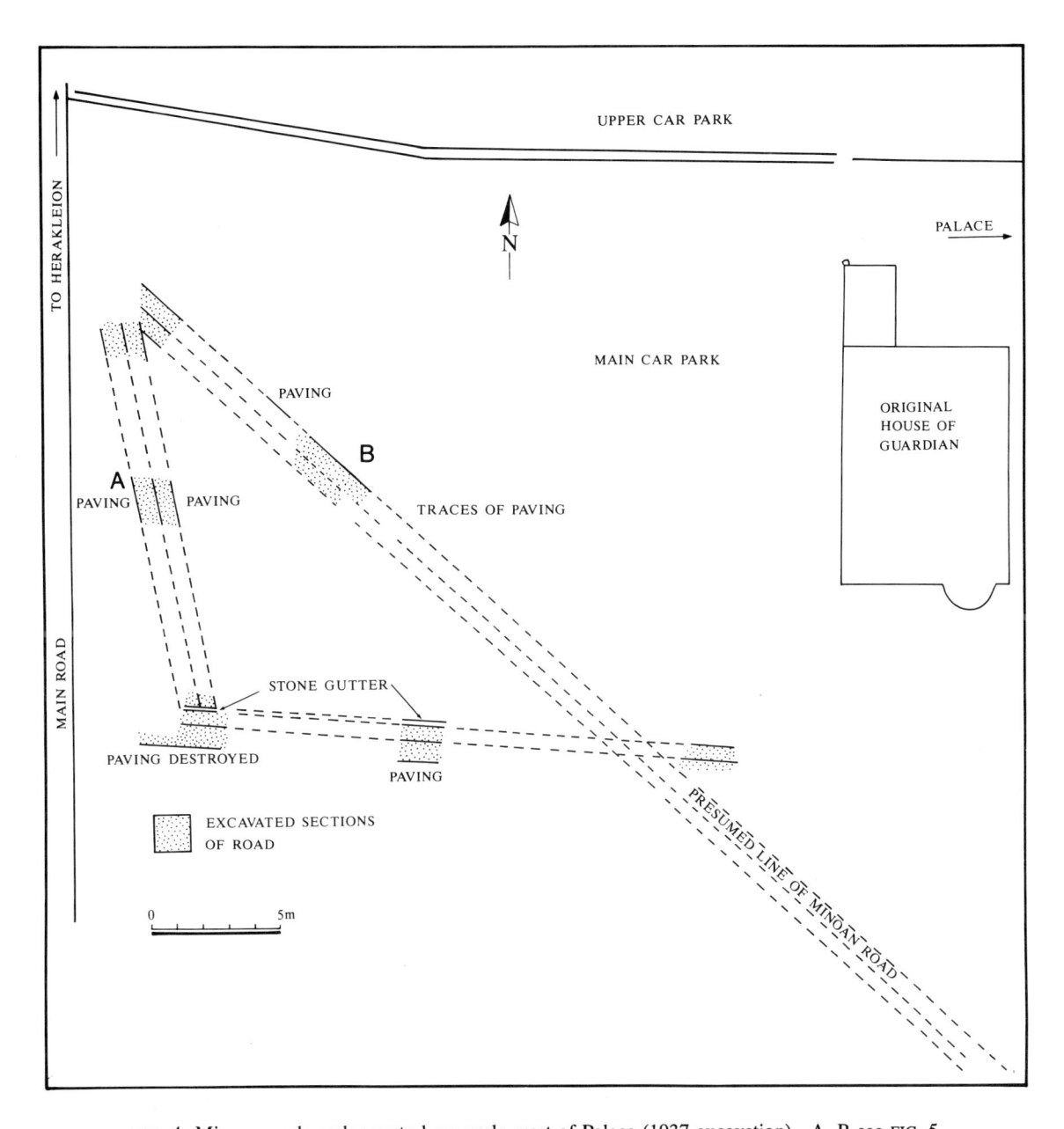

FIG. 4 Minoan roads under central car park, west of Palace (1937 excavation). A, B see FIG. 5

Plans preserved in the British School at Knossos[28] show these roads (and the later remains) and have been adapted to make FIGS. 4 and 5. The roads lay under what is today the central or middle of the three car/coach parks, namely that which lies alongside the ticket office and entrance gate to the Palace. The

---

[28] I am grateful to the Managing Committee of the British School at Athens for permission to use the two plans. FIG. 4 is adapted from a plan drawn by Piet de Jong in 1949 (from trenches left open since Hutchinson's 1937 excavation, or reopened). The original

form of the roads is precisely that of the Royal Road and Royal Road West, namely a double line of poros limestone paving slabs, together 1.40 m. wide, flanked by irregular paving. This paving was found to extend over almost the whole area investigated, so that it resembled the West Court of the Palace.

Each of the directions of the three roads is significant. On the west is the north–south road, adjacent and roughly parallel to the modern main road. At its preserved north end there is a junction with the southeast to northwest road presumed to be coming up from the Viaduct and Stepped Portico (see no. 7 below). At this north junction it appears from the plan (FIG. 4), though it is not absolutely certain, that the north–south road has precedence, with its line cutting across that of the diagonal road. This means that the latter road ended at this point. At its south end, however, the north–south road terminated against the east–west road with its stone gutter. What happened to the north–south road northwards? An obvious possibility is that it is here in the car park the south end of Royal Road West (no. 2 above). But the gap is about 63 metres. Moreover, the two sections of road do not appear to be on exactly the same alignment. Royal Road West runs southwards at about 175o, the car park road at about 170o. If the line of each is prolonged they would meet at a slight angle under the modern road. Other roads might also have entered the system in the 63–metre gap. Nevertheless the general line of correspondence is impressive, and it remains a reasonable possibility that the car park road was the southern end of Royal Road West.

The east–west car park road at its western excavated end cuts across the north–south road, as noted. The three preserved bits of the east–west road give its line. It may be noted that the road runs parallel to the Royal Road 80 metres to the north. How the car park road extended westwards is unknown, but there was occupation extending back to MM IA on the opposite side of the modern main road (*KS* no. 208). It is likely that the car park road continued up the slope westwards to serve the Minoan city here, as did the parallel Royal Road further north. If it did so continue, might the north–south road on the Stratigraphical Museum site (no. 4 above) have linked the two in this western area of the city?

Eastward the east–west car park road ran towards the West Court of the Palace. Within the court the east–west causeway on the south side (FIG. 1) is in reality a paved road, 1.50–1.56 m. wide and set within two lines of slabs like the car park roads, the Royal Road and Royal Road West (PLATE 33). It ends at the West Porch of the Palace, its terminus being the north end of the Corridor of the Procession.[29] If extended westwards it would run some metres south of the car park road. Evans, however, discovered an east–west section of road (about 2.90 m. wide) rising as a ramp (FIG. 1) up to the West Court about 6 metres north of the West Court east–west road (causeway) and he plausibly restored a north–south connecting link along the great terrace or enceinte wall at this point.[30] We may now observe that this road ramp must be right on line with the east–west car park road, as Hutchinson appears to imply, and that we therefore have in effect a continuous paved road from the West Porch of the Palace running west across the West Court and out beyond the modern car park area. The arrangement was surely an arterial route parallel to that of the Royal Road.

---

which I have adapted to make FIG. 5 was possibly drawn by de Jong in 1949 or 1951, but it is more likely to be Hutchinson's own plan. I pencil-traced it at Knossos in 1973 and the inked version was prepared from this by Mr H. Buglass, University of Birmingham, in 1976, and Mrs S. Grice, University of Bristol, in 1992.

[29] S. Hood and W. Taylor, *The Bronze Age Palace at Knossos. Plans and Sections* (*BSA* Suppl. 13; London, 1981), plan.

[30] *PM IV.i*, 56, 59–61, figs. 33–4; Hood and Taylor (n. 29 above), plan, position 14.

The third car park road ran diagonally to the other two, from northwest to southeast (FIG. 4). On the northwest it joined the north–south road, as noted. Its line southeast points towards the Stepped Portico and thus offers a remarkable confirmation of Evans' supposition that the public road, having ascended north beside the Stepped Portico, then swung northwest to link up with the Royal Road at the western end which he excavated (see no. 7 below).[31] Hutchinson, quoted above, also noted this confirmation. We can see now that there was in fact a junction under the modern car park, the great southern route then continuing northwards perhaps as Royal Road West. Excavations in 1992–3 by the present Curator, Dr C.F. Macdonald, in the area west of the South West House, i.e. in the area where the car park–Stepped Portico Road would have run, have revealed 'a post-Minoan (Geometric?) cobbled roadway at the expected level of a Minoan floor'. It is hoped that further work here will determine whether there are earlier road lines.[32]

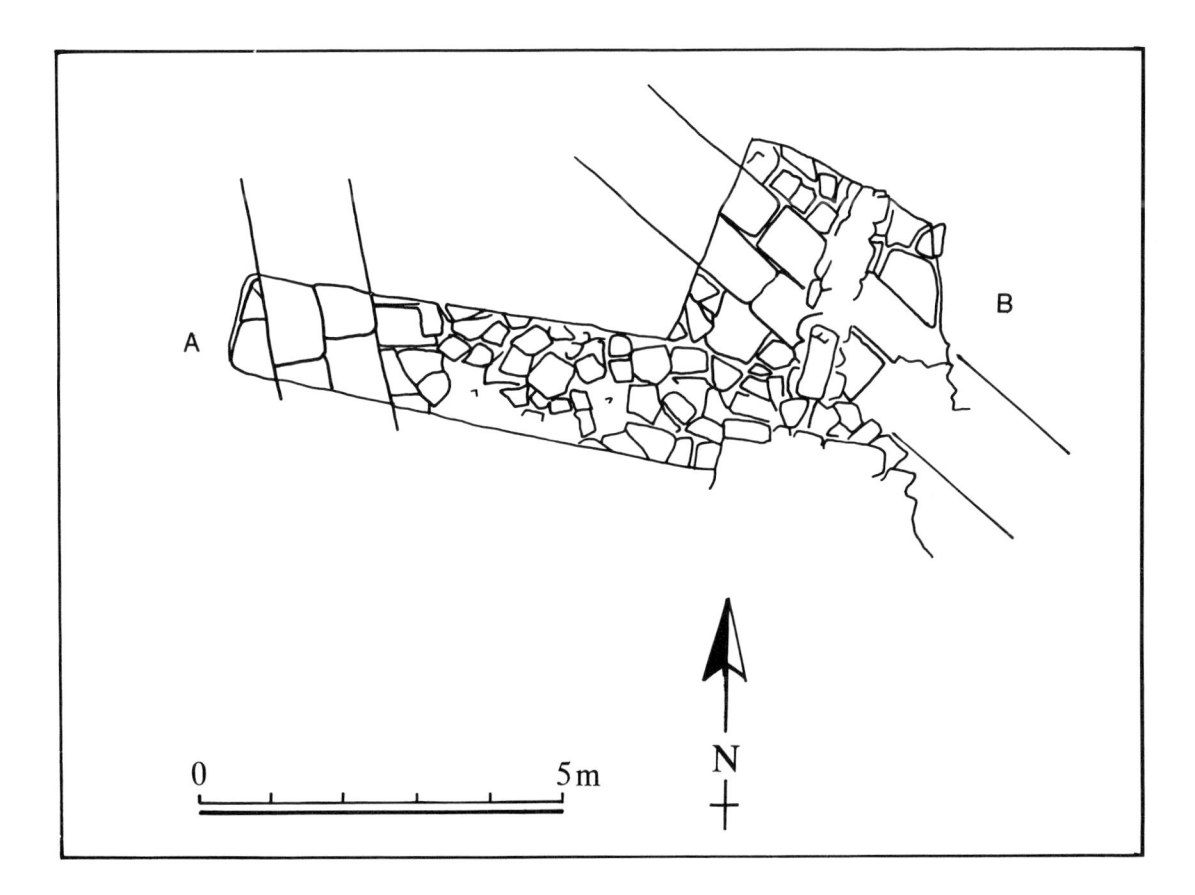

FIG. 5 Plan of central preserved sections of Minoan roads under car park. A, B in FIG. 4

---

[31] *PM II.i*, 150–3, fig. 71.

[32] I am most grateful to Dr Macdonald for permission to refer to his British School internal report. The line from the north end of the Stepped Portico (see PLATE 32) to the NW-SE car park road runs a little to the west of the 1992–3 excavations.

7. The Stepped Portico road (FIG. 1; PLATE 34)

The great tripartite road system southwest of the Palace and north of the Vlykhia stream was described in detail by Evans.[33] On the east the Portico led up to the southwest corner of the Palace. It appears to have passed out of use within LM I, since the South House was built over its eastern side on the upper section. Beside the lower section (PLATE 34) a road ascended to the southeast part of the West Court. The third, western line of the structure was a public road about 3.50 m. wide which Evans, as noted, conjectured to have swung northwest up the slope. On their southern side these roads crossed the Vlykhia, either, Evans thought,[34] on a single bridge about 10.50 m. wide or on two separate bridges with a gap between. The massive foundations of the bridge abutment have survived, bedded in clear river sand which must mark the older, more northerly course of the Vlykhia here, as did bevelled blocks of the bridge masonry itself.[35] This was the point where traffic from the south divided along one of the three routes according to its destination.

8. The Viaduct (PLATE 35)

Immediately after crossing the Vlykhia from the north by one large or two smaller bridges, the road, facing a rocky outcrop of Gypsadhes hill, turned left or southeast and ran along the mighty viaduct to the adjacent Caravanserai (PLATE 35).[36] From here Evans traced a great transit route across the island, conjectured to terminate at the port of Kommos on the south coast.[37] The Kommos excavations under Professor J. Shaw have supported Evans' theory with a fine paved road running beside the huge LM I Building T and Building J down to the sea.[38] The Viaduct itself, whose lower parts were preserved for 21.5 m., was estimated by Evans to have been about 10 metres high and the roadway across it a minimum of 5.25 m. wide.[39]

9. Road on Ailias

On the steep slope of Ailias above the Kairatos stream and east of the Palace massive Minoan walling provides terraces of what may well have been a road.[40] This could have been running north–south along the slope or ascending Ailias to the Mavro Spelio cemetery above. Within the cemetery and about 70 metres higher up Sinclair Hood found a section of Minoan road terrace built over the collapsed chamber of a Middle Minoan tomb.[41] Perhaps this was a continuation of the lower terraced

---

[33] *PM II.i*, 141–53; *KS* no. 282.
[34] *PM II.i*, 152.
[35] Ibid. 149–50, fig. 77 (cf. fig. 72).
[36] Ibid. 93–102; *KS* no. 283.
[37] Ibid. 60–92.
[38] J.W. Shaw, 'Excavations at Kommos (Crete) during 1981', *Hesperia* 51 (1982), 178–80, 192–3, figs. 6–7 and pl. 53; id., 'Excavations at Kommos (Crete) during 1982–1983', *Hesperia* 53 (1984), 257–64, 287. For a more sceptical attitude to Evans' great north–south transit road, when the Kommos excavations were beginning, see J.W. Shaw, 'Excavations at Kommos (Crete) during 1976', *Hesperia* 46 (1977), 201 n. 8.
[39] *PM II.i*, 98–9.
[40] *PM II.ii*, 552–4; *KS* nos. 240, 242–4.
[41] *KS* no. 256.

road. The route could well have continued higher up the slope to give access to the Minoan settlement on the plateau of Ailias above.[42]

Several junctions and forks have been noted above, nodal points within the city's route network. Much of that network, especially in the Minoan city on the western slopes, remains unknown. But let us note the following (FIG. 1): (1) the generally north–south orientation of the buildings of the city; (2) the linkage of the Royal Road to the Palace and its line at a right angle to the building; (3) the east–west road on the south side of the West Court, starting and finishing at the Palace, again at a right angle to it, and with a very probable continuation westwards under the modern car park; (4) the parallel lines of the Royal Road and this southern east–west road; (5) one road running approximately southwards at almost a right angle from the Royal Road (Royal Road West) and another likewise from its continuation (Stratigraphical Museum site north–south road). Given these points it is worth raising the possibility of a layout approximating to a grid plan at Bronze Age Knossos. Considerably more evidence is needed for this suggestion, while the car park–Stepped Portico route runs diagonally counter to such a grid. But whether or not the network was in grid form, with all the consequent implications for city planning, it is surely clear that the main arterial roads, especially the Royal Road and its junction road, Royal Road West, could only have been designed, laid out and built (with precisely the same constructional format) by decision of a single central authority. Put another way, these roads are evidence for such an authority. It will be seen next that the chronological evidence strengthens this point further.

DATING AND HISTORY OF USE

1. The Royal Road

In 1928, reporting his earlier work, Evans noted that the Royal Road had at one point been built over an MM IA north–south drain.[43] He also noted that sherds in its own drain along the south side were MM IIIB–LM IA,[44] which he took to mean that the road in its existing form was a construction of that period. That could be so; but sherds in an open drain could mean construction by the time of the date of the sherds, i.e. a *terminus ante quem*, or even (less likely) a later construction date, loose sherds having got there sometime after their actual date. Evans' excavations of 1929 and 1930 in the Theatral Area showed that the road was here associated with a paved area (North West Court, not the earliest paving here) dated MM IIA, preceding the later construction of the eastern flight of stairs of the Theatral Area.[45] The road itself cut through what he took to be a northern extension of the enceinte wall.[46] Evans' MM IIA date for the road and associated paving was based on polychrome

---

[42] *KS* no. 268.
[43] *PM II.ii*, 576.
[44] Ibid. 533 n. 1; 576.
[45] *PM IV.i*, 50 n. 4; 53–4.
[46] Ibid., 50, figs. 31–2. The enceinte on the west side of the West Court was dated late MM IA by Evans since it cut through walls of the MM IA House B, below and north of kouloura 3, excavated by the Pendleburys (*PM IV.i*, 77). That it cut the walls of corridors 2a and 3 is clear (*PM IV.i*, fig. 42). That it also cut those of rooms 5 and 7, which were at a higher level (H.W. and J.D.S. Pendlebury, 'Two Protopalatial houses at Knossos', *BSA* 30 (1928–30), 57 and figs. 3–4 for these rooms), is less clear. N. Momigliano ('MM IA pottery from Evans' excavations at Knossos: a reassessment', *BSA* 86 (1991), 210) assigns much pottery from these rooms to the Old Palace period, although the excavators clearly concluded that the rooms marked an upper storey (or ground floor, if rooms

sherds with racquet and ball pattern.[47] An MM IIA date was not contradicted by Hood's test below the road surface in 1959: 'It seems that the road restored by Evans belongs to the period of the Last Palace (Late Minoan II, c.15th century B.C.), but beneath it are traces of one or more earlier systems of roadway with drains set in them.'[48] We shall see below that a construction date not later than MM IIA appears firm for Royal Road West. Since this road made a junction with the Royal Road and was of precisely the same form and, in its central slabbing, the same width, it is very difficult to believe that the two roads were not built at the same time.

The Royal Road must have remained open until at least LM II/IIIA, in order to serve the Arsenal (with its Linear B tablets). LM II, possibly into LM III, was also the final period of use of the long 'grandstand' building flanking the road on the south.[49]

2. Royal Road West

Two tests were made in the 1971 excavations, one below the flanking cobbled area on the west (PLATE 28, below), another below the road surface. The sherd material was mostly MM IA, but there were also a few fragments of MM IB.[50] This road system therefore has MM IB as a *terminus post quem*. Since, however, the sherd material stratified immediately below it was as just stated, it may be taken that no long period elapsed between the date of the latest sherds, MM IB, and the construction date. We are dealing here with laid surfaces, not with walls or wells, for example, cut down to earlier levels. Construction in MM IB is probable, beyond MM IIA very unlikely. Since the road is of exactly the same form and width as the Royal Road, and makes a junction with it, the latter was presumably constructed at the same time. This is also the time of the foundation of the first Palatial buildings.

The test below the road, at its southern preserved point, revealed a paved area or cobbled road with a clear west edge, 0.32 m. below the surface of Royal Road West (FIG. 2; PLATE 30). The foundations of the east flanking wall of Royal Road West rested on this earlier paved level. The fill over the earlier paving contained a few MM IB fragments at the top, dating Royal Road West laid over them (see above), but was otherwise EM III.[51] There may therefore have already been a north–south road here in EM III, but not with the double line of slabs providing the actual road, as was to be built above in MM IB.

Royal Road West, unlike the Royal Road, passed out of use with the massive destruction on the site of Knossos in the MM IIIB–LM IA transition.[52] A thick fill of this date overlay the whole area

---

1–4 were basements) of House B (Pendleburys, above, 57). Accepting her ceramic argument (Momigliano, above, 210, fig. 19: 86–124), we could infer an MM II date for the enceinte wall, as she herself suggests (ibid. 212) and as Damiani Indelicato argues in relation to the West Court itself (see n. 6 above, 60). But all that can be said for certain is that the enceinte is later than the MM IA rooms 1–4 of House B; if it preceded rooms 5–8, then it is quite closely dated within late MM IA–MM IB/II; if it followed rooms 5–8 it is presumably later Protopalatial. This has a direct bearing on the date of the ramp road against the enceinte on the west.

[47] *PM III*, 248–50; *IV.i*, 50 nn. 1–2, 53.
[48] M.S.F. Hood, 'Archaeology in Greece, 1959', *AR* 6 (1959–60), 23.
[49] Warren (n. 18 above — 1973), 575.
[50] Warren (n. 19 above), 628, pl. 588.b and e; Catling (n. 19 above), 21, fig. 35.
[51] Warren (n. 19 above), for details.
[52] P.M. Warren, 'A new Minoan deposit from Knossos, c. 1600 B.C., and its wider relations', *BSA* 86 (1991), 333–5.

of road cobbling. At the point of junction with the Royal Road the road, cobbled areas and fill were built over by a wide stairway ascending from the Royal Road (see above, no. 2, and FIG. 2; PLATES 28, above, and 29, right). The stairway might have continued at its top as a road, though none survived. It is much more likely that it gave access to the long 'grandstand' building flanking it on the east.

3. West extension of Royal Road

No dating evidence.

4. Further west extension of Royal Road

Middle Minoan I and II buildings existed on the north side of the road on the Stratigraphical Museum site (excavation trenches D, H, M, and F/FG), at which time it was unpaved and was probably a track. The paving was laid in MM III–LM I and the road continued in use certainly to the LM IB destruction. Pottery of this date overlay it, doubtless from the destroyed buildings and kilns beside it. The road then continued through LM II, probably with an earth surface, with house entrances off it to the north and south into buildings destroyed in that period (FIG. 3, Gypsum House and South House).[53] Later on, LM IIIA levels and walling lay over the North and South House. By then the road would have become a track, no longer serving houses.

5. Road at northwest corner of Little Palace

No dating evidence, although the 'paved way' must have been in use with the Little Palace.

6. Roads under car and coach park west of Palace.

The excavation data, quoted above, together with the form of the roads exactly as the Royal Road and Royal Road West, indicate that the three roads, resting on an Early Minoan level, were built at about the same time as the other two.

No dating evidence is cited by Evans for the ramp road, which appears to continue the east–west car park road eastward. If taken to be built up against a pre-existing enceinte wall or built with the wall it must be later than MM IA.[54] As an eastward continuation of the car park road any date after Early Minoan can be argued.

The date of the West Court east–west road (causeway) is uncertain (PLATE 33). Evans took it to be MM IA,[55] while the dating of the test pit B.I.30 from under its paving is not easy to understand, but might go down to MM III.[56] Evans saw the function of the road as serving an original west

---

[53] P.M. Warren, 'Knossos: Stratigraphical Museum excavations, 1978–82. Part II', *AR* 29 (1982–83), 63–5.
[54] See n. 46 above.
[55] *PM IV.i*, 59.
[56] J.D.S. Pendlebury, *A Guide to the Stratigraphical Museum in the Palace at Knossos* (London, 1933), 6 (location of B.I.30); H.W. and J.D.S. Pendlebury, *Knossos. Dating of the Pottery in the Stratigraphical Museum I* (London, n.d., c.1934), 6 (dating); M.B. Money-Coutts and J.D.S. Pendlebury, *Knossos. Dating of the Pottery in the Stratigraphical Museum III. The Plans* (London, n.d., probably 1935), plan 4 (location of B.I.30 on plan).

entrance to the Palace through the West Façade.⁵⁷ But Momigliano has now shown that the conjectured Protopalatial façade at this point was very probably simply West Court paving and of MM IIIB–LM IA date.⁵⁸ This could well be the date of the road (causeway) too, adjacent to the paving and terminating at the Neopalatial West Porch. On the other hand the car park road seems clearly Protopalatial and Evans stated that the West Court east–west road ran under the later Palace façade (PLATE 33).⁵⁹ There may well have been an original, Protopalatial entrance road of canonical double-slab line form here, perhaps renewed in MM IIIB–LM IA.

7. The Stepped Portico road

A fortunate discovery yielded a *terminus post quem* for this elaborate tripartite system. Under the Portico was an MM IA well apparently filled in at the time of the building, while pottery of the same date underlay other parts of the construction.⁶⁰ While the well gave a *terminus post quem*, construction is not likely to have been any *considerable* time later, since post-MM IA pottery would have accumulated.

8. The Viaduct

Underlying the Minoan road approaching the Viaduct from the east were houses last used at the close of MM III⁶¹ (PLATE 35, above), which Evans took as a *terminus ante quem* for the construction of the Viaduct in its final form. Its initial date he placed in MM IA, since the Stepped Portico, road and bridgehead opposite could have existed only in relation to such a viaduct on the south bank of the Vlykhia stream. Pottery associated with the use of the Viaduct was of LM I and II date, terminal use being equated with the Palace destruction (then dated to LM II).⁶²

9. Road on Ailias

An MM III building was associated with the possible road terrace wall at one point,⁶³ while the Mavro Spelio cemetery above was used in Middle and Late Minoan times. The Minoan settlement on the plateau of Ailias higher still was dated MM I–LM I by Sinclair Hood.⁶⁴

The historical development of the Knossian network is thus clear in broad outline.

1. Throughout most of the Early Minoan period nothing approaching a road system appears to have existed, though obviously the different areas of occupation⁶⁵ must have been connected with each other, probably by unpaved roads or tracks. Settlement had spread westwards from the Kephala knoll

---

⁵⁷ *PM IV.i*, 56, figs. 30, 34.
⁵⁸ N. Momigliano, 'The "Proto-palatial Façade" at Knossos', *BSA* 87 (1992), 167–75.
⁵⁹ *PM IV.i*, 59, fig. 30.
⁶⁰ *PM II.i*, 146, 153, fig. 74 (position of well).
⁶¹ Ibid. 101.
⁶² Ibid. 101–2.
⁶³ *PM II.ii*, 553–4; *KS* no. 241.
⁶⁴ *KS* no. 268.
⁶⁵ P.M. Warren, 'Knossos and its foreign relations in the Early Bronze Age', *Cretological IV, A'2* (Athens, 1981), 628–30, fig. 1.

to north and south of the later Royal Road area in EM IIA,[66] while the earliest *in situ* pottery on the Stratigraphical Museum site, 190 metres west of the later Royal Road West area, extends back to EM II.[67]

2. Towards the end of the third millennium, in EM III, more formal arrangements for communication and transport began to be made. The EM III paved surface of flat cobbles below Royal Road West had a clear west edge and may well have been a north–south road. In this connexion one wonders whether the 'layer of rough stones' under the clay cement level on which the Royal Road was built,[68] which Evans took to be a foundation level of the later road, was in reality an earlier road surface like that below Royal Road West, later incorporated in MM IB or MM IIA as foundation. We recall Sinclair Hood's 1959 test which found 'one or more earlier systems of roadway' below the Royal Road.[69] Again, within the Theatral Area, the MM IA paving below the Royal Road level and its paving[70] may have been associated with a road.

3. In MM IB or MM IIA, 19th century B.C., decisions were taken to institute a major road network on a common, canonical system in the central area. Thus the Royal Road, Royal Road West, the car park roads–ramp–enceinte wall–West Court 'causeways', the Stepped Portico road and almost certainly the Viaduct all appear to have been built at this time. Such a system could surely have been determined only by a single central authority. If there was anything approaching a grid plan network the case is even more persuasive.

4. The road network remained in use for at least two hundred years until the great, probably seismic destruction *c.*1600 B.C. (MM IIIB–LM IA transition). As a result of this destruction Royal Road West was thickly covered over and out of use; but the Royal Road continued and a paved surface was laid on its distant western line, on the Stratigraphical Museum site. The Palace West Court and car park site roads also continued, as did the Viaduct and the public road on the west side of the Stepped Portico, probably linking northwestwards with the car park site diagonal road. The approach road to the Viaduct on the east apparently took its final form after the seismic destruction. Despite the destruction this was essentially a time of continuity, albeit with repairs and disruption in some areas. No new major roads seem to have been added, though fine paved roads or passages were laid between new LM IA buildings.

5. The road system lasted to and beyond the LM IB destruction,[71] through LM II. At what point it passed out of use is bound up with the date of the Palace destruction. The Royal Road must have remained open till then, serving the Arsenal or Armoury, though further west only a track at a higher level well above the paving can have existed. Mackenzie did not believe the Viaduct system survived LM II.[72] It must be noted that destruction at this time (quite separate from the final Palace

---

[66] Warren (nn. 19, 49 and 65 above).
[67] From trench O, level 39, fragments of a decorated jug, bowl and goblet (unpublished).
[68] *PM II.ii*, 574, 576, fig. 359.
[69] See n. 49 above.
[70] *PM III*, 248, fig. 172 ('System 1').
[71] Note Evans' brief but still apposite summary of this point in Knossian history, at *PM II.i*, 101.
[72] Ibid.

destruction in LM IIIA) was widespread, notably in the western part of the city (Unexplored Mansion, Stratigraphical Museum site). Apart from the Royal Road and the roads west of the Palace in the central area there may have been only tracks or earth roads on the old lines. No trace of any system exists after LM IIIA.

CONSTRUCTION

The surface forms of the road network have been described above. There appear to be three main forms of construction, though the second grades into the third. The best and most elaborate is that using a double line of poros limestone slabs, each slab line 0.70 m. wide, thus giving a total width of central, slightly raised road of 1.40 m.; this was flanked by an area of flat paving of irregular cobbles on one or both sides, of varying width. On the Royal Road Evans described[73] a cement coating over the side paving, consisting of small pebbles, clay and pounded potsherds with a hard surface. This surface finish to the side wings does not appear to have been noted elsewhere. A stone drainage channel ran along one side of these Class 1 roads at the edge (FIGS. 2 and 4). The central raised section was an excellent concept for pedestrian usage, with the side wings for animals or larger numbers of people, while the drainage system was an integral part of the total design. Evans well described the Royal Road in 1904 as 'the first European example of road-making on scientific principles', even if the Neolithic wooden roads across the Somerset Levels in England now have precedence.

The widely used and thus clearly planned width of the central raised section of these Knossian roads (PLATES 26–9), 1.40 m. (0.70 m. × 2), may be thought a good candidate for acceptance as a Minoan unit of measure. Was it in fact? J.W. Graham's well-known unit, a Minoan foot of 30.36 cms.,[74] does not yield any whole number of such feet, nor even a half unit (1.40/0.3036 m. = 4.61 units). J. Cherry, in re-examining Graham's unit,[75] has, however, proposed a best fit quantal value of $c.46.8$ cms. from Graham's 87 measurements. If this proposed value is applied as a unit to the Knossian road we get 1.40/0.468 m. = 2.99 units and 0.70 (width of each line of slabs)/0.468 m. = 1.496 units. These results are so close to 3 and 1.5 units that they can be seen as supporting Cherry's unit or, alternatively, as suggesting that such a unit was used for determining the width of the roads. If so, the argument advanced above for a central authority planning and designing the roads is further strengthened.

Below its surface the Royal Road was set on a clay cement level and this in turn on a level of 'rough stones'. We noted that the latter may originally have been a road in their own right, later reused as foundation material with clay cement. On Royal Road West the central slabs and side paving were simply bedded on hard earth, small stones and sherds; the paved level below this bedding (FIG. 2; PLATE 30) was an original and separate entity.

The second form of road or passage construction is that with flat slabs, usually large, irregular in shape, but carefully laid over the underlying surface. The passage between the Little Palace and

---

[73] *PM II.ii*, 574, fig. 359.
[74] J.W. Graham, 'The Minoan unit of length and Minoan palace planning', *AJA* 64 (1960), 335–41; id., 'Further notes on the Minoan foot', *Cretological II, A'* (Athens, 1968), 157–65; id., *The Palaces of Crete* (Princeton, 1969), xi–xii, 222–8.
[75] J. Cherry, 'Putting the best foot forward', *Antiquity* 57 (1983), 52–6. Note that neither Graham nor Cherry used the 1.40 m. road width as part of his database.

Unexplored Mansion[76] and the north–south road on the Stratigraphical Museum site (PLATE 32, left) are examples, LM I in date, as is the Stepped Way south from the Theatral Area. The slab paving was simply bedded on the firm mixture of earth, stones and sherds noted above.

The third form of construction again used paving of irregular slabs, but smaller than those of the second class. The east–west road on the Stratigraphical Museum site, as it survived, varied from neat areas of such cobbled paving to a more casual arrangement, and to areas without paving and simply a hard surface of earth and small pebbles. Roughly arranged slab steps were built to deal with the slope ascending west. Along the south side of this road was an unpaved drainage channel (PLATE 31, above). The road may have had a neat paving throughout at the time it was in use. The Stepped Portico public road had no surviving surface, but there were slight remains of irregular step slabs on the adjacent road on the east.

The careful engineering techniques and drainage arrangements of the roads described[77] were developed much further when uneven or strongly sloping grounds was being traversed. The Viaduct with its stepped culverts (PLATE 35) is an outstanding instance, as is the massive terrace walling of the probable road on Ailias.

Whether or not there was any element of grid-plan, and however many junctions or angle bends (never curves, no Grande Raccordo Anulare like that of Gournia) are observed in the Knossian roads, the overall arrangement is one of straight lines, of whatever length. This means that construction was preceded by planning and design of road lines. Once again, as with the canonical form of Class 1 road and the probable use of a fixed unit of length for its width, we see the mark of a central, decision-making authority.

FUNCTIONS

The functions of urban roads may be defined in terms of movement, that is of circulation and destination, and in terms of different kinds of traffic and its purpose. The two are of course related, all traffic having both destination and purpose. Knossian traffic will have included driven animals and conveyed food, raw materials and finished products, as well as people moving without goods, for example on administrative or religious duties, or for social purposes, and all with a specific destination. From the outset the traffic was pedestrian. The Knossian roads are excellently designed for people on foot or with pack or driven animals. They were not designed for wheeled traffic.[78] The Palaikastro wheeled cart of EM III date[79] may have been a country vehicle. Chariots were of course used by the time of the Palace destruction, but a raised road only 1.40 m. wide (and hundreds of years old) seems inconveniently narrow for such vehicles, particularly moving at speed.

In terms of circulation and destination urban roads have single or plural functions. Single-function roads gave access to a particular building or destination. Such roads at Knossos vary from short sections or passages, such as that which connects the Little Palace and Unexplored Mansion, to longer sections. Examples of these are the final eastern section of the Royal Road in its last period of use,

---

[76] *PM II.ii*, fig. 345.
[77] Cf. Shaw (n. 38 above — 1982), 178, on the engineering of the great paved road at Kommos.
[78] Cf. ibid. 178, n. 31.
[79] *PM II.i*, 156, fig. 78.

when it led only to the Theatral Area (originally it led east beyond it), or the Stepped Portico and its accompanying 'private' road giving access to the Palace.

The relationship of roads to the Palace is an important question, as the great debate about the date and orientation of the Palace of Mallia in relation to the city has shown. At Knossos the matter is complicated by uncertainty about the precise form of the 'Palace' in MM IB–II. What emerges now is that no fewer than three roads have in their final sections the single function of giving access to and from the Palace: the line of the Royal Road branching southeast from west of the Theatral Area (PLATE 27), the east–west road (causeway) across the West Court (PLATE 33) and the 'private' road immediately beside the Stepped Portico (PLATE 34, below). At least two of these (Royal Road and Stepped Portico Road) were built at the same early date, MM IB/MM IIA, and the third may date from then too. Whatever the form of any 'Palace' at this early date, these road directions once again provide evidence for a central authority.

Like the single-function roads, those with more than one function also varied, from roads for intra-city circulation to different houses and other buildings, such as the north–south road or passage on the Stratigraphical Museum site, to major arterial roads which both had this internal, multi-service function and gave access to destinations beyond the city. These destinations were (1) the agricultural hinterland, (2) more distant, often mountainous territory for grazing and raw materials, (3) other population centres, including ports, (4) religious sites.

Evans' Great South Road passed out of the city beyond the Viaduct. Evidence for other routes south and north has been carefully summarised by Sinclair Hood in the detailed evidence of the Knossos Survey.[80] The route west may now be added, the more so if the Stratigraphical Museum site east–west road (no. 4 above) is accepted as the continuation of the Royal Road. Their direction is slightly north of west (282°). Tylissos lies due west of Knossos; a straight-line projection of our west road therefore runs a little north of Tylissos, a little south of Gazi and very near Giophyrakia.[81] It would in fact have made good sense for a road to Tylissos to run a little north of west for much of its course, in order to avoid the dissected valleys and spurs on the direct line and to take advantage of the easier ground just north of them. A slight turn down to Tylissos from the northeast would have been easy, and this is just what the modern road does. Beyond Tylissos lay Sklavokampos, then Gonies with its peak sanctuary, and then the Minoan serpentine quarries at Lepria,[82] from which a route to Knossos was needed. Further west is Anogeia and the inland route through Axos to Stavromenos and Rethymno. This must have been a main route in Minoan as well as more recent times, avoiding the formidable Mt. Kouloukonas between this line and the north coast.

If the west road from Knossos ran across to Giophyrakia, a branch could have left it there to go southwest to Aghios Myron and Krousonas, then west up the steep valley beside Mt. Gournos to emerge at Zominthos. The great Minoan building here, high up *en route* to the Idaean Cave (and currently under excavation by Professsor Sakellarakis),[83] was surely not built without some relationship to Knossos. The old track down from it to Krousonas is the direct route to the Minoan

---

[80] *KS* pp. 14–15.
[81] For MM IA vases from the settlement at Giophyrakia, see S. Marinatos, 'Γιοφυράκια', *A.Delt.* 15 (1933–5), Παράρτημα 49–51.
[82] P. Warren, *Minoan Stone Vases* (Cambridge, 1969), 138–9.
[83] Μεσόγειος, 17 September 1988, 5. H.W. Catling, 'Archaeology in Greece, 1988–89', *AR* 35 (1988–89), 101–2, fig. 139.

capital. The mountain zone is likely to have provided the capital with timber, cereals (grown around Zominthos earlier this century), aromatic herbs, sheep, and spirituality.

CONCLUSION

Minoan towns and cities developed out of Neolithic or Early Bronze Age villages of much antiquity. The early 'road' systems are largely unknown, but the 'roads' (arterial passages) of Early Minoan II Myrtos-Phournou Koryphe[84] unsurprisingly show the same communicational pattern principle as the later urban roads; at this early stage the main determinant of road direction was direct communication, with allowance for any constraint of terrain, between the village and the agricultural hinterland; a secondary function was service to different buildings within the village. As Minoan villages expanded into towns the internal service or circulation function grew in importance. For towns not built as new, planned foundations like later Greek colonies, but developing over time, it is impossible to say whether decisions about buildings determined road lines or *vice versa*. Dr L. Platon rightly makes this point[85] and cites good examples of both decisions. Nevertheless at Knossos we can see a remarkable example of several planned city road lines being decided upon at what appears to have been about the same time, MM IB/IIA or the 19th/early 18th century B.C. This decision clearly had priority over existing buildings. Evans noted that MM IA structures were sacrificed to the construction of the Stepped Portico System;[86] the Royal Road was set into EM occupation levels and ran over an MM IA drain; the car park roads were also reported as overlying EM remains. The priority decision (or decisions) here is surely explicable only in terms of a central authority directing the enterprise, a conclusion strengthened by the use of the same road type, with a raised central section 1.40 m. wide, probably on a standard measure of three units, for different roads in the city. The start/finish points of these roads, namely at some element of the central building, makes the same point, as do the essentially straight lines and perhaps even grid-plan elements of the system. Authority prevailed. Later modification or rebuilding of the Viaduct road used parts of ruined MM III houses in its foundations.[87]

The Minoan roads of Knossos currently relate to an area of about 217,000 m² (21.7 ha.) (FIG. 1; PLATE 25), but they must originally have provided a network for the estimated 750,000 m² (75 ha.) of intensive settlement in MM I–LM I.[88] The roads formed an integral part of the built space, that

---

[84] P. Warren, *Myrtos. An Early Bronze Age Settlement in Crete* (*BSA* Suppl. 7; London, 1972), plan opp. p. 11; nos. 64–65–44, 32–33 and 67 are three routes leading to the central open area 45; 12–15 is an east–west passage at the north end of the site. Id., 'The genesis of the Minoan Palace', in R. Hägg and N. Marinatos (eds.), *The Function of the Minoan Palaces. Proceedings of the Fourth International Symposium at the Swedish Institute in Athens ... 1984* (Skrifter ... Svenska Inst. i Athen 4°, 35; Stockholm, 1987), 49, fig. 2.

[85] Platon (n. 7 above), 382.

[86] *PM II.i*, 153.

[87] Ibid. 101.

[88] *KS* no. 10 and fig. 2. P.M. Warren, 'The place of Crete in the thalassocracy of Minos', in R. Hägg and N. Marinatos (eds.), *The Minoan Thalassocracy. Myth and Reality. Proceedings of the Third International Symposium at the Swedish Institute in Athens ... 1982* (Skrifter ... Svenska Inst. i Athen 4°, 32; Stockholm, 1984), 40.

It has been suggested that the main Harbour–Palace road at Zakros, 'with its central causeway of poros stone slabs', resembles roads at other palaces (presumably Knossos) (N. Platon, *Zakros: The Discovery of a Lost Palace of Ancient Crete* (New York, 1971),

is, they were part of the material correlate of social, political, economic and religious systems. Materially the roads helped to articulate the expression and meaning of those systems.

89; cf. Shaw, n. 38 above — 1982, 193 n. 84). But published plans and photographs do not appear to show any central line of rectangular, raised slabs as at Knossos; rather they show a well-paved road of irregular slabs, like our second type above (N. Platon, above, figs. on p. 90–1; id., ''Ανασκαφὴ Ζάκρου', *PAE* 1973, 154–6, pl. 163a; 1975, 369–71, pl. IB'). Platon does, however, well compare the Northeast Entrance passage leading off the Harbour Road into the Palace to the Knossian type (Royal Road etc.) (above — 1971, 90–1, fig. on p. 91); this entrance way had a middle strip of slabs like 'a carpet covering the central part of the ramp'. This strip is about 0.70 m. wide, i.e. half the Knossian standard width. If this constructional connexion is accepted, it adds to the evidence for a special relationship between Zakros and Knossos.

PLATE VI Knossos — The Way Back (etching and aquatint)

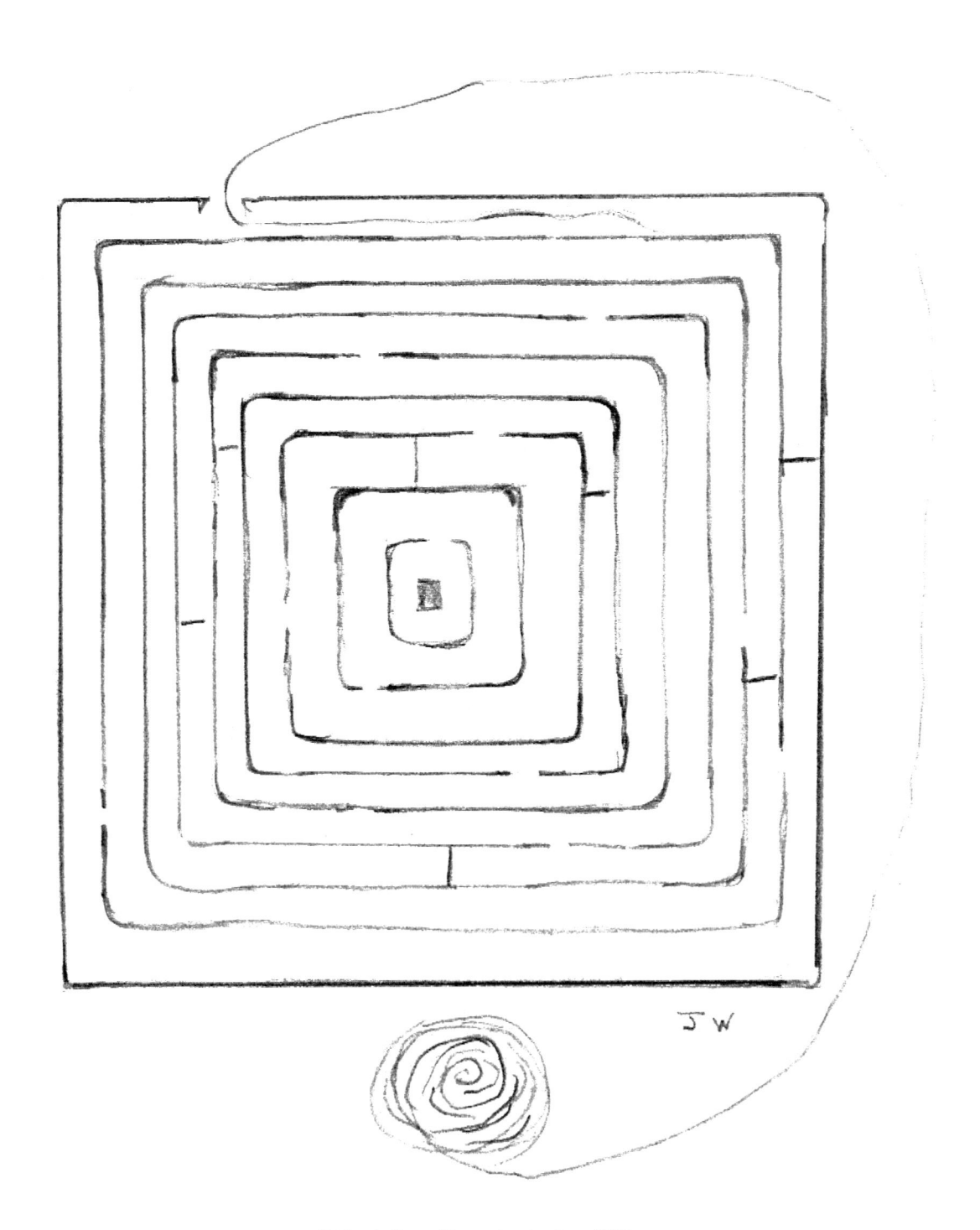

Labyrinth — illustration by Jane Willetts

Ariadne

"My gifts are twofold.
Firstly, my love;
And then this thread.

"Yet be warned, my love,
That speech may distinguish,
But life will weave

"These as a single fetish.
Be warned, my love,
And never distinguish

"In heart or in mind
What can be spoken twice
But which leads you to find

"Your way through the maze
Only if grasped together,
Woven again at each phase.

"Nor have they any tether.
Be warned, O my love,
Only each ties the other.

"Be warned, as you go,
And find, as you go,
And finding, return to me. So!"

R.F. Willetts

Plates

PLATE 1

a Mudbrick walls in Aceramic stratum, area ZE;   *b* Mudbrick building, Stratum IX, area AC;   *c* Pisé *building, Stratum VII, area AC;*   *d* MN building, area K/N

PLATE 2

a EN I potsherd with pointillé *decoration*; *b* EN II incised bowl; *c* Ripple-burnished carinated bowl, MN; *d* Two-handled jar, MN; *e* Storage vessel, LN; *f* Incrusted bowl, FF

PLATE 3

a Clay figurine from Aceramic deposit, Stratum X;   b Clay figurines, later N;   c Stone male figurine, Stratum VIII pit;   d Clay seated male figurine, LN

EVANS

PLATE 4

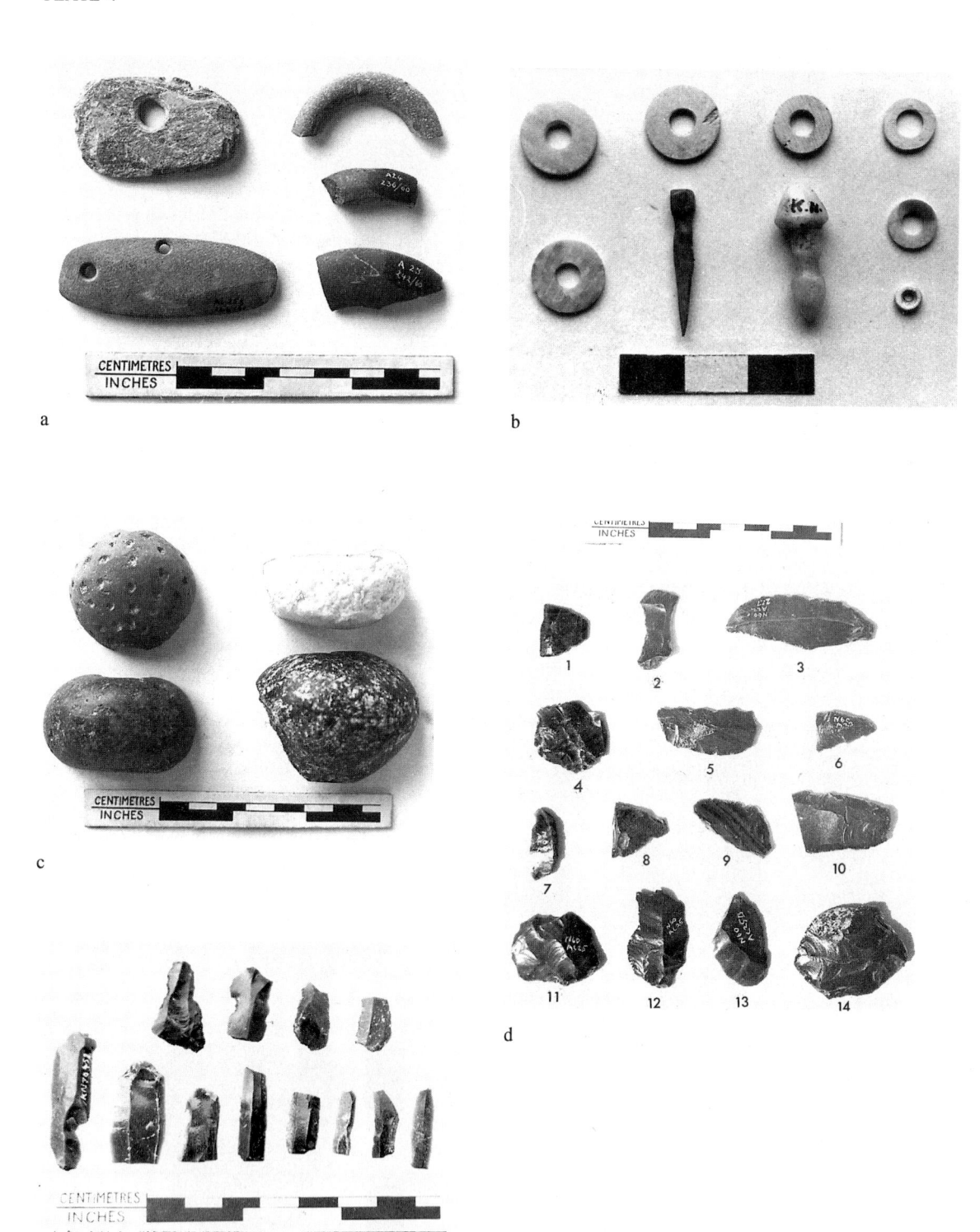

a Bracelets and pendants;   *b* Disc beads and ?pendants;   *c* Stone mace-heads;   *d* Obsidian and chert, all levels;
e Obsidian blades, FF

PLATE 5

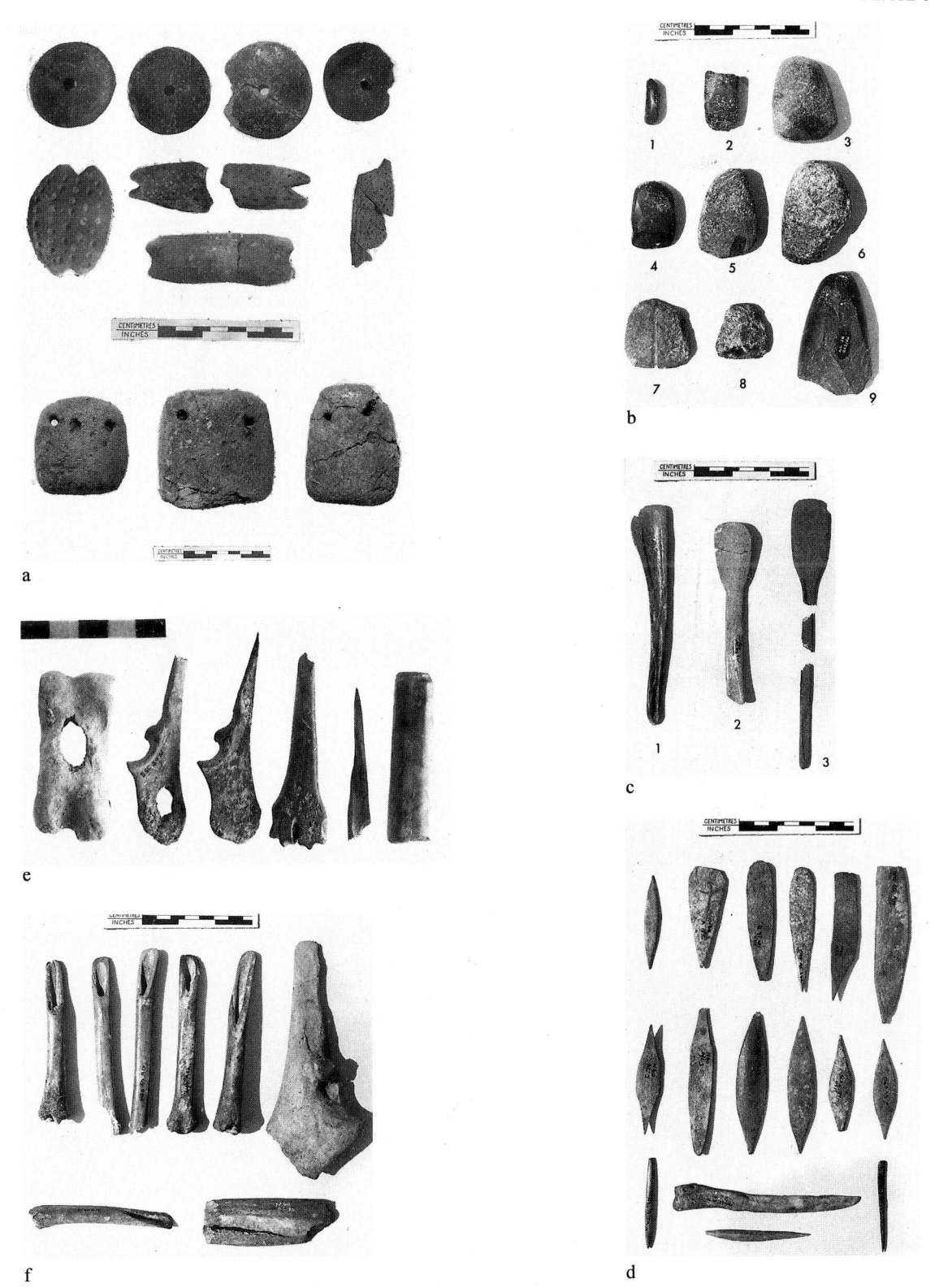

a Clay spinning and weaving equipment;   *b* Stone axes;   *c* Bone spatulae;   *d* Bone double points, from ribs;
e Bone points, on ulnas;   *f* Bone 'chisels'

EVANS

PLATE 6

Militarism at Knossos in LM II to early LM IIIA
a Palace Style jar from Katsamba depicting helmets; b bronze helmet; c–f weapons and details of their decoration; g fragment of a vase depicting swords or daggers   Various scales

PLATE 7

Mycenaean features at Knossos in LM II to early LM IIIA
a chamber tomb with long keyhole-shaped dromos; b squat alabastron; c Linear B tablet listing a cuirass,
chariot and horse; d Tomb of the Tripod Hearth   Various scales

POPHAM

PLATE 8

a b

c

d

e f

Knossian vases of LM II to early LM IIIA
a–b LM II 'Ephyraean'-type goblets;   c–d cups depicting floral sprays in LM II/III A1 and LM IIIA2;   e–f cups
decorated with a frieze of flowers in LM II and early LM IIIA   Scale 1:3

POPHAM

PLATE 9

Knossian vases of LM II and early LM IIIA
a–c Palace Style jars;   d–e LM II cups;   f early LM IIIA cup   a–c) no scale; rest 1:3

PLATE 10

Vases decorated with birds in LM II and early LM IIIA
a LM II jug from Katsamba;   b LM IIIA alabastron from Phaistos;   c LM II pyxis from the Unexplored Mansion;   d LM IIIA1 cup fragments from the Palace;   e LM IIIA pyxis from Mycenae   b–e) scale 1:3

POPHAM

PLATE 11

Early LM IIIA vases: a, b and d from Knossos; c from Prosymna in the Argolid; e–f from East Crete   Scale 1:3

PLATE 12

LM IIIB (a–e) and LM IIIC (f–g) vases
a cup from the Little Palace;   b mug from the Palace;   c bowl from Phoenikia;   d kylix from Milatos;   e stirrup jar from the Palace;   f restored drawing of the bowl from the Kephala tholos;   g stirrup jar from Mouliana
Scale 1:3

PLATE 13

a EPG coarse pithos 285.58;   b EPG kalathos J 37;   c and d PGB pithos 283.11, with lid 283.31

PLATE 14

a EG pithos G 6, with lid G 7;   b EG lid 107.138;   c LM II oval-mouthed jar G 37;   d MG pithos and lid Eph. 58

PLATE 15

a LG pithos and lid Fortetsa 824;   b and c PGB coarse lid with stamped decoration

PLATE 16

a

b

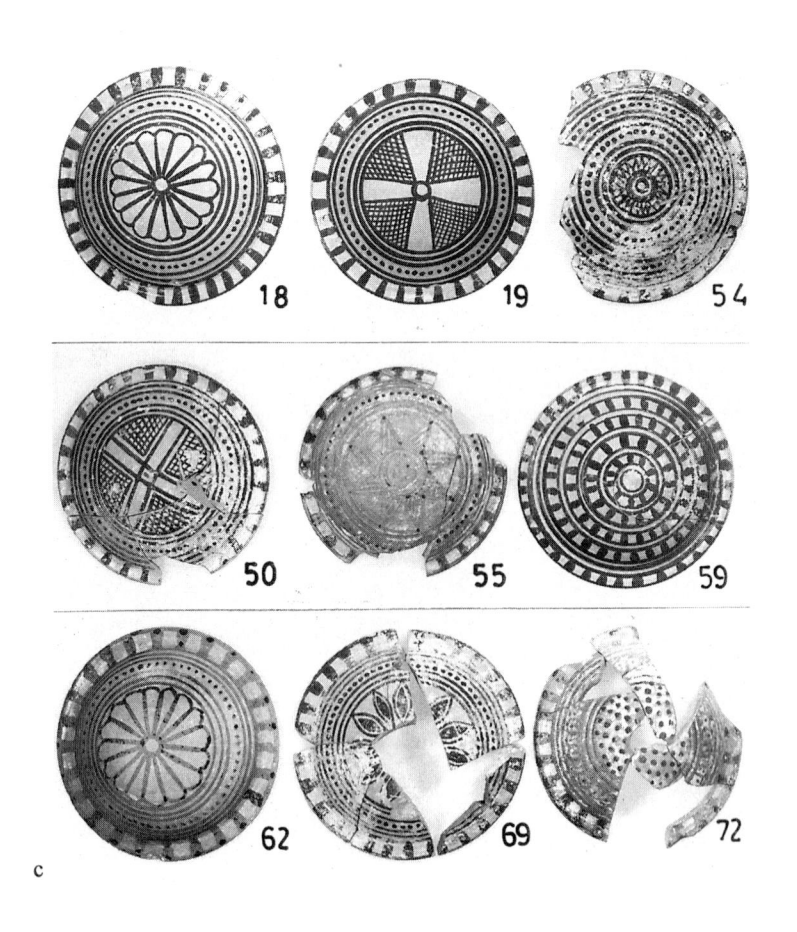

c

a EG domed lid 293.123; b LG domed lid 163.2; c MG set of miniature domed lids from Tomb 134

COLDSTREAM

Villa Dionysos, mosaic panels (photos Michael Gough)
a Pan with pipes; b Maenad with flute

Statue of Hadrian, found in the Villa Dionysos in 1935: showing bucrania *on the greaves and other joining fragments recently identified by D.E.H. Wardle (photo Graham Norrie)*

PLATE 19

a Seal impression on MM IB nodulus;   b Hieroglyphic seal impression on Class VI, from South-East Pillar Room (CHIC 03-08)

PLATE 20

a

b

*Seal impressions on two-sided oval nodulus, from South-East Pillar Room
a double-axe (= CHIC 03?);   b 'barley-corn' (= CHIC 08?)*

PLATE 21

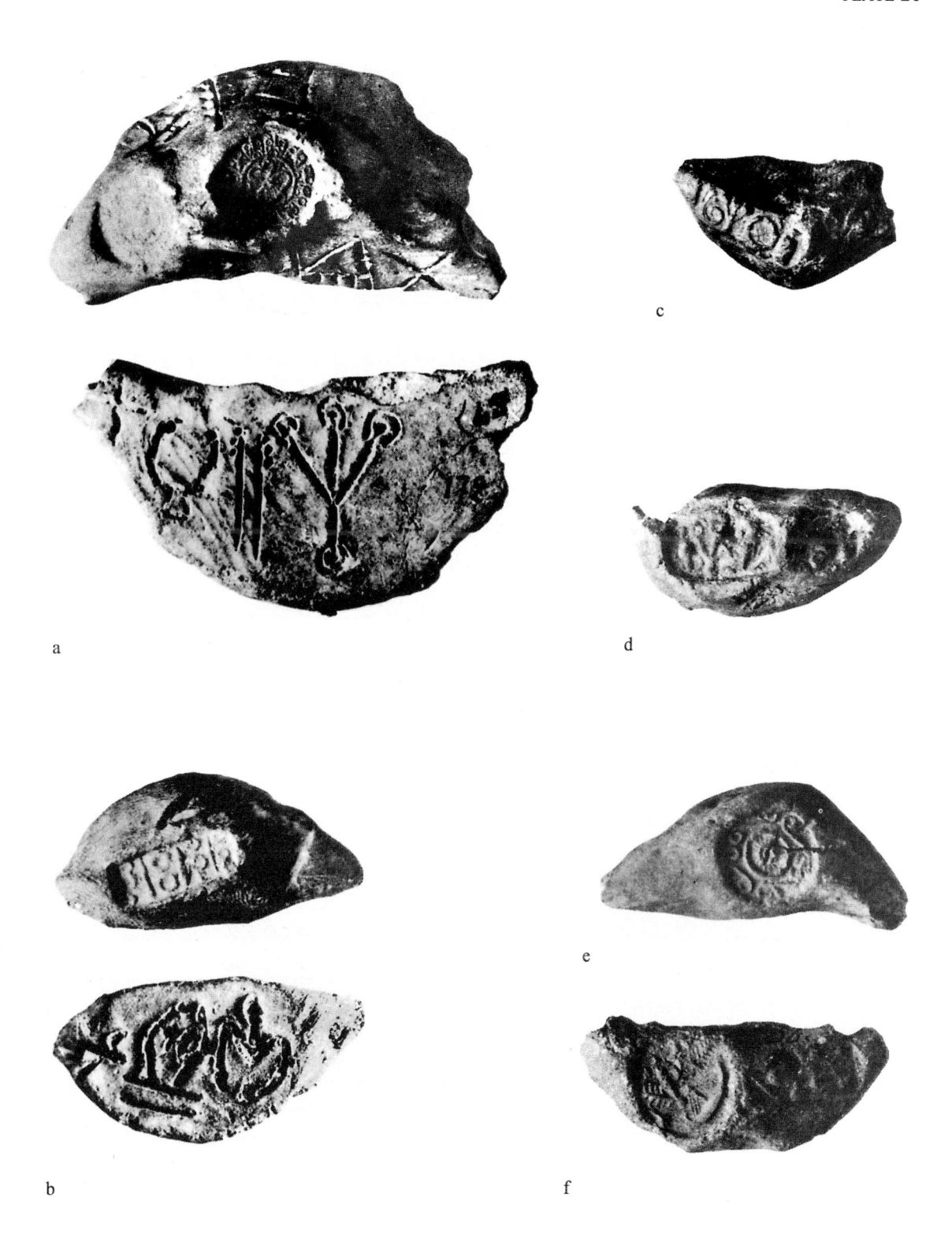

Hieroglyphic deposit – crescents
a P64;   b P65;   c P69;   d P60;   e P68;   f P63

PLATE 22

a

b

Look-alike seal impressions on noduli, from Temple Repositories: a and b

WEINGARTEN

PLATE 23

a

b

Look-alike seal impressions on noduli, from Temple Repositories: a and b

WEINGARTEN

PLATE 24

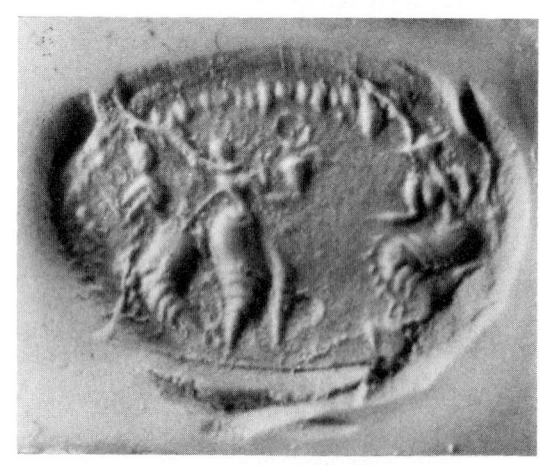

a Class XII sealing – *note both the stringhole and imprint of wickerwork;*   *b* Ring impressions: *top Knossos sealing;*
middle Knossos matrix – photographically reversed;   *bottom Zakro sealing.*

WEINGARTEN

PLATE 25

Knossos central area (photo Whittlesey Foundation. May/June 1976)
1 Royal Road;   2 Royal Road West;   3, 4 West extensions of Royal Road;   5 Little Palace Road;   6 Car park roads;   7 Stepped Portico;   8 Viaduct

PLATE 26

Royal Road from west (23/7/73)

PLATE 27

Royal Road and Theatral Area, with branch road southeast to Palace (right). From west (21/8/73)

Above. Royal Road West, with cobbled area and flanking walls: A Royal Road, B Staircase over Royal Road West. From south.   *Below.* Royal Road West, after restoration (test area below cobbles on right). From north

PLATE 29

Left. Royal Road West: road, cobbled drain and east flanking wall. From south
Right. Staircase from Royal Road (foreground), over Royal Road West (top right). From north

Early Minoan III cobbling or road (scale 0.5 m) below Royal Road West (left), with flanking wall of Royal Road West on top of cobbling. From west

PLATE 31

Stratigraphical Museum site, East–West Road, with drain.
Above Trench L (scale 1.0 m). Below Trench M (scale 2.0 m). From east

PLATE 32

Left. Stratigraphical Museum site, North–South Road, with drain on left (scale 1.0 m). From north   *Right.* Royal Road. Stone column base which had been built into later wall beside Minoan Staircase (pl. 29 right) (scale 0.5 m)

West Court, East–West Road (causeway). From west (25/5/93)

PLATE 34

Above: Stepped Portico. (scale by foundation column, A–2.0 m). From northeast. (27/5/93).
Below: Stepped Portico (A) and area of side roads (B). From southeast (27/5/93)

PLATE 35

Above. Viaduct. From northeast (30/7/78)
Below. Viaduct. From northwest (6/75: photo V. Hankey)